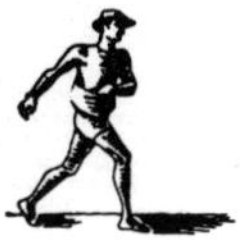

PORTRAIT IN OIL

*The
Autobiography
of
Nubar Gulbenkian*

SIMON AND SCHUSTER

NEW YORK

Contents

Acknowledgements

———————

I would like to express my appreciation to Viscount Radcliffe of Hampton Lucy and Doctor José de Azeredo Perdigão for their permission to reproduce their correspondence concerning the constitution of the Gulbenkian Foundation as an appendix. I am also indebted to Feliks Topolski for permission to reproduce his portraits as a frontispiece and on the wrapper.

Most of the photographs between pages 160 and 161 are family snaps but I should like to acknowledge some of them. The two photographs of myself in uniform as the Commercial Attaché to the Iranian Embassy are by Lafayette and P. A. Reuter. 'Gate-shutting' with the Whaddon Chase is by Fox Photos Ltd. and the photograph of myself and my wife at Richmond Horse Show 1963 is by Sport and General. The Lambeth Palace photograph is by Kingsley Mitchell and the Old House at Hoggeston by the *Sunday Dispatch*. The two portraits are by Associated Newspapers (Relaxing at Home) and Vivienne.

I should like to thank George Scott for his valuable help in assembling this book for publication. I should also like to thank Mrs. Lyons, Mrs. Kruger and Mrs. Price for all their care and energy in transcribing my dictation and in preparing the manuscript.

N.S.G.

1

Escape in a Gladstone Bag

MY GRANDFATHER had a servant whose sole occupation was to make coffee for him every twenty minutes or so. He was good at his job but inclined to be lazy. One day, when my grandfather clapped his hands, there was no response, and the *kahveci*, as he was called, who should have rushed in with a cup of fresh coffee, was found sleeping. My grandfather was very angry. He told his other servants to give the *kahveci* a good beating-up to teach him to stay awake on duty. Unfortunately, they carried out their orders all too thoroughly and the poor man died. This was a double misfortune, for my grandfather had also lost the services of a very good coffee-maker.

'*Vur dedik öldur demedik*,' he shouted at his servants. 'I told you to beat him, not to kill him.' This saying, the equivalent, I suppose, of Horace's *auream quisquis mediocritatem diligit tutus*, has been handed down in the Gulbenkian family and is used whenever anyone exaggerates.

My grandfather lived in a small village called Kadi Keui on the Asiatic shores of the Bosphorus and I think I can say, without exaggeration, that he must have been an important person in the village. The schoolmaster, for instance, knew he would be beaten up, on my grandfather's orders, unless my father was first in his class. (This may not be the way to win friends but it was no doubt at that time and place a most effective means of influencing people.) When the weather was bad my father was carried to school on the back of a faithful retainer who chanted as he went, 'Here comes the cleverest boy in the village, the son of the all-powerful, Mr. Gulbenkian.'

I was born, on the 2nd of June 1896, in that same village of Kadi Keui, which was the ancient Chalcedon, the seat, in the

9

year 451, of the fourth Council of the Christian Church, to which
I belong, by tradition, if not always by deepest religious conviction.
I am an Armenian. My father came from a family of Armenian
merchants who were engaged in trade within the old Ottoman
Empire and also in export business. He was a member of the
family firm which had a branch in England; my mother was the
eldest daughter of an Armenian banking family from Constantinople. I was their first-born.

I was only a few weeks old when we left Kadi Keui and fled
from Turkey, for the year 1896 was the time of the Armenian
massacres. The Armenians, deeply attached as they were to their
Church, were one of the Christian minorities in the old Ottoman
Empire, and although, by their financial and commercial abilities,
they rendered great services to the Empire, they were apt to look
towards the Christian Great Powers; they were also used by those
Powers, not only against each other, but also against the already-
decaying Empire. 'The Armenian Question' was a problem of
long standing and Abdul Hamid the Second, known variously as
the Sick Man of Turkey or the Red Sultan, was determined to
find a solution to it. He set about it in a very logical way. If there
were no Armenians, he reasoned, there could be no Armenian
Question: hence the massacres.

All Armenians who had the means and influence to leave the
country did so, my parents and grandparents among them. After
much pulling of strings and probably a great deal of bribery, the
necessary exit permits, passports and all the paraphernalia
required for a fairly large family to travel were in order and cabins
had been secured in a ship sailing from Constantinople (as
Istanbul was called in those days) for Egypt. All seemed to be
ready for the departure; my grandfather gave the order to leave
the house for the quayside and the embarkation. But my grandmother protested. 'The laundry hasn't come home,' she said,
and another family saying was born.

It is also said in the family that the infant Nubar was transported either in a Gladstone bag or (perhaps a later embellishment) in a roll of carpets. (This legend was referred to in a case
at the Law Courts in 1937 to decide my domicile. Mr. Justice
Langton held that 'a bag or portmanteau' did not represent 'a
domicile of choice'.)

We went from Constantinople to Egypt and thence to make our home in London and Paris; we used to spend the winter in the south of France and it is there that I see my grandfather, in the only image I retain of him, an old man with a neat, pointed white beard, sitting or lying on a couch. He died in 1900. His wife, my maternal grandmother, survived him until after the First World War. She eventually managed to sell up her property in Constantinople and elsewhere in Turkey and then settled in the south of France; she had a large flat, behind Nice, overlooking the Mediterranean in Cannes, at that time a most attractive part of the world. She spent much of her time playing bridge with old cronies or playing the Oriental game of backgammon, known in the East as tric-trac. Members of the Afghan Royal Family lived in the same block of flats. One of them, Shah Wallih Khan (who later was Ambassador in London for some years), often helped her out of her car and into the lift. She was very fond of her grandchildren and especially of myself, as the first child of her eldest daughter. She gave both my sister and myself a gold cross; my sister chewed hers, so my grandmother gave her another and, lest there be any jealousy, she also gave me a second one. I wear them both round my neck to this day. We were very attached to her and we treated her with that respect for age which even now is a characteristic of Armenian family life.

We Armenians come of a long-lived race and our women marry early. When I was born not only had I two grandmothers alive but also a great-grandmother and a great-great-grandmother. (American oil-men who came to Lisbon to talk to my father after the Second World War were shocked to find themselves in the presence of a man who had talked to a man who was older than the United States; my father as a small boy had talked to his grandfather, who lived to be 106.)

I remember hearing of the death in the early 1900s of my paternal grandmother. We were at Deauville. My sister had to wear a large black sash, with black bows for her pigtails and her hat; the rest of her was dressed in white. I had to wear a dark suit and black tie. We were in mourning for one year.

My father, following the exodus from Turkey, based his life on Western Europe, but our first stop on the way was Egypt, where both my mother's and father's families had friends and relations.

One of these friends was the famous Nubar Pasha who had just retired, the year before, after fifty years' outstanding service to Egypt. Nubar Pasha, the son of an Armenian merchant, had been the pillar and prop of his country, the regime and of Western influence, with profit to each of them and to himself.

He was very successful in missions abroad on behalf of his master, the Khedive Ismail, when the Suez Canal project was being brought to completion. He served both Ismail and his successor, the Khedive Tewfik, as prime minister and, later, co-operated with Lord Cromer to further his policy. It was after him that I was named Nubar. I was too young at the time for me to remember him but I knew his son Boghos Nubar Pasha and his grandsons very well.

From what my mother told me later it is clear that life in Egypt then, for the ruling classes, must have been quite fantastic. For instance, when my mother went driving with Nubar Pasha in a carriage and pair through the streets of Cairo the fellahin used to bow deeply and some even prostrated themselves as the Pasha's carriage passed. The horses were preceded by a runner, called a *sais*, who carried a stick with five horses' tails; the number of tails, one, three or five, was determined by the rank of the Pasha; the Khedive himself warranted seven tails. This tradition (which also existed in Jordan, or Transjordan as it then was) went on right down until 1952 when King Farouk lost his throne. (The late Lord Cadman, the great Professor of Chemistry and Mineralogy at Birmingham University, who was subsequently a Government adviser on petroleum during the First World War and became the Chairman of the Anglo-Persian Oil Company, now B.P. Petroleum, was granted by the Amir Abdullah of Transjordan the rank of Pasha with Three Tails. This, without his knowledge and much to his apparent annoyance, caused a great deal of banter about him by his family and friends.)

During those early days, after leaving Turkey, we were often on the move, living in hotels, and my first clear recollections are of the time when the family had arrived in London and had settled in the then newly built Savoy Hotel. I remember some of the staff who were there. There was the floor waiter called Paul, with large black side-whiskers, who looked immensely tall in the eyes of a small boy. There were also two little page boys with whom I used to play and whom I knew later as cloakroom attendants; one was a Mr. Joseph and the other, called Mr. Byron, for many years looked after my hat, gloves and umbrella whenever I had a meal at the Savoy and never gave me a cloakroom ticket.

At that time our family spent part of the time in London and part in Paris. We had a big apartment in the Ritz Hotel, overlooking the Place Vendôme. My father was one of the earliest clients of the Ritz, having helped to finance the great César Ritz in his very early days. (This was a good investment, not merely from the financial point of view, but because in the hotel and restaurant world my father was remembered for the help he had given César Ritz in the difficult moments of his career. This inspired a sense of gratitude which has been passed on to the second and even third generation of hoteliers. I find that in my travels on the Continent there is always some waiter, young or old, who knows my father's name and reputation and I benefit by getting more than adequate service and attention. True, I am vain enough to think this is not due solely to the wealth my father acquired, but also to his knowledge and mine of the arts and graces of the table. At the same time I admit that the plant of gratitude and appreciation needs nourishment for it to grow; it needs to be tended pretty regularly, not merely with water or with oil but with the proceeds of the latter.)

I was four years old when I was first allowed down into the restaurant of the Ritz in Paris. It was on Christmas Day, 1900, and this was a special treat for me, the apple of my parents' eyes (as I remained until their deaths). They asked what I would like to eat. Seeing other people eating oysters, I asked for one, tried it and was immediately sick, much to the disgust of the august patrons of the Ritz. The restaurant there was under the guidance of the famous Olivier Dabescat whose boast it was he could supply anything his clients might order. On that same Christmas Day an American, perhaps more eccentric than most, had asked for elephant's feet.

Not even this could daunt Olivier. He bought an elephant from the Jardin des Plantes (the strange name of the Paris Zoo) and served up the four feet to the American eccentric's party. He also kept back a small portion for my father's table and I was given a small mouthful: it tasted like something between sponge and flannelette.

Just before 1900 my parents bought their first house. This was in London, at 38 Hyde Park Gardens, and the family occupied it for twenty-five years. From there I often saw Queen Victoria on her way to Paddington Station to take the train for Windsor. She drove from Buckingham Palace across Hyde Park, out of Victoria Gate and along the Bayswater Road in front of our house. I heard the call 'The Queen's coming', and I ran to the windows to watch. First came a mounted policeman with helmet and baton, his flesh bulging out over the top of his high-necked tunic, and then the Queen's carriage.

I recall the Relief of Mafeking in the South African War, not for its historical significance but because I heard my parents discussing whether or not to dismiss the butler, a man called Warrior. He had come home rolling drunk and had made a general nuisance of himself; as it was such a special occasion, however, he was forgiven.

Warrior was an apt name for him; to me, he looked ten feet tall, and like so many others of his profession at that time, seemed most imposing even to grown-ups. Butlers in Victorian days could seem to condescend even to their employers who had to fight hard to preserve their own sense of status. There was one woman in our household, however, who had scant respect for his dignity or person. She was the cook, a Frenchwoman called Louise. (She is now ninety-three, in possession of all her faculties and living in Cannes, where I see her twice a year when I go to the Riviera.) Louise was a wonderful cook, trained by the great Escoffier, but she had a foul temper. One day Warrior was unwise enough to provoke a row with her and the moment came when Louise abandoned mere words and turned to a more effective and conclusive form of argument: she turned over a dish of hot spinach on to his head. Warrior dashed into my mother with the dish jammed firmly on his head and the spinach pouring down on either side of his face. I could not help laughing, but my mother kept a serious face.

'Don't aggravate the situation,' she said, and proceeded to sort out the trouble. Then, after peace had been restored and we were alone again, she turned to me.

'I must teach you not to laugh at other people's misfortunes and you must learn to exercise self-control,' she said. Another spanking.

It was in the house in Hyde Park Gardens that my sister Rita was born; I remember being called in to see her when she had had her first bath. Perhaps I was jealous of her and perhaps even at that stage I was already an odious little boy. Anyway, I remember she was in a swinging cot and I used all my strength to swing that cot over a wider and wider arc until finally I managed to achieve a full circle. My infant sister was thrown out on to the floor. I was soundly beaten and the cot was secured so that the same thing could not happen again.

I had no real cause for jealousy, for the Oriental preference for boys rather than girls and, in particular, for the first son, was very marked in our upbringing. For instance, my parents always told us that while my sister had been found on a cabbage patch I had been found on a rose bush.

I had a French nurse and my sister had an English nanny. When I progressed to a governess, at the age of six or seven, the English nanny was dispensed with and my French *nounou* was passed on to my sister. This ensured that both of us would be bilingual. My *nounou* was called Clémence. She was from the peasant class and conformed to traditions in her dress. She always wore a white *coiffe* and on high days and holidays this *coiffe* was surmounted with a sort of crown of tartan-plaid ribbons; two long ribbons hung down her back and two large golden balls of hatpins fastened the *coiffe* on her head. My sister was brought up in the English way and had a pram (which I never had); her nanny had the conventional black bonnet with a bow under her chin. The two nannies did not like each other. This was before the days of the Entente Cordiale, and the nannies used us to express their warm feelings about each other. My *nounou* referred to my sister as a '*sale petite* English'. Rita's nanny called me, 'that nasty little French boy who must eat frogs'.

We were very strictly brought up. Although we were allowed to make a fair amount of noise playing together on the nursery floor, it was drummed into us that when our elders were around we must never disturb them: children should be seen and not heard. Sound beatings were a regular occurrence and many of the incidents I remember from childhood ended that way.

There was, for example, the day I went into short trousers. In those days boys wore dresses until quite a late age: I think I was about five before I was taken out of them. The first day I was put into shorts, I naturally felt all grown up and entitled to whatever is the five-year-old's equivalent of the key of the door.

Clémence took me into Kensington Gardens, established herself on a seat, and settled down to spinning the thread with which she made lace, a nimble and delicate operation in which she became absorbed, though still keeping an eye on me. I began to play further and further away from her; she called to me to come back, but I took no notice. I felt I was now emancipated from having to obey the commands of a woman. I continued to ignore her calls and to move away from her, until Clémence was goaded into action. She put down her *fuseau*, rose, armed herself with her sunshade and set out to recover her charge. Seeing her coming my way, I quickened my own pace: in other words I ran as hard as I could, and reached the Bayswater Road, which even in those days was a busy and hazardous thoroughfare. I dashed across, escaping the hooves of the horses pulling the broughams, the victorias and the hansom cabs, made the other side in safety and attained what I had imagined to be the sanctuary of our front door. But the front-door bell was beyond my reach and so I had to stand there, waiting ignominiously and apprehensively until a panting and furious Clémence arrived.

She did not wait for the door to be opened before she began to belabour me with her sunshade, employing such force that she broke it on my back. That was not the end of my punishment. I was put on bread and water for the rest of the day and, unkindest cut of all, which shook my faith in human justice, my pocket money of three whole pennies a week was stopped until enough had been saved to pay for a new sunshade for Clémence.

As children, my sister and I had to submit to certain conventions and disciplines which also amounted to punishment. Every other Wednesday, for instance, Mother was At Home. Rita and I had to be dolled up in our Sunday best and our hair was curled into beautiful ringlets round a curling stick with which we were belaboured if we did not keep quite still. When we were finally considered fit to be seen by adults we were made to sit on a high table where we could not move until the time came for our summons to the drawing-room. There we were exhibited before critical eyes and we had each to recite a piece of poetry—a new one for each occasion; our reward was a *petit four* or *friandise* from the grown-ups' tea. The ritual over, we were packed off back into our nursery.

We children were regularly chastised, left, right and centre, by my mother, the governess or the nurse or by Clarisse Genie, my mother's lady's maid, but never by my father himself. Clarisse Genie was more than an institution in our family, becoming a housekeeper and general assistant during her fifty-three years in our service. She would not hear of the idea that she should be retired on pension. The thought of retirement was wholly unacceptable to her, even though she had saved quite a lot of money and her savings had been invested very successfully, from time to time, by my father. She came from a coal-mining village called Bruay, near Lens, a typical French peasant from that north-east area of France. She had the virtue of economy instilled in her from her earliest childhood and that virtue she never abandoned. When, after an illness lasting several years, she was dying, she called her son and grandson to her and said that, whatever happened, they should not waste money on buying either a wreath or flowers for her funeral; she was quite sure, she told them, that 'Monsieur Nubar' would provide all the flowers that were necessary. Which, of course, I did. She was devoted to my father, my family and myself, but this did not prevent her from chastising me from time to time. This was done whether I deserved it or not, because it was 'good' for me and because she probably considered that whether I deserved it or not at that moment I probably should before the day was out.

From Clémence I graduated to an English governess to whom I was devoted although she also beat me regularly and soundly. Her name was Miss Brockway and it is as Miss Brockway that she is still known by my sister and myself despite the fact that she has been married and a widow for many years. She is still alive, at a ripe old age well over eighty, and has been on my pension roll ever since my father's death.

My sister was just as often in trouble as I was. I remember one particular incident when she was about six. For a long time she had suffered from exhortations to emulate another little girl who was cited as a perfect example of how well-brought-up little girls should behave. There came the day when Rita could stand no more. She took hold of a large stone and threw it at the head of the unfortunate paragon, who was quite badly hurt. My poor sister was put on a bread-and-water diet for a week, she was spanked, her pocket money was stopped and she was made to apologize most humbly. My mother also apologized to the parents and gave the paragon a huge doll.

Holidays we spent either at Deauville or at Cap Martin in the south of France. Among the other children with whom we made friends on the beach at Deauville were the d'Erlangers, whose family had a very large villa there, the Villa Louisianne, which I believe stood on the site where the Casino has now been built. I was very jealous of little Leo d'Erlanger because he had a sailor suit with horizontal stripes; mine had mere vertical stripes. (I was quite shocked to read in the *Observer* recently a description of that little boy as he is today, 'silver-haired and urbane'; he is also the chairman of the Channel Tunnel Company, having succeeded his uncle in that position.)

We passed the winter months at Cap Martin at the Villa Paulette. That is to say, my mother and the children spent the winter months there: my father used to join us from London or Paris from time to time whenever business allowed him. I am writing of the time before motor-cars. We had a hired victoria with a spanking pair of large horses and a coachman with a large cockade and an even larger moustache. I remember that the victoria had red wheels and I remember the colour spinning. Sometimes the past catches up with one in agreeable ways. A year or two back I was rather thrilled, when I went to a garage in Nice to hire a Cadillac, to hear an echo from my childhood. The manager of the garage, a man of about fifty, recognized my name; his father had told him about supplying our family with horses and carriages during the winter season. For that reason the garage manager gave me his best car (although it had been promised to another client who was ready to pay much more than I). Tradition should not be underrated: it is quite remarkable that in this materialistic age the fact that somebody's father worked for and knew my father has so many times resulted in some sort of advantage to me.

As a small child at Cap Martin, I used to meet, almost every day, the old Empress Eugénie, the last Empress of France, who also had a villa there, the Villa Cyrnos. She was always very sweet and kind to a little but rather grubby boy who had been taught to doff his straw hat very courteously whenever he saw her. I saw quite a lot of her garden, for I was taken there while her chef was courting Justine, the sister of Clarisse Genie (who, as I have told, was my mother's lady's maid).

Whether it was winter or summer, whether his family was at the Cap Martin or at Deauville, my father used to go backwards and forwards from London or Paris, spending as much time as he could with us. I do have a memory, a rather shocking one, of his arrival one night at Deauville; 'shocking' because he had shaved off his beard. It is with his beard that I think of him now: a dark, bristly beard. That is my first recollection of him, a rather fierce-looking man with very bushy eyebrows and beard.

I did not see much of my father when I was small, either because he was away at the office or on business. By the time he came home in the evening I was generally in bed or being put to bed. When he was back in time he used to come up to the nursery and spend a few minutes or so with me, but at no time during my early childhood were we really intimate. He was very stern, had a great sense of duty and responsibility and stuck to his principles, perhaps to the point of obstinacy. My sister Rita and I were terrified of him; so was everyone else, the governess, nurse, servants, probably even my mother. Yet he was devoted to me as his eldest son and nothing was too good for me; as a result, I was hopelessly spoilt as a small child and quite unbearable.

On my sixth birthday I was given my first pony. I was rigged up at Swears and Wells—the Young Gentlemen's Outfitters, as I think it was known in those days—with a pair of breeches, cloth gaiters with buttons, short covert coat with pearl buttons the size of five-shilling pieces, a tam-o'-shanter and a very jaunty feather, a hacking stick and a pair of gloves. At that early age I was taught that a gentleman always carries a stick and gloves, whether walking or riding. I still do, although a neatly rolled umbrella replaces the walking stick nowadays. I was led around the Park (one could ride round the whole of the Park in those days in comfort and safety) by the family coachman, 'Mr.' Ashton. I was on the leading rein for about a week and then, probably because Ashton did not relish my wish to be trotting the whole time, I graduated to being led by him from one of the carriage horses.

Father used to ride at seven-thirty, before breakfast and before leaving for the City. I used to ride at nine o'clock and mother used to ride at eleven. (When we gave up horses and carriages a larger pony was hired for the season for me, and two saddle horses for my parents and Ashton, from W. J. Smith. This was the same firm of Job Masters from whom we hired, under contract, the carriage horses for the victoria and the brougham, and who then supplied horses to the majority of people in London.) At the beginning of each season Mr. Horace Smith (then a very young man but now dead) or his father came to demonstrate the horses he proposed to hire to my father, trotting them up and down the Bayswater Road.

I first became a capitalist when I was nearly ten years old. It was 1906; we were in the south of France and I had scarlet fever; I must have been fairly ill because I was in bed for some five or six weeks. The hotel, the Riviera Palace, was kept open for several weeks, especially for us: at that time the season was over by the middle or end of April. My father brought me a money-box and each day while I was ill he put in a twenty-franc gold piece, worth something under a sovereign in those days; on Sundays he put in a gold 100-franc piece, which was used a great deal in those days for gambling in the Casino at Monte Carlo.

When I recovered, my father told me I had about £50 or £60 saved and asked me what I wanted to do with it. My ideas were pretty vague, so he suggested I should hand it over to him to invest it. Later on, he came back and told me he had bought me some Shell shares; I had become a capitalist, but my father kept the shares and, from time to time, told me what they were worth. When I went up to Cambridge their value had reached between £400 and £500 and I wanted to use them to buy a car. Father frowned upon that idea, however, and in the end I do not recollect having profited directly from my long-term abstinence: I suppose I should say that my savings were lost in the wash.

As children we naturally saw much more of our mother than of our father. We used to go into her room when we first got up, when she was having breakfast in bed, and we used to see her at lunch. My memory of her in those days, an image which lasted throughout her life, was one of a very beautiful, affectionate, but efficient person, always smartly dressed. I remember how, before the First World War, I waited hours for her while she tried on dresses at Callot Sœur of Paris, in the Rue Taitbout, then the finest fashion house in Europe. The house, servants, children, all had to respond to her orders; she insisted on cleanliness, tidiness, a rigid sense of discipline.

We had to eat what was thought to be good for us. If we did not finish up our greens—I took a great dislike to cabbage and spinach—they were kept and served up cold at teatime: until we had eaten them we were not allowed to have a slice of cake or any jam. After one or two attempts at insubordination we found it was simpler and less nauseating in the long run to eat up everything at lunchtime as we were told.

It was silly to try to put one over on my mother. I remember once I had committed some misdemeanour or other and had been told I must go without sweet and fruit at lunch. I was sitting at the other side of the table from my mother. When the fruit came round my eyes fixed upon a beautiful, small peach, furry, rosy and appealing. Sitting next to me was our old family tutor, Monsieur Devgantz, who felt rather sorry for me. He peeled the peach, winked at me and then left it within my grasp. I snatched it and put it in my mouth. But my mother had seen me and she was not going to have her authority thus flouted. She jumped up from her chair, came round to the other side of the table, took hold of my head and shook it until I had to regurgitate the peach.

In the mornings it was either the Park or the Gardens for my sister and myself. In the afternoons, in the summer when it was fine, my mother generally went out in the victoria with a woman friend, going round and round the Park, bowing to their friends and acquaintances: the smarter the equipage, the better it was, of course, a sort of equivalent of the modern keeping-up-with-the Joneses. The coachman was 'Mr.' Ashton, who took me out on my first pony. (He stayed with us from just before 1900 until after the First World War; when we gave up horses, he was taught to drive an electric brougham and after that a petrol-driven car.) Beside him sat the footman, his hands rigidly on his knees, according to custom. Both of them were supposed to sit bolt upright and, lest they should forget, they were prodded in the back periodically by Mama's sunshade; it was all an essential part of the show. I was often taken out on these drives, which meant my sitting on a tiny seat with my back to the horses. I invariably ended up by being sick, and then I was spanked for not having sufficient self-control and for disgracing the equipage.

A much more pleasant memory is of my mother taking me to watch the Coronation of Edward VII. I was only four but as a great treat she took me to the Carlton Hotel, at the corner of Haymarket and Pall Mall, to watch the procession from a balcony window. I remember the glittering military escorts and the various crowned heads including the Kaiser, Wilhelm the Second. Yet perhaps just as exciting to the small boy was that I was allowed to lunch in the Carlton Restaurant for the first time, listening to the string band, sharing in the privileges of the grown-up world.

My first chance to see the country in which I was born came in 1910 when mother took Rita and myself on a holiday to Turkey to visit our grandmother. It was then that we were taken to see our great-grandmother. She was living in a large and very imposing old house at Yedi Kuli along the Golden Horn, which is an arm of the sea which runs on one side of the old Constantinople. The old lady was very frail. My mother knelt down and kissed her hand; my sister and I followed her example.

At that time, although the Young Turk Revolution had just taken place, Turkish women were always veiled. Sometimes they were accompanied by a eunuch from the harem. They were kept apart and, of course, no man was allowed to look at them. On the steamboats which plied the Bosphorus, for instance, there was always a section of the boat set aside for the Turkish ladies and children. During our visit to Turkey in 1910 we travelled on one of these steamboats and my mother took me with her into the special cabin for the ladies. This caused one of the eunuchs much consternation. He protested that I had no right to be there, that I was no longer a child (I was fourteen) and therefore ought not to be among the ladies. The argument was rich and voluble and had still not exhausted itself by the time we reached our destination, but my mother had been unmoved in her determination to keep me by her side.

My mother's sense of responsibility for me lasted a long time. It expressed itself in the most emphatic way when I was seventeen. I was on holiday in Paris and staying with my parents. Their Paris home at that time was a large flat on the fourth floor of 27 Quai d'Orsay. They had acquired it in 1906 and they did not give it up until 1925, when the house in the Avenue d'Iena was ready for them. (The word 'flat' may be misleading to many English readers. In Paris people of all classes live in apartments; very few indeed have private houses, which are known there as *hôtels particuliers*. This was so even before the First World War, but 'flats' in Paris for the well-to-do were, and still are, much larger and more luxurious than their London equivalents.)

I had been out for a long and most enjoyable evening and it was five o'clock in the morning when the fiacre, bringing me home from Montmartre, arrived in the Quai d'Orsay. The noise of the horse's hooves shattered the quiet of the sleeping street. I stopped the fiacre about a hundred yards away from the house. I was supposed to be in by midnight, so I let myself in quietly with a latchkey and walked up the four flights of stairs with my shoes in my hand to avoid a disturbance. I was greeted by the yapping of my mother's Pekingese and I saw a light under her door. There was only one thing I could do. I rushed into my room and dived under the covers of the bed. A few moments later my mother came in. She was not to be fooled. She whipped back the bedclothes and saw me still dressed in my evening clothes. She did not actually spank me but she slapped me hard on both cheeks, slaps I remember to this day with affection. It was the last time my mother physically chastised me.

During my childhood we lived modestly. Our standards were not those either of the nobility or of the newly rich like Sir Ernest Cassel. Our house in London was on 'the wrong side' of the Park; it was at the wrong end of the Bayswater Road, much too far away from Park Lane to be fashionable; we shared a garden and our horses were 'jobbed'. The servants (especially the nannies) always emphasized how frugal our establishment was. I was acutely conscious of the fact that though both my sister and I each did have a nurse, there was no nursery footman and not even a nursery maid.

I am saying all this to correct any false impressions which younger readers in particular, looking into the mirror of the present day, may be inclined to draw of my life as a child of the so-called 'Upper Class'. It is difficult, I know, for anyone who was not alive before the First World War to realize what a gulf existed then between the haves and the have-nots. The general attitude towards wealth and poverty was so different from that prevailing today. To be poor was considered rather shameful, the probable consequence of sloth, drunkenness or wasted opportunities. Again, it is useless to ask me how I felt as a child towards the poor and the slum-dwellers of London: I did not know they existed. My world in my early years was a small one bounded by my family, the servants, by Hyde Park and Kensington Gardens; a world governed by strict conventions, by commonly acknowledged codes of behaviour and by an unquestioning acceptance of the *status quo*.

In those first years of the twentieth century English Society was still almost rigid in its class structure; it was enormously difficult to move upwards from one class to another. It was still held to be non-U to admit to earning one's living. Many people would have said, on hearing that my father went each day to the City: 'But fancy *having* to go to the City!' There was all the difference in the world, too, between an eldest son looking after the family 'estates' and his looking after the family 'business', no matter what the scale of it might be. Similarly, a man who had made his fortune in retail trade would meet the most formidable obstacles to acceptance by Society. First-generation wealth was disdained. Only large contributions to Party funds, the acquisition of a country 'place', a pack of foxhounds, a polo ground and, eventually, of a baronetcy, might open the door. Even then the emphasis is on the word 'might'.

Before the 1914–18 war the St. James's Club rarely accepted professional men as members. An eminent barrister or a medical specialist good enough to earn a knighthood might be admitted but not a solicitor or a G.P. There was a general feeling that to have men who, by their professions, might have knowledge of the private affairs of other members could be embarrassing and undesirable.

It is by the standards of this world I have described, the only world I knew, that I say we lived 'modestly' when I was a child. Indeed, I can go further and say it was not until after this last war that I personally had any awareness of being rich. That, whatever others may have imagined my feelings to be, or could wish them to be, is how it really was.

2

An English Gentleman:
First Stages

———◆———

AFTER I had recovered, in the south of France, from the bout of scarlet fever I went to a preparatory school at Harrow called Orley Farm. I had been well trained, by my governess Miss Brockway, for initiation into this important first stage in the life of an English gentleman.

'When you go to school,' she told me time and again, 'you will be a man. Being a man means that whatever happens you must keep a stiff upper lip.'

My mother took me to the prep school and, on the journey there and while waiting for her to take her leave, I kept repeating to myself, 'Remember, Nubar, keep a stiff upper lip, you're a man now.' We met the Matron, Mrs. Miles, a woman of very forbidding looks, with hair parted in the middle and drawn tightly back into a bun. I parted from my mother by shaking hands with her very manfully in a fashion my governess would certainly have approved. It was not until the Matron took me upstairs, and from a window I could see my mother leaving, that my self-discipline cracked and I started to cry. Mrs. Miles was very understanding and tried to comfort me. I was bitterly unhappy for the first twenty-four hours but I soon settled down.

My illness meant that I was starting school rather later than was customary. I was ten and suffering from certain disadvantages. I was not allowed to play any games, I knew no Latin and either my parents or my old tutor, Monsieur Devgantz, came down every weekend to see how little Nubar was getting on. Their visits were not very popular in the eyes of the Headmaster. I understand that nowadays parents are encouraged to see how their offspring are faring at school, but it was certainly not so in the first decade of the century, when parents were held to be an unsettling influence.

In other ways I enjoyed advantages over my schoolmates. If I was behind them in Latin, my knowledge of French was certainly superior to that of the other little boys and, though I say it myself, to that of the so-called French master. I had another advantage in that, being Oriental, I developed much more rapidly than English boys of the same age so that my mental abilities were equal to those of boys two or three years older than I was. As a result, I was considered something of an infant prodigy, coming out at the head of my class or form for each weekly placing and likewise at the end of each term throughout the whole of my stay at Orley Farm; later, at Harrow, I ended up as head of the sixth form when I was still just under sixteen. I also collected a large number of prizes. (Fortunately, however, I realized the reason for my earlier successes some years afterwards when I went up to Trinity College, Cambridge. There, I failed to pass both the Entrance and Senior Scholarship exams and managed only to scrape through a Third Class Science Tripos. It was a salutary awakening for me and during the rest of my life I have never considered, or found, that I was in any way mentally superior to any other people with whom I have come into contact: far from it.)

While I was at Orley Farm I had my first lesson in financial timing, a lesson from which I hope I have profited in later life. In the High Street there was a very fine confectioner's, the Cornflower Tea Rooms. Behind its large plate-glass window, on a grid, lay a perpetual enticement, five rows of strawberry tarts, twelve tarts in each row, each tart consisting of three strawberries and a dash of whipped cream. Each tart cost a penny. I can see them still and I feel again the agony of frustration of the small boy gazing upon them from outside. At that time my arithmetic was good enough to work out the capital investment which would have been involved in buying up the whole grid: for an outlay of sixty pence or five shillings I could eat up the lot. However, my total income was threepence a week and I worked out that it would take me the best part of two terms' pocket money to be able to indulge my wish. To this day, as I remember that tray of strawberry tarts, I think the tragedy of life is that when one has the appetite to eat sixty strawberry tarts the financial wherewithal is lacking and that when one can afford the five shillings, the childhood desire and the child's capacity have gone. Yet the failure to fulfil that desire is remembered.

(Another desire which I shall now never fulfil is to ride in the Grand National. The nearest I got to it was in 1937. Top weight and well fancied for the National that year was a horse called Royal Mail, owned by Sir Hugh Lloyd Thomas, then Minister in the British Embassy in Paris, a man approaching fifty. Sir Hugh broke his neck steeplechasing a few weeks before the race. As a consequence, Royal Mail was put up for sale by auction. The weight of 12 st. 4 lb. had been allotted to it and, although I was forty at the time, that was the weight I could just manage after a great effort. I had dreams of riding Royal Mail, perhaps even to victory, in the National. Because I was afraid of my father hearing about it, I sent an agent to the auction to bid for the horse; I also thought of a *nom de course* I would use to prevent my father from hearing of my activities. I authorized my agent to bid up to £4000 for the horse. That was all the cash I could raise among my friends at the time, because, as they kindly but not very encouragingly explained, they thought that was quite enough to ensure my death in public. It was not enough; Royal Mail went for £6000 and went on to win the National at 100-6.)

I was put down for Harrow soon after I was born, thereby ensuring that I would follow in the footsteps of my uncle and grand-uncle. Fortunately, I did not suffer the same kind of experience as my grand-uncle, who was very unhappy there and for good reason. During his first term, for instance, his schoolfellows persecuted him by putting drawing-pins on his seat in Chapel. When he sat on the pins and let out a yell he was punished for behaving improperly in Chapel. He could not have been spanked to learn self-control as I had been.

My uncle, by contrast, always talked with affection of his days at Harrow, a feeling which I share. I had to endure a bit of ragging at the start but, by making friends with three or four other new boys and finding strength in numbers, I survived without too much discomfiture. I played no games and had an unpronounceable name, and, quite soon, I was recognized as something of an oddity. However, even though I did not strictly conform, which is normally a most heinous offence at a public school, I was accepted on my own terms.

Once you were at Harrow you were *of* Harrow and there was little curiosity about the background of one's schoolfellows, either who their parents were, whether they were rich or titled or what their homes were like. Much of this was taken for granted and being a Harrovian admitted one to a closed circle. A great deal of snobbery attached to being a member of that circle, which manifested itself in a common attitude of condescension towards the world outside, as, for example, in the saying, 'Harrow we know, Eton we know, Winchester we've heard of, but who are ye?' when referring to any other public school.

On the other hand, let me disabuse younger readers of any illusion that the rich young men of Harrow lived a life of plushy luxury. Living conditions at Harrow were, admittedly, not unduly hard by the standards of the time. Many ex-public schoolboys have written of the tyranny of the cold bath, allegedly an essential ingredient in the forming of character. We were relatively fortunate in that respect, yet even so we had only one hot bath a week. In the mornings we filled a jug with cold water from a tap on the landing and washed at the wash-hand-stand in our rooms. As is still true today in some colleges at Oxford and Cambridge it was deemed desirable that a rich intellectual life should be accompanied by a degree of physical privation. The beds we slept in at Harrow were folded up during the day into wall cupboards, a space-saving device frequently adopted today in modern flats. Although it was strictly forbidden, the custom was to burn or carve one's initials on the door of the cupboard and, for many years after I had left Harrow, I made a point of revisiting my room and looking, with nostalgia, upon my own initials. Then the day came when it was decided that keeping a bed in a cupboard by day was unhygienic. The cupboard doors were removed (and with them the hand-engraved memorials of the former, perhaps ultimately illustrious, occupants of the beds) and replaced by curtains.

The standard pocket money at Harrow was two shillings a week, but one could bring down a certain amount of money from one's parents and hand it over to the Housemaster who doled it

out each week. I used to come down each term with a fiver so
that I had something over ten bob a week as my average weekly
income. This was a bit above average but not unduly so. For
instance, Prince Karamjit Singh, of Kapurthala, the son of a Sikh
maharajah, used to have a weekly income of several pounds to
spend. Amounts of this size were frowned upon by the authorities,
but it should be remembered that out of this pocket money we
had to supplement our daily diet—as all schoolboys do if they
get a chance. School food was wholesome, clean and, I suppose,
very adequate, but between one period or lecture and another
there was generally a period of three-quarters of an hour or an
hour, during which one had to prepare for the next lesson. This
was usually done in the Hill Tea House, to the accompaniment of
a cup of tea and such gastronomic heresies as sardines and strawberry ice or sausages and raspberries.

By and large, we held the masters in awe, although it was considered good form to try and score off them. Some masters,
generally the newer ones, had a rather unhappy time, for schoolboys of fifteen to eighteen can be very plausible and ingenious in
devising ways of discomfiting masters.

The older boys were held in much greater awe by their juniors.
This was especially true of the Monitors, the members of 'Phil',
the Head of the House, the sixth-formers and members of the
School, or even the House Elevens at football or cricket. Many of
them were endowed with delegated authority from the Headmaster or Housemaster. At Harrow, then as now, the fagging
system was in full force and a very good system it is. It teaches
you to obey before you can command and it deflates any precocious tendencies you may have.

On reaching the heights of the sixth form one had one's 'sixth-
form privs' or 'privileges'. These meant that the small boys in the
Lower School took it in turns to stay in and be at the call of the
older boys; they were summoned by a loud call of 'Boy' resounding through the House and the 'day boy' on duty had to rush to
take instructions about an errand a sixth-former wanted him to
perform. Another sixth-form privilege was to award an extra
day's fagging to a delinquent youngster or to remit one day. I
was reminded of this some forty years after I had left Harrow,
when attending one of the Harrow dinners. I was sitting next to

a portly and important business man whom I had not seen since our schooldays together. He asked me if I remembered what had happened the day I attained my 'privs'.

'No,' I said. 'What did happen?'

'You really don't remember?'

'No,' I repeated, 'but you tell me.'

'Well, I haven't forgotten,' he said. 'I was very grateful to you at the time.' It seems that I celebrated the great occasion by remitting one day's fagging to each of the Lower School in my House, thereby earning the gratitude of all the youngsters concerned— quite undeservedly for, of course, everyone was in exactly the same position as before. To remit a day's fagging for all cost nothing; the rota remained unchanged and the fagging went on as usual. But I had seemed to be generous. I had completely forgotten the episode but it had remained in the mind of one of the 'beneficiaries' for some forty years.

As at Orley Farm, my bilingual upbringing served me well at Harrow, in one respect at least. I won for Harrow the Gold Medal presented by the Association of French Professors in England. To receive the medal I had to go to an awe-inspiring ceremony at the Mansion House. The Lord Mayor of the day was there and the medal was handed to me by the French Ambassador, the famous Paul Cambon, in front of a large gathering. Even a fifteen-year-old boy as odiously precocious as I was could not help feeling nervous, but there was ample compensation: I was given a day off from school and a large tea with ices at the Mansion House.

On another occasion, I had reason to regret my fluency in French. One of my friends asked for my aid in translating from English into French a piece of prose which had been set for prep. It would have involved him in a long and not necessarily successful struggle with his dictionary and grammar. I found it as easy as pie and I rattled off an excellent French translation for him. But, alas, it was so excellent that the French master, rightly convinced that its quality was much beyond the capacity of my pal, subjected him to cross-examination in which the truth came out that he had indeed received assistance. The master did not need the skill of Sherlock Holmes to suspect me and I, too, had to confess my guilt. We were both sent up to the Headmaster, the Very Rev. Lionel Bridges Justice Ford, whose son, Sir Edward Ford, is now

Assistant Private Secretary to the Queen. We were both severely lectured as to the heinousness of our crime, which amounted, said the Headmaster, to cheating if not to dishonesty.

'Gulbenkian,' he said to me, 'you will wait outside.' While I waited, I saw a large birch being brought in by the official called at Harrow 'Custos', whose perquisite it was to supply at a cost of seven shillings and sixpence the implement of torture. I heard my poor friend receiving six of the best administered by the Headmaster and suffered all the agonies of listening to his fate, firmly convinced that I should suffer the same five minutes later.

My friend limped out, very sore in the lower part of his back. Then I was summoned into the presence; I expected the order to bend over, but it did not come. Instead, I was once more admonished and condemned to write out I do not know how many lines of Vergil. I do not know which I should have preferred: to have received at once the physical punishment which I knew according to the rules I had incurred or to have the mental anguish, which I remember to this day, of expecting it without receiving it.

Beyond the formal education I received at Harrow was the informal education devised for me by my father who thought, for instance, that during my holidays he would conduct, for my benefit, certain experiments involving foreign travel and the value of money. Once he sent me off to Switzerland with the family tutor, Monsieur Devgantz, under very exceptional conditions.

'You can spend as much as you like,' said my father, 'and you can spend it on what you like. But,' he added, 'at the end of the three weeks you must present me with an account of every penny you have spent.'

This was almost too good to be believed, but I did not stop to question it. Monsieur Devgantz was by now an oldish man but one for whom I had great affection and whose company I enjoyed. He had been born during the Crimean War, had been tutor to my uncles and devoted to the family for many decades. (He now lies buried with my mother—he was 'in the family' when she was born—and with her brother, in the cemetery of the Caucade at Nice, a beautiful cemetery overlooking the Mediterranean.)

So Monsieur Devgantz and I went off to Switzerland, staying at the best hotels and eating the best food at the best restaurants. What is more, I was able to indulge my passion for horses. At that time, many of the Swiss roads were not open to motor traffic. So, when going out from Interlaken, for instance, where we stayed a week or so, the normal means of making an excursion or of crossing the Alpine passes was either by the public vehicle, a *diligence* with a post-horn, carrying some ten or twenty people, and pulled by four or five horses, or by private carriage with a pair of horses. I decided, however, that I should like to have a private carriage and *four* horses and so my tutor and myself did ourselves proud in a landau, behind a spanking team of four chestnuts, driven by a dour Swiss *kutscher* who rejoiced in the name of Fleurie. But I had to pay for my pleasures by spending hours every night trying to balance my accounts, setting out in detail how every penny was spent, down to the cost of each post-card and each stamp.

Whether or not my holiday taught me the value of money, I certainly had a wonderful time, the kind of time that only money can buy. It also instilled in me a hearty dislike of accounts and accountants which persists to this day for, although I now have very efficient and very clear-minded accountants who watch over my financial affairs, I dread the weekly morning I spend in their company. I am full of inward groans (and occasionally outward ones, too) as they try to explain to me what I have spent, what liabilities I have incurred, what monies I have received, what is owing to me and what taxes I still have to pay: an ordeal by addition and subtraction, and particularly subtraction.

My father had very firm ideas about the value of money and how it ought to be spent. By this, I do not mean that he was un-generous, but that he was indifferent to the kinds of external show that pleased other people. In 1911, he was one of those approached by a tout offering to sell him a peerage. This was the time of the famous Lloyd George Budget which the Peers threw out. The then Prime Minister, Mr. Asquith, secured the King's promise that if, after a General Election, the Peers again rejected the Budget, the King would agree to the creation of a sufficient number of docile Peers to ensure its passing through the Lords. This resulted in many people, some authorized, some unauthorized, touting around for rich men who would be willing to contribute to Party funds in exchange for a peerage. The standard donation was £100,000. My father sent the tout on his way; decorations and titles were not his line of country. But I remember the conversation in the house in Hyde Park Gardens between my sister and myself when we heard of the offer.

'What fun it will be if Papa gets a peerage,' said Rita. 'He'll be Lord Bayswater and we will be the Hon. Lancaster Gates.'

At that time my father was Financial Counsellor to the Ottoman Embassy in London and in this role, and in pursuit of his business interests, he entertained a good deal at Hyde Park Gardens.

Whenever a mission from Turkey came to London, he played host to its members at a luncheon or dinner party; of these guests, the most memorable was Djavid Bey, a man of Jewish origin who was a very able Minister of Finance with a wonderfully astute brain, but who, between the wars, following a political trial instituted by Kemal Ataturk, was hanged. Of course, the oil people were often there: Henri Deterding, Frederick Lane, the Rothschilds' representative, and Dr. J. Th. Erb, the great oil geologist who seemed to smell out oil as by instinct; business friends, too, such as William Lever, later Lord Leverhulme, and his very tall, good-looking and statuesque wife whom I remember much better than him.

Whether in London or in Paris, my parents liked to entertain not only useful and 'important' people but also amusing and talented ones. They knew many theatrical folk, like Seymour Hicks and Ellaline Terriss and Charles Wyndham and Mary Moore. Wyndham was a very old man with a slightly wandering mind when I saw him and it was hard to imagine him in the role of David Garrick, which had earned him the tribute of being 'the greatest actor of our time representing the greatest actor of all time'.

In France we knew the whole Coquelin family, father, brother and son, who were almost as famous for their wit as for their acting. It was the great Coquelin *aîné* who was credited with the perfect retort to a tiresomely ostentatious hostess. The lady in question was anxious everything she offered should be of the best and that her guests should realize and appreciate the fact. As dish followed dish, she told them with what difficulty and at what cost each had been obtained. When the time came for brandy, she told Coquelin of its great age, quality and price. Coquelin waved aside the attempt to pour him some. 'Oh, no, dear lady,' he said, 'not in the glass, I beg you—it's too precious—just give me a drop on my handkerchief.'

But of all my parents' guests, the most curious was undoubtedly Yussuf Izzedine, the heir to the Turkish throne. He had come to London to represent the Sultan at the funeral of Edward VII. (As at the Coronation, I watched the ceremony with my mother, this time not from the Carlton Hotel but from a public stand in the Edgware Road. Once more I remember the solemn parade of the crowned heads of Europe, in particular the King of Bulgaria, controlling his restive horse with difficulty, and again the Kaiser, Wilhelm the Second. I retain, too, a vivid image of King Edward's charger led by two Royal grooms with top hats and cockades, fully caparisoned and with the King's jackboots in the irons reversed. Behind trotted his little fox terrier, Caesar, bereft and pathetic.)

My parents gave a largish lunch party at home for Yussuf Izzedine, who, even then, was slightly mad and was later to commit suicide, perhaps under pressure, by cutting the veins of his wrist. I do not think our dining-room held more than twenty-four and on this occasion some eighteen or twenty sat down to table. It was rather a grand affair but the beginning of the lunch was somewhat marred, almost disastrously so. Being Royal, the Crown Prince was served before all the other guests. The first course was caviare which, by all European standards, is a delicacy and a luxury. Naturally, when my parents entertained they did so without stint and the caviare was served in a large dish. Even so, they were taken aback when Yussuf Izzedine seized the dish incontinently, placed it squarely before him and proceeded to eat out of it. Fortunately there were some spare dishes of caviare so that the other guests did not go without; equally fortunately they did not feel compelled, out of courtesy, to follow His Imperial example by eating one dish apiece.

The Crown Prince was a remarkable character. Like all heirs to the throne in the time of the Ottoman Sultans he was excluded from normal public duties and was regarded with the greatest suspicion by the reigning Sultan. (It had been common practice in the history of the Ottoman Empire for heirs to the throne to be put to death by the reigning Sultan as a means of self-preservation but eventually it was recognized that this was a futile exercise, for as soon as one heir to the throne had been despatched another automatically sprang into his place.)

By any criteria, Yussuf Izzedine could be rated an eccentric of high degree. It was but a short time after he had arrived in London that he set tongues wagging with stories of his activities. He sought my father's help in ordering some suits and my father took him to his own tailor, T. & F. French, in Dover Street. This, however, caused some difficulty. Being a member of the Ottoman family, it was beneath his Imperial dignity to be touched by an infidel and the poor cutter at French's had to take his measurements from a distance without touching him. For all the skill of that establishment I doubt whether the dozens of suits he ordered were a very good fit. The Crown Prince also refused to wear the same pair of boots or shoes more than once, an idiosyncrasy from which his valet must have profited handsomely; though some today may think that little enough compensation for serving such a man, the honour of being in Royal Service, even if badly paid, was much sought after.

When I became head of the sixth form at Harrow, although I was just sixteen, my father thought there was nothing more that Harrow could teach me and took me away. I have always greatly regretted this because I think the last year or two at a public school bring the biggest benefits: they instil an abiding sense of responsibility and they are the time when friendships are made which last throughout life. Even so, I can look back at my time at Harrow with a genuine warmth of affection and with respect for its traditions and for the qualities it represents. I made many friends there and, I must confess it now, I have laid claim for years to a degree of familiarity with others which is quite unjustified by the facts. For instance, I have been in the habit of saying, quite truthfully but entirely misleadingly, that I was at school with boys who later became very distinguished, such as Lord Alexander of Tunis and Viscount Monckton of Brenchley. Our time at Harrow did overlap by one term, but they were my seniors by three or four years and the only contact I had with them was to be privileged on occasion (though I must say it was not very often) to be kicked in the bottom by, as they seemed to a small boy in Lower School, these lordly and superior creatures.

When the moment came for me to leave Harrow I was really unhappy. Even though I was 'a man' of sixteen and head of the sixth form, neither my governess's injunctions of years before nor all my Harrovian training could prevent me from bursting into tears on my last night at the school. Try as I might, my upper lip just would not remain stiff.

My father decided that from Harrow I should go to Germany, primarily to learn the language but also to study science. At Harrow I had been on the classical side. (I am most grateful to my father for having given me, first of all, a classical education, for I have found great solace in the Classics and especially in Horace. This has been particularly true in later life. Each night before I go to sleep I try to read a Horatian ode and I have now achieved membership of the Committee of the Horatian Society, a Society which meets in distinguished surroundings once a year, has a good dinner and is addressed by two speakers. For our president we have that great classical scholar, Professor Wilkinson, and Lord Justice Harman is our chairman. Some years ago I was given the honour of addressing this eminent audience in the dining-room of the House of Lords. With the help of a 'devil', a young barrister whose briefs, or rather their scarcity, allowed him time for other activities, I produced a speech in which I commented on the superior attitude of Horace who was equally disdainful of the Persians and Armenians on the one hand and the British on the other. I mention this not simply out of a real sense of pride but also because my address rated a leading article in *The Times*, albeit only a third leader, which itself caused some small commotion. The Lord Great Chamberlain remonstrated against this publication on the grounds that even the august *Times* is a part of the Press and that the Press were not allowed inside a Royal Palace, which term included the dining-room of the House of Lords where the Dinner had taken place that year.)

My father was, as I have already suggested and as all my memories of him will show, thorough in everything he did. This applied as much to my upbringing as to his conduct of business. There could be no better example of his thoroughness than the very special appointment he made for me before I went to Germany. I was sixteen and more developed mentally than the average English boy of that age and probably more developed physically also. My father, on medical advice, decided it was time my sexual life should start. He arranged for me to call one afternoon on our family doctor, an Armenian, Dr. Kemhadjian, a little hunchback with a pointed grey beard who, thanks to my father, had become the official doctor to the Ritz Hotel in Paris.

It was in Paris that I went to see him. He was very much a man of the world and a considerable wit. He conducted our interview with a sort of amiable amusement that was combined with serious instruction and advice. He introduced me to a very respectable-looking young woman of about twenty or so. She was well dressed and appeared rather shy. I gathered that she had just been examined by Dr. Kemhadjian and he had passed her as being sound in wind and limb and everything else. The doctor told me to go with her in a taxi to a *maison de rendezvous* (which is something quite different from a *maison de passe*) in the Place de la Madeleine.

'When you get there,' said the little doctor, 'you must ask for a room. When you ask for it, don't look as though you are frightened or shy about it; you must behave as though you were completely at ease and you must speak firmly and with assurance. Then you should have no difficulty.'

Frightened and shy as I undoubtedly was, I took the young woman, who by then had shed some of her shyness, in a taxi to the *maison de rendezvous* and, in what I hoped was an assured, matter-of-fact manner, asked for a room. I could have one, I was told, provided I paid in advance.

The young woman and I went upstairs to the room and there my sexual initiation took place. I was too concerned about my own feelings to pay much attention to hers, but looking back now I remember her repeated remark, 'How young you are.' Thus, safely, I was introduced to the mysteries of sex. *Safely*. My father's reason for arranging this appointment was that if the adolescent sexual urge was not properly guided a young man could well end up in trouble. Either, he said, he would get V.D. or find himself involved in some unnecessary and unhappy complication, or both. His attitude to sex was characterized by the saying of Napoleon which he always quoted. Women, according to Napoleon, were 'all right in bed and on the bidet but nowhere else'.

It was upon medical advice that he himself had one mistress, of no more than seventeen or eighteen, whom he changed every year until he was eighty. He used to say, and the late Lord Evans agreed on this, that while it is very unkind on a young girl to have sexual relations with an old man because she loses her youth, it does rejuvenate the sexual functions of the old man. This was always recognized in the harems of the East and even today at the court of King Ibn Saud of Saudi Arabia or that, until his death, of the Pasha of Marakesh, the harem contains one or two young girls just past the age of puberty who are kept, and regularly replaced, for precisely that purpose.

I went to Germany in the autumn of 1912, accompanied by our old family tutor, Monsieur Devgantz, to attend Bonn University. Bonn, as I knew it then, was a pleasant little town on the banks of the Rhine and the centre for agreeable excursions in the Siebengebirge at Godesberg which was later (in 1938) to become notorious as the place where Hitler and Neville Chamberlain met before the Munich crisis. Now, of course, Bonn is the capital of Federal Germany, and the university takes a poor second place to the busy world of politics and diplomacy and is dwarfed by the official buildings which were rushed up to accommodate the new dignity of the city.

But life was pleasant then. During my first year I lived in the house of Professor Wilcken who was the world's greatest authority on papyrology.

German universities, then as now, gave much more freedom to their students than English ones. In Bonn I had merely to register on the first and last day of each semester. There were two semesters a year. Where you lived, where you slept, or if you slept; how often you went to lectures, if at all—none of this was regulated. There were no exams to pass until you felt fit to prepare a thesis which, if approved, entitled you to be called a Doctor—of Philosophy, of Law, of Medicine, and so on—which explains why so many Germans are 'Doctors', of course.

However, I must be careful not to give a false impression. If there was very little imposed discipline, there was a deal of self-discipline among the students, as elsewhere in Germany in every walk of life. The accepted thing was to work; this was the purpose of living. If you stopped work from time to time it was only in order to eat or sleep or take just enough recreation to make you fresh enough to go on working. Compare this with the English universities, where the object was to get the work out of the way as soon as possible to leave more time for 'living'. I believe the English way makes for a fuller life and certainly a more pleasant one; it is ideal training for a gentleman, but it is not, I grant, the best way to obtain a thorough and comprehensive knowledge of any subject. As an Armenian, I do enjoy the advantage perhaps of belonging to a people who have had to adapt themselves to their surroundings and who have managed somehow, while remaining Armenians, to identify themselves with their adopted countries. Yet I must say I found English university life the more agreeable and even now, when there are so many countries with so many different attractions for me, I always feel that life in England is the most satisfying. That is why I have made it my home, although I heartily dislike the climate.

I followed the custom in Germany and worked pretty hard, while finding time also to enjoy myself. There were pleasant rides on horseback along the banks of the Rhine and into the adjoining countryside. Although I was still too young according to the law to drive a car, I did hire one and drive to Cologne or to Coblenz or up the Moselle or the Taunus. With other students I spent evenings in cafés overlooking the Rhine, drinking beer and singing rather ribald student songs. When funds were high, we went to the night clubs, where there were plenty of feminine attractions. No doubt those night clubs were much the same as night clubs all over the world, but when one is sixteen or seventeen the atmosphere produced by low lights, an illuminated glass floor and cabaret turns involving a certain amount of exposure of the female form, seems glamorous and exciting. Not, I should add, that there was as much nudity among German cabaret artistes then as there is now anywhere. Naturally, there was a lot of drinking, generally of *Sekt*, German 'champagne'; we drank French champagne, costing three or four times as much, only if we were with a girl whom we wanted particularly to impress.

The great time for letting off steam was the Carnival, or *Fasching*, season of February and March, a sort of close season for morality. There were Carnivals at Munich, Cologne and at Düsseldorf, which was only about an hour's run by car from Bonn. During *Fasching* there was a great deal of promiscuity between the sexes and even married women were freed from normal ties of morality. Behaviour which would have given offence at other times, leading to a challenge and duel, was tolerated. Fancy dress and masked balls helped to disguise identities and so avoid embarrassment when the next day, or the next week, one met intimate acquaintances of the night in more sedate surroundings. No doubt a cold and detached analysis of the Carnival would seem shocking, but the normal standards of reason were suspended when one was taking part. Any who felt strongly disapproving obviously refused to join in, but it seemed to me that everyone took part and because of this and the wine and the general atmosphere of gaiety and abandon one was free of any sense of moral reprobation. One should remember, too, that if there were orgies, they were strictly limited to the period of the Carnival. Once it was over, whatever had happened was forgotten, and everyone returned to normal.

There was one moment during my time in Germany when I questioned whether I had enjoyed myself all too well and when it seemed my father's good advice had been ignored. I received through the post an official-looking form whose contents caused me much anxiety. They constituted a maintenance order, condemning me to pay five marks per week for the next sixteen years for each of three triplets, named Caspar, Balthazar and Melchior. They were alleged to have been produced by one of the beautiful young ladies to whose charms I was known not to be entirely insensible, and I was supposed to be their sire. I did not immediately appreciate either the honour or the degree of my achievement. I was really very troubled. Luckily, however, Monsieur Devgantz was there to help me; I had the greatest trust in him and confided my worries to him. He looked at the form and a smile began to spread over his face. My own sense of humour failed to rise to the occasion until he assured me that the form was not authentic. Even then I could not rid myself completely of my doubts until we discovered for certain that the whole thing was nothing more than a hoax played on me by some of my more sophisticated university friends.

The German students belonged to Corps or Corporations, whose memberships indicated the demarcations of class in Germany. The Borussia, for instance, was reserved for the sons of Prussian nobility; the Kaiser and his sons had all been members of it. The Hansea chiefly comprised the sons of bankers, industrialists and so on. The Rhenania took its members mainly from local people of the Rhineland and did not rate anywhere near so high as the others.

The prime purpose of these Corps was to indulge in the manly sport of the *Mensur*. The *Mensur*, which Hitler abolished but which has been reinstated recently, is a safe but disfiguring form of duelling. The eyes are shielded by goggles, the neck, the arms and all the vital arteries are well padded. The two opponents stand within an épée's length of each other and exchange blows—which really means they gash each other's cheeks. There is a doctor in attendance who disinfects the wounds but is honour bound not to apply any *blutstillendesmittel*, in other words any product which will stop the bleeding. The duel continues until one of the protagonists faints through loss of blood. It is unquestionably a rather messy proceeding, but in those days unless, after his first year, a student could sport two or three gashes on his left cheek—this was the one most easily attainable—he ranked low in student estimation. I bore no such scars, for my father, who objected to having his only son disfigured for life, forbade me to join any of the Corporations. Happily, for the sake of my life there, I was excused by my fellow students on the grounds that I was a foreigner and it was appreciated that marks which might seem honourable to a German could be misunderstood abroad. Instead, I became a member of the International Students Association, which did not allow duelling, a restriction which applied also, I believe, to certain of the so-called Christian Corporations. However, apart from the absence of scars on our cheeks, this also deprived us of the right to wear the distinctive headgear which denoted membership of the various Corporations. Members of the Borussia, for instance, wore, in the street, a white bonnet or cap with a tiny coloured fillet of (I think) gold. The lowly Rhenania tried to ape this headgear by having a white cap of similar shape but with a slightly different-coloured fillet.

The Germans were very helpful and friendly to foreigners but there was in their attitude, as in their acceptance that duelling scars might seem less than honourable to non-Germans, an assumption of their own superiority over all other peoples, of being the *Herrenvolk*. This could make itself manifest in the smallest ways. For instance, when I was studying chemistry in the laboratory, a fellow-student, a Hungarian, and I talked Italian together to practise the language. The *Privatdozent* Doktor Gewecke shut us up rather firmly. 'For God's sake,' he said, 'can't you speak German?' He said it in a way which indicated that German was a superior language. That same professor, who coached me in chemistry, smoked, like most Germans, very pungent cigars which nearly made me sick. I was much too young and too shy to make any open protest but I found a tactful way of protecting myself from regular bouts of nausea. Or so I thought. I gave him a box of excellent, mild, Havana cigars. He was most grateful, he said; but the next time I had a lesson with him he was still smoking his own pungent brand. 'Your cigars are much too good to smoke every day,' he said to me with a beaming smile. 'I keep them for Sunday afternoons.'

Then was the heyday of Prussian militarism. Before the 1914–18 war the officers' corps and the conscript soldiers conformed to a strict discipline, not only because it had been instilled into them but also because they believed in it as a matter of pride. If a soldier was beaten up in a brawl by a civilian, or even, as could happen, by a whole mob of civilians, he was immediately put on a charge by his commanding officer and could expect severe punishments. This was not, as one might have supposed, because he was guilty of unruly conduct, but because he had dishonoured his uniform by allowing himself to be beaten. The man himself felt a sense of personal shame. In any conflict with civilians, a soldier was expected, if needed, to use his side arms or any other weapon he might have with him, to defend himself and the honour of his uniform.

On Sunday mornings, the Poppelsdorfer Allee in Bonn, a broad street about a mile long, resembled the 'church parade' in Hyde Park in the early 1920s. It was the place where everyone walked up and down, taking the air, wearing their best, acknowledging friends and acquaintances, pausing to chat. The officers and soldiers from the local garrison in Bonn walked in small groups or squired their girl friends. When an officer passed, soldiers sprang to attention, saluted, remained stiff as ramrods, until he had gone on his way. On one occasion I saw what happened when a soldier neglected this observance of respect and discipline. Strutting along one side of the road was a young whipper-snapper of a second lieutenant, obviously full of a newly bestowed importance. Walking on the other side of the road, in the opposite direction, was a private soldier, six feet tall, an impressive figure in his gleaming *Pickelhauber*, the pointed helmet then worn by the German Army. With the soldier was a girl friend to whom he was talking and who so engaged his attention that he did not see the little junior officer across the road. The latter, clearly on the look-out for punctilious recognition, stopped, and called to the soldier, who left his girl and crossed over to the officer. The second lieutenant, in the midst of the promenaders, cursed him roundly, tweaked his nose and kicked his bottom. During the whole of this humiliating episode the soldier remained stiffly at attention without saying a word. The only person who appeared shocked at the whole affair was myself. No one else took it as other than a wholly natural occurrence, merely a moment's distraction from conversation; no one else even bothered to stop and stare.

During the Christmas vacation of 1913 I went from Bonn to spend a fortnight, alone with my father, in the south of France. The weather was wonderful. I exchanged leaden wintry skies for the sun and the blue, blue sea, and although I was comfortable enough in Germany I was now translated into a place where the service was incomparable and where luxury was taken for granted. Monte Carlo was the meeting-place for the highest of international society. From St. Petersburg, by sleeping-car express, came Russian Grand Dukes, travelling in the opposite direction to the flowers which were shipped regularly from the Riviera to the rich and noble houses of Petersburg. There were the wealthy from North and South America and the 'Milords' from England. In short, Monte Carlo was a hot-house in which the rich and the titled of the world bloomed. On the whole, however, this did not include French people who were too conscious of the virtue of thrift to be seen flaunting their wealth as the foreigners did. The pervasive feeling was that if one asked for something, for anything, there was always someone in Monte Carlo whose duty and even whose pleasure it was to supply it. That it cost money and might involve the suffering of others was never considered or, rather, considered to be in the natural order of things, for this after all was before the cataclysm of the First World War and the 1917 Russian Revolution.

The clientele of Monte Carlo expected the best and expected to pay for it. The Hôtel de Paris, where we were staying, had the best cuisine and the best cellar in Western Europe. (Even now, since Mr. Onassis bought the Société des Bains de Mer, the curiously named Company which owns the Casino, the standard has been fully maintained. I say 'even now', for some business men might have been concerned only to turn it into a more commercial property, but that has not been true of Aristotle Onassis. Sir Winston Churchill, of course, has for years spent much of the winter, as Onassis's guest, in a suite on the top floor of the Rotonde, as it is called, overlooking the harbour, when not on his yacht, *Christina*.)

By day, one of the big attractions of Monte Carlo was pigeon-shooting from boxes on a terrace below the Casino. By night, there was the parade of ostentatious wealth and high fashion, of beautiful women and priceless jewels. To serve the needs of this society were men whose own names were to become no less famous and, in some instances, more enduringly so than their patrons. There was the original Ciro, a small, brown, fat man, who founded, in the Gallerie Charles Trois, the first Ciro's restaurant. Afterwards this great restaurateur was to open branches in Paris, Deauville and London, but this was where he began. I remember his manager, 'Philippe', coming up to our table. (My father and I were dining alone there but wearing dinner jackets, for we should not have been allowed in any Casino or restaurant without them.) 'Philippe' sought my father's advice on a new development he was considering.

'I want to make it possible,' said 'Philippe', 'for the young people to dine here.' He knew that, however fine or wealthy their families, the sons did not always have unlimited supplies of money with which to entertain themselves and their friends. 'I want to offer them a dinner *prix fixe*'—at a fixed price—'so that they need not worry, you understand. How much do you think I should charge?'

'Philippe' and my father consulted together and agreed that it should be ten francs for a five-course dinner and twelve francs if it included fresh asparagus. That meant that for about ten shillings a head a young man could eat excellently at a great restaurant, a fine idea which in itself made no small contribution to Ciro's reputation in later years.

Our holiday together was another stage in my initiation by my father into grown-up behaviour. This included gambling, although my father was fanatically anti-gambling. By this he meant gambling on horses, on cards, in the casinos or in any game of chance. He did not mean the gambling of any successful business man, the difference being that in business the risks taken are calculated ones and, to a considerable extent, the outcome is dependent upon your own character and your own judgement. Despite my father's opposition to gambling he did allow me to go one night to the Casino. He took me in although I was only seventeen and the law denied entry to any under twenty-one. He lent me his own card and as he was very well known himself he merely nodded at the *physionomiste*, the functionary at the entrance to all casinos whose job it was to know everybody by sight.

In those days, people did not play with counters but with twenty-franc gold pieces, called Louis d'Or, which were worth about sixteen shillings, and with Five Louis pieces (100-franc pieces) which were about the size of an English crown or five-shilling piece. To give me pleasure, or perhaps to teach me a lesson, my father allowed me to stake twenty francs on a number. Naturally, I lost it and he then dragged me away, sharply and firmly.

Gambling was the great diversion at night, if diversion is the right word for so obsessive an activity, but there were many other attractions. Among them were the demi-mondaines who flourished at this time and whose extravagances have been reported in so many contemporary memoirs. There was great competition between them, particularly at that time between one called La Belle Otero, a Spaniard, and her rival, Liane de Pougy, who were always trying to score off each other. One evening while I was there Liane de Pougy made a startling entrance into the Casino covered with beautiful jewellery and wearing a priceless diamond necklace which her latest admirer had given her. News of this display was taken to La Belle Otero who, when she made her own entrance the next night, was wearing a plain, black velvet dress, without a single jewel. But she was accompanied by her maid whom she had decked out with even more jewels than Liane de Pougy had worn.

My holiday over, I caught the train back to Bonn, a twenty-four-hour journey, leaving behind the blue skies and waking up to see the banks of the Rhine and the surrounding landscape covered in snow.

Life at the University during the first half of 1914 went on as before. Neither was my mother deterred from her normal arrangements for that summer. She came to Germany to follow the Edwardian fashion of 'taking the waters' at Bad Homburg. She was accompanied by her maid. My sister, Rita, who was then fourteen, joined her later with her governess, Mlle Soulas. My father, however, who was in London, was less sanguine. As the political horizon grew darker and darker, he sent telegram after telegram telling us all to return home, but my mother was enjoying her waters and in no hurry to leave, especially as she was now under the protection of the Turkish Ambassador to Paris. The Ambassador, Rifaat Pasha, and his wife had also gone to the German spa and as my father was at that time an official of the Turkish Embassy, my mother came under the ambassadorial wing.

My father, of course, was right (as he usually was) and when general mobilization was ordered in Germany, we knew we could dally no longer. With the greatest regret, my old tutor and I packed up our books and our belongings and made ready to leave Bonn. I took leave of my friends, Germans and foreigners alike, with cheerful assurances to each other that we should meet again soon after Christmas; we could not, as yet, imagine the reality of war, even less of a long one.

Monsieur Devgantz and I chartered a car and set out for Bad Homburg to join my mother and sister. We motored away from the main roads which were already packed with military traffic and reached the spa without too much difficulty. The Turkish Ambassador had given orders for his party to return, for he was anxious to get back to his post in Paris before the war began. His presence there was most fortunate for my mother, indeed for all of us, for we were able to join him and to travel as members of the Ambassador's suite. This simplified so many matters which otherwise would have been very awkward. Without his diplomatic influence, for instance, we should certainly never have had the aid of the German General Staff, who gave us cars and lorries to take us to the Franco-German frontier, nor, later, that of the French General Staff, who sent us vehicles to help us on our way to Paris.

We were quite a party: Rifaat Pasha and his wife and his valet and her maid; my mother and her maid; my sister and her governess; myself and my tutor; and our family chauffeur, Ashton. Through the Ambassador's influence we secured enough sleepers for all of us in the train from Frankfurt to Paris. The only thing we could not take with us was my mother's car, a Delaunay Belleville Landaulette with basketwork of the kind I now have on my 'taxi'; we had to leave it behind in the care of Herr Ritter, the owner of Ritter's Park Hotel at Bad Homburg. (Some six months after the end of the war, nearly five years later, we received a letter from Herr Ritter. The car, he said, was there to be picked up at our convenience. He assured us it had been well looked after during the war, cleaned regularly, and that the lamps and fittings which, in those days, were of brass—chromium was unknown—had been properly greased. He regretted only that the tyres had been requisitioned by the German Army and taken away. He enclosed a bill for five years' garaging. Ashton was sent over to Germany and he drove the car back. We continued to use it for another couple of years until cars could again more easily be bought.)

We went to bed in the train, thinking that soon we should be in Paris and that would be that, but when we got as far as Metz (which then was German), a few miles from the French frontier, we were awakened in our beds and told the train could go no further. Our luggage was taken off the train and dumped on the platform and there we stood, a large party of travellers, surrounded by mountains of luggage, as we watched the train steam off back to Frankfurt. It was about four o'clock in the morning, it was still dark, there was a slight chill in the air and, with the sleep still in our eyes, we hunched and huddled as travellers do throughout the world.

As dawn broke and we began to set about the task of organizing the next stage of our journey there was consternation. On examining our baggage we found that one trunk, belonging to the Ambassador, was missing.

'My boots!' cried Rifaat Pasha. 'Where are my boots? I must have them. Where's the trunk with my boots?' The trunk containing them, it seemed, had not been offloaded and was now on its way back to Frankfurt. War might be about to break out at any moment but there was no more pressing problem, at that instant, than the loss of His Excellency's boots.

We spent at least an hour protesting. The Ambassador, using his monocle to gesticulate, was expressing his wrath in a rich mixture of Turkish and French. As the chief German scholar in the party it behoved me to translate his protest into somewhat more tactful German. Even so, given all the willingness of the German station staff to help, the most I could manage to secure was the *Gepäckschein*, the luggage ticket for the rest of our belongings, in the hope that after the war the necessary enquiries could be made for the missing trunk and the missing boots.

Apart from a few railway staff the station at Metz was desolate and we felt as though we, too, had been abandoned. We herded the women of the party into the waiting-room and the Ambassador, his valet and myself set out to get help. There was no transport to be had so we started off on foot. This had its difficult moments, for although the town was also virtually empty we did meet the occasional policeman or armed soldier who shouted to us.

'Halt! What are you doing? Where are you going?'

We tried each time to explain our predicament, but there were obstacles to overcome. For instance, if we chanced to stop a civilian merely to make enquiries, the three of us and the man we were talking to made a group of four and that meant trouble from the military.

'Assemblies of more than three people are *verboten*,' we were told. 'It is against the law. Why are you meeting together?'

Eventually, however, we reached the German *Kommandantur*. We persuaded first the sentry and then the sergeant of the guard of our innocent purposes. Then we were taken to see a very correct and very courteous staff major who spoke French. Through his good offices, we were given the necessary passes to help us on our way and two cars and a lorry to carry us and our baggage to the frontier.

We set off towards France. Every two miles or so we were held up at road blocks, usually composed of a farm cart. Soldiers pointed rifles at us, examined our passes carefully; but, once they had established that our papers were in order, they saluted smartly, rolled the cart back and let us through. The strong impression I received, as we drove onwards from Metz, was of thorough German organization. This was a nation prepared for war. The soldier's uniforms, like those of our excellent drivers, who wore the symbol of a little motor-car on their sleeves, were of good material; the guards at the roadblocks looked smart, their rifles gleaming; the officers with their gloves and field glasses seemed the epitome of military efficiency. This, I thought, is the end product of that Prussian militarism I had seen at first-hand in Bonn.

When we reached the frontier, which was lined with German troops, we were left once more to our own devices. The Germans had done all they could to help us and now, as they said, it was up to the French. War had not yet been declared, but that formality was only a matter of hours away. Our luggage was unloaded from the lorry on to the side of the road and we got out of the two cars to join it. Then the lorry and the cars went back to Metz. We were the last people to cross the frontier before war was declared.

We were in France but this did not help us much for, pending the declaration of war, the French authorities had withdrawn their troops ten kilometres back from the frontier to avoid frontier incidents. We found ourselves in a no-man's-land ten kilometres wide and, for the first time, perhaps, a little concerned at the possible dangers of finding ourselves involved in a local clash or skirmish between the two armies. At last we were aware of the imminence of war but even then, to recall our feelings honestly, we were still more worried about the discomforts and inconveniences of the journey than of the potential dangers.

Three of us walked into France to the nearest village, about a mile away, leaving our luggage at the frontier. There we found some farm carts and, after some gold had changed hands, these were sent off to the frontier to pick up the rest of the party and the luggage and to bring them back to the village where there was, at least, a barn to shelter us. Luckily, as it was August, the weather was fine and, if anything, too hot; at any rate, it was not yet raining. Next, we found a man with a bicycle who, again for payment in gold, agreed to cycle to the nearest French outpost some five miles away, to explain our plight.

We sat down in the barn and awaited his return or the arrival of the French military. While we were waiting, however, we had a bit of luck. We heard that there was a car in the village; it had been abandoned in a garage. If we were willing to take the risk, we were told, it might get us as far as the nearest French Command post or even as far as Nancy, where the French Army Commander had his H.Q.

We were prepared to try anything. We decided to put the women in the car, while the men stayed behind. In we piled, my mother, the wife of the Turkish Ambassador, my sister and her governess, Mlle Soulas, and myself at the wheel, all squeezed into what was a very tiny car. We drove off, with little knowledge of where we were heading, with no papers except our passports, towards what we hoped was the nearest outpost. As in Germany, we were stopped at roadblocks, manned by French troops, and this time, having none of the official authorization which had carried us through Germany, we had to talk and bluff our way through. We did meet the captain in charge of a Command outpost who, as he could do nothing himself, allowed us to go through. It seemed that our best bet was the nearest town, Pont-à-Mousson, on the Moselle, where we were told we should find the Army Commander. Unfortunately, when we reached there, we found he was away on inspection, so we explained our plight to the civilian authorities.

Much sympathy and much shrugging of shoulders was the response to our story. 'It is difficult. . . .' 'We will try. . . .' 'The war will be declared any moment now, you understand. . . .' We understood all too well.

'You should make your request for assistance through Diplomatic channels,' we were told, 'but . . .' The idea of 'Diplomatic channels', ten miles from the German frontier, with war about to break out, was enough to make us all smile, even in the face of our anxieties. However, we decided to go on in the car, hoping there was enough petrol to reach Nancy. We did get there but by that time it was pouring with rain, which did not increase our optimism.

We managed to find the French General in command and to him we told our story yet again. He seemed a somewhat harassed man and obviously not prepared for the war that was about to break out. Compared with what we had seen on the German side of the frontier, everything and everyone in France appeared to be in confusion. This is the kind of comparison which can often be made between French and German organization and yet it is unwise to draw too many conclusions from it. The Germans frequently seem to have worked out everything most thoroughly in advance, but the French are much better and more successful when called upon to improvise to meet the unexpected. (This was seen time and again in the battle of wits between the German Army and the French Resistance during the Second World War.) The French may talk and gesticulate a great deal; the Germans may seem more stolid and unimaginative; experience has taught me only to judge by results and not to generalize.

The French General sent off a lorry and a car to return to the frontier and pick up the rest of the party and the luggage. Unfortunately, he forgot to give his drivers the necessary passes so that, at the first roadblock, they were turned back. More delay. Meanwhile, the Turkish Ambassador, his valet, Monsieur Devgantz, the two lady's maids and Ashton, our chauffeur, had set off from the village where we had first sheltered in the barn. They had persuaded the owner of the farm carts to load up the luggage again and to take to the road; they followed the carts on foot. Eventually, by midnight, they had been rescued by the French Army and they rejoined myself and the ladies of the party at an hotel in Nancy.

At Nancy, we had another wait because there was no train to take us to Paris or even on the way to it until the next morning. Still, there was the chance to sleep after the exhausting experiences of the past day and once again Diplomatic influence enabled us to get two compartments to ourselves on the train into which we squeezed ourselves and our luggage (minus the Ambassadorial boots).

The journey to Paris, which normally should have taken about six hours, took a full twenty-four hours. Confusion of one kind or another caused many hold-ups and more than once we found ourselves on a siding alongside long trainloads of trucks, the

Quarante Hommes ou Huit Chevaux (forty men or eight horses) so well known to veterans of that war. These trucks were packed with men on their way to what was still the frontier but which, in a matter of hours, was to become the Front. War broke out while we were on the train between Nancy and Paris. Many of the trucks had '*À Berlin*' scrawled on them in chalk and the men aboard them generated a feeling of enthusiasm and great confidence. We leaned out of our compartments to call to them but conversation was rudimentary.

When, at last, we reached Paris, we thought all our troubles were over, that it was now merely a matter of buying railway tickets to get back to London. But it was not quite as easy as that. The Turkish Ambassador, his wife and their two servants, had left us and we discovered that not only had our supply of gold run out but that all the banks were shut; there was a moratorium on all withdrawals and it was impossible to get hold of any cash. Luckily, as a constant traveller between London and Paris, my father was well known to the station-master and numerous subordinate officials at the Gare du Nord. Where, not unnaturally in the circumstances, people of much higher rank and influence had been too preoccupied to bother with our party, the staff at the station managed to help us. The bulk of the luggage had to be left in Paris but once again we found a place on the train for ourselves and our most necessary belongings. The station was in chaos, invested by great crowds of people trying to get home from Paris, but some railway inspectors, who were grateful for the largesse they had received from my father in happier times, pushed us through the throngs, on to the platform and packed us into a train for Calais.

After another all-night journey, we arrived at the port, only to find that no one knew whether there would be a boat going to England or whether, even if there were, we should be allowed to board it. This time a tramp around Calais located the Mayor whom I persuaded to give us exit permits and permission to go on board the *Pas de Calais*, the cross-channel steamer which, in the meantime, had docked. The purser was a Mr. Hart who had known my father for many years and also knew my mother and myself. He smuggled us past all the struggling and shouting mob, up a side gangway and into the cabin de luxe. We expected either to be torpedoed by German submarines or to be bombarded by the German Fleet, which was about to sail into the Channel to shell the French ports, but in the end the worst thing to happen on the voyage was that my sister was sick. Of the German Fleet we saw and heard nothing.

At Dover, the now familiar story continued, with the British authorities coping inadequately with the flood of semi-refugees from the *Pas de Calais*. However, here again, Diplomatic influence came in useful, as did the familiarity of the name Gulbenkian to the harbour officials; we achieved a compartment on the boat train into which we all piled, along with such luggage as had survived that far. We reached London and home without further trouble.

In England the war was welcomed as something of a sporting adventure in which everyone wanted to take part before it was all over; that meant, in England, before Christmas. That was what everyone, except Lord Kitchener, expected. Like all youngsters of my age and like all my friends, I was anxious to join up and to try to get a commission. This was much against my father's wishes, who met my enthusiasm with a combination of commands, solemn entreaties and a deal of sarcasm.

'I can see no grounds for believing,' he said to me, 'that it will help the Allied war effort if you, a callow youth, get yourself killed or maimed for life. Furthermore, it would be a great displeasure and disappointment to me if you were to allow your childish whims to take precedence over your first duty, which is to your family. I have done everything for you and I do not wish to see your life thrown away.'

Apart from the respect and veneration I felt for my father, I was also, as throughout my life, terrified of him, and so long as he was there to press his appeal I found it very difficult to withstand him. However, because he thought my education should now proceed, I went up to Cambridge and there, out of his sight and away from his immediate influence, I did as I had wished. I joined the O.T.C., the Officers' Training Corps. Even as I did so, I felt frightened at my boldness in having flouted what I knew were my father's desires. This was one of the first important occasions on which I had to face a clear conflict of loyalties.

In the O.T.C. I formed fours assiduously with my fellow-undergraduates, performing rifle drill with dummy rifles. I was not a success as an embryonic soldier.

' 'Shun . . . left, right, left—Halt! . . . Quick march! . . . Jump to it there, Mr. Gulbenkian!'

The sergeant-major's voice so impressed and so frightened me that I was reduced to confusion. So was my squad when he gave the order to about-turn to the right and I did an about-turn to the left. This was not the reason, though, why I did not get my commission. When the time came to fill up the forms to apply for one, I faced the question, 'Are you of purely European descent on both sides?' As an Asiatic, I was precluded from holding His Majesty's commission. Almost ignominiously, I had to leave the O.T.C.; my belligerent days were cut short at their very inception. Then Turkey entered the war on the side of Germany and, though Armenians in Britain were exempted from the restrictions applicable to enemy aliens, yet that fact, too, militated against my warlike ambitions. I settled down to enjoy Cambridge.

I had been accepted for Trinity College, chiefly, I think, because the Master, Dr. Henry Montagu Butler, had been Headmaster of Harrow. When I first went up in the autumn of 1914 I had rooms just outside Trinity Great Gate. Later, when all the undergraduates were moved into College, I had rooms in Great Court.

The war touched Cambridge very little. There was a fairly strict blackout, the Corps did drill (or tried to) in Great Court, there were troops billeted in some of the colleges and khaki uniforms were a common sight in the streets; yet those of us who were still up at the University were left free to carry on their normal activities. The war seemed close only when the casualty lists were published containing, as they invariably did, the names of friends from school. But, for myself, my attempt to get a commission having failed, my conscience was free and I enjoyed myself. (Throughout the war my mother and sister stayed in England. My father travelled fairly often between London and Paris on business. He had negotiated contracts on behalf of the Royal Dutch Shell Group to supply petroleum products to the French Government and was actually appointed delegate of the Royal Dutch Shell Group to the French Government. He was also in charge of a Dutch hospital, which Henri Deterding, head of the Group, maintained in France.)

I made quite a large circle of acquaintances, chiefly among the variegated foreigners who were studying there. I took up hunting seriously, getting two or three days a week, mainly with the Cambridgeshire Hounds but also occasionally with the Puckeridge who, even in those days, had a Barclay as Master. (I believe the Barclays have been Masters of that pack for nearly a century and certainly some fifty years after my first hunt with them there is still a Barclay as Master, the grandson, I think, of the one I knew—or rather of whom I was in awe.) On other days I rode with the Fitzwilliam Hounds, boxing my horse by railway to Huntingdon (motor horse boxes were unheard of then) and hacking on from there to Graffham, which was the most convenient meet.

Some of us organized a point-to-point meeting with the help of one or two sporting farmers and the joint proprietors of a livery stable. One was a Navy captain, a Captain Taylor, who was later torpedoed and went down with his ship, and the other a tall, lanky fellow called Tebbs, who remained in the horse-coping world for many years.

We also held one flat race, in which my Cambridge friend, George Ansley, who was then known as George Ansbacher, took part. Unhappily, George, who was not much of a horseman, fell off when his horse shied at a puddle on the course. This was not an episode of which he was unduly proud and he was much abashed when, at a point-to-point meeting twenty years later, we were joined by Tebbs who reminded him of it in front of a fairly large circle of racegoers. (George Ansley is now a distinguished international banker and the owner of a champion steeplechaser. He has organized his life well, living partly in France and partly in Ireland, carrying on some of his business there and some in London, where his parental firm of bankers and stockbrokers, Henry Ansbacher and Co., have their headquarters.)

Apart from hunting, I also learned during my time at Cambridge how to take the train to London and assist at the matinée of a musical comedy—taking out one of the girls of the chorus for tea and early dinner before she had to return for her evening performance. I had to get back on the last train in order to be in College before midnight. (I am told that nowadays the gyps, the College servants, whose duty it is to report when an undergraduate has not slept in his bed, are not so keen-sighted as they were in my time and are known to turn a tolerant blind eye when the occasion arises.)

George and I were enamoured, or so we thought, of the same girl, called Phyllis, who had been recently promoted from the second to the first row of the chorus at the Hippodrome and we found out we both had a date with her on the same day in London. Obviously, one of us had to give way, but neither of us volunteered to do so. I was unsporting enough to ensure his absence by pouring surreptitiously a generous amount of Epsom salts into his whisky and soda the night before the appointed date. He stayed in Cambridge. I kept the date with Phyllis.

There was also Connie. She was a Gaiety Girl who lived in Ladbroke Grove. We used to meet at Notting Hill Gate station. She was always very punctual for our meetings; so was her youngest sister, Billie, who succeeded Connie. My finances limited my entertaining and there was no exclusivity on either side, asked for or received. I was one of many young men who took them out; we enjoyed ourselves, promised to meet again and that was that.

There was another girl, a girl who was third from the left in the second row of the chorus at the Gaiety; she caught my eye when I went to see a new play put on by the 'Guvnor'—the famous George Edwardes. I found out the name of the lovely and, having invested £2, a week's pocket money, in buying some flowers, I went round to the stage door. I sent the flowers up to her with what I thought was an amusingly written invitation to come to tea—and waited expectantly.

'Sorry, sir,' said the stage doorkeeper when he came back, 'the lady's in Birmingham this week.'

Having been brought up by my father on sound business principles, I thought it a pity that a week's pocket money should be wasted on flowers for a girl who would never see them.

'Will you please go back to the dressing-room,' I said to the stage doorkeeper, 'and say that if the lady is in Birmingham could I have the flowers back.' Off he went again but came back very soon with an unexpected answer.

'She's not there—she's in Birmingham like I told you,' he said. 'But her husband's in the theatre and he says if you want the flowers back will you go and see him about them.' I am afraid neither my *sang-froid* nor my *savoir-vivre* was up to that test and I took myself hurriedly and ignominiously, as fast as my legs would carry me, along the Strand to find a taxi to catch a train back to Cambridge.

Perhaps I was more successful in entertaining male friends at that time, for I had developed quite a taste for playing the host and I gave some quite good dinners supplied by the College kitchen. When I look back on some of those menus—menus which were quite common even in wartime—I am amazed at our capacity. I offered eight or ten courses and, halfway through the dinner, a sorbet (a water-ice) was served to stop the digestive processes and to enable my guests to enjoy the food which was still to come. I suppose one could compare it, *mutatis mutandis*, with the vomitorium of the Romans, or the Trou Normand when a glass of Calvados is, and was, taken halfway through the meal to hasten digestion.

Once, my enjoyment for entertaining led me into trouble. The son of a business friend of my father's, Sir Henri Deterding of Royal Dutch Shell, came to Trinity to pass an exam and, on his father's instructions, looked me up. Unfortunately, I had quite forgotten he was coming and, the day he arrived, I was giving one of my dinner parties in my rooms. The young Deterding came to my staircase and was appalled, apparently, at the number of champagne bottles in ice waiting there in anticipation of my feast; he went away without letting me know he was there. He told his father who told mine. I had a very unpleasant homily from my father.

'The very good money I am spending,' he said, 'is meant for your academic education. Not—*not* to teach you to recognize the vintages of wines and champagne.'

(I always remember that episode because nearly forty years later, when a young nephew of mine, my father's only grandson, was at Balliol, a rather similar incident occurred but with very different consequences. Another friend of my father's, and of mine, Lord Radcliffe, called on my nephew and found him out. Lord Radcliffe wrote to my father a letter which I saw. He said he had called on my father's grandson but found him out, 'probably attending some lecture'. My father was delighted to receive that letter. He beamed and showed it to me. 'You see,' he said, 'how different my grandson is from you. He gets on with his work at the university. You remember what you were like. . . .')

In the spare time which my hunting, trips to London, entertaining and card-playing—I learned to play bridge at Cambridge—left me, I attended lectures and worked with my tutors.

While still young I started to follow the principle that one's work must never be allowed to interfere with one's pleasure, but I also believed, and still believe, that one's pleasure should not interfere with one's work. At Cambridge I did manage to scrape through two Honours courses in three years and am now the proud possessor of the degrees of M.A. and LL.B. After passing my Science Tripos, I read Law for a year there; I got a second-class Honours and was placed equal with my friend, George, who had been studying Law for four years.

George Ansley reminded me recently of the remark I made when the results came out: 'I thought I was intelligent—until I found I was only equal to you.' His sense of humour has improved with age—he was a bit pompous at times at Cambridge—and I was told he said this of me: 'Nubar is so tough that every day he tires out three stockbrokers, three horses and three women.' I am not sure whether that was meant to be complimentary. I doubt whether it was entirely true. And, in any case, I am afraid he said it quite a few years ago.

3

The Three Requirements of
Monsieur Nubar

ONE of my regrets is that the lack of £100 prevented me from being called to the Bar. During my last year at Cambridge I put my name down for the Middle Temple and ate a few dinners with a view to being called; it was also a good excuse for going to London. The atmosphere in the Middle Temple was much to my liking; I appreciated its dignity, its traditions and its customs. It was there that I was initiated into the practice of taking snuff, because in those days smoking was not allowed in the Middle Temple Hall, and I also developed a taste for port which has stayed with me throughout my life. Unfortunately, however, I never ate the requisite number of dinners to enable me to sit for my Bar examinations and eventually to be 'called'. The pleasure of being able to drop into the Temple to lunch with one's fellow barristers, even if one is no longer practising, has been denied to me, and simply because I was hard up at the all important time. I had deposited £100 which allowed my name to go on the Boards of the Middle Temple. The money had been called for as a guarantee, though as a guarantee for what, whether of good behaviour or financial integrity, for instance, I am not sure. Faced with my need for funds, it seemed to me the easiest thing was to take my name off the Boards and recoup my £100. This I did, to my subsequent regret.

When I left Cambridge, I went straight into my father's office. Above my desk I found a large notice which displayed the ominous words: 'There is no fun like work.' Fifty years later I wonder if that is really true. I am very ready to agree that work is fun and that if you do not find your work fun you will never be any good at it. But I certainly cannot accept that work is the only possible source of enjoyment.

My first job in the office was far from onerous: I was put to addressing envelopes and copying letters. In those days every office had a copybook. Letters were typewritten with a purple ribbon and then placed in this copybook with a damp sheet and a board on top. The next step was to press down on them with a huge letter-press in order to transfer a copy of the letter on to a page of the copybook. If the cloth was not damp enough the copy would not come through; if it was too damp it would smudge not only the copy but also the original, so quite a bit of skill was needed.

After a few weeks of that routine job I was promoted to keeping, or endeavouring to keep, a set of books. I was initiated into the mysteries of bookkeeping by Mr. F. W. Stephens, who always wore a morning coat and top hat. From him I learned the first golden rule of bookkeeping: that every debit has a credit with the result that the greater the loss a company incurs the greater the amount on the credit side of its balance sheet. To those who understand such mysteries this will seem an inane remark, but it will help to understand why even to this day I find the sessions with my accountants nerve-racking and perplexing to say the least. (The firm which looks after my affairs is still F. W. Stephens & Co., a firm founded by the same man who conducted my initiation and now run by his son with partners. I should add that however much I fear the appointed day with them, I am more than grateful for what that firm has done for both my father and myself. In particular, I owe much to their Mr. Simmonds.)

At that time, the latter part of 1917, my father was in close alliance with the Royal Dutch Shell Group, whose big noise, Sir Henri Deterding, was his bosom friend. My father produced from the public large amounts of money for what was then, compared with what it is now, a small company. I propose to deal in detail later in this book with the oil negotiations which are so important to the Gulbenkian story—to my story, indeed—although I have no intention of inflicting a pompous or solemn history upon my readers. The record has been distorted by certain other writers and I should like to straighten it out a bit.

For the moment, however, I want to give just a few examples of my father's activities and hence of the work in which I became involved after leaving Cambridge. Towards the end of 1917, my father negotiated an issue in New York of Royal Dutch and Shell shares, both through the banking firm of Kuhn Loeb and Company. The name of this firm or that firm may mean little to anyone not closely concerned with international finance, so let me at once personify Kuhn Loeb and Co. by a quick sketch of the men behind it. One of the partners was Otto Kahn, dapper, very well dressed, Maecenas of the arts and a pillar of the New York Metropolitan Opera. His prominence in American financial circles and his own persistence helped him to succeed in another ambition: to meet all the important people in the world. One might almost say he 'collected' them. At one time he came to London and had a house in Regent's Park which, eventually, he gave to St. Dunstan's for the blind; this is the same house which was later sold to Barbara Hutton and is now the residence of the American Ambassador in London. A beautiful house, beautifully situated and a sort of monument to Otto Kahn's success.

Another partner was Morty Schiff whose father, Jacob Schiff, had been born in Germany but had come to America as a boy and whose financial genius had been recognized while he was still a young man. Morty Schiff had followed his father and had become a great banker. Unlike my father, he enjoyed gambling and in the smart places of Europe, like the Deauville Casino, he could be seen in the private rooms nonchalantly tossing 50,000-franc plaques on to the tables. Like my father, however, he was not always exclusively in the company of his own sex.

These were the men behind Kuhn Loeb and the issue of the Shell and Royal Dutch shares in New York, and it was part of my job to act as liaison between them on the one side and the Royal Dutch Shell over here. This required a certain exercise of tact for Kuhn Loeb, in sponsoring the Shell issue, and Shell, in granting Kuhn Loeb those rights, each thought they were doing the other a favour. Telegrams from one to the other passed through my father's office and as time went on their wording became more and more tart. Before passing them on, I toned them down, endeavouring to keep both parties reasonably sweet.

At the London end I had to deal with Walter Samuel, son of the first Lord Bearsted who was the founder and original owner of the Shell Company. A comprehensive book has been published recently about the first Lord Bearsted and although I do not believe in hereditary vendettas I do want to take this opportunity of pointing out that this book contains a few gratuitously unfair remarks about my father. I think, too, I may be permitted to state that though the first Lord Bearsted certainly had a great deal of prescience in hitching his chariot to Deterding's, he might have done it on a 50/50 basis but he missed that chance. Still, he was wise enough to make the 'marriage' even though he got the worst end of the 60/40 agreement, which is the present basis of the relationship between the Royal Dutch and Shell in that combine. There was a moment in 1917 when Lord Bearsted's foresight definitely failed him. My father had been responsible for bringing to the Royal Dutch Shell Group a concession in Venezuela which involved them putting up £100,000 between them. Lord Bearsted accosted my father in the corridors of St. Helen's Court where the Royal Dutch Shell had their London office and told him: 'Gulbenkian, you ought to be ashamed of yourself for bringing such muck into the Group.' The 'muck' has since brought tens of millions of pounds' profit to the Royal Dutch Shell and has been the whole basis of their interests in the Caribbean. Still, I suppose it fair to say that at the time neither Lord Bearsted nor anyone else had a crystal ball to see into the future. I am glad to say that his grandson, the present and third Lord Bearsted, and his charming and amusing wife, Heather, are good friends of mine and so is his grand-daughter, Mary Elliot Blake.

In 1918, the year after I started in his office, my father was negotiating the taking over, by the Royal Dutch Shell, of the controlling interest in the Mexican Eagle Oil Company. The Mexican Eagle had been founded by the first Lord Cowdray, a very shrewd Yorkshireman, who, as a contractor, had been responsible for building Dover Harbour. While he was surveying the Isthmus of Tehuantepec in Mexico, for the purpose of building a railway from the Atlantic to the Pacific to compete with the Panama Canal, Cowdray became interested, as a side-line, in the mineral rights in that area and especially in the oil rights. He began in a very small way but went on to obtain oil concessions from the Mexican Government in Mexico's famous 'Golden Lane'. He built a refinery at Tampico and founded a distributing organization in England. He also had a fleet of tankers which were by far the largest in the world at that time. The average tanker then was about 6000 to 8000 tons; his were around 18,000 to 20,000 tons. Nowadays, tankers of over 100,000 tons are almost commonplace.

For all this, Lord Cowdray felt that the oil business was not really his line and some years before he and Sir Henri Deterding had met together to try to agree an amalgamation of their two companies. They were both stubborn men, however, and their personalities and temperaments had clashed: Cowdray, the quiet, shrewd Yorkshireman, was the antithesis of the brilliant, mercurial Deterding. They had failed to reach agreement. This had turned out to be much to Cowdray's advantage for, in the years that followed, his shares had become much more valuable. Now, both men wanted to try again. This was where the Gulbenkians came in but the prospects were not good.

'If we are to have any chance of success in these negotiations,' my father told me, 'it is essential to keep Cowdray and Deterding away from each other.'

We managed it. I had to spend a good deal of time at 47 Parliament Street, the huge, palatial headquarters of S. Pearson and Son, the contracting firm founded by Lord Cowdray, and also of the Cowdray group of enterprises. As I saw for myself, Lord Cowdray knew how to surround himself with devoted assistants. There was J. B. Body, the white-haired, rather petulant but charming man who was in charge of the technical side of the oil-field management. There was also J. H. Macdonald, a Scots accountant who had been with Deloitte, Plender, Griffiths and Co. Macdonald was a worldly and very cheerful man, extremely tough and very, very loyal to 'the Chief', as Cowdray was generally known. There were moments when this loyalty could become exasperating. On one occasion when dealing with Macdonald, my father, tired of being reminded of the interests, direct or indirect, of Lord Cowdray, shouted out, 'Macdonald, I think you'd give your mistress to the Chief, if he wanted her.'

The contract for the Mexican Eagle deal was very complicated. I was engaged in drafting it early in November, 1918, and even on Armistice night, because I was trying to evolve a most difficult clause, I was the only person who did not go out to celebrate. Gradually, we hammered out a scheme whereby the Royal Dutch Shell bought for cash a large number of Mexican Eagle shares.

They paid 98*s*. each for them. These shares were then formed into a succession of 'pools', under my father's management, and re-sold to the public. The arrangement was that whatever they fetched above the 98*s*. they had cost in the first place should be distributed, 40 per cent of the proceeds going to each of the two large participants and 20 per cent to my father.

The first 'pool', of half a million shares, sold at 105*s*. Thereafter, Mexican Eagle shares rocketed to a price of £11. One oil-field after another 'came in' and every day, it seemed, the news was rosy. My father was responsible for placing millions of shares and, at one time, he showed, as his slice of the deal, a paper profit of £1 million, a lot of money in those days.

It was also part of the deal that my father should receive 50,000 Mexican Eagle shares at par. Although the shares were then standing at around £5 or £6, the par value was only ten Mexican pesos or £1 0*s*. 6*d*. each. They were always referred to, in fact, as £1 shares. For his 50,000 shares, my father, believing the par value to be just £1, sent a cheque for £50,000 to Lord Cowdray's office. Mr. Macdonald, from Parliament Street, wrote back, pointing out that the par value of the shares was not £1 but £1 0*s*. 6*d*. 'Please,' Mr. Macdonald asked, 'could we have the odd sixpence.' My father promptly sent round a cheque for the 50,000 'odd sixpences' but he gave me a wigging for not having reminded him of the exact par value of the shares.

Unhappily, before the whole Mexican Eagle transaction had been completed, news came that salt water instead of oil had appeared in the 'Golden Lane' of Mexico. At that time, wells were produced at full blast and no one was sufficiently advanced, technically, to know that the flow of a well should be so regulated that the salt water which lies under the oil should not be sucked up with the oil. There was just one man, de Golyer, who predicted that the appearance of salt water presaged the beginning of the end. At first, his forecast met only with scepticism, but he was right and thenceforward his reputation as a consultant geologist in the United States was made; for the next twenty years no oil company would venture to go to the public for capital without a certificate from de Golyer.

As a consequence of salt water appearing in the Mexican wells my father's profit of £1 million was turned into a loss of half a million. It was many years after the original deal before the last shares, which my father had bought at 98*s.*, were liquidated; by that time they were selling at 12*s.* The loss of half a million pounds was a big blow to my father for he had made his first million only just after I had come down from Cambridge to start work in his office. I knew that because I kept a note on a slip of paper which summarized his fortune, a fact of which no one else in the office was aware. These figures, as I say, meant a great deal because a million pounds then is probably worth £10 million today. After all, Mr. Paul Getty, the present holder of the title 'the world's richest man', is quoted as having said that a billion dollars is not worth what it used to be. (About Getty, by the way, another tycoon— Charles Wrightsman, who generously allowed the National Gallery to buy the Goya Duke of Wellington which was stolen in 1961—once remarked, 'Paul?—Why, he's not worth a cent more than half a billion dollars!')

During the same period as the Mexican Eagle transactions, the Royal Dutch Shell were liquidating some of their holdings in one of the Trinidad oil companies and because my father was away it was left to me to negotiate the sales. I obtained firm offers from the Royal Dutch Shell Group of the price at which I could buy lines of shares on the understanding that I would try to find buyers for them and that the difference between the price fixed by the Group and the price I could obtain from outside buyers would go to my father. A firm of stockbrokers, Vickers da Costa, helped me. They formed a syndicate prepared to pay 50*s.* for 100,000 shares which the Royal Dutch Group had offered to me at 30*s.* I 'married' the offer and the bid without risk and, in half a day, cleared £100,000 for my father. I felt rather pleased with myself, even deserving, perhaps, of a little time off on a Saturday afternoon or a Sunday. But when I reported my efforts to my father I received, instead of praise, a sound telling-off for having mishandled the deal.

'You should never have accepted 50*s.* for the shares from Vickers da Costa,' he said. 'They immediately went up to over 60*s.* The proper profit you ought to have made on the deal was £150,000.'

I was in a bit of trouble in another way over both the Mexican Eagle and the Trinidad ventures through trying to do a good turn to my Cambridge friend, George Ansley (the one who fell off his horse in the flat race). George was then a young apprentice in his father's stock-brokering firm and, naturally, I had let him in on the brilliant prospects foreseen for both these deals. He bought the shares from the respective syndicates early and at handsome prices. The following day the shares soared high above the prices he had paid but, perhaps because he was too greedy or, as all good business men are, a bad seller, he had not taken his profit. He had kept his shares which eventually fell. He reproached me with not having told him to take his profit, something I did not think it proper for me to do. He groaned and moaned that Mexican Eagles would never again reach the price he paid for them, which was £11. I bet him £1, quite a lot of money for me in those days, that they would. Three or four weeks later, the shares crept up and there was one marking in the *Stock Exchange Gazette* at $11\frac{1}{16}$.

'There, I told you so,' I said. 'One pound, if you please, George.'

He paid up, but unfortunately the shares fell again immediately afterwards so that the poor man not only lost his bet but still kept his shares. He has told me he has remembered me in his will by a bequest of one Mexican Eagle and one Trinidad share. Unfortunately, as he is very much alive (having had two wives and two daughters), I do not know whether I shall live long enough to enjoy his munificent legacy.

Yet another of my father's activities was to represent the Royal Dutch Shell in their negotiations with the French and Italian Governments for the supply of petroleum products, initially for war purposes and later for peaceful ones. He set up the sales organization in both countries. I was attached to the French Ministry of Supply to facilitate the working of the various contracts between the Royal Dutch Shell and the French *Commissariat aux Essences*, as it then was. This involved my receiving cheques from the French Government and passing them on to the Royal Dutch Shell Group. As with all good Government departments in all countries, the payments by the French were not always very prompt and it was part of my job to jog up their financial representative in London, who was first of all the Marquis de Chasseloup-Laubat and then Monsieur Hannonet de la Grange. The French Government had a fortnight in which to pay up, after which interest was charged, with the result that the cheque used to be delivered by hand at 2 p.m. on the fourteenth day. I remember one occasion when over £1 million came into the office and I had to get it over to St. Helen's Court within the next half hour so that it could be paid in within banking hours. I was feeling rather pleased with myself for having chivied the French representative sufficiently to obtain payment for what was, after all, not a negligible sum. At St. Helen's Court, I handed it over to B. A. Fenwick of Royal Dutch Shell. Both he and his father were good friends of ours, but instead of giving me a pat on the back Fenwick blew me up.

'What the devil,' he said, 'is the good of bringing me a million pounds at this time of day? It's like heaving a gold brick at me— what on earth do you expect me to do with it?'

My work meant spending quite a lot of time in Paris. In those years immediately following the end of the war, Paris had an abundance of Russian night clubs, all of them run by men who were, allegedly, members of the exiled and penniless Russian aristocracy. Grand Dukes and cousins of the Czar were a commonplace (or so it seemed) and every waiter had been a member of the Chevaliers Gardes, the crack Russian regiment. The Russian émigrés told the story of the dachshund which, when scoffed at for its size and asked what it was, replied, 'Now I am only a dachshund, yes, but before the Revolution I was a borzoi.'

Among the exiles was a Russian-Armenian called Adjemoff, a tiny man, with a face like a fox, a black moustache and a small, pointed beard. In the Czarist days he had been a deputy in the Duma, the Russian Parliament, as representative of the Don Cossacks. On one occasion when the Czar granted Adjemoff an audience he remarked on the incongruity of this unimpressive little man representing the tall, handsome Don Cossacks. Whatever Adjemoff may have lacked in his physical appearance he made up for in his mental abilities: he was very astute and sharp as a needle. By profession he was a lawyer and a very good and persuasive one. He was also a man of courage. As a member of the Cadet (Constitutionalist Democratic Party) in the Duma he was opposed to the autocratic powers of the Czar. He also resented the pro-German and anti-Russian activities of the German-born Empress, but to have attacked her directly would have led to his immediate arrest and probable banishment to Siberia. He managed to avoid this fate while still leaving no doubt in anyone's mind of his views about the Empress. He made a speech in the Duma attacking German princesses in other countries, who had influenced their husbands and the politics of their country in favour of Germany and against the Allies. He instanced the wife of the King of Greece who was a sister of the Kaiser and the King of Sweden's wife who was also a German princess. He then went on to say: 'We have seen how foreign princesses influence their countries against their countries' interests. We have seen it in Sweden, we have seen it in Greece. And now—what is happening in Russia? What is happening? (Pause.) Why the transport system has broken down and in my constituency we cannot get coal although coal is available only a short distance away . . .' His inference was plain, the implicit attack on the Empress obvious, but he had said not a word with which he could be justly reproached and nothing happened to him.

Later, when the Czar had been deposed and was about to be put on trial, the Czarists paid Adjemoff the doubtful honour of choosing him to defend the Czar. Adjemoff agreed to take on this dangerous role, but only after being satisfied that plans had been made to smuggle him out of the country as soon as the trial was over. The trial was never held for the Czar, with all his family, was murdered.

Adjemoff turned up in Paris in about 1918, with his wife, her brother and her two sons by a previous marriage. They had only some £200 between them but Adjemoff, blessed as he was with the gift of the gab, bluffed and blandished their way into an hotel. His wife, however, could not accept the reality of their straitened circumstances. In the past, when she had come to Paris, she had patronized the famous fashion house of Vionet. What should she do now when, as she explained to her husband, here she was in Paris without a stitch of clothing to her name? What else should she do but go to Vionet? Adjemoff, who was devoted to his wife and wholly under her influence, gave her half their total fortune of £200 to spend on clothes.

We got to know Adjemoff because of his professional connection with the Mantacheffs, an Armenian family which had large properties in the Baku region. Father had known old Mantacheff who, when he died two or three years before the first war, had been worth £10 million sterling, a terrific fortune by any standards. Old Mantacheff was a huge, bearlike sort of man, by turns most generous and very stingy. He came to Paris for a month or two every year and while he was there Cartier's always remained open throughout the night because of Mantacheff's habit, in the early hours of the morning, of splashing out, thinking nothing of spending, say, £3000 on jewels for the favourite of the moment. He was a very good client of the night clubs and, like so many Russians, had a weak spot for the gypsy bands of which there were many, both before the war and again afterwards. He loved to take a handful of gold coins, louis d'or, from his pocket, throw them on the floor, and then watch the band scrambling for them. But old Mantacheff was a shrewder and much less generous man by day.

Despite his wealth, he had brought up his three sons in the harshest way. Even at the age of thirty, he allowed them only 300 francs a month, say £12. Naturally, as soon as their father died and they inherited his wealth, they behaved outrageously. When they arrived in Paris after the Revolution, they had little more than the clothes on their backs but this did not prevent them from hitting the high spots.

Because of my father's friendly relations in the past with old Mantacheff, the sons now approached him for help. He also helped Adjemoff. It was Adjemoff who suggested that a wonderful opportunity existed for the Royal Dutch Shell Group to obtain a footing in Russia cheaply by doing a deal with the impoverished Mantacheffs. The Group's contract with the Anglo-Persian was coming to an end and Deterding was afraid of running short of crude oil. Everyone thought the Bolshevik regime would fall quickly and it was in that expectation that we negotiated with the Mantacheffs and reached an agreement whereby they were paid £625,000 in cash as an advance against their properties in Russia. The Mantacheffs managed to blow that little lot in a matter of two years, whereas Adjemoff, who had received 3 per cent of the cash as his fee, hung on to his share and prospered.

What was even more important to Adjemoff's future than the money he made on that deal was the impression he had made on both my father and on Deterding. From then onwards he was closely associated with them and came to wield great influence on them both. He knew how to play on people's weaknesses. It is said he introduced Deterding to a succession of good-looking, homeless, aristocratic Russian women, with results that were pleasant on one side and profitable on the other. Deterding ended by marrying

Lydia Pavlovna, who was still married to a White Russian General, the Armenian General Bagraduni, when she first arrived in Europe after the Revolution. She is really a charming and very generous woman, always ready to help any cause. She gives wonderful parties, and I am personally very fond of her and of her daughter, Olga.

Adjemoff introduced my father to Diaghileff, when he brought his Ballet to London. There was a party at the old Carlton Hotel after a first night of a new Diaghileff ballet when all the ladies of the company were presented to assembled business men, including my father and myself. This most agreeable occasion ended with my father lending Diaghileff a few thousand pounds to help him. Unfortunately Diaghileff treated the word 'loan' as a euphemism and even when he became well off he made no attempt to distinguish between a loan and a gift. That led to a row between them. It was Adjemoff who eventually brought them together again and Father helped Diaghileff once more, this time by paying the cost of Olga Spessivtseva's treatment in Switzerland when she became ill.

At another party given to the Diaghileff Ballet, at the Hungaria Restaurant in Lower Regent Street, I saw Tamara Karsavina give a demonstration of technical perfection. First, the young girls in the Ballet had given an exhibition of some of their steps, very prettily and, as it seemed, with great polish and delicacy. Then it was Karsavina's turn. I had seen her before the war in Paris, dancing with Nijinsky in *Le Spectre de la Rose*. She was now some ten years older, a little plumper. She wore a long skirt which she lifted just enough to reveal the calf. She executed a sequence of steps with such grace and mathematical precision that the other girls who had preceded her were made to appear gauche and clumsy, like cart-horses next to a thoroughbred. Even I, who am not a balletomane, was immediately aware of and enormously impressed by that demonstration of technical excellence.

When the great row came between Deterding and my father, Adjemoff very loyally broke with Deterding and stuck to my father. It is quite possible he thought he would do better with a fellow-Armenian than with a Dutchman but I am convinced that genuine feelings of loyalty to the Gulbenkians had much to do with his decision. In fact, as a result of the exercise of his brains and his gift of the gab and of his association with the Gulbenkians,

Adjemoff ended up with a very fine apartment in the Avenue Foch, a big car and a daughter who was the joy of his life. He wanted my father to be godfather to the little girl but my father, with his hatred of publicity, refused to handle the infant in front of the large party Adjemoff had invited for the christening and I actually held her during the ceremony.

I saw a lot of Adjemoff. He knew his way around the night clubs in Paris and I spent many a boisterous night with him there. He had a great hold on me, as he had on Deterding and on my father. So far as I was concerned he was always a good friend to me, but my father became jealous of the influence Adjemoff had over me and eventually my father broke with him.

Working with my father was certainly stimulating and I could not have wished for a better school in which to learn about business. To see how his mind worked and especially to observe how he obtained the last ounce or last farthing out of anyone who came into contact with him was the kind of education only a day-to-day relationship with such a man can make possible. He always felt that if he did not get the last farthing out of a deal or the last ounce of energy out of an employee it showed a lack of self-control and an intolerable slackness on his part. It was a standard he applied to others in turn, such as myself. But he was also essentially a negotiator, for although he would fight to get that last farthing he could always recognize when his position was not strong enough and he would give in gracefully long before he was forced to do so. He could be very generous, too, when he felt like it or perhaps when he felt it might be to his ultimate advantage; any act of generosity was the result of premeditated thought on his part.

Our relationship was based on the fact that I was the apple of my father's eye and all he wanted was my welfare—according to his lights. In practice, this meant that I had to endure a great deal of interference by him. He justified this on the ground that, first, he was older and more experienced than I was and therefore knew better than I did what was good for me and what I ought to want and, secondly, that we were an Oriental family, which meant it was not only his duty to interfere, even in the smallest details of the lives of his family and particularly that of his beloved only son, but also his undoubted right. He always wanted to know where I was and I had to telegraph him when I arrived after any journey, whether it was by car to the south of France or by plane to, say, Paris, Lisbon or Switzerland. He was most particular about my diet, enquiring assiduously whether I was over-eating and whether I was eating the foods which his specialist doctors advised him were not good for health.

His solicitude for me was extremely practical. This was exemplified by an incident in 1920. I had been suffering slightly from colds and sore throats and the doctors had recommended that I should take a cure at a spa in France. They suggested a place called Mont Dore, which was said to be very good for health but otherwise was deadly dull. On the day I was supposed to set off there, I went to see my father in Paris and we had lunch together at the Ritz. Before ordering the meal, my father sought the help of Olivier Dabescat. Olivier was the man whose resourcefulness and devotion to the needs of his clients at the Ritz I had first encountered (as I related in Chapter One) at the age of four. Since then his reputation, deservedly, had grown even greater and he was the model for the hero of a famous play called *Le Sexe Faible* by Edouard Bourdet which was produced between the wars. It featured that fine actor Victor Boucher and portrayed Olivier as a sort of *deus ex machina*, meeting all the multifarious desires of his clients and receiving their gratitude and more tangible tokens of appreciation in return. Olivier not merely satisfied all needs, he anticipated them. This I can confirm from my own experience.

'My son is leaving for Mont Dore this afternoon for three weeks,' my father told Olivier when he came to our table. 'I don't want him to go alone. He hasn't got a valet and he hasn't got a car over here —will you please see what you can do to help him?'

'Certainly, sir,' said Olivier.

We ate a quiet lunch, exchanging news and views and thinking no more for the moment about my trip or about the arrangements Olivier might be making. After lunch, he came back to us.

'I have a valet for Monsieur Nubar,' he said. 'He is waiting in the hall for interview.'

I found there a perfect valet by the name of Fernand and engaged him on the spot. I gave him my keys, told him where my luggage was, and away he went to do the packing. Then Olivier came again.

'I have a car and a chauffeur I can recommend,' he said. In the Place Vendôme was a 40 h.p. Renault. Monsieur Nubar was invited to inspect it. I did so and found it eminently suitable in every way. When I returned to the hotel, Olivier was still at my service.

'Will Monsieur Nubar be good enough to go into the *Salon de Lecture*?' he said. 'I can present there his last requirement as ordered by Monsieur Nubar's father.'

I went in. Waiting there was a very charming lady, *très comme il faut*. But I felt that this service was perhaps a little too perfect: there are some things a man may prefer to arrange for himself.

If he could have done so, my father would certainly have prevented me from hunting or riding in point-to-points, so afraid was he that I might hurt myself. But eventually he had to resign himself to these hazards and, in fact, I have broken my collar-bone three times, also a few ribs and one shoulder, as well as being concussed on several occasions.

Throughout our joint lives I was terrified of him, while feeling, even at the time, and especially now on looking back, the greatest admiration for him as a man and also gratitude for his affection towards me although I did not invariably relish the forms it took. I think he gave me credit for a certain amount of intelligence and I do not remember in the many years we were together his criticizing any decision I had taken in business on the ground that it was foolish or due to stupidity. But he always said, 'You should have done better,' and he was ever ready to jump in, asserting the value of his superior experience.

'Nubar,' he used to say, 'you are like a very powerful engine. Now if that engine is properly directed it can do anything and get anywhere. But, my son, from time to time it needs a guiding hand and it needs the brakes applied to it.' I often found this 'stop—go' business irksome and our relationship was blotched with rows resulting from my resentment of his interference in matters, big and small.

The first important row between us came to a head in 1922 but it had been festering for years before that. Although I had no idea at the time, of course, of what was to come, I can date the beginnings of that row to a day in November 1918, just before the end of the First World War. I went to the Hyde Park Hotel for what would now be called a 'deb's dance', a gathering of more or less eligible young men and heavily chaperoned young ladies of good family. At that dance I met a Spanish girl. She was wearing an electric-blue dress. Her dark hair was parted down the middle, her features were striking but irregular, she spoke very slowly: to me she seemed a ravishing beauty and the dearest of attractions. A few days later, I met her again when I went to the Victory Ball, a fancy-dress affair at the Albert Hall. I turned up as an Indian rajah, complete with huge turban with a large aigrette, baggy, red, silk trousers, a short, green jacket and a cummerbund into which I inserted various daggers, pistols and the like. The shoes I wore had long, curling, turned-up, pointed toes; no sooner had I put them on than my feet got entangled and I ended up flat on my face. (My costume had been produced for me by Willy Clarkson, the famous theatrical costumier in Wardour Street, a small man with a pointed beard and a great character in his day. Earlier, when I was at Cambridge, I had gone to him for a suitable disguise so that I could pass incognito when in London, and came away sporting a large and luxurious moustache. Unfortunately, a friend of my mother's had seen me in London only two days before and I was then clean-shaven. Although I was an Oriental and inclined to be hirsute— hirsuteness is said to be a sign of virility—no one would believe, nor was I prepared to try to make them believe, that this magnificent moustache had sprouted almost overnight.)

The Victory Ball, however readers may now imagine it, was, though gay enough, still a decorous affair. The formalities observed were fewer than at a dance in a private house but formal it was, nevertheless, and tickets at £5 apiece were an effective bar against any lowering of social tone. Standards, in the matter of social etiquette, as to where it was proper for a young lady to be seen and where she could not go, were still strictly upheld. If my sister wanted to dance, for instance, she could do so only at a private house, at a carefully chosen *thé dansant*, but never at a public ball —and always with a chaperone. No young lady could be seen at a night club. If a young man went there, it was with one of the 'other sort', probably a chorus girl. Conversely, it could be said that no woman of the stage would be accepted in Society unless she had passed the age of sixty or had married into the peerage. Even married women in Society were debarred from the night clubs unless, on very rare occasions, they went there with their husbands in large parties. So rare were these occasions as to be memorable in the lives of the families of those days. Once, in 1914, for example, some business people from abroad whom my father and mother had been entertaining wanted to go on from the theatre to a night club. My father looked dubious but felt obliged to agree to take them; my mother was very excited at the prospect. Too excited, it might be said, for in the night club she overstepped the limit.

'Do you think we might dance?' she asked, timidly. My father was greatly shocked.

'No. No. *No*.' I might just as well have asked if I could bring the girl from the third row of the chorus back home for dinner.

Formalities, decorum, chaperones: none of these could inhibit my joy when, at the Victory Ball, the would-be Indian rajah saw his beautiful Spanish señorita. We danced and we talked and I knew, if I had not known it at our first meeting, that I was head over heels in love with her. She had the resounding name of Herminia Elena Josefa Rodriguez de Feijóo.

We met again at various parties. We danced together and whispered sweet nothings to each other and my parents realized I was infatuated but they did not take it very seriously. Not at first. They reasoned that, after all, I was only twenty-two and could not possibly be serious about it myself. But they were wrong and when they understood that I really was serious they started to agitate against the attachment. There is no doubt, although she did not express her views so forcefully, that my mother fully shared my father's hostility to any suggestion of marriage. They were still imbued with the Oriental idea that the eldest son, the heir-apparent to the dynasty, should marry a hand-picked girl of their choice. (I can say now, though I did not respect the tradition then, that there is much in favour of marriages arranged by parents regardless of the wishes of the young people concerned. The idea of arranged marriages is still widely accepted on the Continent, even though it has gone sadly out of fashion in England.)

My parents' main objection to Herminia was that she was a Roman Catholic. Their hostility was reciprocated by the feeling of Herminia's mother and father towards me. Her father was a tall, impressive-looking man, who travelled frequently between Europe and Cuba, where his interests lay. At one time he had had slaves on his plantation there and he liked to tell a particular story of that time. One day, in the pouring rain, he saw a slave walking along with a hat under his arm.

'Hi, Pedro!' he called. 'You are getting your head wet—why don't you put your hat on?'

'Ah, Massa,' the slave replied, 'the head belongs to Massa but the hat is my own.'

Herminia stayed in London with her mother, a very formidable Spanish duenna, of whose eye I certainly was not the apple, and a maiden aunt, Doña Lala, who showed much more understanding of the young people's feelings. During 1919, the year following our first meeting, we continued to meet at parties and generally contrived to make sure we were both going to the same parties. More and more strongly, we pressed upon our parents our intention to marry. After we had been meeting in this way for over a year, we were allowed (or rather a very determined Herminia flouted the conventions of her redoubtable mother) to go out together. Not alone, at first, for this would have been altogether too much of a transgression, but frequently with just the discreet and sympathetic Doña Lala. I hired a car and we used to go out to dinner in the countryside to Virginia Water, some twenty miles from London. Often, I popped into the Curzon Hotel, where they were living, either on my way to the office or on my way back. Certainly we enjoyed nothing like the freedom allowed to youngsters nowadays but we were somewhat less trammelled by the existing conventions than most people.

I may be giving the impression that parental opposition marred what was otherwise an idyll of young love in which never a cross word was exchanged between boy and girl. That was certainly not the way of it. Herminia had been spoiled by her parents; I was not without a wayward streak of temperament; we had plenty of rows. One such eruption happened when we were together at the Curzon Hotel. Heaven knows what provoked it but it was serious enough for Herminia to snatch from her finger a ring I had given her and thrust it back at me. In my temper, I threw the ring, which consisted of a large, flawless ruby, into the fire. The next moment Herminia, who had the thrifty outlook of a woman from the north of Spain, and I, an Armenian who had been taught the value of money, were both on our hands and knees, grubbing the ring out of the fire. Although there was no sign of damage on the outside of the ring, it had been cracked on the inside.

Our semi-engagement lasted for perhaps two years, with the

families on both sides trying persistently to break it, but Herminia was just as obstinate as I was. Then her father decided the family should return to Spain. The packing began at the Curzon Hotel and applications were made to the Spanish Consulate for passports, visas and so on. Since efficiency was not her greatest characteristic, Herminia's mother became slightly flustered over the various arrangements she had to make for the journey. At the Consulate, in the midst of an already confused conversation with the Spanish Vice-Consul, she suddenly exclaimed, 'What about the gramophone?' She had just remembered it and I think she had panicked at the thought that she might need a licence to import it into Spain or that she ought to make some declaration to allow it to come back duty free into England. The Vice-Consul could not be blamed for not understanding this curious intrusion into a discussion about passports.

'But, dear lady,' he said, very courteously but rather bitingly, 'the gramophone does not require a passport for Spain.'

The attempt to break up our affair by taking Herminia back to Spain did not succeed. What it did do was to provoke a visit by me to her home at Coruña, as an uninvited guest. With Spanish courtesy, the family bowed to the inevitable and took me to see the sights, including Santiago de Compostela, a Christian shrine for many centuries, where the Cathedral and the Bishop's Palace are gems of Gothic architecture. (Santiago, St. James in English, is the patron saint of Spain.)

Herminia's uncles and cousins were military men. One uncle was a General, and she had a cousin who was a cavalry officer; as a consequence Spanish army horses were always available for Herminia and myself to ride, accompanied by a Spanish Army orderly.

The return home to Spain made no difference to our determination to be married and nor, a little later, did a move by her family to France. Indeed, while they were staying there, Herminia and I actually tried to get married but that attempt was successfully defeated by my father. In France at that time a couple were not allowed to marry under the age of thirty without the written consent of their parents except by special application to the Court for permission. There was no question of my father consenting.

Nothing he could do, however, no amount of legal obstruction of that kind, nor dissuasive argument, nor appeal to my sense of filial duty, could lessen my resolution. So my father played his last and what he probably thought was his trump card.

'You know how strongly I disapprove of this marriage,' he said. 'If you go ahead with it, despite my opposition, then you can no longer work with me. Make your choice.'

I did. As I had been in close contact with the Royal Dutch Shell Group and my father was very friendly at that time with the Chairman, Henri Deterding, and with the Acting Chairman, H. Colijn, I asked them for a job and got one.

Freed of my dependence upon my father for an income, the last obstacle to our marriage was removed. Nothing could stop us now, we felt, and, in 1922, we were married at the Princes Row Registry Office. It would be difficult to describe it as a gay occasion. The only people present were Herminia's mother, Doña Lala, Herminia and myself. Herminia had dressed at first in black, but her mother had protested. 'Whether this wedding is popular or not, you must wear something more cheerful than that.' This time, Herminia bowed to her mother's wishes. But a telegram from her father on the morning of the wedding did not help much. It said merely: 'I regret the decision of Herminia.'

Once the marriage was over, my father, faced with the accomplished fact, insisted on a religious ceremony according to the rites of the Armenian Church. At that time, he had not built the Armenian Church in London and the nearest ones were in Manchester and Paris. So the Armenian priest in London, the Reverend Nazarian, came to our first married home, a suite on the fourth floor of the Ritz Hotel. The service was held in the sitting-room. A table was brought in and a white tablecloth, usually used for breakfast, was laid on it. Candles were added and the table became an *ad hoc* altar. This time two of my friends were with me, Tommy Frost, who has been present at all my weddings and is known as my 'permanent best man', and Constantine Chadinoff. It was Chadinoff in fact who was my best man on this occasion for, according to Armenian Orthodox rites, one must have a godfather at the wedding who is of the Armenian Church. After the ceremony the priest, Chaddy, Tommy Frost, Herminia and myself, drank a bottle of champagne. Now we were well and truly married.

We went for our honeymoon to Deauville. On the way back the

Rolls-Royce, loaned to us by Chadinoff and driven by him, skidded and turned complete turtle. Herminia was thrown out, clutching her little Pekingese dog, and broke both her collar-bones. Chaddy's pelvis was smashed by the steering wheel and he was in and out of hospital for over a year. I escaped with nothing worse than a shaking and a bruising. But there have been more auspicious beginnings to a marriage.

4

Oilmen Are Like Cats

I SHOULD find it difficult to present a tidy chronicle of my work either with my father or with Henri Deterding. Certain negotiations in which I was involved were carried on over a period of years and were the cause of endless meetings at which oil interests and governments haggled over terms. Much of the present pattern of the world's oil supplies and ownership was settled in those days and I want to tell not only of the arrangements which were then arrived at, for these are to be found elsewhere, but also of the men who made them.

My father was early in the field. As a very young man in the 1890s he was sent by my grandfather to the Caucasus and he visited Baku which was just starting as an oil-field. At that time oil was used to some extent as the basis for making lubricating oil but vegetable oils were considered to be much superior for this purpose and the chief reason for producing oil out of the ground was for lamps. On my father's return from the Caucasus, although he was still in his early twenties, he published a most learned article in the *Revue des deux Mondes*, a very highbrow French journal; what was even more remarkable was the foresight he showed of the possible developments for the oil industry.

However, he was also aware of the risks involved and his caution led him to reject an opportunity which, later, was proved to have been a golden one. At the beginning of the century, a fellow-Armenian, called Haladjian, who was then employed by the Persian Government, tried to negotiate a concession for the production of oil in Persia. He offered it to my father who discussed it with his friend and crony, Henri Deterding, but they agreed that it was much too risky and certainly not worth the money. The price being asked for the concession was £20,000. This same concession eventually became the basis on which the Anglo-Persian Oil Company was founded and developed, the company which changed its name to the Anglo-Iranian at the time of Reza Shah and is now known as B.P. The Company has endured many relative vicissitudes but in 1963 its profits before tax were £191 million though, of course, this figure is achieved not only from its interests in Persia but also in Kuwait and elsewhere in the world.

During the first decade of this century, German interests were making great progress, both politically and economically, in the old Ottoman Empire. The British Government were rather perturbed about this and asked Sir Ernest Cassel (grandfather of Countess Mountbatten) to go to Constantinople to see what could be done to develop British economic interests there. My father went with Sir Ernest and, as a result of the trip, the National Bank of Turkey was founded for the purpose of furthering British interests in that country. My father was on the board and so, too, was the Hon. Hugo Baring, son of Lord Revelstoke, and a member of the famous Baring banking family who have five peerages, the Earldom of Cromer and the Baronies of Ashburton, Northbrook, Revelstoke and of Hawick of Glendale. (The present Lord Cromer is Governor of the Bank of England.)

The National Bank of Turkey formed the Turkish Petroleum Company, with an issue of capital of 40,000 £1 shares, of which only one shilling was called up, and the Company began trying to obtain an overall petroleum concession in the Ottoman Empire, or at any rate in the Mesopotamian provinces (or *vilayets*, as they were called) of Baghdad and Basrah. But other people had similar ideas including the Anglo-Persian Oil Company who had been trying in vain for the past ten years to get concessions in that part of the world. It soon became clear that the only people with any rights there at all were the German Baghdad Railway. They had the rights to build a railway from Constantinople to Baghdad and to the Persian Gulf; they also had the mineral rights for a strip of land, twenty kilometres wide, on each side of the railway. After much fruitless negotiation and quite a lot of intrigue, it became clear that while it was easy enough to stop the other parties from getting a concession this was a game two or more could play and no one was going to get anywhere.

As so often, the only solution was compromise. The British and

German Governments, both of whom had been backing their national groups throughout the futile negotiations, were brought directly into the business. They entered into two agreements at the Foreign Office, one in 1912, the other in 1914, by which, instead of opposing each other, they joined together to back the reorganized Turkish Petroleum Company. The Company's capital was doubled. One half was allotted to the Anglo-Persian Oil Company, a quarter to the Royal Dutch Shell Group and a quarter, in fully paid shares, to the Deutsche Bank German interests in return for giving up their rights to the strip alongside the railway. My father was to receive for his lifetime a 5 per cent interest, half of it to be provided by the Anglo-Persian and half by the Royal Dutch Shell Group. This was all that was left to him of his original 40 per cent holding. He had started by ceding 25 per cent to the Royal Dutch Shell. The remaining 15 per cent was finally reduced to this 5 per cent life interest, which some people might regard as rather hard on him, but he always reckoned that it was better to have a small slice of a big cake than a big slice of a small cake and that unless one co-operated with competitors one would never get anywhere. Which, by and large, is a very sound principle.

The next stage, after the British and German Governments had seen the wisdom of pursuing their interests jointly, was to put pressure on the Ottoman Government which, at that time, under the Capitulations,[1] could not increase its import duties without the consent of the Great Powers. This is just what the Ottoman Government wanted to do, but the British and German Governments refused to give their consent to the proposed increase unless the Turkish Government gave the petroleum concession to the Turkish Petroleum Company.

In the spring and summer of 1914, the Ottoman Government sent to London Hakki Pasha to negotiate with the British Government on a number of questions relating to the desired concession, including the Baghdad Railway. My father was then Financial Counsellor to the Ottoman Government and as such often entertained Hakki Pasha to dinner at our house in Hyde Park Gardens.

1. Capitulations: Under the capitulatory system the subjects of foreign nations living in Turkey enjoyed complete personal, religious and commercial freedom and immunity from Ottoman jurisdiction. Each foreign colony became a sort of empire within an empire. The First World War swept away the old system of capitulations in many places, including Turkey.

Hakki Pasha was a very astute man. He was small, not much more than five feet high and nearly five feet round, wore thick glasses and had a marvellous appetite to which he gave free rein. He was certainly nobody's fool.

He and my father held long discussions and although I was just eighteen at the time and not allowed, of course, to join in the talk, I was permitted to sit and listen to them. I found it fascinating to observe the inner workings of diplomacy, to gain an insight into the kind of arguments and calculations that precede the eventual publication of a bland official communiqué.

These negotiations in London bore fruit and on 28 June 1914 the Grand Vizier, Said Halim Pasha, a dignitary whose functions corresponded to these of a prime minister, wrote letters to the British and German Ambassadors stating that it had been agreed to issue the concession to the Turkish Petroleum Company.

That was as much progress as the Company could make until after the first great war, for the German Government's ratification of the agreements was handed to the Foreign Office on the day in August 1914 before Britain declared war on Germany. Then the Turkish Government's so-called concession 'went to sleep' for the duration and the Germans' 25 per cent holding was taken over by the Public Trustee. War was not the only obstacle to the progress of the Turkish Petroleum Company. For quite a long time the Anglo-Persian Group, which was headed by Mr. Charles Greenway (later Sir Charles and then Lord Greenway of Stanbridge Earls) showed no inclination whatever to fall in with the Foreign Office agreement. Indeed, one could hardly blame them for they had been encouraged by the British Government to hope that after the war, instead of sharing the concession with the Germans, the Royal Dutch Shell and my father, they would have the whole thing to themselves. Not surprisingly, after all the work they had done to get the agreements, neither my father nor the Royal Dutch Shell were very happy at the idea of being elbowed out in this way and in order to baulk any such development the Royal Dutch Shell kept the Turkish Petroleum Company alive throughout the war. My father was one of the directors and I was his alternate and I well remember attending my first directors' meeting in the Royal Dutch Shell Building at St. Helen's Court, in 1917, I think it was. Among the items on the agenda was how to find office accommodation and £500 a year as the salary for the company secretary. Other directors there were Sir Eric Hambro and Lancelot Smith, who represented the Public Trustee's holding of 25 per cent of the shares, taken over from the Germans. Sir Eric, very tall with a black moustache, was a well-known banker; Lancelot Smith was a stockbroker, a partner of the well-known firm of Rowe and Pitman.

Deterding, on behalf of the Royal Dutch Shell Group, offered the orphan company office space and the services of a secretary. This was enough to keep it going, but as Deterding was beginning to realize, the Royal Dutch Shell needed the help of some Government in what had now become world-wide negotiations for oil concessions. The Anglo-Persian Group could well look to the British Government for encouragement, because the Government, as the result of the foresight of Winston Churchill and Jackie Fisher (Admiral of the Fleet, Lord John Fisher), when they were at the Admiralty as First Lord and First Sea Lord, were the majority shareholders in the Anglo-Persian. The Standard Oil Company always had the backing of the American Government when dealing with outside interests, although the U.S. Government, from time to time, launched anti-Trust suits against the Standard and all the other oil companies.

Henri Deterding knew that justice was an abstraction when it came to disposing of oil concessions and that the Royal Dutch Shell's best advocate in any negotiations would be the strength of some Government's support. So, at my father's instigation, he turned to France.

In order to understand the part my father played in all this, I should explain the nature of his association with Deterding and the Royal Dutch Shell. He and Deterding were very close for over twenty years. One never knows, as another oilman said, whether in the end it was Deterding who used my father or my father who used Deterding. Whichever way round it was, their association was very fruitful to them both as individuals and to the Royal Dutch Shell Group as a whole. In those early days the finances of the Group were tiny, both actually and also in comparison with the oil giants of the time like the Standard Oil. There was no question then of 'auto-financing' (the financing of an enterprise out of its profits, without resort to outside capital) which the oil groups have enjoyed since the last war. At that time, the money had to be found and to find it meant going to the bankers or to the Stock Exchange and that was where my father's experience, his business contacts and his negotiating ability came into play.

The oil industry, generally, was still in the early stages of development and there were still concessions all over the world to be obtained and, when obtained, exploited. Some had been developed, some had lain idle. Some had begun to be developed but, through lack of finance or technical ability, were in danger of floundering. It was my father's role to bring these sinking companies to the Royal Dutch Shell, arranging by his negotiating skill for them to become closely associated with the Group. The pattern of these negotiations rarely varied. My father arranged for the Group to take an option at a low price on part or the whole of the capital to be issued by the failing Company, thus enabling the Group and my father, who was always personally involved in the deal, to make large profits and the Company to obtain the finance much needed for its development. That is a statement, in simple terms, of his activities but I ought to enlarge a little on the way it was done. A contract was made between the new company and the Group by which the Group achieved a majority on the Board and also provided the management of the new company. In exchange, the new company gained the technical and commercial experience of the Group plus their financial resources. After the contract had been agreed, shares had to be issued and sold to the public to raise finance, for the Royal Dutch Shell in those days could not afford to buy a 100 per cent interest in these new companies. Of course, as soon as word went round that a company was coming into association with the Group the shares went up and that gave the Group and my father the chance, not only to interest the public, but also to make a handsome profit at the same time in some of the shares on which they had taken the low-priced option.

The underlying intention, an entirely genuine one, was that the new company should benefit from the association and that, for their part, the Group should have assured supplies of oil or facilities for producing it, or both. But the Group were not content with this position nor with the profit they made on the original share deal. They were apt to look on these companies as cows to be milked and certainly as mere subsidiaries whose interests were subordinate to those of the Group as a whole. It was this attitude of mind which was the origin of the troubles between my father and Deterding and led ultimately to a permanent break between them.

My father felt that as he had been responsible for interesting the public in these companies, he also had a responsibility to see that they were run fairly for the benefit of the individual companies and their shareholders, even though their Boards of Directors contained a majority of Group nominees. He held, for instance, that the oil a company produced should be sold at a fair price and that having paid a large sum or a percentage of its profits to the Group as a management fee, it should really benefit from the association and not be regarded merely as a cog in a large wheel. Deterding himself did try, on the whole, to keep the balance between the interest of the Group and that of the new companies; on the other hand, there was an element in the Group who said that once in control the Group were entitled to treat the new company entirely as a subsidiary. Things came to a head over the Venezuelan Oil Concessions and led to the break-up of my father's long association and friendship with Deterding. But the details of that row belong later in my story.

Arising out of the struggle for the Turkish concession, Deterding wanted the backing of the French Government so that the Royal Dutch Shell's strength in negotiations could match that of the other Government-backed oil companies. It was my father who had directed Deterding's interest towards France and it was now his job to use his many contacts in that country to make the French Government 'petroleum-conscious'. In this, the French met him halfway, as it were, for they, too, had anxieties, although there is no doubt my father did much to foster them. He worked on and through Senator Henri Berenger, who was Senator for Guadeloupe and the head of the *Commissariat Général aux Essences*—the equivalent of the British Minister of Fuel and Power. Berenger was an impressive and colourful personality, whose conversation was laced with quotations from Greek (one of his favourites was εὖ πράττειν, which I should translate as 'behave well' or 'be a gentleman'). Berenger, who had himself in his younger days achieved a considerable reputation as a poet, wore a big slouch hat, glasses and a flowing moustache *à la gauloise*. He had full confidence in my father and was a ready receptacle for the fears about the French position, genuine and justified as they were, which my father instilled into both him and his staff. When Berenger came to London on his official visits from Paris he very often lunched or dined at our house in Hyde Park Gardens and Georges Bénard, another old friend of ours (then working as a mobilized captain in the *Commissariat Général* in a small office in the Champs-Élysées) was usually there as well. I sat in on the discussions. (When Berenger was in Venice during the 1914 war he was shown the famous statute by Verrocchio of the Colleone who was a Gran Condottiere of the Renaissance and had remarked to Bénard: 'There goes Gulbenkian.' A year or two back when I met the late Enrico Mattei's representative in London I sent him a message saying that like my father half-a-century before, Mattei was a Gran Condottiere.)

The French quickly perceived that it was all very well having contracts with the oil-producing companies but without direct access to sources of production they must always be at the mercy, in peace or in war, of the oil groups—'*Les Trusts*' as the French called them. My father suggested to the French that, as a beginning, they should ask the British Government to let them have the 25 per cent share of the Turkish Petroleum Company which had previously belonged to the Germans and had been taken over by the Public Trustee.

The question of oil supplies could not be isolated from the general political discussions going on at the time between the Allies, England and France, and, until the Revolution, Russia. France wanted the Rhine frontier which the British were not over-keen to allow. The Russians wanted Constantinople and access to warm water in the Mediterranean, a centuries-old ambition. Britain wanted balance of power and a good many other things, including preservation of the route to India. The influence of France in Turkey and the Middle East—or Near East as it was then known—was paramount but the British, by backing the Hashemite dynasty and the cause of the Arabs against the Turks, gradually increased their influence until, finally, the Sykes-Picot Treaty was signed which defined the spheres of influence of France and Britain. One result of this was the granting to Britain of the

Mandate over what was then called Mesopotamia, previously a French sphere, and it was only some time later that the French woke up to the fact they had lost, or given up, the '*Pétroles de Mossoul*'. In that phrase was contained the dream, the fantastic dream, of oilmen of the riches that might be. Today, we merely talk of Middle East oil and the dream has become a reality. However, the French were eventually compensated for this loss by the Treaty of San Remo which guaranteed them 25 per cent of the '*Pétroles de Mossoul*', either in the form of oil or shares.

My father was successful, from all points of view, in his negotiations with the French. He was much less than successful in his dealings with the Anglo-Persian Group who, throughout the war, continued to sit on the fence, conceding nothing, waiting to see which way to jump. I remember going with my father to see Sir Charles Greenway and Sir Hugh Barnes, directors of the Anglo-Persian, to discuss what they were going to do about the Turkish Petroleum Company. In particular, we wanted to know when they would meet the obligations of their agreed 50 per cent holding by taking up their shares and contributing towards the expenses which would be involved in starting to develop the concession. The answer we received, in short, was that they intended to do nothing. The Anglo-Persian gentlemen talked to my father courteously and knowledgeably about Persian manuscripts, Persian ceramics, Persian architecture and about his collection of objets d'art, but when he tried to steer the conversation round to business matters he encountered a very polite but very stubborn wall. Good negotiator though he was, he could not get a word in edgeways about oil.

What my father failed to do, the Americans achieved, though this was far from their intention. After the Treaty of San Remo, the Americans, never backward in coming forward, made claims for the Mesopotamian concession. The United States Government, in the person of Mr. Secretary Lansing, and Lord Curzon, for Britain, exchanged a series of very acid notes. The American argument was that the 'Allied and Associated Powers', having won the war together, should now share the fruits of victory. The British Government accepted the American argument in principle but insisted that it could not apply to rights which had been acquired before the war. According to the British Government, the Turkish

Petroleum Company was in this position and the American Government had not been a party to the agreement or to the concession. The only rights the Company actually possessed were contained in the letter of 28 June 1914, from the Turkish Grand Vizier to the British and German Ambassadors, in which the Turkish Government promised the concession. The Americans were unconvinced by this argument but the immediate effect of their démarche was a closing of the ranks. The Anglo-Persian Group lost no time in taking up their shares in the Turkish Petroleum Company, the French took up theirs, and the French and British Governments together stoutly defended the 'acquired rights'—a phrase much in vogue—of the Turkish Petroleum Company.

The Americans, however, were not to be kept out as easily as that and continued to press for a share of the spoils, claiming with some justification that the Turkish Petroleum Company had no rights whatsoever, certainly no more than the promises various Americans—Admiral Chester for one—had obtained from previous authorities of the Ottoman Empire, promises which were equally as binding or non-binding as the one given in 1914 by the Grand Vizier.

My father used his influence with all concerned to persuade them to make room for the Americans. He ultimately succeeded and to his death he was very proud of a letter he received from Sir William Tyrrell, Head of the British Foreign Office and former secretary to Lord Grey, thanking him for being 'so instrumental in bringing in the Americans'.

Between his making the first moves in that direction and the concluding of the final agreement, however, lay long years of tortuous negotiation. It was one thing to agree in principle on the admission of the Americans and to accept their demand for 'the open door' policy, by which there should seem to be free competition and no violation of anti-trust laws, but it was quite another to arrive at the detailed settlement. First, it was agreed, again in principle, that all the American companies who were wanting an interest in the Mesopotamian oil concession should combine to form the Near East Development Corporation, and that this N.E.D.C. should be granted a 'proportionate' share of the capital.

That did not suit Deterding. He pointed out that on that basis the Anglo-Persian would have the largest share and could always gang up with one of the other three groups to get a majority. He insisted that all the shareholdings should be equal: one quarter to the Americans, one quarter to the French, one quarter to the Royal Dutch Shell and one quarter to the Anglo-Persian, all the holdings subject, of course, to my father's 5 per cent. This meant cutting down the Anglo-Persian 50 per cent shareholding by half. To persuade them to accept this, Deterding suggested they should receive in lieu a royalty on the oil produced. After more negotiations the Anglo-Persian agreed to take a 10 per cent royalty on the oil produced from the twenty-four plots which the Turkish Petroleum Company originally were to retain.

That brings me to another aspect of the negotiations and while I recognize that the story of these discussions, which went on over years, is a complicated one, I think it necessary to tell it in some detail, if only to give readers some idea of just how complex was the business in which my father and I were involved. As everyone now knows, the prizes at stake were magnificent ones and it would be silly and misleading to suggest that everything was settled once for all and the spoils divided in the course of a few hours' cosy chat.

To meet the American insistence on 'the open door' we worked out that the Turkish Petroleum Company should be allowed to select twenty-four plots, each of eight square miles, and after that to offer by auction every year other plots for which everybody could bid. This satisfied the American Government and the Anglo-Persian agreed to the 10 per cent royalty from these twenty-four plots.

There was more trouble to come, this time over the question of income tax. The Americans said that if the Turkish Petroleum Company were to be run as an ordinary company producing oil and making profits, those profits would be subject to British income tax and they had no wish to pay income tax to the British Government. So the Americans devised a scheme whereby the Company should merely cover its expenses and sell its oil to its shareholders at cost, plus a very small margin for profit. This suited everyone but my father. It certainly suited the French, for what they were after was not so much profits as reliable supplies of oil; oil at cost seemed to them an admirable arrangement. The

Royal Dutch Shell were quite content to receive cheap oil instead of dividends. So said the Anglo-Persian as well and, naturally, since they had put forward the idea, the Americans.

Not so my father, who had worked for years to obtain the concession and who wanted, not the right to take oil in the desert or even from the seaboard, but dividends on his investment. But, as so often happens in this world, my father, having worked hard to get the four oil groups together and to secure their participation in what had been his 'cake', now found them uniting against him.

Many years of strenuous negotiation followed. Time and again we worked into the small hours trying to find a solution. Let me recall just two of those countless meetings. The first of them was between my father, myself and Sir John Cadman. Sir John had been a professor at Birmingham and had joined the Petroleum Executive as a Government official in the war. It was thought that after the war he would probably join the Royal Dutch Shell but, in fact, he joined the Anglo-Persian and, at the time we met him, he was to be their next chairman. (When in later years he chose his title, Lord Cadman of Silverdale, some of his colleagues made the unkind jibe that he ought to be called Lord Crude of Abadan, the port of Southern Persia where the great refinery was built.) Sir John was a great friend of my father and the family. On this particular night we were in Paris, where we talked for two hours at my father's flat before going to the Ritz for dinner. We chose blue trout as being both light and nourishing. After dinner we went back to the flat and went on talking until two in the morning while we hammered out a draft agreement. It seemed acceptable at the time but, in the end, the oil groups did not ratify what Cadman had agreed; I mention this meeting as an example of many such long evenings which failed to bring a solution.

The other meeting I want to recall was one which laid the foundations of our final agreement. It took place on a Sunday in a sitting-room of the old Carlton Hotel at the corner of the Haymarket and went on for several hours. With us were the President of the Standard Oil Company of New Jersey, Walter Teagle, and one of their directors, Heinrich von Riedemann. Teagle was a man of uncertain temper, at any rate when he was undergoing one of his drastic cures to cut down his weight. Riedemann I knew quite well and regarded as a good friend of mine. He was of German origin, tall, upstanding, with the bearing and appearance of a Prussian officer, poker-faced but often very helpful and resourceful.

These men from the American company suggested to us that the simplest way of solving the whole business was for my father to convert his holding into a royalty and that the proper price, in their view, would be a penny a ton.

'A penny a ton?' my father repeated in astonishment.

'Yes,' said Teagle, 'we think that would be about right.'

'Well, I most certainly do not think so,' said my father. Small wonder at his shock, when we both knew from their published accounts that the oil companies made an average profit of something like £1 a ton. Anyone with the most rudimentary perception of arithmetic could work out that if 100 per cent was £1, then 5 per cent, my father's holding, must be not one penny, but one shilling. When dealing with millions of tons of oil, the difference between a penny a ton and a shilling a ton could be of some interest to the person at the receiving end. That meeting at the Carlton was just the start of another long period of haggling over the royalty to be paid to my father on each ton of oil. I had an argument about it with Morry Bridgeman; he is now the chairman of B.P. but, at that time, he had just joined the Anglo-Persian. He tried to explain to me that a penny a ton was the fair price so I showed him his own company's published accounts.

'Do you see?' I said, pointing to the figures. 'Where you have a ten million ton production you also have a ten million pound profit. Therefore, one ton earns one pound, and 5 per cent of one pound is one shilling.' Morry was taken aback for a moment but he was a resourceful man.

'Ah, I can see where you are being misled by these figures,' he said. 'These public figures include the profit made on the purchase and sale of oil, not just on its production.'

'You can't be trying to suggest,' I retorted, 'that buying and selling oil is more profitable than producing it? If that were true, then there would be very few people who would bother to produce it.' I must say that Morry is a most charming person, with an endearing, if sometimes caustic, sense of humour. In personal relationships, he is the kindest of people who goes to a lot of trouble for others. I heard only the other day how my wife, without my knowledge and, of course, had I known, against my wishes, had written to Morry about the son of an old governess of hers who wanted a job with B.P. Morry went to very great trouble to help; he sent her a long, handwritten letter and eventually arranged everything to everyone's satisfaction. I was angry with my wife for having bothered him but he genuinely did not seem to mind.

All the others eventually agreed that my father should have a shilling a ton royalty and no doubt they breathed a sigh of relief, thinking all was settled. Not quite, however, for my father then raised the question of a guarantee against the depreciation of money or the devaluation of the pound. This was not a very popular move on his part, especially at that time when the pound sterling was regaining, or trying to regain, its pre-war stability and, thanks to Winston Churchill and a million unemployed, was able once more to look the dollar in the face. Nevertheless, my father proposed he should be given a golden shilling or a shilling in gold for each ton. Such a suggestion had never been heard of before and for some time he was known in an inner circle as Mr. Gold Shilling. (This preceded the title 'Mr. Five Per Cent' by which he was more widely known in later life.)

The other parties jibbed at this one and for some while we were stuck again. Then, finally, I suggested to him that we should achieve our safeguard against the loss of the purchasing power of money if we were paid in oil itself which, after all, was the source of the profits, if any. We asked the opinion of the great economist, Sir Josiah Stamp, and he confirmed my belief that this arrangement would be as safe an insurance against loss as we could want. In effect this was coming back to what the oil groups had desired originally, that everybody should have their profits in oil instead of in dividends or in cash. We had objected to that proposal (as shareholders in a coal mine, offered pieces of coal rather than money from selling the coal, would have objected). They had wanted us to take the oil but had made no offer of an assured market for it. What I was now proposing and what was ultimately agreed was that we should put up our 5 per cent of the capital and have our 5 per cent of oil at cost, like the other Groups, and that there should be a contract whereby our oil would be taken over every year at a fair market price at our option. This would be our protection against any fall in the value of the pound. As we were very friendly with the French Group, we suggested that our contract should be only with the French because it would be much easier for us to come to terms with our friends than with the others, who by now were getting quite exasperated, and because the French were anxious to obtain as much oil as they possibly could.

On this basis two agreements were negotiated: one, an overall agreement, known as the Red Line Agreement, concerning all the interested parties, and a second one, a Sale of Oil Agreement, which decided how the Gulbenkian 5 per cent of the oil production should be bought. Father left the negotiating of this second agreement entirely to me. He never attended the Board meetings of the Iraq Petroleum Company, as the Turkish Petroleum Company had been re-named. He was always represented by me. In the early days he was a director by virtue of the contract he had with the Royal Dutch Shell to put a Gulbenkian on the board. But between 1925, when the row between my father and the Royal Dutch Shell over the Venezuelan Oil Company resulted in the breach with Deterding, and 1928, when the Red Line Agreement was signed, the position of the Gulbenkian director on I.P.C., in effect myself, was somewhat anomalous. The other Royal Dutch Shell director during these years was Sir Andrew Agnew, a very experienced and able man who had spent a lot of time in Singapore and knew the East like the back of his hand, but who was far from tactful and apt to show the subtlety of a sledgehammer when dealing with delicate situations. I was young, just about 30, and very anxious to defend the Gulbenkian interests. During one discussion he was interrupting me so much that I told him, also with a certain lack of tact perhaps, 'Hold your tongue!'

This was rather unfortunate because within a week the Royal Dutch Shell, who had the powers, removed the Gulbenkian director and for a whole year no Gulbenkian director attended the meetings of the I.P.C. Board. However, because of our close and friendly relations with the French, we were kept well in touch with what was going on. The French directors always had a long talk with me the day before the meetings and dined with me the day of the meeting, showing me all the papers.

The Sale of Oil Agreement I negotiated with Louis Tronchère, the managing director of the Compagnie Française des Pétroles.

He was a tremendously hard-working man, with a very meticulous mind, who loved everything to be precise. It was this latter quality, so admirable in other circumstances, which led him to make a very grave error in our negotiations together. The suggested basis on which we sat down to talk was that the price at which the French should take over our oil should be fixed each year, in advance, by an arbitrator or expert and that we should then have a limited time in which we could either accept the price or sell the oil ourselves. We had assumed that the price proposed by the arbitrator would be based on a forecast of the ruling price for the following year. Monsieur Tronchère, however, did not like the idea of the expert having to look into a crystal ball to guess what the price would be for the following year, although it is normal for contracts to be made ahead and it would not really have been very difficult. Still, Tronchère insisted that he could not tolerate this kind of imprecision and said the price offered to us must be based on prices ruling during the previous years. This certainly did not perturb me for the result, of course, was that we had been handed a very valuable option. If the price of oil was rising at the time of the offer we could sell the oil ourselves at the higher prices then prevailing. If the price of oil was falling then we should be in the happy position of accepting the inevitably higher price—the price for the previous year—fixed by the arbitrator. It is remarkable that Tronchère never realized that. I made the agreement on his basis but, in fact, for twenty years, although we were in a period, by and large, of rising prices, which would have allowed us to cut out the French and sell the oil ourselves, we never took advantage of that provision. To have exploited Tronchère's error in those circumstances would have been unsporting and, when we came to re-negotiate our position at the end of the Second World War, our attitude was appreciated.

'Oilmen are like cats,' my father used to say. 'One never knows when listening to them whether they are fighting or making love.' I must say that in the oil business not even one's best friends are to be trusted and this proved true at the very moment of my negotiating the Sale of Oil Agreement with the French. I negotiated that contract on the general basis that the French interests and ours, the two smallest and weakest members of the outfit, were likely to be the same or very nearly so. Furthermore, my father had lived in France for a long time and had a genuine affection for the French who had shown more consideration for him than the others. Which does not mean that he could not look after himself very well in his dealing with the Royal Dutch Shell, the Anglo-Persian and the Americans, but he knew he always had to be on the lookout for any move that might be made to squeeze out his interest.

After negotiating the Sale of Oil Agreement, when oil was finally being produced and was available for the following year, our contract with the French came into force and that involved finding an arbitrator to fix the price. In our innocence, as it turned out to be, we thought he could be a member of the Anglo-Persian, Sir William Fraser, for instance, who was very well up on oil prices and was the vice-chairman of the company. We thought he would be a fair and impartial arbitrator who ought to be equally acceptable to the French. However, when I went to see him at his offices in Finsbury Circus to ask him to accept the role, he hummed and hawed, looked a little uncomfortable, and gave a dozen excuses for not taking it on. None of them was very convincing and I was puzzled by his attitude for he had always been very friendly to us and I considered what I was asking him was a sign of great confidence in his integrity.

I understood what it was all about two days later when Monsieur Cayrol, a very good friend of my father and myself, and the vice-president of the Compagnie Française des Pétroles, came with Monsieur Tronchère to see me. Never have I seen two men looking more embarrassed. But as they began to talk I soon understood why. They explained to me that although they had negotiated the Sale of Oil Agreement with me on the basis that we, the Gulbenkians, were selling our oil to our friends, the French, they had in fact also been acting on behalf of all the other Groups. They were all in on the deal. This, they were sorry to say, they had never revealed to us. Because of that, it was obvious that an interested party, like Sir William Fraser, of the Anglo-Persian, could not be an impartial arbitrator of the price he would have to pay. I am afraid I told my French friends a few home truths about loyalty and straight dealing but I did not take it too far: there is no point in having avoidable rows with anyone, least of all in the oil business, and having eased my mind I let the whole thing pass over. Later, we did find an expert, a truly impartial one, to act as arbitrator; this was J. H. Macdonald, of S. Pearson and Son, Lord Cowdray's firm, to whom I have already referred.

To round off this short narrative of the way oil production in the Middle East began and developed, I must tell of the signing of the Red Line Agreement, the main settlement which was also known as the Group Agreement of 1928. This famous Agreement, which was negotiated simultaneously with the agreement with the French for the sale of the Gulbenkian oil, covered what was roughly the Ottoman Empire before 1914. It laid down that within that area none of the prospecting Groups in the Iraq Petroleum Company could have independent concessions; any concessions they possessed had to be given to the I.P.C.

The Agreement was finally in order and approved by all the interested parties and required only the formal execution. For fiscal reasons it had to be executed outside England so I chartered a plane from Imperial Airways, as it was called in those days. The pilot was my old friend, Captain Olley, who was their first charter pilot and who later made a small fortune by running a private charter line called Olley Airways; a cheerful, resourceful, little man who had often flown me before and continued to do so right up to his retirement. He died in 1958.

We flew from Croydon to Ostend in a fourteen-seater Handley Page. In the party as well as myself (in the role of President or Vice-President of a Gulbenkian company formed specially to hold our interests in the I.P.C. venture), were my brother-in-law, Kvork Essayan, Duncan Smith, Tommy Frost and Miss Everest. My brother-in-law had been working in my father's office. Duncan Smith was a partner in a firm of solicitors called Freshfields, Leese and Munns. A man with a little blond moustache and a gammy leg from the First World War, he was most able but very stubborn. Scrupulously honest and devoted to his clients, he always stuck to his guns, which was a great quality but had its drawbacks. Even if something he had said turned out to be wrong, he would not budge, but he was an excellent lawyer and it was a matter of learning how to handle him. Miss Everest was the secretary, a lady who had come to my father's office for a fortnight as a temporary typist and was to stay for some thirty years before retiring to a well-earned rest and pension near Reading. Miss Everest had never been in a plane before and was quite terrified until I reassured her by pointing out Crystal Palace below us, as we headed for the Channel. Tommy Frost, as mentioned before, my 'permanent best man', had come for the ride; I had arranged to play golf with him over the weekend at Folkestone, after signing the Agreement.

We flew to Ostend, went to the Royal Palace Hotel and ordered champagne and an excellent lunch, with turbot as a first course because Ostend is famous for its turbot. We signed the Agreement, had our signature witnessed by the necessary authorities, sent off a few telegrams to New York, enjoyed our lunch and champagne and prepared for the journey home again. My only anxiety was that the pilot, Captain Olley, might have had more champagne than was good for him but he was a very conscientious man and drank just one glass and nothing more. We landed first at Folkestone so that Tommy Frost and I could start our golfing weekend; the rest of the plane-load then flew on to London.

And that, some fourteen years after the letter from the Grand Vizier promising the concession to the Turkish Petroleum Company and even more years after the first attempts to secure a concession, was the beginning of the real development of the Middle East oil-fields.

After the signature of the 1928 Agreement a Gulbenkian director attended the board meetings of the I.P.C. by right, and from then onwards I represented the Gulbenkian interests on the Board. The French Government wanted to recompense my father for all the work he had done for France for, after all, it was thanks to him that France had a petroleum policy at all or had an interest in the Mesopotamian oil-fields. Philippe Berthelot, who was then Secretary-General at the French Foreign Office, offered my father the Grand Cross of the Legion of Honour, the highest decoration in the power of the French Government to award. Berthelot, whom I had often gone to see during the negotiations, was a man of the highest intellect, a great patriot, a subtle diplomat who always thought of the interests of France, and very watchful, perhaps too watchful, of his friends' interests. He was a man who never feared to take decisions.

My father refused the decoration, just as later he was to refuse an English knighthood. But he told Berthelot that it was I who had done all the work, which was very kind and generous of him. He suggested that I should be given the Legion of Honour instead of him though, of course, for a young man just over thirty, it was out of the question that I should receive the Grand Cross. Berthelot prepared a recommendation for me to be made a Commander of the Legion of Honour. He put it to Briand, the Foreign Minister, for signature. Briand, of the 'silver tongue', a great parliamentarian who could sway the Chamber of Deputies or any other audience he addressed, could never be bothered with details and used to sign almost any paper that was put before him without reading it. He signed Berthelot's recommendation for my award but a decoration of that distinction required not only the signature of the Minister concerned but also the counter-signature of the President of the Republic. This was Poincaré, who was the antithesis of Briand, being coldly mathematical of mind and paying the greatest attention to detail. He would never sign anything without going into it, almost too meticulously.

When the decree for my decoration came before him, he said to Briand, 'I see you want to decorate Gulbenkian for all he has done for us.'

Briand said, rather surprisingly, 'Oh, I didn't realize what I was signing.'

However, Poincaré duly counter-signed it and I became a very proud Commander of the Legion of Honour, for many years the youngest to hold that rank. That decoration is about as high as a French Ambassador ever rates, even at the end of long years of service. For that reason my possession of it impresses all Frenchmen of the rank of Ambassador and below, down to the Customs official at the port and airport.

When I received my decoration, Philippe Berthelot, with his usual quizzical smile, informed me that if I died in France, I would be entitled to have a gun carriage to carry my coffin and a platoon of infantry to accompany me to my last resting-place! Alas, since the last war, there is apparently no horse artillery in the French Army, and all the military honours which my sorrowing widow might have claimed for my mortal remains have been done away with.

I have lived too long.

5

A Chihuahua for Herminia

———————

AFTER the honeymoon with Herminia I took up my job
with the Royal Dutch Shell. I felt proud of the fact that I had been
able to defy my father's threats, had found a job for myself and
was now standing on my own feet. What I did not know at the
time, however, was that he had had a hand in this as well. He had
arranged that while the Royal Dutch should give me a job they
should send me out to what was then the Dutch East Indies (now
Indonesia) to the oil-fields which were at that time the basis of
the Royal Dutch Shell position in the oil world. All I knew was
that I was to go out there for about a year, at a salary of £1000
a year, and I was quite happy about the idea. I understood I was
on trial, as it were, and if I shaped well I could hope for promotion.
I ordered some tussore suits for the tropical climate, and prepared to start a new stage in my career. All this had been arranged
before my marriage and perhaps my father had hoped that the
prospect of going to the East Indies would be enough to stop
Herminia and myself going ahead with the wedding. When we
were actually married, my father realized this plan had failed and
arranged that I should not go out there after all. So I was left with
my tussore suits and though my shape has altered somewhat in
the past forty years and I have put on a fair amount of weight I
still use them occasionally.

Instead of cutting a figure in the Dutch East Indies I joined the
London office of the Royal Dutch Shell Group in St. Helen's
Court. Rumblings of a row between the Group and my father
(over the way the Group tried to exploit the companies brought
in by my father) could already be heard. In this situation, Henri
Deterding, who was a very wise man, assigned me to a particular
role, that of taking charge of the Mexican department of the Group

in London. As I have already related, my father negotiated the deal between Deterding and Lord Cowdray which brought the Mexican Eagle into the Royal Dutch Shell orbit and Deterding now saw my appointment as fulfilling a dual purpose. On the one hand, he felt that if my father should attack the Group for their handling of the Mexican Eagle affairs he would be attacking his own beloved son as the man responsible; this might either dissuade my father from his attack or, if he went ahead, I might be able to pacify him. On the other hand, Deterding also thought I might be more independently minded than others in the Group's employ and stick up for my department and the Mexican company which formed part of it against the encroachments of other interests in the Royal Dutch. As I suggested earlier, Deterding did not go all the way with those who wanted to treat the associated companies as mere subsidiaries.

I gradually became Deterding's personal assistant, although I was never given that formal title. Whenever awkward letters addressed to Deterding arrived, his secretary, Miss Blom, used to send them on to me, on the principle, 'When in doubt send it to Gulbenkian.' This gave me a wonderful opportunity to meet all the oil kings of the time. (They were not called 'tycoons' until much later.) I met, for example, the leaders of the Standard Oil of New Jersey, the Chairman, A. C. Bedford, the President, Walter Teagle, and Heinrich von Riedemann, an important director. I have told in the previous chapter of my encounter with Teagle and Riedemann at the time of the negotiations leading up to the Red Line Agreement. The present meeting came about during negotiations between all the companies which had had properties in Russia to form a so-called 'United Front' to boycott Russian oil; this was to be a retaliation against the action of the Bolsheviks in nationalizing all the oil properties on Russian territory. These companies met once a month in Paris, passing resolutions and plotting ways of getting their own back on the Soviets. (It has been said that it was not only sound business reasons which dictated Deterding's hostile attitute towards the Bolshevik regime. There was, too, his involvement in White Russian circles, the result of Adjemoff's influence which in turn had led to his marriage to Lydia Pavlovna; this, it was suggested, also played a big part.) The oil business, however, is probably not one where there is much hope of achieving any concerted action if any of the companies involved sees a chance to further its own interests. So it was with the 'United Front'. The Vacuum Oil Company was the first to break away from the boycott on Russian oil. They bought from the Russians, at a very cheap price, 500,000 tons of kerosene for the Indian market. Their excuse was that if they had not done so, the Russians would have sold direct in India and would have collared the Indian market. The other companies were not entirely convinced by this argument; they suspected the motives of the Vacuum Oil were something less than altruistic. But the 'United Front' crumbled overnight. Within twenty-four hours the Royal Dutch Shell started buying Russian oil and it quickly became a question of the devil taking the hindmost. (Of course, since those days, the Russians have found other ways of selling their oil. At the time of writing, for instance, the British Government do not allow Russian oil into Britain. In theory, that is. In practice, what happens is that men like the late Enrico Mattei and the Italian Government entity buy Russian oil, sell it in Italy among other places, and thereby release other oil for sale on the British market. Oil boycotts have little hope of success although the boycott of Mexican oil just before the last war began and that of Persian oil in the early 1950s, after Mossadeq had expropriated the Anglo-Iranian Oil Company, did have some effect.)

In the period 1923–4, however, before the 'United Front' was shattered, I accompanied Deterding at the negotiations and on trips to discuss ways of beating the Russians. I also went with him on a visit to the United States which was partly concerned with discussions about the Russian position, but we combined this visit to the U.S. with one to Mexico to inspect the Mexican Eagle installations.

We sailed in the 56,000-ton *Majestic* from Southampton, Deterding and his son, Ronald, my faithful valet, Bailey, and my private secretary, Miss Ward. I had to make all the day-to-day arrangements for the comfort of the party, make minutes of all meetings, take notes of all decisions and keep the various departments of the Group fully informed. There was plenty of work to do, but life was certainly not without its moments of relaxation or the means to enjoy it. Although prohibition had just started in America, I have never drunk so much alcohol as during those few weeks' stay in the States. I had been given letters of introduction to business associates of the Royal Dutch Shell and to my father's friends over there; I had scarcely arrived in New York before they started to send me gifts, cases of gin, whisky, champagne. Before long my cupboard at the Ritz Carlton Hotel could rival a well-stocked cellar and certainly contained more bottles than are stocked at this moment in my London flat.

We held meetings with the Standard Oil at 26 Broadway, where they then had their headquarters. Then, for our tour through the United States and on to Mexico, we travelled in a private Pullman car, first to St. Louis, Missouri, where the Royal Dutch Shell had oil-fields and a refinery, and thence south towards the Mexican border. It was now that I appreciated for the first time the size of Texas. I know that Texans are supposed to be blow-hards and loud-mouths about their state, claiming among other things that it was they who annexed the other American states, but one is bound to admit that when it comes to size, at least, Texas really has something to boast about. We entered Texas, at San Antonio, at eleven o'clock at night. We travelled all that night and when I asked next morning what state we were in I was told 'Texas'. We travelled the whole of that day, too, still passing through Texas, the track running through cotton country, so that I was able to see the cotton-pickers at work in the fields from the Pullman window. It was not until the following morning, after a second night on the move, that we came to Laredo, still in Texas, but at the Mexican frontier.

We went on to Tampico, where the Mexican Eagle had a huge refinery, and at last our travelling hotel came to a halt. The Pullman was put into a siding, Deterding stayed at the house of the managing director, a Dutchman called Van Gothen, and I was the guest of the general manager and his charming Mexican wife. Wherever Deterding went supplies of Poland water, an American mineral water, had to go too, and when I reached my host's home I realized I had forgotten to arrange for the Poland water to be taken off the Pullman. So poor Bailey, my valet, who was also serving Deterding and his son, had to go back for it before Sir Henri called for it and him. The Pullman car was some miles away and Bailey went off in one of the company's cars but he ran into trouble on the way back. The trouble took the form of

an election meeting which consisted of Mexican cowboys galloping in from the countryside on their cow ponies, firing their guns
wildly in the air. Bailey escaped injury but when he finally arrived
he was very shaken.

During our visit to Mexico we were accompanied by J. B. Body,
one of Lord Cowdray's right-hand men. Body became very
wealthy as a result of this association, for Lord Cowdray had the
good habit of giving all those who worked for him or with him an
interest in his business.

We spent some days in Tampico inspecting the oil refineries
and offices, working very hard on a tour of inspection. A great
deal of work devolved upon me for I had to be present at Deterding's side throughout, including all meals, breakfast, lunch and
dinner, at which business was usually discussed. Then I had to
sort out what had been discussed and what decisions taken and
dictate reports to Miss Ward. One night, I had finished work by
midnight and though I was rather tired I felt the need of distraction. I was glad to accept the offer of an official called Marcuse
(whom Deterding had met in England when hunting in the Shires
and had engaged there) to see the sights of Tampico.

Tampico was a small but booming oil-town on the seashore and
much like all such towns. The company had put up houses in the
suburbs, the size of the houses and the comfort of them varying
according to the rank of the occupant. All the unskilled labour
in the oil-fields was drawn locally—'native' labour as it was called
then—and wages were low. They must have been because I remember Lord Cowdray defending himself against the accusation
that he was using old-fashioned human labour to move earth in
sacks—carried on the backs of peons—instead of using the earth-
moving machinery and excavators which elsewhere were in fairly
general use. He explained it was cheaper to use native labour than
to install the comparatively expensive machinery.

Tampico at night was as brightly lit in the main streets as
Piccadilly is today. It had all the crude, wild vigour of an oil
town, as we soon discovered on our trip into town. There were
three of us, Marcuse, myself and Wellings, a very experienced
geologist who was a constant companion during our trips to the
oil-fields and who later became the chief geologist of the Iraq
Petroleum Company. As our car was pulling up outside a night

club called Casa Africa, we saw two American drillers, both drunk, having a fight in the street. Like drillers of any nationality these were a couple of toughs, big and hefty and, especially at that moment, in no mood to give a damn for anybody. They certainly were not taking any notice of a diminutive Mexican policeman, with his large sombrero and double bandolier of cartridges, who was trying to separate them. Of course, in those days, no American would take the slightest notice of any 'native', an attitude of mind which caused a great deal of ill feeling and brought its own consequences in later years.

When the policeman found that persuasion was having no effect on the two drillers, he drew his revolver, not with the idea of shooting anyone but of hitting them on the head with the butt. Unfortunately, the revolver went off by accident and shot an innocent passer-by on the other side of the street, just in front of the entrance to the night club. The poor man went down with a grunt and just lay there (and, in accordance with Mexican law, he would have to go on lying there until a *Juez*, a judicial inspector, had certified the exact position of the body). My appetite for entertainment suddenly vanished. I had the wind up and, with teeth chattering, I suggested to Marcuse we should call it a day.

'After all,' I said, 'I've had a pretty hard day, a lot of work and I've got to be up early in the morning. I think perhaps I'd better g-g-go home.' I looked down at the man who had been shot and turned back towards the car. The doorman of the Casa Africa, realizing he was about to lose three customers, took me by the arm and almost pushed me into the night club.

'*Pasa usted, señor,*' he purred, with an ingratiating smile, '*es un muertito nada mas.*'

I have remembered those words all my life. 'Pass in, sir, it's only a little man they've killed, nothing more.'

Touring the oil-fields in Mexico in the early twenties was altogether an eventful business. Although we did not have time to go to the famous Mexican Golden Lane, we did inspect some oil-fields in Panuco, which was joined to Tampico by a railway. This railway had been bought by the Royal Dutch and was part of my responsibilities, but as there was no money to spare the equipment and old rolling stock was degenerating more and more; the result was that never a day passed without some sort of accident.

We had a special train to take us the ninety miles from Tampico
to Panuco. It was a single track, but with only two scheduled
trains a day it seemed a fairly safe assumption that no other train
would be on the line. We were wrong. As we were on our way and
approaching a bend a little rail car hurtled towards us from
around the corner. It was hand-propelled and carrying four workmen. They had not been told of the special train running that day.
There was no time for either them or us to stop but, as the rail
car crashed head-on into our engine, the workmen jumped off
and rolled over in the dust beside the track. There was some rich
oathing for a time but, although the little car was a write-off and
the cowcatcher of our engine was bent, no one was hurt.

Further on, we passed a huge lake, more than a mile across, of
thick, black, glistening Panuco oil. The lake had been formed by
oil which had got out of control. It would have looked sinister
enough in any circumstances but now it looked macabre for the
surface was covered with hundreds of birds which had been
attracted by reflections in the mass of oil and had alighted on it,
never to rise again. The lake was supposed to be guarded by
watchmen but I was told that one man had walked into the lake
at night, had sunk into the oil and was never seen again.

On our way down the Panuco River by launch to see some of
the outstanding installations, we saw a couple of tents on the river
bank. They had been pitched there by a detachment of *rurales*,
the Mexican Gendarmerie, a very formidable body of men whose
task it was to keep order in the countryside. They had just caught
a gang of bandits, one of whom had been hanged and was dangling
from a tree. I was young in those days and perhaps guilty of bad
taste but as we stopped the launch I took a photograph of the
bandit's limp body hanging on the tree. A sergeant of the *rurales*
tried to stop me.

'Hey, señor,' he shouted. 'Don't waste your film on just one
bandit. Come back tomorrow morning. We'll be hanging two
more of them at dawn.' His Latin courtesy rather overwhelmed
me and all I could say was that while I appreciated his offer, one
man was enough to make the point in my picture and anyhow I
should not be there at dawn the next day. Latin courtesy was not
to be so simply baulked.

'Oh, well, señor,' said the sergeant, 'if you're not going to be here tomorrow, just give us a quarter of an hour and we'll get the bandits out and hang them right away.' In the face of such politeness and consideration, it was difficult not to seem ungracious, but I managed to make suitable excuses; I jumped back on to the launch and off we went.

Back at Tampico, on our last night there before moving on to Mexico City, Deterding gave a company dance to which all employees, male and female, were invited. A great deal was drunk and when Deterding got up to make a speech he had an enthusiastic audience. But some of their enthusiasm dimmed as his own took hold of him. He praised the work of the staff in glowing terms, which was fine, except that he did not confine his praise to the North American and European members of the staff; he praised the 'natives' too.

'I have been much impressed,' he said, 'by the way the Mexicans are working here. What is more, I will say this; I like the Mexican people so much that if I was not a Dutchman I would like to be a Mexican.'

I was the one who got into trouble over this. We were all pretty high by this time and the American members of the staff became very hot over what they considered Deterding's gross indiscretion in praising the 'natives'. It was no good my telling them I had no means of controlling an off-the-cuff speech for they held me responsible just the same for allowing him to make it. Still, when you have the advantages of travelling with the boss, you have to take the rough with the smooth.

I found Mexico City, which is nearly 7500 feet above sea-level (1500 feet higher than St. Moritz), exhilarating at first but then very tiring to the heart. At first sight, it had a certain magnificence, with its main street, the Avenida Juarez, as it was then called, a fine wide avenue leading to Chapultepec Park and rivalling the Champs-Élysées, fringed with beautiful buildings. But fifty yards away from this splendid street, down the side-roads, the houses were no more than hovels and the roads themselves not only had no surface but were a quagmire. I was reminded of this aspect of Mexico City when I went to Moscow in 1958, whose back streets at that time also mocked the splendour of the main thoroughfares.

Deterding made the necessary round of all the authorities in

Mexico City, meeting Ministers of the Government and the representatives of the American and Dutch Government. With the exception of his interview with the President, I accompanied him on each occasion. This was my role throughout the tour, aide, confidant, the man to whom he could turn at an interview for factual information, a sounding-board for opinions and ideas; and, whenever our special car stopped for a while, his deputy in entertaining officials and big-wigs, whether Governmental, local or company, who came on board the train to present their respects to Deterding. When he had retired or was actually sleeping, I had to undertake the dual function of the host who observed the courtesies on his behalf and at the same time kept his guests quiet. Often it was amusing, never a bore, and in all provided me with an insight into the personalities and affairs of the places through which we were passing.

One obvious virtue of the trip was that it gave me a first-hand acquaintance with many of the people and locations for whom I, as head of the Mexican department in London, was responsible. These duties included, for instance, the 'defence' of the Minatitlan refinery, which was owned by the Mexican Eagle. This refinery was on the river Coatzacoalcos and the river itself was sited in a strategic position: fighting often broke out between various revolutionaries who wanted to cross the river. Now the Mexican Eagle, although a Mexican-registered company in order to save income tax, was owned predominantly by British capital and the British Government, at the request of the Mexican Eagle, accepted the responsibility to protect the Minatitlan refinery. Whenever fighting broke out on the Coatzacoalcos, the British Government held that no warlike acts must take place within one mile upstream or one mile downstream of the refinery. As the means of giving practical effect to that, a naval gunboat patrolled the stretch of river running one mile upstream and one mile downstream from the Minatitlan refinery. When we, in London, heard from the Mexican Eagle people on the spot that fighting had broken out again, it was my job to telephone to the Director of Naval Operations at the Admiralty and ask for a gunboat to be sent to the scene: it became known as the 'G.G.' ('Gulbenkian Gunboat').

From Mexico we went to Tallahassee in Florida to meet Walter Teagle and von Riedemann of the Standard Oil again; United

States Senator Walter Edge, who was later American Ambassador in Paris, was also in the party. Teagle had a 'hunting box' in Florida (what would be called in England a shooting lodge) which consisted of a one-storey wooden building, with other accommodation alongside for the Negro servants. Teagle met us at the nearest station, Thomasville, which was twenty miles away and then took Deterding on ahead, leaving Bailey and myself to come on later with the luggage. I had packed a pair of 'Napoleon-topped' snake-proof gaiters, bought at the famous stores of Abercrombie and Fitch in New York, where I had been warned that Florida was notorious for rattlesnakes. Napoleon tops came up above the knees; my gaiters were made of canvas covered with thin wire mesh. If a rattlesnake tries to bite you, he hits his nose on the wire mesh, retreats discomfited, leaving you safe. That, at any rate, is the theory as put to me.

Bailey and I had some difficulty in making our way to the hunting box for our driver lost his way and Bailey's efforts to get directions from the local coloured people were far from successful. They spoke a language, or a dialect, which was quite impossible for us to understand, so that although they knew what he was saying their replies made no sense. Still, we got there in the end and in the first few moments after our arrival wished we had not. As we approached the steps leading into the 'box' we nearly jumped out of our skins, for there, lying across the threshold, was a huge rattlesnake. This was not my idea of Southern hospitality, especially as my Napoleon tops were still in my luggage, not yet unpacked. However, our hearts quickly settled back into their proper places when we realized it was a dead rattlesnake, put there for our special benefit.

The idea of the trip was to combine business with pleasure and there were matters of high oil policy to be discussed which kept me busy, making notes and sending telegrams. This meant my motoring to and from Tallahassee to send and receive the cables which were in code and to dictate to my secretary, Miss Ward, who had been left in the hotel there as the shooting party was all-male.

The game was quail and turkey; the quail, about the size of English partridge, with white flesh, made very pleasant eating, though as they formed the staple diet for days on end I became tired of them. To 'hunt' them, we left in two wagons, each drawn by two mules; a negro on another mule rode ahead. On the wagons, or dog-carts, were what the Americans call quail-hunting dogs. We rode into the bush, as high as a man's shoulders, for what was both complicated and dangerous sport. All of us wore white coats so that, concealed as we were by the bush, the rustle of our movements should not be mistaken for that made by the game. Yet even though I stayed with the mules, the negro drivers and the dog-carts, safely as I thought, I was peppered by Senator Edge; a few pellets hit my shoulders but did not penetrate 'the flesh'.

When the discussions were ended and the cables had been drafted and despatched we had to wait over the weekend for reactions from our departmental experts and the other directors in London. Deterding, Teagle, Riedemann and the Senator decided to put in some serious shooting and I was given the weekend off to pop over to Cuba for a day to see Herminia's father in Havana. This meant my taking a train down to Key West, the furthest tip of Florida, to catch the boat. On the way there I met an example of the average American's kindness. We had to change trains at Jacksonville and wait some hours for our connection. I went to a restaurant where the waiter was a Greek recently arrived from Europe. When he heard that I was an Armenian and my train was not leaving until the early hours he offered to show me round the town after he had finished work at eleven that night. I found the Americans everywhere tremendously helpful and friendly. In New York, people who were friends of my father and to whom I had letters of introduction not only sent cars to fetch me from my hotel to their homes for dinner but also came themselves to accompany me. They did this, although I was only in my twenties and they were often thirty years older than myself. I also admired the way they cut out red tape in the States, sometimes to a degree startling to people brought up with the ideas of the Eastern Hemisphere. For instance, we ran out of cash on one stage of our trip and I cabled our New York bankers to send a thousand dollars to meet me at one of our scheduled stops. The cable, authorizing the money, arrived after we had already moved on, but the very efficient Western Union telegraphed to a wayside station ahead of us. On our arrival there a man walked up and down the train shouting my name. When I answered it, he said, 'Say, man, I guess I've got good news for you—a thousand bucks!' He never asked me to identify myself in any way and I do not remember even signing a receipt.

In Cuba, although I was having a weekend holiday, I managed to find time to do a little business, inspecting a site which had been mooted in London as a potentially good purchase for oil installations. Bailey, who always wanted 'his gentleman' to be correctly attired, had put out for me an immaculate pair of white trousers and white and brown shoes, the correct wear for the tropics. Unfortunately, the site was partly on a bog and in my anxiety to appreciate its advantages and defects I walked a little ahead of the local Company manager and floundered right up to my knees in mud; I was less immaculate than Bailey could have wished at lunch with the local officials.

In the evening, Herminia's brother took charge of me and we had a night out on the town. Havana was very gay and wealthy American visitors made it gayer still. About half a dozen of us had a party in the leading night club in the city, consuming more champagne than was good for us, plus some more, to the point where glasses and champagne bottles started flying out of the windows. A Cuban policeman came in and summoned the proprietor, but Cuban policemen were no more effective than Mexican ones. The proprietor, it is true, was fearful of losing his free-spending customers but he need not have worried. The offer of five dollars easily persuaded the policeman to see his hat go the way of the bottles through the window. Another twenty dollars and he agreed to be thrown out himself. Luckily, the party was on the mezzanine floor, only about ten feet above the pavement, and the policeman landed unhurt and twenty-five dollars better off; we were left in peace, if that is the word, for the rest of the night.

I got back to the hotel at six in the morning, to find the faithful Bailey waiting up for me. We just had time to get me out of my evening clothes and packed before catching the boat, which was leaving the harbour at seven.

I was less than pleased to find that the local manager had not failed in his duty to get up to see me off, bringing with him further details about import duties on gasoline I had asked for the day before. I was feeling like death and probably looked it but managed, I hope, not to give myself away. Still, I was rewarded when, on my return to London, on the strength of my personal inspection and my report, it was agreed to build a million-pound refinery in Cuba.

Back in New York, we stayed at the Ritz Carlton and on the day we were leaving to catch the *Berengaria* back to Europe, I was paying my bill when I saw an unexpected item of 300 dollars.

'What is this for?' I asked.

'That, sir,' I was told, 'is for carpets ruined by the dog.'

The dog was a chihuahua, a tiny dog weighing about a pound and a quarter I had bought in Mexico for my wife. I had given him to Miss Ward to look after and she had had a certain amount of trouble, especially at the Ritz Carlton, because he was not entirely house-trained. Not a carpet was left unsoiled and the Ritz Carlton was run by business-minded people.

'Can't the carpets be cleaned?' I wanted to know.

'I'm afraid not, sir—they're completely ruined and we shall have to replace them with entirely new carpeting.'

I did not argue with this but I had learned a little business-sense too, by now.

'I quite understand,' I said, 'but, as there are a couple of hours yet before the ship sails, would you mind having the carpets wrapped up and I'll take them with me.'

The cashier was somewhat flustered by this and he retired to consult his superiors.

'On reconsideration,' he said when he came back, 'we feel that perhaps a charge of twenty dollars to have the carpets cleaned would meet the situation.'

The journey home was uneventful, but it did provide an example of Deterding's tolerant and considerate attitude towards his staff. J. B. Body and Riedemann came with us and we still talked quite a lot of business during the day. Unlike on the way over, when the weather had forced Miss Ward to retire to her bunk for the whole voyage, the sea was fairly smooth and I was able to do a fair amount of dictation. As we were sailing eastwards and losing an hour or more every day, Deterding went to bed at about eleven o'clock and I was able to enjoy a little relaxation. I made the acquaintance of a very attractive American, a blonde with a white fairy-queenlike dress, who did not immediately repulse my advances when looking at the stars in a dark, lonely part of the deck. The next morning, Deterding and Riedemann tackled me.

'What on earth were you up to after we went to bed?'

'Where have you been? Explain yourself.'

I flushed and stuttered my answers.

'I-I-I finished all the dictation.'

'Yes, yes—and then?'

'I don't know what you mean. Really, I don't see—I was on time for breakfast at half past eight.'

'Oh, yes, we know you were, but that's not the point. What we want to know is what you were doing *after* you finished dictating and *before* you appeared for breakfast.'

They played the game for a little while longer and then Deterding ended my embarrassment. It appeared that he had found it stuffy in his cabin, although it was December, and had decided to take a walk along the deck. He had seen me with my 'fairy queen' but he had not spoken to me because he had not wanted to spoil my fun.

At Cherbourg the party broke up. Deterding and J. B. Body went on to London; von Riedemann and Bailey caught the boat train to Paris and I got into my Hispano Suiza which was waiting for me at the dockside. I had been bitten by the speed-bug and, like many of my friends, bought faster and faster cars and drove them more and more recklessly in order to knock five minutes off a three-hour journey. On this occasion, despite my stopping for a good lunch at Evreux, I managed to reach Paris before the boat train arrived. I saw Miss Ward, took possession of the little chihuahua and handed him over to Herminia who was waiting for me. It had been a good trip.

When we were in Paris, Herminia and I lived at the Hôtel d'Iena. This was where her parents had lived for a while after leaving the Curzon in London. The Hôtel d'Iena was smallish, respectable, comfortable while not unduly luxurious, but very good style; perhaps rather like Brown's in Dover Street.

In London, for the first few months of our marriage, we lived in the suite in the Ritz where our marriage service had been held. The suite was a very pleasant one, overlooking Green Park and consisting of a large bedroom, a bathroom and quite a big sitting-room. It was my father's idea that we should stay in an hotel for he was very sceptical about how long the marriage would last. After we had actually married, my parents no longer showed hostility towards the union; it would be fair, I think, to describe their attitude as one of strict neutrality. They did not try to interfere with us but nor did they do anything to help us. It was because of their reluctance to spend money in setting us up in a house that we lived either in hotels or in furnished flats.

After about a year, we moved from the Ritz and took a flat, quite a posh affair, at the bottom end of Park Lane. We had a small staff, including a very good cook, my valet, Bailey, and Wooster, a chauffeur who had joined my service in 1920. (One night in Paris, when Chadinoff and I were doing the rounds and had reached a night club called Zelli's, I was surprised to see my chauffeur and valet among the patrons already there. Each of them was dancing with one of the young ladies of the establishment and they were fairly enjoying themselves. I was not sure whether I should discharge them immediately for impertinence or send them a bottle of champagne. After little hesitation I chose the latter course of action and I am glad I did for I could not have wished for greater loyalty than I received from them in the years that followed. Wooster was pensioned off in 1950 and I am happy to think he enjoyed his pension until his death in 1964.)

We entertained and were entertained chiefly in fashionable restaurants, in parties of not more than six. We did not entertain business friends because I suppose I was too unimportant to need to do that. For a long time, indeed, I kept my private life and my business life in separate compartments and I was always shocked when I saw a banker or an oilman, with whom I had been doing business during the day, in the same restaurant or dancing place as I, even if he was with his own wife. If he was with somebody else's wife I became, subconsciously, rather puritanical, though I certainly had no right to be. Dining out in those days invariably meant stiff shirt, white tie and tails. Our table was always the cynosure of neighbouring eyes. This was not because of me for I was not at all well known then; I had no beard and looked rather insignificant. Nor was it because of Herminia's behaviour for I must say, in all fairness, that she did not make a fuss of summoning waiters or show off in that sort of way at all. No, it was undoubtedly because of her looks and appearance. With her typically long Spanish face and her dark hair parted down the middle, she looked strikingly attractive and, while she did not dress flashily, she did carry her clothes well. She was a good dancer and enjoyed it; so did I up to a point, although I have always been a very bad dancer, rather like a bear on hot bricks waddling around the room.

Herminia also enjoyed driving cars but her driving was not in the same class as her dancing. She had a small model T Ford; it had a special body in white with red wings and red wheels, quite a smart little job. I think her father had been given it for Herminia as an extra commission when, after the war, he did a deal with agents for the French Government to buy up surplus stores; he bought some 50 or 100 second-hand lorries and shipped them to Cuba where lorries were worth their weight in gold. Herminia drove the little Ford about perilously, the peril being to those who were in the vehicle and also to those who came within range.

There was also the Hispano Suiza. The Hispano was about the *ne plus ultra* of cars at that time. My father had just given me one and we had taken it to Baveno on Lake Maggiore where Herminia and I were spending a few days. One day we went from Baveno to Stresa. Herminia wanted to drive so the faithful Wooster had to take the back seat. I think his heart was in his mouth once or twice but he had been used to sitting next to me when I was driving and this must have inured him somewhat, for I think I may have been more occupied with getting somewhere quickly and with passing the car in front than with caring for the safety of others. In fact, with Herminia at the wheel, we proceeded along the main road from Baveno to Stresa without undue mishap and managed to get as far as the Grand Hotel et des Iles Borromées which was, and is still, a smart hotel at Stresa. Although the Grand Hotel had, and still has, a fairly wide entrance gate which is always kept open, this gate was flanked by two massive stone pillars. The Hispano was a longish car and, therefore, one had to take quite a wide sweep. Herminia, however, decided—or the car decided for her—to go in partly through the gate and partly through the gatepost. The result was that the two frame members of the Hispano, which had been scrupulously parallel hitherto, gave the impression of a dancer doing the splits, as the member which hit the gatepost progressed a deal less quickly than the member which was going through the gate. The gatepost itself was shifted out of true by about two or three inches. No other damage was done to the hotel property but the Hispano was out of commission for four days and my holiday money was reduced by the astronomical sum it cost to bring a mechanic from Paris to Stresa to repair the Hispano. Some thirty-five years later, in 1960, I was again on the shores of Lake Maggiore; I passed the same Grand Hotel, I looked at the gatepost and saw that it was still out of true. It has been suggested that a plaque should be mounted there to record the incident for posterity and perhaps some kind reader, or the hotel proprietor, will feel inclined so to do.

Herminia and I had both been spoiled by our parents; she was also a very attractive girl who was used to getting her own way. When the first glamour of married life had worn off, our clashes and rows became more and more frequent. They must have been for very trivial reasons for I cannot now remember what started most of them. I do recall, though, the one which followed the dinner we gave at our Park Lane flat for Chadinoff and Adjemoff. I have always been rather particular about my food and when I entertain, whether my guests be good friends, as they were, or acquaintances, I like to give them as good a dinner and as well served a dinner as possible; I personally take quite a lot of trouble over it. That was why I was very cross with Herminia. She had no staff problems but she had forgotten to tell the cook about the dinner and no food had been brought in. The meal was so awful that Chaddy and Adjemoff left early, about ten o'clock, and went to a restaurant to get a square meal. This I learned afterwards and of course I had a row with Herminia about it but it achieved little: just a scene in front of the servants and a fraying of our own tempers.

6

A Corner in Caviare

AFTER our return from the States, Deterding arranged to meet von Riedemann again at St. Moritz to carry on the negotiations. I went along, too, and so, this time, did Herminia.

This was rather against Deterding's wishes though he did not assert them positively. She behaved rather foolishly, trying to throw her weight around and showing too little respect for Deterding who clearly did not take to her. She was, perhaps, snobbishly inclined and preferred people, especially men, of aristocratic background; but she liked them with low ethics. She liked what might be called 'good-looking scoundrels'—possibly just a youthful enthusiasm—and she liked to have them around her: she certainly found them more amusing than solid business men. Having been spoilt, she was used to being the hen of the walk and when we were at St. Moritz she did not care to have her meals at the times which suited Deterding. Nor did she like having to fit in our excursions and our life together to suit the unpredictabilities of the business conversations between Deterding and Riedemann.

Herminia's behaviour, however, did not affect my progress with the Royal Dutch Shell. My salary was quickly doubled from the initial £1000 a year and then it went up to £2500 and I started 1925 at £3000 a year. I was kept hard at it but I enjoyed it. I worked at the London headquarters during the week and then, on Saturday night, I went down to Deterding's country house near Melton Mowbray, where he hunted five or six days a week, to spend Sunday with him, returning with his general instructions and keeping him informed regularly of developments. Though the work was strenuous and continuous, it was often done in pleasant surroundings. I used what little influence I had to arrange for meetings to be held in agreeable places: once a month in Paris, for instance, another each month at The Hague and from time to time at Deauville where, although I had little free time, I did manage two or three hours off to go to dinner at the Casino. At that age, sleep does not matter so much and provided I had sorted out the day's notes and minutes before going out I was able to manage all right. There was also the occasional week or ten days in the south of France, at the Carlton Hotel in Cannes, a very good hotel belonging to a friend of mine, Frankie Goldsmith, at which for the last few years I have spent two or three weeks each winter.

It was generally thought that I was being groomed to be a director and possibly Deterding's successor: Riedemann always used to refer to me as the Crown Prince. Whether I might have succeeded Deterding one day I do not know, but I should say that at that time it was of course only a matter of speculation. Whenever Deterding went away for any length of time, either on business or for a prolonged holiday, the running of the Royal Dutch Shell was taken over by the acting chairman, H. Colijn. Deterding arranged this. Each winter for the past few years, Deterding had taken a winter holiday of several months in order to hunt at Melton Mowbray where he maintained a large hunting box and where he kept a very fine string of hunters. His inordinate fondness for hunting brought serious remonstrances from other directors of the Group who urged upon him that it was not right for a man, with responsibilities to a world-wide company with its thousands of shareholders, to take such risks; he had had one or two quite bad accidents. (Actually, Deterding's fondness for hunting had un-expected results. Many people in the Royal Dutch Shell took up hunting because he, the chairman, was doing it; this, in turn, involved their being asked down to Deterding's place for a Saturday's hunting and also to discuss business on the Sunday; although on holiday Deterding kept his finger on the pulse of all that was going on.)

H. Colijn was paid by Deterding himself who refused to allow him to be employed directly by the Royal Dutch Shell. He received £50,000 a year out of the quarter of a million or so which came to Deterding. Colijn was a tall, big, quiet, dour Dutchman, very sound but with none of Deterding's fire or quick perception. He had been Minister of War for Holland during the 1914–18 war (when Holland was neutral) and he used to tell stories of his negotiations with von Bissing, the German Commander-in-Chief and Governor-General of Belgium, about maintaining mutual respect of the Belgian-Dutch frontier. He was the soundest of the Dutch statesmen and subsequently became Prime Minister on a number of occasions; he was in that office when the 1939–45 war broke out. Colijn was not used to the kind of money Deterding was paying him; until then he had always lived in modest style. I remember hearing him say to my father in his grammatical but halting English, 'I do not know what to do with all this money. I cannot spend more than ten thousand pounds a year. I already have a large house'—in Sydenham—'and a Mercedes car'—which he had bought for next to nothing in Germany after the débâcle of the German currency. But, as many readers may agree, not knowing how to spend a lot of money is the least of life's problems, and I do not think it embarrassed Colijn too greatly.

Deterding was an autocrat and whenever his colleagues dared to criticize him he flared up and threatened to resign; this was enough to squash effectively all opposition and to make his very strong position even stronger. But there was opposition and there were many people jealous of his power and position. There were strong currents running within the Group. One was the Dutch influence which, with Deterding at its head, was predominant; the other was the Jewish influence, with Lord Bearsted and his son, Walter Samuel, and, more actively concerned in the business, Robert Waley Cohen. (Waley Cohen, who disliked my father intensely, was engaged during the First World War in negotiating, on behalf of the Royal Dutch Shell, the supply of oil to the Admiralty. In that war, the Government had not taken the powers it took during the second war and there was some difficulty in arriving at agreeable terms. Waley Cohen tried to apply pressure with the rather rash remark, 'What would the Admiralty do if the Royal Dutch Shell refused to sell any oil?' 'Well,' came the reply from 'Blinkers' Hall—Admiral Sir Reginald Hall—who was Director of Naval Intelligence, 'there will always be a lamp-post in the street on which to hang Robert Waley Cohen. His son, Sir Bernard Waley Cohen, has been Lord Mayor of London and is chairman of the Devon and Somerset Staghounds; he is a good friend of mine, I am glad to say, for, as I have said earlier in this book, I do not believe in hereditary vendettas.

When Deterding's younger son, Ronald, wanted to go into business, his father took him into the Group and put him under me in my department. I had been very friendly with his brother, Henry, at Cambridge, a very fine gentleman rider who retired from riding after winning a hundred steeplechases and after having ridden in the Grand National. He was still riding and very much so when Ronald was put under my charge and this sometimes put me into an awkward position. I remember Deterding ringing me up at my flat and asking that young Ronald should be given the day off in order to attend a race meeting at which his brother was riding; he could then be at hand in case of accidents. That was not the kind of request to refuse, of course. On the other hand, I was criticized by other directors who said it was subversive to discipline to give any employee a day off merely to go to a race meeting. They probably found it a convenient way of criticizing Deterding indirectly but I was the one who was in the line of fire.

Deterding was apt to be much influenced by various women he met, women to whom he was most generous, not only while their association lasted but also when he had moved on to fresh woods and pastures new. He was uxorious by nature and my father had his work cut out to prevent his making utterly unsuitable marriages. However, when Deterding fell in love with the Russian exile, Lydia Pavlovna, there was no holding him. My father tried to dissuade Deterding from the marriage and I have always heard it said that the Royal Dutch directors were opposed to it, but Deterding went ahead. They married at the Princes Row registry office and my father was Deterding's witness. I had a flat at that time overlooking Princes Row and when Deterding and Lydia Pavlovna left the registry office I threw an old shoe at them from my window for luck. I gave a small party in my flat to celebrate the wedding to which my father, Deterding's sons and his brother-in-law came, but Lydia and Deterding did not come themselves for he was afraid to show what might seem to be undue favouritism to a junior employee of the Group. I did attend their religious wedding afterwards, conducted according to the rites of the Orthodox Church, in the Russian Cathedral in London.

My relations with Lydia Pavlovna (the mother of Olga Deterding, who goes out to Lambarené in Equatorial Africa to work for Albert Schweitzer) were always of the friendliest kind. She was a cheerful, good-hearted woman with a characteristically Russian ignorance of the value of money, although she had been through very hard times after her escape from the Revolution. She spent money, or rather had money lavished upon her, in a really overwhelming way. Deterding, for instance, bought her an emerald parure, worth several hundred thousand pounds from Cartier's, if 'bought' is the right word. In fact, Deterding was not able to lay his hands comfortably on that amount of cash at the time and my father had to arrange with Cartier's to wait payment for a few months, until the following summer, when Deterding would receive his salary from the Royal Dutch Shell Group. It is often said, but I do not know whether it is true, that Lydia was jealous of my father's influence over Deterding and egged her husband on to the final break. If that were true, then I suppose it could be said she contributed to the end of my career with the Royal Dutch Shell, but I must say it cannot now alter the affectionate friendship I feel for her. Certainly, I was not aware of any part she may have played at the time, and I can only tell the story as I saw it and as it affected me. I became involved, unwillingly, in the row which was brewing between my father and Deterding and the Royal Dutch over the Venezuelan Oil Concessions. The full story of that row must be told separately; for the moment I shall deal only with my side of it.

Trouble had blown up in Venezuela about the Royal Dutch Shell oil concessions there and Deterding said I was the best person to go out to try to settle matters with the Venezuelan Government. All the necessary arrangements were made for me to go there with a Dutch lawyer, Professor Oppenheim, my secretary, Miss Ward, and the inevitable Bailey. I was very flattered at having been chosen but it turned out that the reason for choosing me was not quite so flattering as, at first, I thought. Deterding, aware of the row brewing with my father over the way the Venezuelan Oil Concessions was being used by the Group, decided that if he were to put me in charge of the operation it would deter my father from excessive criticism.

I arranged to take a few days' leave before the trip and decided to spend Easter—this was 1925, the *Anno Santo*—in Rome. On the Good Friday I travelled by the Rome Express and spent Saturday, Sunday and Monday in the Italian capital. As soon as the London office reopened on the Tuesday, Deterding sent me a wire telling me to return at once. I was to go to Paris and get my Venezuelan visa there, the idea being it would create less attention there than in London. When I got the cable I thought of my poor grandmother, fleeing from Constantinople, for I had sent my laundry to the wash and it had not yet come back. I managed to retrieve it, undried, and caught the Rome Express back to Paris. I was met at the station there by the Royal Dutch Shell representative and given further instructions; there were one or two other jobs to do in Paris before I left for Venezuela.

My father was in Paris at the time. He took myself, Riedemann, who was also there, and Nobel, a Russian of Swedish nationality whose family had large properties in Russia before the Revolution, and who instituted the Nobel Prizes, to lunch at a very famous restaurant in the Rue de la Banque. It was run by Madame Génot, a great character, who did not think it worth while to cook for fewer than four people and who felt it was too much trouble to cook for more than eight. You had to order your lunch the day before and you sat in a *bistro* on chairs with cane seats but the food and wine were superlative. Her sole au vin blanc was a poem and her Jacquet de Pommes I can never forget.

At that lunch, my father discussed my trip to Venezuela.

'A very unhealthy and very uncomfortable place,' said Riedemann.

'Would you let your son go there now?' my father asked.

'No, Mr. Gulbenkian,' said Riedemann, 'I would not.' I doubted whether Venezuela was quite so bad a place as all that but Riedemann gave his opinions with a poker-face and I could not tell what he was thinking. It was clear that my father, with all his love and affection for me, had decided to do all in his power to stop me from going.

'I am a servant of the Royal Dutch,' I said, 'and if they want me to go, I certainly must go. Anyway,' I added, 'I think it is a wonderful opportunity for me and very important to my career with them.'

It was all to no purpose. We did not have a real row but father again brought the utmost pressure upon me and even suggested I should leave the Group rather than go. This I refused to do but he was not put off so easily as that. When he found he could not persuade me to disobey orders, he set to work on his friend,

Deterding, and managed to get my trip cancelled. Deterding argued that it was indeed a great opportunity for a young man and that, however much he liked me, I had spent virtually all my working life at headquarters in London; I should not be able to rise to the top, he said, without having had some experience of work abroad in a responsible and independent position.

My father did not change his mind. My instructions were countermanded just two hours before I was due to leave London. All my trunks had been packed and I had had all my inoculations and injections; I was bitterly disappointed. This feeling was aggravated when my place was taken by General Sir George Macdonogh, who had been taken on from the army after the First World War to act as a Relations Officer between the Royal Dutch Shell and Government departments. Sir George, a tall, bulky man, charming with a keen sense of humour, had been Director of Military Intelligence in the latter part of the war and Adjutant-General to the forces immediately afterwards; and was a believer in strict military discipline: what he was told to do, he did. He was also punctilious in observing the courtesies and, though he was some thirty years older than I was and in no sense my subordinate, whenever he was dealing with anything concerned with my department he always asked my instructions. When General Macdonogh came back from Venezuela, having agreed to all the Venezuelan Government's demands, I could not help telling myself that whatever might have happened if I had gone I could scarcely have done worse.

I settled down again to my normal activities in London, with trips to Paris and The Hague, but tension was mounting between my father and the Group and it became clear that a showdown was inevitable. Anticipating this, Deterding was, I must say, very fair to me, recognizing that my position in London would be untenable if my father and the Group had a public row. He offered me the job of general manager in Spain, a post of independence and great responsibility. Because I could speak fluent Spanish (one of the advantages of having married Herminia) Deterding was able to quash the criticisms that came from fellow-directors who said I was much too young for such an important position. My salary was to be £5000 a year plus a lot of 'perks', which in 1925 was quite a lot of money for a boy of my age. I was already getting £3000 a year which was worth something then. I do not think I had reached that salary through favouritism because there was a great deal of jealousy in the Group and if I had not been able to do the job there were plenty of other men only too ready, willing and able to do it.

Once again I was excited by the prospect ahead of me and once again my father intervened. He told me he did not want his only son 'banished to Spain' for three or four years and that he badly needed me by his side once more. I did not think he was right in regarding the Spanish job as 'banishment' and I listened with much misgiving and self-doubt to his attempts to persuade me that it was now my duty to leave the Royal Dutch Shell and my assured career with them to return to working with him. I had a terribly difficult decision to make but, in the end, my filial feelings and, possibly, my fear of my father won the day. That is to say, I decided not to take the job in Spain. I told Deterding on Christmas Eve, 1925, and that was a particularly bad day to have chosen. It was a Monday and someone had decided, without consulting Deterding, that the Royal Dutch Shell offices should be closed on that day. As soon as Deterding heard of the instruction, he cancelled it and turned up himself on the Monday to find that half the staff had not been contacted in time to get them to work. He was in a towering rage. When, on top of that, he found a young man of 29, turning down what was undoubtedly a magnificent offer, he exploded and sacked me on the spot.

'You will have to go back and work with your father, which is surely no catch for you,' he said. I had neither taken it for granted that I should get the sack and nor had I decided definitely that I would return to my father. In the back of my mind was something Riedemann had said to me some time before, a sort of promise I had cosseted against an evil day. Riedemann had said, 'If Deterding ever leaves the Royal Dutch and you feel you can't go on with the Group, I'll give you a job with the Standard Oil like a shot.' If I was now thinking of cashing in on that insurance policy I was to be disappointed. Even before he sacked me, Deterding had written to Riedemann and had told him it would be regarded as an unfriendly act for the Standard Oil to take me on. Riedemann wrote me a very friendly and flattering letter which did not reach me until after Christmas, by which time I was already out of my job. He said he was sure the row between the Gulbenkians and the

Shell would not come to a crisis but, because of the relations between the Royal Dutch Shell and the Standard Oil and in view of what Deterding had written, the Standard could not fulfil his promise.

I was forced to go back to my father. For quite a long time I felt that I had given up my independent career, which had a reasonable prospect of taking me to the top, only because of my duty to, and perhaps because of my fear of, my father. That may have had some bearing upon our relationship. I could not grumble about money for my father was always very generous to me in that respect. On the other hand, I was always improvident because, I suppose, I felt at the back of my mind that it did not really matter if I spent a few hundred pounds too much with Papa there to help me out. To be fair to myself, I liked to justify my improvidence on strictly economic grounds. I argued that, in an inflationary cycle, if you overspend in one year you are really saving money because in the future the same amount of cash would purchase fewer goods and services. This may have been merely my way of justifying myself, but it was an argument I was happy to accept. As to my losing the career with the Royal Dutch and Deterding and working again with my father, the regret lingered but the die was cast and I accepted it.

Working for my father now meant spending some time in our office in Paris, in the house at 51 Avenue d'Iena. This house had taken several years to build. It was really two or three houses which had been gutted and knocked into one; it stood at a corner where three streets met. Father held a competition in which he invited architects to build large-scale models of how they thought the house should be rebuilt; these models were given as dolls' houses to the children of various friends. He built the house to provide a home for his 'children', the works of art which he had been accumulating all his life. The rooms were designed to house his collection and to display his treasures to the best advantage. For instance, the house was really built around the dining-room and the dining-room was built around the set of Italian gold and silver thread tapestries which had been woven in Ferrara in the sixteenth century for Cardinal Gonzague of Mantua.

The house was wasteful of space. A huge hall led on to a mag-

nificent staircase at the foot of which my father placed the treasure
of eighteenth-century art, the Diana of Houdon, which had been
purchased for the Empress Catherine of Russia and which he
had bought from the Soviet Government when they were very
hard up for cash and were selling a few of their finest things. The
curators of the Russian museums were much opposed to the disposal of this Russian artistic patrimony—even in those days in
Russia, it seems, museum curators criticized the political authorities. To avoid this criticism, the works of art to be sold were sent
from the Hermitage Collection in Leningrad, on loan, to one
provincial museum after another and eventually shipped abroad.
The agreement was consummated in Berlin, being halfway between Russia and France. The Russians sent the works of art to
Berlin under the care of one or more of their officials and father
sent to Berlin Monsieur Aucoc, a famous French silversmith and
art expert. The treasures were handed over in Berlin against
father's cheque and Aucoc saw to their repacking and forwarding
to Paris. It was feared the statue of Diana might get broken in
transport if it were laid down, so it was transported, standing up,
by sea all the way from Petrograd and by barge up the Seine to
Paris. Apart from the Diana the deal included two very fine
Rembrandts, one a self-portrait of the artist when he was old and
another of a young man or young woman, variously known as
the Pallas Athene or as Titus. These were the pride of my father's
collection but though they were priceless pieces in themselves they
were not really missed out of the abundance of riches in the
Hermitage from which they came.

The Hermitage was a palace in St. Petersburg, as large a
palace, I think, as any in the world and now a public museum. It
has, I believe, twenty-two miles of galleries and it has been worked
out that if someone went through the Hermitage and looked at each
item for one minute it would take them ten years of day and night
inspection to look at every item. The wealth of the Hermitage
cannot be imagined; a visit there, such as I made a few years ago,
is, of course, an incomparable artistic treat but an exhausting
one. In the Rembrandt room, with its illustrations of his styles
from the very earliest to that of his old age, I saw at least a dozen
paintings which might compare in quality with the two my father
bought. That is why the Soviets were willing to part with them.

Father was the first to do a deal of this kind with the Russians. Later, Andrew Mellon (who built the National Gallery of Art in Washington) and Duveen, the famous art dealer (who persuaded him to do so), bought quite a lot of stuff from the Russians and spent much more money than my father did, but the pick of what was for sale had already gone when they got there. Duveen offered my father a million dollars for the statue of Diana but that only made father all the more anxious to keep it. Also included in the deal was magnificent eighteenth-century French silver by Germain. There was very little French silver of such importance to be found in Europe because, during the Napoleonic wars, most of it had been melted down. There was some in Portugal and some in Russia, the two countries which Napoleon never actually occupied.

The house in the Avenue d'Iena, built for these treasures, had over a hundred rooms but consisted chiefly of a large suite of reception rooms leading off a picture gallery which was specially air-conditioned and had the latest form of lighting designed to show his paintings to the best advantage. My sister and I each had a bedroom with its own bath and my mother had a suite of rooms which included her favourite boudoir built around some really beautiful Chinese tapestries. On the top floor, father had his own suite of a sitting-room, a bedroom and bathroom, the latter designed by Lalique, and a huge roof terrace paved with Italian mosaics. A team of Italian workmen were specially imported for the making of this terrace for no one else had the necessary expertise. The whole terrace was shaded by a six-foot yew hedge, but at one end, also to give shade, he had three trees planted. They were planted in three feet of earth, however, and this subsequently caused a great deal of trouble for the trees had to be watered and it proved almost impossible to water them without water percolating into the rooms below. Father generally slept at the Ritz in Paris but when he slept at the Avenue d'Iena he used to have his breakfast on the terrace and in the summer it was very pleasant to have dinner there. Further along there was an aviary in which he kept exotic pheasants and other rare and beautiful birds. He tried to have them walking loose on the terrace but this was not successful for they kept flying over the yew hedge and they then had to be rescued from the traffic below in the

Avenue d'Iena. The police were quite used to rescuing the birds but eventually they had to stay in the aviary with wire all round to keep them in.

There were always four services for every meal. My mother with my sister and myself had lunch and dinner at normal hours, say one o'clock for lunch and eight o'clock for dinner. But Father was never in for his lunch until two and, more often, it was half past two or a quarter to three; he did not dine until nine or half past nine. There were also two services in the servants' hall so that there could always be someone on duty, irrespective of their mealtimes; my father's secretaries also had their meals provided, to say nothing of the housekeepers who had to have separate meals.

One of the housekeepers was the unmarried sister of my brother-in-law, Kvork Essayan; she was first taken in out of kindness as the whole of Essayan's family were penniless and his father and mother were also kept until their death by my father. Among the secretaries was Madame Chanet who was my father's secretary with the Royal Dutch Shell Group and who left the Group to stay in my father's employ when he had his row with Deterding. She was in charge of all the works of art and the catalogue; she was really the director of his museum and was known as the *conservatrice*. Madame Chanet was very devoted to my father and the family and had worked for him for thirty-five years up to his death. The accounts were kept by another French lady, Mademoiselle Latournerie, but the main secretarial work was in the hands of Madame Theis who later went with my father to Portugal; she accompanied him wherever he went and was really his shadow. The main office work was in the hands of Madame Berthelot who ran practically everything else. There were, of course, a butler, four footmen and a doorkeeper (*concierge*) whose wife was the telephonist and had a remarkable memory for voices: a person need telephone only once for her to recognize the voice the next time.

The domestic staff consisted of twenty-four indoor servants plus my father's two valets and my mother's two maids, twenty-eight in all. I got into trouble with my mother because in one of my divorce cases I said that the staff consisted of a couple of dozen as I really did not know the exact number. My mother, who was very proud of the way she ran the house, reproved me. Nobody, she said, could run a house of that size with *only* twenty-four servants.

The kitchen staff comprised the chef and I do not know how many helpers in the form of staff cook, kitchen maid, scullery maid, cleaning woman and so on; there was also my father's Oriental chef who accompanied him wherever he went as he was fond of Turkish cooking and very particular about its quality. His Oriental chef was always either a Turk, a Greek or an Armenian. One of them caused quite a sensation. He left my father's service in 1928 or thereabouts and was engaged by the Turkish Ambassador in Moscow. The Oriental chef who succeeded him did not seem able to turn out *beurek*, the wafer-thin Oriental pastry my father relished so much. My father kicked up a fuss and the new chef explained that he, too, could turn out good *beurek* but he needed a special rolling-pin which he did not have. With my father's usual care for detail he remembered that some years previously he had had a special Oriental rolling-pin sent from Istanbul, a rolling-pin the intrinsic value of which was a few shillings; even allowing for the trouble of having it sent from Turkey could not make it worth more than a pound. But my father became very annoyed. 'How is it,' he wanted to know, 'that you haven't got the rolling-pin when I remember quite well having bought one from Istanbul specially for this purpose?' There was a great hullabaloo in the house and my poor mother was reduced to tears when the rolling-pin could not be found.

Eventually, it transpired that the departing Turkish chef had taken it with him to his new job; the rolling-pin was now in Moscow with him. That meant nothing to my father. He sent two detectives from Paris to Moscow to interview the departed chef. In the end, they recovered the rolling-pin. What it cost my father to send them there, both in cash and in getting them visas to go to Russia, can be better imagined than calculated. But that was my father all over. He would not allow anyone to take advantage of him in the slightest respect. It became for him a matter of principle.

In January 1924 the minority Labour Government recognized the Soviet Government. The Conservative Government which came to power at the end of the same year were anxious that Britain should benefit from this political recognition by increased trade with Russia. Trade with Russia then, even more than now, could take place only on the basis of a two-way traffic; unless Russian commodities were sold in this country, the Russians were unwilling, and probably unable, to buy anything from Britain.

The Gulbenkians came into the picture when the Russians wanted to do a deal with the caviare which they had and which they could obtain from the Caspian Sea. They were offering a monopoly in the sale of their caviare for the following season against an advance of £50,000. The Russians had some fifty tons for sale and the Gulbenkians went into the caviare business along with a few other people. Among these was a refugee from Russia, an Armenian from the Caucasus called Vanetzian, who had had a great deal of experience in the caviare trade, as manufacturer, distributor and salesman. We paid over our £50,000 to the Soviet state organization called Caviaretorg on the understanding that they would not sell caviare through any other channels. Mr. Vanetzian handled the marketing of the fifty tons very satisfactorily, making 100 per cent profit on the deal. That was pleasing and so was the fact that we had helped a fellow-Armenian to get on his feet again in a business he knew. (His son still deals in caviare, trading as Grivan Products, in Denman Street, near the Regent Palace Hotel, and I still buy my caviare from him.)

The next year the Russians approached us again to see whether we would do the same kind of deal. This time, we were told, instead of fifty tons of caviare for sale there would probably be seventy-five tons and they wanted an advance of £75,000. As the first deal had gone through very well and we had made £50,000 profit we agreed to do another deal with them. Much to our surprise, after a month or two, Vanetzian came and told us he could not sell any of the caviare. Whenever he went to his usual customers, he said, he found that no matter what price he quoted another source quoted a lower price. He could not understand it and nor could we. We did not know where the other caviare could be coming from. At that time there was no Rumanian caviare on the market. French caviare from sturgeon brought to the Gironde estuary was only an invention of the Second World War, as were the sturgeons in the Manzanares river in Madrid.

In the end, we discovered that our Russian friends were selling caviare and, as they were not inhibited by ordinary commercial considerations, they could afford to underbid us every time. We remonstrated with them, pointing out that they were not abiding by the letter of the contract with us. We were told, however, that our contract was with Caviaretorg and that Caviaretorg had scrupulously carried out its obligation to us; it had sold not one ounce of caviare, other than to us. But Gostorg, another Russian state trading organization, had no such obligations to us and it was free to sell all the caviare it could get. We went into the matter fairly thoroughly but we found we had no legal remedy; we were not even able to accuse our Russian friends of having acted in anything but the utmost good faith; they had proved to be better business men than we were.

As a consequence, the Gulbenkian family was left with twenty-five tons of caviare, which was entirely unsaleable. There was only one thing to do—eat it! I was very fond of caviare but when one realizes that the average helping of caviare in a restaurant is one or two ounces it is easy to understand that the eating of twenty-five tons was beyond my capacity. We gave it away to all our friends and acquaintances and achieved quite a reputation— deservedly, I suppose—of being remarkably generous. So generous were we that almost the first question we put to anyone we met was, 'Do you like caviare?' If the answer was 'Yes', we made an immediate present of a one- or two-pound tin of caviare. One of those to whom we gave caviare was Douglas Hogg, the first counsel I ever retained. At that time, he was a rising young junior; eventually he became Lord Chancellor and the first Lord Hailsham. He remained the Gulbenkian counsel for many years and his son, Quintin Hogg, said to me a few years ago, 'It was the Gulbenkian connection that made my father.' He also recalled the huge tins of caviare which arrived at the Hogg home and how the Hogg children, Quintin and his brother, used to regale themselves with it.

For my part, today, I am rather allergic to caviare.

7

The Break with Deterding

THE great row between my father and the Royal Dutch Shell
and Deterding started coming to a head over the Mexican Eagle
but there, Lord Cowdray and the Pearson interests, who were the
largest shareholders, were sufficiently powerful and important to
make their protests effective. Arguments there certainly were and
tough ones at that but the Group's ambitions were checked. It was
different with the Venezuelan Oil Concessions, where there was
no one except my father to stick up for the purely V.O.C. interests.
Before I explain just how he did that, however, and bring the story
to its climax, I must tell how his connection with the Venezuelan
interests began.

Before the First World War, a Venezuelan, General Antonio
Aranguren, obtained oil concessions over several provinces of
Venezuela and approached a group of British financiers who put
down a few thousand pounds and founded the Venezuelan Oil
Concessions, known later to everyone in the oil business as V.O.C.
A leading light was Mr. Duncan Elliot Alves, of Bryn Bras Castle
in Wales, who conformed to the popular image of a city financier.
He was a tall, good-looking man, with a shiny top hat, a frock coat
(not a morning coat), a huge cravat with a pearl pin, a large signet
ring and a wide gold chain across his ample stomach; he smoked
eight-inch cigars. Alves got in touch with Baron von Ofenheim, an
Austrian who was interested in the oil-fields in Galicia, Poland, as
well as in many other deals. Baron Ofenheim was one of the most
astute international financiers who did not even allow the war to
disturb or disrupt his interests. He remained an Austrian subject
but in 1914 he arranged for all the family Ofenheim interests, which
were in England and France, to be transferred to his brother, who
was a naturalized British subject, a doctor by profession.

At the same time, the British brother transferred to his Austrian brother all his interests in Central Europe. All these transfers and contracts were handled in London by the best solicitors and Baron Ofenheim then sent them to the Board of Trade, asking the British Government, in effect, to note and approve what had been done. This was something without precedent and the Board of Trade told him it was no part of their functions to approve contracts. Baron Ofenheim was intelligent enough to insist and as a result he obtained irrefutable evidence of the ownership of these properties. When war broke out in 1914 neither brother lost his interests. The doctor stayed in England as a British subject and the Baron went back to Vienna; when the war ended they were happily (and prosperously) reunited.

It was before the war that Baron Ofenheim came to my father and asked him whether he could use his influence with the Royal Dutch Shell to persuade the Group to take an interest in the Venezuelan concessions. This was the pattern of so much of my father's activities. During the forty years I worked with him we handled many deals, which, on balance, were certainly financially rewarding to us, but which again, on balance, also resulted in the development of natural resources which otherwise would have lain fallow.

My father was, in effect, the founder of the Venezuelan oil industry, though he receives scant credit for it these days. Ofenheim had no direct relations with the Royal Dutch Shell because years earlier he had had a row with Deterding who could not stand him. My father made a deal whereby the benefits in the Venezuelan concession should be 65 per cent for the Group and 35 per cent to himself, out of which he would give Ofenheim 11 per cent. The Group obtained options on the whole of the capital to be issued by the V.O.C. at par. In accordance with general practice, as I explained in chapter four, they obtained the right to nominate the majority of the Board of the V.O.C. and also a Management Contract, whereby the Royal Dutch Shell Group or one of its subsidiary companies were appointed managers. The total capital put up was not much more than £100,000, but because of the prestige of my father's name and that of the Royal Dutch, a wide, flourishing market was established on the London Stock Exchange. The options on the V.O.C. capital were taken up and the shares sold at

prices which were equivalent to something like £15 taking into
account the new issues. The upshot was that the V.O.C. brought
a great deal of financial profit on the Stock Exchange to my
father and to the Royal Dutch Shell Group who had had no
more than £100,000 at risk for just a few months. What is
more, as a result of my father's activities, work began which was
eventually to make Venezuela the world's second largest oil
producer.

When oil was found on the V.O.C. concession, the Royal Dutch
Shell Group took advantage of their Management Contract and
their majority on the Board to try to run V.O.C. as a branch of
the general oil business. The V.O.C. concession was on the shores
of Lake Maracaibo, out of reach to deep-sea-going oil tankers; the
only way to remove the oil in those days was by a fleet of shallow
lake tankers which could sail over the bar at the entrance to Lake
Maracaibo. The Group refused to allow the V.O.C. to build their
own tankers and therefore were in a position to buy the oil at a
very cheap price and much below its real value. The Group argument was that, without their knowledge, experience and technical
skill, the V.O.C. concession could not be developed at all and so
they felt entitled not only to all the co-operation they could get
but also very cheap supplies of oil. It was a ruthless exploitation of
their powerful position.

The Group encountered the same kind of opportunism from the
Venezuelan Government who, seeing the potentialities of the oil
production, wanted to improve the terms of the concession they
had given. That, of course, is a natural failing of all governments.
They sign a concession and agree terms and then, as soon as the
concessionaire can be 'squeezed', they ask for a better deal and
invariably get it. However morally wrong it may seem—and there
has been a degeneration of moral standards since before the first
war—one must admit that a concession, or even a contract, is
valid only so long as it continues to be of advantage to both
parties. When it ceases to be satisfactory to either side, respect for
the pledged word or one's signature no longer exists. The 'squeez-
ing' of oil companies by the governments of the oil-producing
countries is also the result of the way in which in the past many
companies took advantage of ignorance to make unfair contracts.
In this instance, as I told earlier, General Macdonogh went out to

Venezuela instead of me and agreed to all the Venezuelan Government's demands.

My father was strongly opposed to the Group's treatment of the V.O.C. He felt that as literally thousands of investors on the Stock Exchange had bought shares on his recommendation and were relying on him to safeguard their interests, it was up to him to see that the V.O.C. got a fair deal and especially the minority shareholders of whom he and General Aranguren were the principals. Here was a situation where both high morals and financial interests were identical.

The Group tried many manœuvres to deter my father or to weaken his attack and his support. There was Deterding's proposal to put me in charge of the 'controversial' companies in the hope of restraining my father and of achieving a balance between conflicting interests. There was the attempt made to 'get at' Alfred Chester Beatty, one of my father's colleagues in the V.O.C. row. Chester Beatty, an American by origin who became a British subject, an engineer who made, lost and re-made a fortune in Rhodesian copper and is a founder of the Consolidated African Selection Trust, was a man of very colourful vocabulary. He was asked to lunch at New Court, which is the home of the Rothschild interests in the City, and such an invitation was always held to be a great honour. The Rothschilds had—and still have—very large holdings in the Royal Dutch Shell Group, originating from the time, long before the First World War, when they sold their Russian properties to the Group. The Rothschilds were four-square behind the Group in the V.O.C. rumpus and they tried to talk Chester Beatty over into leaving the Gulbenkians. They failed. Chester Beatty reported on the meeting to my father with the comment, 'They thought they could buy me with a cutlet.' Chester Beatty also had a vivid way of summing up his feelings about the Royal Dutch Shell Group at the time.

'If they were inside a steel safe,' he said, 'and the combination had been lost and the key had fallen into the Thames and there was a dog on guard outside—I still wouldn't trust them.' Chester Beatty obtained a baronetcy and during the last few years he has retired to Ireland where he has built a wonderful museum of which the Irish are very proud. Whenever I go to Ireland I make a point of visiting him to pay my respects for I remember with affection all his co-operation with my father over the years.

In order to fight effectively for the V.O.C. interests, my father had to organize public opinion and the moral feelings and pecuniary interests of the thousands of shareholders. The position was reached where the Group were being publicly attacked by the independent shareholders under my father's leadership. This was lamentable from many points of view and, when I got the sack, Lord Cowdray tried to mediate between Deterding and my father. He was urged on by J. H. Macdonald and by feelings of gratitude for the services my father had rendered to the Pearson interests by realizing millions of shares belonging to the Pearsons at a huge profit. These friendly efforts, however, came to nothing. Certain elements in the Royal Dutch Group were only too pleased to take every opportunity of getting rid of my father's influence with Deterding and the Group.

The final act could not be delayed any longer. Early in 1926, a general meeting of V.O.C. shareholders was called to protest against the attempts of the Group to 'crib, cabin and confine to the Caribbean' the V.O.C. oil, by selling it to the Group at a very low price. 'Crib, cabin and confine to the Caribbean' was a phrase coined and used with great effect at the meeting by one of my father's associates, George Marsden.

It was a stormy meeting which lasted from eleven o'clock until twenty past two. Speeches on both sides were long and heated. The senior Group representative, the Hon. Walter Samuel, son of the first Lord Bearsted, the founder of the Shell, made much play with his 'honour'. In reply to attacks made on the way the Royal Dutch Shell had been behaving, he said, 'My personal honour is at stake.'

'We are not asking you,' said a shareholder, 'to arbitrate about your personal honour. We are asking you to arbitrate whether this is a fair contract.'

At the end of the meeting the Royal Dutch Shell seemed to have won the day. The directors representing the minority shareholders resigned in protest at what the Group had been doing, but the Royal Dutch took no notice, appointed nominees to take their place and proceeded to push through a series of contracts whereby they took V.O.C. oil at a cheap price.

It seemed, too, as though the Gulbenkians had been completely beaten, but for my father that row over the V.O.C. was only the declaration of open hostilities which were to persist for more than twenty years. He waged unremitting warfare against Deterding and the Group from then onwards, attacking them right, left and centre. He took advantage of the Slump in the early 1930s, for instance, to launch a savage assault on the Royal Dutch shares in the markets of the world and managed to make quite a comfortable sum from his efforts. He had a great public following; all the people who had bought shares on his recommendations, though making quite a lot of money, were anxious to make more—in respect of the V.O.C. it was, in all fairness, due to them. One of the great qualities of my father's business career was the way in which he always seemed to arrange that his public attitudes were not only morally admirable but also resulted in financial benefit to himself.

Although in the long run it is probably true to say that neither the Group nor my father suffered, the final and permanent break between Deterding and my father over the V.O.C. seemed to a great many people, including myself, a matter of great sadness. They had first met in the early 1900s through Frederick Lane who was the representative in London of the Paris Rothschilds.

The work Henri Deterding and my father did together before the break was undoubtedly of great value to all concerned. Their friendship was a rich one, cherished equally, I believe, on both sides. I myself retained the highest regard for Deterding and could only regret the circumstances that had made them clash so decisively.

On the occasion of that stormy and decisive V.O.C. general meeting, a photographer came up to my father and said, 'Are you the millionaire Gulbenkian?'

'No,' said my father, 'I only wish I were. Won't you photograph *me* though?'

The photographer rejected the idea as 'nonsense' and cleared off. That was the nearest escape my father ever had from being photographed by the Press, the thought of which he hated, for he loathed any sort of personal publicity.

Venezuela is a good example of all the mistakes which even the most well-informed people, either oil companies or individuals, can make. In the 1920s, General Aranguren brought to my father an important Venezuelan personality, Señor Gil Fortoul, a former Minister in Paris and a former Minister of Commerce in his own country. He was a little man, with a bald head, and a large mouth which he kept opening and shutting like a trapdoor. He wore the Legion of Honour of a high grade in his buttonhole. This man had obtained the concession from the Venezuelan Government of the Lake Maracaibo oil rights; he now offered it to my father. At that time, drilling in water was unknown and was considered very risky. We had negotiations in Paris which lasted more than a week, talking until four or five each morning, hammering out a contract. As partners, we had Bénard Frères and the American firm of Blair and Company. A deal was agreed in principle but we had to have the approval of the Venezuelan Government and to get the necessary decrees issued. We sent out Edward Keeling, who was M.P. for Twickenham for many years, a very able negotiator, dry as a stick with a very quiet sense of humour and, to look at, a typical blue-blooded, reactionary Blimp. He had, however, an uncanny knack of getting on with the most unlikely people. He had negotiated and signed the concession with King Faisal the First of Iraq which established the rights of the Iraq Petroleum Company in Mesopotamia. He had also negotiated on behalf of the Anglo-Persian Company in Iran. He used to go out into the blue without much money, because he was very careful with his expenses, and come back three or six months later with a concession, already signed, in his pocket.

Keeling carried out his talks with the Venezuelan Government successfully but, on this occasion, in the end, and in spite of all the hard work, we could not find an outlet for our concession. No one wanted to develop it and we merely managed to recover our expenses from Blair and Company.

This was the Lago Concession, which was to become famous. It was turned down by the Shell, to whom it was offered on modest terms. It was taken up, finally, by the Creole Company which itself was taken over by the Standard Oil Company of New Jersey. That concession, which we had to abandon, is now the basis of all the Standard Oil production in Venezuela.

8
More Comfortable than Happy

MY FATHER turned out to be right about my marriage, in that it did not last very long. During our life together, Herminia and I had a number of tempestuous scenes in which she gave free rein to her full-blooded Spanish temperament. As I have already mentioned, Herminia did not go down very well with my boss, Deterding, and this was a factor, though not a very significant one, in drawing us apart. My relations with my mother-in-law were also strained at times and she accused me of being responsible for a nervous rash which broke out on her stomach. However, I think it would probably be both tedious and false to try to draw up a list of reasons why we did not stay together: the simple fact is that I met someone else.

I met her one night in the Casino at Cannes. I was walking round the gambling room, just watching others playing baccarat. I never sat down at a table, either out of respect for my father's views or from terror of him; he thought gambling one of the mortal sins. I did do the occasional Banco, though, as I did on this particular evening when I saw an attractive girl running a bank. I turned up an eight. Perhaps I was feeling lucky that night, or, more likely, I wanted to curry favour with the girl; whatever the reason I was not content to leave well alone.

'Do you want me to draw a card?' I asked her. 'I'll do just whatever you like—you have only to ask me.' At that, she gave me a card, which was an ace, so not only had I the small natural to begin with but the larger natural when the draw had been done. On the strength of that I asked her to have a drink with me and took her out to dinner the following night. Her name was Doré. She was tall, she had a wonderful figure and, when I first met her, reddish hair, though as with all women the shade changed with the fashion. She had been on the stage in the Charlot and Cochran shows and a star of revues at the Alhambra although I could not remember having seen her. She was married to a man called Freeland but they were not getting on too well.

Our friendship developed and ripened; I began to see a lot of her, sometimes in London, sometimes in Paris, sometimes on a trip together; when I went to Rome for the Easter holiday of 1925—and was recalled to Paris to prepare for Venezuela—I went with Doré. Our meetings were reported by kind friends to Herminia, who had me watched by detectives, the kind who made their money by double-crossing their clients. On one of my business trips to Paris, when Doré came with me, I had a telephone call from the detective who had been paid to follow me. She said she had collected a large amount of evidence: she was ready to scrap it if I was ready to offer the right inducement.

I listened politely—I try to be polite under all circumstances—and then reported the matter to my very efficient solicitor, Sir Charles Russell, in London. One thing led to another and the lawyers got busy and eventually I received a formal letter from Messrs. Lewis and Lewis who were then, as now, the *crème de la crème* of society divorce lawyers. The next stage was an appearance in the divorce court before Mr. Justice Darling, who made a few witty remarks; some tough and protracted financial negotiations finally resulted in an agreement that the proceedings should be dropped. Instead, a French divorce was arranged on the grounds of *injures graves*—grave insult—which meant that Herminia wrote to me asking me to 'reintegrate the conjugal domicile' and I replied that nothing on earth would so induce me. I also had to establish a French domicile, but in those days that was not difficult for foreigners; it was merely a question of persuading a compliant *concierge* to sign a certificate of residence. It had become the smart thing for all Americans who wanted to change their spouses to come to Paris for the divorce. So fashionable and so easy had the process become, however, that the American Government had to protest to the French authorities against the way in which they were prepared to assume matrimonial jurisdiction over American citizens who had come to Paris for only a few weeks.

The French decided to stiffen up on the procedure and referred

all foreign divorces to a particular court—Number One, I think
it was—which would examine very carefully the authenticity of
domicile. This might have made things awkward for me but, not
for the first time, I realized the value of having friends in the right
places. One such in Paris at this time was Adjemoff, who acted
as adviser to my father and myself for many years and who, as
I said in an earlier chapter, exercised a great influence over us
both, not just in legal matters but in all our affairs. My father's
own influence in French Government circles was also put to good
use at this moment for he was desperately anxious for my marriage
to Herminia to break up. So it was arranged that my divorce
should not go to the special court for foreigners but to another
judge to whom word had been passed that, because of the great
services rendered to France by my father, his son's divorce should
go through quickly and without undue enquiry.

That was how my marriage to Herminia, for which, in the first
place, we had fought against such heavy opposition, ended. There
were more noisy scenes during the period of our final separation
but on the whole the transition was achieved fairly comfortably.
The breaking up of any close association is very sad, of course,
but the world is made up of one succeeding sadness after another
and I have always tended—certainly I did at that time—to look
forward rather than look back.

Doré's divorce went through quietly enough in England, with
me being cited as co-respondent, and after a certain amount of
tidying up and sorting out of our respective affairs we were both
free. I proceeded to enter into the state of holy matrimony for the
second time on a Saturday morning in 1928 at the Princes Row
Registry Office. Tommy Frost was one of my witnesses again and
there was also another old friend of mine, Geoffrey Hart, whom
I had known even before my Harrow days. Geoffrey, Tommy
and I did not take the occasion very seriously, though, and after
a glass of champagne we all went off to Wentworth to play a
round of golf.

At first, of course, my parents did not think Doré the ideal
wife they would have chosen for me but they came to like her
for she went out of her way to be pleasant to them. Whenever she
was going to Paris, for instance, she took some haddock with her
for my mother, who was very fond of haddock; what little of

it there was to be found in Paris in those days was generally stale.

On one trip I made to Paris I took with me not haddock but a baby. Doré and I were living at the time at 35 Grosvenor Place, in a flat on the second floor of an old converted house. In the flat above lived Dorothy Dickson, the famous dancer, and once, when I was off to Paris, she asked me to look after her baby. The baby was Dorothy Hyson, who also went on the stage later. Her mother was precise in her instructions: baby Hyson must have her milk warmed at five o'clock. Lest anyone should get too sentimental a picture of me warming the bottle and feeding the baby I should say I found other hands more competent than mine to take over the baby during the Paris trip.

After a while we moved to a flat in North Row, Park Lane, overlooking the Park at Marble Arch. We gave a dinner party there every Wednesday. Doré was very social and loved entertaining. She took a great deal of trouble about the house and the servants to make everything just so. Our dinner parties at the flat were for ten or twelve because that was as many as the dining-room would hold, although we did cram in fourteen on one occasion. We managed these dinner parties with our usual staff or, at most, by bringing in one extra man to wait.

Adjemoff pointed out that when it came to mixing with business friends and their wives Doré did drop little bricks at times but, generally, she was very popular, especially with the other wives. She got on well with the Persians and, on the whole, with all my Diplomatic friends. She was recognized as a good sort, always trying to help people and make herself agreeable.

Life with Doré was centred very much in what is now known as 'café society' and we went regularly to the smart clubs. Each Thursday, when our staff had their day off, we gave another party, smaller than those at home, usually at the Embassy Club. Thursday was the smart day at the Embassy. It was the club where the then Prince of Wales (later King Edward the Eighth) and one or more of his brothers were generally to be seen, the Prince of Wales with the reigning beauty of that time (Thelma Furness comes to mind) and the Duke of York (later King George the Sixth) with the present Queen Mother, whom he had married a few years before.

The Embassy was run by the famous Luigi Naintre, a small, white-haired man, with a small moustache. Luigi was a very good restaurateur, whose standards of service and ready tongue had brought him his deserved reputation and success. He had started at Romano's Restaurant in the Strand which, at the beginning of the century, had been the haunt of the Gaiety Girls and the gilded youth who pursued them; then he had opened Ciro's Club in Orange Street where, again, all the so-called Smart Set used to congregate.

It was while Luigi was at Ciro's that my father's favourite injunction to check, re-check and counter-check served me well. After licensing hours, Luigi would serve you a bottle of champagne in a glass jug, strictly against the law, of course. He started by charging 18*s.* a bottle, then pushed the price up to £1, then to 21*s.* and eventually to 25*s.*, all in the course of a couple of months. I never pay a bill without inspecting it item by item and I never order anything without first asking the price: this has probably saved me from some unpleasant surprises and it does not put temptation in the way of others. At Ciro's one night, after hours, I asked Luigi how much he was charging for the champagne; he quoted the price of 25*s.* I refused to pay. I pointed out what I had been paying in the past few weeks and that this upward progression must stop. He reduced the price to 21*s.* and it remained at 21*s.* so long as Luigi was there.

The Embassy Club, which he took over after Ciro's, was at the bottom of Bond Street, in the same premises in which, just before the First World War, the first night club in London, called the Four Hundred, had been opened. Between the wars night-clubbing was a much more formal affair than it is now and I must say I regret today's casual manners. At that time it was usual for men to wear white ties and tails and for the women to put on long dresses and all the jewellery they could muster. On the nights when Courts had been held, it was no uncommon sight to see half a dozen débutantes, with their white feathers and tiaras, coming in, probably to show off that they had just been presented or possibly merely to supplement the good supper which one had in those days at Buckingham Palace.

Doré usually accompanied me on my business trips, to see my father in Paris, or to visit business contacts in Switzerland and

Liechtenstein. From 1920, Liechtenstein, the tiny but independent principality, nestling between Austria and Switzerland, had been in a Customs union with Switzerland but as its company law was based on the old Austrian law all sorts of anomalies arose. These, plus its low taxation, attracted international financiers who were very welcome there and who were not slow, with the help of expert lawyers, to take advantage of the situation. (One of these was von Riedemann, of the Standard Oil, who travelled on a Liechtenstein passport when he accompanied Deterding back from our visits to the States and Mexico.) On these business trips of mine I was generally meeting lawyers or accountants or bankers; with them, as with our other friends and acquaintances, Doré fitted in well.

We took a different kind of trip together to North Africa, on the French Line, from Marseilles to Algiers. The boat was carrying a cargo of raw cotton. On the return trip a fire broke out in the hold. I think the cotton smouldered rather than burned; there were no flames to be seen but we saw a little smoke and the decks became rather warm. Quite a lot of people seemed fairly excited, marching up and down, speculating on what might happen, but there was really little to worry about. The night was calm and there were plenty of ships on the route if we did have to abandon ship. My wife and I thought it might be unwise, however, to get undressed and go to bed, so, having come to the conclusion that nothing we could do about the fire would help, we lay back in our deck chairs to enjoy a perfect moonlight night. As it was getting rather late, we dozed off and snoozed for about a couple of hours until we were awakened by the sounds of general relief when it was announced that the fire had been brought under control. Our behaviour was commented upon by other passengers, chiefly Latins, as an example of *flegme britannique*, but I could not see anything remarkable about it: for once, I felt, I had handled the situation in a commonsense way.

Doré's social inclinations led to our taking a box at Covent Garden every Monday and every Thursday during the season for several years; the opera was as much of a social occasion as a musical one. The men were always in white ties and tails and the women, especially those in the boxes, wore their tiaras and just about everything else, except the kitchen stove. As a result, I suppose I have heard—or perhaps I should say, more accurately, I have been present at—the performance of every opera. I have been to Bayreuth to hear *Parsifal* when Wagner's widow, Cosima Wagner, was still alive and reigned as Queen there. I have been to the Scala at Milan and the Opéra in Paris but I am afraid music was and still is a closed book to me. I had so many friends who really enjoyed music that, as one might feel about religious faith in others, I felt I was missing something by my utter ignorance and incomprehension. I have to confess that the great virtue to me of our box at the opera was that there was no telephone there and that no one came in to interrupt a very discreet slumber at the back of the box—except when my snores happened not to synchronize with the time of the aria being delivered on the stage. (I do like Oriental music, however, and I remember particularly an excellent programme of Turkish music given on the B.B.C. one night after the ten o'clock news. I must add, too, that the unaccompanied choirs in the Armenian Church, especially their singing of the Lord's Prayer, is very impressive to me, but perhaps that is because of the emotional appeal of the environment, of the incense and the candles as well as the music.)

I am bound to say I enjoyed our golfing weekends more than our nights at the opera. When I could manage it we went down, late on Friday night, to the Grand Hotel at Folkestone; on the Saturday and Sunday we would play three rounds on the Hythe course; the exercise was good and the air was excellent. Geoffrey Hart or Tommy Frost, who had been at our wedding, often came to stay with us there.

When we were by ourselves, quietly, I enjoyed Doré's conversation, comparatively trivial though it may have been. She had not had a very extensive higher education but she had a very sweet character. She tried hard, too, to provide the dishes I specially enjoyed. I was extremely fond (and still am) of *bécasse au fumet*, which is rather a complicated dish to make. Doré decided to try it. She supervised our cook, a very good cook, in the making of it, but the result was not a success. Some weeks later I came home at about seven, feeling rather tired and having worked harder than usual.

'I have a nice surprise for you,' said Doré.

'What is it?'

'You're going to get *bécasse au fumet,*' she said.

I must have been feeling churlish as well as tired for I replied: 'Well, I hope it will be better than last time.'

There were just the two of us for dinner and, when it came, I found she had imported the second head waiter from the Embassy Club for the evening. He had prepared an excellent *bécasse au fumet.* Doré had also thought of getting out some burgundy which, although it is a wine I normally avoid because it gives me gout, goes very well with that heavy and richly spiced dish.

Doré was always anxious to please and she certainly tried to make me comfortable and happy. She succeeded in making me, perhaps, more comfortable than happy.

I first went to Buckingham Palace in 1926. It was in that year I joined the staff of the Persian Legation (as it then was) in London and thus became a member of the Diplomatic Corps. (My father had been Commercial Counsellor to the Persian Legation in Paris since 1920.) The Persian Minister in London under whom I was to serve was Ovanesse Khan Mossaed, an Armenian and an old friend of our family. He was a very cultured man who had translated Shakespeare into both Persian and Armenian; he was also a very kindly and helpful man. This latter quality came out on my first appearance at Court. He noticed that I had forgotten my white gloves which, then, were *de rigueur* at Court, and he sent me home at once to get them.

'It is much better that I should send you home now,' he said gently, 'than for you to go into the Throne Room without them. If you were to do that you can be sure that the Marshal of the Diplomatic Corps, Major-General Sir John Hanbury-Williams, will send you home. It's much better I should do so than an English Court official.'

All the women had long trains, hanging from their shoulders and carried over the arms. They wore three white feathers and a tiara on their heads and when the Royal procession came into the Throne Room all the women curtsied and the feathers bobbed: a wonderful sight, like a field of waving corn or a crescent of white billows on the sea.

The Royal procession of King George V and Queen Mary

walking hand-in-hand, was preceded by the Lord Chamberlain and two or three officials, bearing white wands and walking backwards. The rest of the Royal Family followed and took their places on the dais; they remained standing while the Diplomatic Corps filed past. This, of course, was done according to a strict ritual just as much as every part of the ceremony. First, the Marshal of the Diplomatic Corps announced the name of the Chef de Mission. (In those days there were only just over a dozen Ambassadors, all the others were Ministers.) The Chef de Mission, having made two bows, one to the King and one to the Queen, then named the oncoming members of his staff, one by one. They, too, bowed, first to the King and then to the Queen. Everyone was in uniform except the American Ambassador and his staff, who wore evening tail coats and knee breeches; one American Ambassador, General Dawes, had refused to wear knee breeches and an exception had been made in his case, but his successor reverted to the normal custom out of courtesy to British Royal tradition. 'Uniform' in the context I have just mentioned must be understood to include the gorgeous ceremonial clothes of the Indian maharajahs who attended these occasions.

After the members of the Corps Diplomatique had passed before the King and Queen, they remained in the Throne Room, the women sitting, the members of the Embassy staffs standing opposite the throne, and the Ambassadors taking up their positions on the left side of the dais. After their presentation those not in the Diplomatic Circle now passed out of the Throne Room and went on to enjoy their supper, but the diplomatists had to wait until all the presentations were over. This took between an hour and a half and two hours and then the Royal procession reformed with the officials walking backwards in front of the King and Queen, followed by the Royal Family, and thereafter the Ambassadors and the Heads of Mission, each of whom had been asked to take a particular lady in to supper. The other members of the Diplomatic Corps who had not been assigned a lady, had to make a grab for whomever they knew or fancied. The procession then wound through several of the drawing-rooms, lined on either side by the less-favoured guests, and went on to two supper rooms. The further one of these rooms was for the

Royal Family, the Heads of Mission and the more important diplomatists, and the doors were guarded by the Vice-Marshal of the Diplomatic Corps. The atmosphere was one of unqualified grandeur and opulence: gilt chandeliers, gold plate, servants in knee breeches, gorgeous liveries and powdered hair. The buffet was abundant and of the highest quality; champagne was served but all the labels had been washed off the bottles before serving, for it was not considered proper that the Royal Family should advertise any particular brand of champagne.

(I must take this thin excuse to recall what happened when Sir William McClintock, an accountant and an old friend of my father, was appointed at the end of the first war to reorganize the finances and expenditure of the Royal Family. He was told to make economies in the running of Buckingham Palace but that he must not discharge any member of the staff. At first sight, with a staff of several hundred, it seemed that the one way of making useful economies had been barred to him; but then he discovered that certain servants were entitled to 'perks', such as a bottle of brandy a week, or even one bottle a day. In the cellars of the Palace he found priceless brandies which had been laid down by George III and which had been handed over to the servants as their 'perks'. McClintock forthwith sold the stocks of these old brandies and bought a current three-star brandy. The old brandies fetched between £4 and £5 a bottle, the price of the three-star was 12s. 6d., and the Royal servants enjoyed the new brandy better than the old because it had more 'kick'. He had made a big saving and everyone was pleased.

The exclusion of divorced persons from the Royal circle did not apply to diplomatists and especially not to Oriental diplomatists and so there was no difficulty about Doré accompanying me to the Palace. The first time she did so, we gave a small party in our flat for our friends to see us in our finery before we set out. Doré was wearing a Worth dress; the couturier's description of it had been sent to *The Times* which liked to publish a list of the people at the Court and descriptions of their clothes. We had a glass of champagne each but the excitement of the occasion was more intoxicating for her, I think, than the drink. When her turn came to pass the throne, she found some difficulty in executing the manœuvre whereby she had to let her train fall from her arm and spread out on the floor and to have it handed back to her after she had passed the Royal presence. Furthermore, she thought she was seeing things and had to pinch herself for reassurance when she saw the Aga Khan the Third, the grandfather of the present Aga Khan. We knew him well for he had been our guest many times but now Doré saw a very different man from the one she knew. There he stood, resplendent and majestic in his star-spangled silk purple robe with a gold sash, the robe stretching from under his chin down to below his knees; on his head he wore a black hat the size of a lampshade.

My experience over the years since I first went to the Palace enables me to make some comparisons. I remember how George V, though looking very regal, was rather bored with watching the endless procession and from time to time he waved it forward. Queen Mary, on the other hand, was always very gracious and gave everyone a very special personal smile. Standing, as I had to, for about an hour and a half in front of the King and Queen there was nothing else to do but observe these small matters; talking was forbidden except in whispered asides. King George VI was most punctilious and the Heads of Mission were always told they must name the members of their Embassy carefully and distinctly as they passed the Presence; we were also told to bow from the neck, as this King did not like what he considered the exaggeration of bowing from the waist.

When I first had the privilege of being presented to the present Queen I asked what the correct procedure was: 'Should I bow from the waist or should I bow from the neck?' It was the Vice-Marshal of the Diplomatic Corps who answered my query and I still think he was pulling my leg.

'You should bow from the third button down,' he said. I tried for an hour to bow from the third button down, but apart from getting a pain in the neck and almost ricking a shoulder I was unsuccessful.

When Queen Elizabeth II was gracious enough to have a few words with me and heard I had been coming to Buckingham Palace since 1926—the year of her birth—she asked me whether I had noticed any changes that had taken place. I told her the story of the white kid gloves, for earlier that evening, on arrival at the Palace, I had been reminded of my first attendance there.

I went to the cloak-room to leave my silk hat, silk scarf, overcoat and stick.

'Don't you want to leave your gloves, sir?' the page said. The formalities have not been so strictly observed since the Second World War, but I am a member of the Old Guard.

'Leave my gloves?' I said to the page. 'Not on your life! I was sent home twenty-five years ago for not having them.'

In these post-war years people attending parties at Buckingham Palace wear only ordinary evening dress with long trousers and their decorations. They wear full uniform only on very rare occasions, as when a new ambassador presents his Letters of Credence to the Sovereign. When I returned home to Arlington House (the block of flats near the Ritz) where I live in London, after accompanying my Ambassador to that kind of formal ceremony, wearing my full uniform, complete with sword, cocked hat and white gloves, the porter asked: 'Have you sunk the ship, sir?'

When I first joined the Diplomatic Corps I had to leave cards, together with the card of my Ambassador, on every other member of the Diplomatic Corps in London. Today, with over three thousand names on the Foreign Office list, it would be quite impossible and the custom has been dropped. I remember giving a farewell dinner party not long ago at our flat at Arlington House for two friends, both Ambassadors, who had been recalled and were returning to their own countries; one of them confided to me that though he had made his *visite* to the other, the latter had not yet returned it and now never would. That was almost unthinkable before the war.

It was as a Diplomatic Member that I joined the St. James's Club in 1929. It was a very exclusive club in those days, exclusive, that is to say, from the point of view of anyone who was neither a diplomatist nor a member of his Majesty's Foreign Service. It had a cosmopolitan membership and one heard more French spoken there than English. The St. James's Club occupied premises which had housed the French Embassy in the time of Talleyrand and for that reason the Club was asked to allow its rooms to be used for a farewell dinner given by the Corps Diplomatique to the French Ambassador, Monsieur Chauvel, when he left in 1962. (I was on the Wine and Food Committee of the Club at the time and was very proud of my share in encouraging the chef to surpass himself.)

A good deal of heavy betting and gambling went on at the Club but I was happy enough merely to wager the odd pound either way at any bridge table. By betting in that way I had the right to see the hands and to criticize the play afterwards. This, not the betting, was the pleasure for me. In the same way, although I loved to call Banco at the casinos, this never became anything important to me; it was never in any way obsessive as gambling was with some of my friends.

It was certainly not just for the gaming that Doré and I used to make our frequent trips to Le Touquet but for the wider pleasures of the place. We used to fly over there; it did not cost very much to charter a four-seater, single-engined plane and within an hour or so after leaving Croydon we would land at Berck, a few miles away. (This was before the polo ground at Le Touquet was taken over and made the site for the present airport.)

Life at Le Touquet or Deauville or Cannes, as in the smart restaurants of London, was very gay and I managed somehow to snatch quite a bit of time from business to spend an hour or two, or even a day or two, at those places. When I look back now I realize the snobbery and perhaps the lack of consideration for others which was typical of everyone there. For instance, no one would ever have thought of walking or of going by taxi from the Normandie Hotel in Deauville to the Casino, a distance of less than 100 yards; the result was that rows and rows of chauffeurs had to wait up until the small hours to take their masters back that short distance.

Although I was not a gambler, I did buy a ticket in the first Irish Sweep, which was widely advertised in England. I thought no more about it until one afternoon, when I was sitting in the large room at 17 St. Helen's Place, which was my father's office for many years, the old sergeant commissionaire came in with the evening paper. He had a big grin on his face and he said: 'You're in luck, sir.' He pointed to the paper. 'You've drawn a horse in the Irish Sweep.' And so I had. It did not win but I was still entitled to £1500 for my £1 ticket. I too thought I was in luck when I first saw the news but, unfortunately, with the publishing of my name in the papers, the news got around. I worked out afterwards that it had cost me, in the tips and parties and presents I had to give, considerably more than the £1500 I had won.

A couple of years after marrying Doré, I took up hunting again. After leaving Cambridge I had had to put my nose to the grindstone and, apart from hacking now and then with Herminia, I had done little riding and no hunting. I started again with the Old Berkeley.

The Old Berkeley are descended from the hounds which belonged to the Earls of Berkeley who used to say they hunted on their own lands all the way from Berkeley Castle in Gloucestershire to Berkeley Square. Unfortunately, the fortunes of the Earls of Berkeley waned slightly and the packs were split up. The country around Berkeley Castle remained Berkeley country while that from Berkeley Square up to about fifty miles from London became Old Berkeley country. It was Lord Rosebery who said of the Old Berkeley, 'They're all right—after all they can draw the Zoo if they like—it's in their country.' At that time, Lord Rosebery was Master of the Whaddon Chase whom I had joined later on. He made this comment when the Whaddon Chase hounds had been stopped by an outbreak of foot and mouth and we were discussing what other packs were doing.

Lord Rosebery was a terrifying person, but a very good Master of Hounds and a great nobleman. He was no respecter of persons and could afford to blast, not only his field, but all farmers, tenants, policemen and anyone who interfered or might interfere with the noble sport of hunting. In the days of my youth nothing so heinous as the shooting of a fox occurred. Farmers were required by their tenancy agreements as well as by public opinion to take down any wire they might have put up lest they impede the progress of the hunt across the country. Mind you, they may well have made a good income from poultry claims for many must be the chicken that lived to lay many an egg after its owner had received compensation for its alleged demise at the teeth of the fox.

I look back with envy upon those times when hunting was certainly better. But if we had continued in that way hunting would not have survived at all. The only chance of it surviving now is for it to become more and more a sport enjoyed by more and more people, by farmers, farmers' children and their pony clubs, by the foot followers and followers in cars; as long as it remains generally a part of the English countryside, and not just a sport imposed on the many for the sake of the privileged few, it will continue.

On my first time out with the Whaddon Chase I was subjected, as are all new members of a hunt, to a searching scrutiny, of a courteous but not necessarily over-charitable kind.

'What is that flower you are wearing in your buttonhole?' I was asked.

'An orchid,' I replied, 'I'm very fond of them.' I have, indeed, always been very fond of orchids and have worn one in my buttonhole for the last thirty or forty years; I saw no reason to refrain from wearing one because I was in a scarlet coat, astride a horse. But my questioner persisted.

'Oh, an orchid!' he said. 'Well, I've never seen anyone out hunting with an orchid.'

'Ah,' I said, 'but have you ever seen an *Armenian* out hunting?'

That reply, which came spontaneously and happily, was enough to establish my position with the Whaddon Chase and I have had many days of great pleasure with them over the past thirty years.

Hunting is a sport I enjoy thoroughly but very often I cannot help drawing a comparison between my feelings and those of the neutrals at the time of the Napoleonic Wars. Arthur Bryant, in his book, *Years of Victory*, quotes Canning in describing how the neutrals were confronted with 'a balance of opposite dangers'. When any country tried to remain neutral during the Napoleonic Wars they found it quite impossible; if they did anything which pleased England, they were immediately overrun by Napoleon's armies; if, through fear of Napoleon's military might, they did what France wanted, they would be bombarded by the British Fleet—twice, in the case of the unfortunate Danes. Similarly, when I come to a large fence, I never know which is the more frightening prospect, that of putting my horse to the fence and trying to clear it or of being seen to turn away from it. At least, that was so in my younger days; now I am approaching seventy, I hunt to enjoy myself and to hell with what people think.

When subject to terror or when out hunting—which sometimes

amounts to the same thing—one expresses one's feelings very clearly and, on occasion, amusingly. I remember once riding a seventeen-hands thoroughbred brute of a horse, a magnificent galloper and a formidable jumper; I could do anything with him in the hunting field except pull him up. When hounds were running that was all right; but, when there was a check, disaster was usually ahead in some form or another. On this day hounds checked and I endeavoured to pull up my horse, but quite unsuccessfully. As we galloped on, entirely out of control, we collided with another member of the field whose horse, though fairly large, was not to be compared with mine for size; the other man was nearly knocked for six.

'Where the hell do you think you're going?' he yelled at me, and he had every justification.

I had no intention of being funny and indeed it was in the nature of a *cri de cœur* that I replied, 'I wish I knew.'

A sense of humour, however, is a great help in life and I have always found it so out hunting as much as anywhere else. There are plenty of times when one is needed. The first time I went out with a neighbouring pack, the Bicester and Warden Hill, I ordered my best horses, put on my best scarlet coat and nearly new top hat, and sallied forth. There had been a lot of rain and the country was flooded. When we came to a ford, which had to be crossed to have the slightest chance of keeping up with hounds, most of the field looked at it and found good reasons for waiting. But not I. Being much younger than I am now I put spurs to my horse and led the field, or so I thought, into the ford. Unfortunately, when we were halfway across and the water was over my saddle flaps, my horse, being wiser than I was, decided he had had enough. He reared up and fell over backwards. I had visions of being drowned as I gurgled under the water; I remember feeling how unfair it was. That I should break my neck out hunting was one of the accepted risks of the game; to be drowned was something quite unpardonable. However, I rose to the surface and, according to those who were watching, first of all two white gloves were seen swimming for the shore; then an orchid floating downstream. Eventually, I managed to cross the stream and clamber safely on to the bank. Unhappily, I was the only one of the field to have crossed the ford; even my horse had gone back to the other side.

So there I was with a swollen stream between me and my horse and the rest of the field. What was there for me to do but swim back again, which I did, accompanied by the cheers of the onlookers. When I got back to the other side, I lay on my back and about two pints of water came streaming out of my boots. I wish I could say now that I went on with the hunt and was the first at the kill but . . . Frankly, I was sodden and shivering—it was December—and I mounted my steed and made for the nearest road, the nearest telephone and the nearest pub, handed over my horse to my second horseman, had four whiskies and hot water in the pub and then went home and retired to bed. I was none the worse after it.

They say that hunting is all the fun of war with 25 per cent of the risk and I must say that in half a century with hounds I have known only five fatal accidents.

Once, with the old Berkeley, a farmer, on the way to cover, dropped off his horse. I was closest to him so I jumped off my horse and went to him. I managed to loosen his stock, although I was slightly hindered by the dozen safety pins with which that poor worthy had secured it; he was already dead, from heart failure.

Another time, hounds were running near Calverton in the north part of Whaddon Chase country and the field took a stream. A man one length in front of me jumped it, but his horse stumbled on landing, came down on its nose and threw its rider on to his head. Three or four of us got hold of the nearest gate (a damned heavy gate it was; ever since then I have learned to look for a hurdle, not a gate, when there is an accident). We laid the injured man on the gate and struggled to carry him to the nearest farm a couple of fields away. I did not realize it until the doctor told me afterwards but on the way to the farm we heard the man's death rattle. The doctor had come to the farmhouse where we had laid the man on a couch; one look at him, a feel of the pulse and of the heart, and the doctor said: 'He's as dead as mutton.' The dead man was known to everyone as Uncle Percy, a seventy-year-old who was very popular with the hunt. He had been a partner in that eminent firm of accountants, Deloitte Plender Griffiths & Co. He had been accompanied that day, as usual, by a very charming lady much younger than he was; she was naturally very distressed and burst into tears on my shoulder. There was also the ticklish business of telling his wife, who was in London, and no one was quite sure just how much she should be told.

I remember, too, the time when one of the McCorquodales of Winslow Hall had a fall into a wet ditch, caught pneumonia, and was dead within twenty-four hours. A year or two ago, a young man out with us recognized a loose horse as belonging to his father, General Philip Mead. By filial duty, as well as by custom of the hunting field, the boy went after the horse, caught it and started to go back to restore it to his father; but we found his father sitting up, under a fence, with his neck broken, dead as a doornail.

The worst accident I recall happened to another seventy-year-old, a fine old man called Digby Whitehead, partner in a wine merchants firm, a man with rugged features and grey hair and a wonderful horseman. His horse rolled over on top of him and smashed his pelvis. We carried him on a hurdle to a car—no gate, I had learned my lesson—and sent him to hospital. Complications set in, however, and within two days he was dead. I attended his funeral and was somewhat shocked to hear the parson, in making the funeral oration, say that if at his age Digby had confined himself to playing bowls he would still have been alive. I recognized that this might have been true but it seemed hardly tactful; still, I suppose being a diplomatist in my spare time for the past forty years had made me more sensitive to such remarks than some might be.

Out of the nearly 2000 days' hunting I have enjoyed, on each of which anything from one to two hundred people were out, five fatal casualties is surely not an excessive toll. So long as one's affairs are in order and proper precautions have been taken to provide for one's widow, or widows, and other dependants—it is far from easy these days to make proper provision with the skill of the Treasury's civil servants pitted against one—then I think I would as soon die quickly from a broken neck out hunting as I would from a lingering illness, when one's physical and mental powers gradually deteriorate and one is reduced to a wreck. I saw just that happen over the last three or four years of my father's life; knowing what a brilliant brain and active body he had always enjoyed, the sight of him in decay was one of the saddest of all my experiences.

9

The Most Expensive Chicken
in History

IN THE spring of 1933, I went out to the Middle East on an
inspection tour of the Iraq Petroleum Company and its activities.
I went out by air, by Imperial Airways; what would take a matter
of hours now then took days. The first stage was a flight in a
Handley Page Heracles from Croydon to Paris, followed by a
train journey from Paris to Brindisi which meant two nights in a
sleeping car. At Brindisi, I boarded a Short Scipio flying boat for
Athens, arriving there at about four o'clock in the afternoon. At
least this gave me the chance of seeing the Parthenon for the first
time but I did not get the Greek food I had been hoping for.
Greek food is much the same as Turkish food, of which I am
rather fond, but the Hôtel d'Angleterre where I was staying in
Athens was so superior they served only French cuisine and a
rather indifferent one at that. I suppose I could have been adven-
turous and gone to a Greek restaurant but as we had to leave very
early the next morning and I was already extremely tired I went to
bed instead. The flying boat took me next day to Alexandria,
arriving there three days after leaving London. I had arranged for
a car to take me from the landing stage at Alexandria to Aboukir
airport and there to board one of the I.P.C. planes, a single-
engined De Havilland 50. I knew this particular aircraft very well
for it had been a charter plane of Imperial Airways and I had used
it many times to take me between London and Le Touquet or
London and Switzerland. We crossed the Sinai Desert by following the railway line, but we were flying against strong headwinds
and the range of the DH 50 was strictly limited. The pilot looked
worried.

158

'We've only about ten minutes' more petrol,' he said. 'It shouldn't take us more than five minutes to Gaza but with these headwinds and the light going I'm not sure we'll find it. There's an airfield by the Canal—do you think we ought to put down there?' I did not think this was a fair question to put to me; piloting the plane and getting us down to earth safely was his responsibility and he knew what was and what was not possible much better than I.

'You must do what you think best,' I said. 'Whatever you decide I shall be happy.'

Actually, with a small aircraft like that the risk of accident was not very great; even if we had run out of petrol the worst that could happen was a landing on the comparatively flat desert alongside the railway line. As it was, we were able to make Gaza just in time. Having reached Gaza, I then had to decide whether to stay there the night or to push on. There was at that time no airfield at Haifa so my choice was between flying the next morning from Gaza to the airfield at Samakh, which was by the Dead Sea and about an hour by road from Haifa, or hiring a car at Gaza and driving the whole way. I was younger then and imbued with a restless spirit; after thanking the pilot I chartered a car, a rather ramshackle one at that, and set out into the night. With me, as he had been throughout the journey, was a young English valet called Card, a very devoted and helpful servant. (Bailey, who had been my valet previously, had had a row with my second wife and had had to go. Card was in my service for seven years.) We arrived at Haifa in the early hours of the morning and I turned into a very uncomfortable bed; I slept the sleep, not perhaps of the just, but at any rate of those who are extremely tired, for I had been up since four o'clock the previous morning.

The next day, Dunkerley, the I.P.C. general manager for the Middle East, contacted me and we worked out a plan for my trip. The first thing was another flight, this time to the airfield at Homs in northern Syria where Sir John Cadman and Willie Fraser (now Lord Strathalmond) were due; they were on their way back from negotiations in Teheran in connection with the Anglo-Iranian concession which had been cancelled by the Iranian Government. It was worth another journey to make contact with them, so I arranged for a company plane, a French single-engined, four-seater Farman to fly me up from Samakh. We had time for an hour's talk before they flew on to Cairo and London in their aircraft chartered by Anglo-Iranian; I flew back to Samakh. On the way back from the airfield to Haifa my car collided with one of the camels of a camel caravan; one wing was dented but the camel seemed all right and I told the driver to carry on, although with some lurking unease of mind. When I got back to the hotel at Haifa, I soon forgot about the incident and enjoyed the surprise of the hotel-keeper who had never met anyone before who had flown to northern Syria and back between breakfast and tea.

The main work in progress was the laying down of the twin pipelines to carry the oil from the Iraq oil-fields to the Mediterranean, a matter which had been the cause of yet another argument between the various interests in the I.P.C., an argument which the Gulbenkians had lost, or at least had not won. On purely financial grounds it was obvious that the pipeline should take the shortest and surest route to the sea and that meant taking it to Tripoli, where there was good anchorage and where there was no need to build a harbour. However, that meant it would run through French-mandated territory and therefore be under French control, which, for political and commercial reasons, suited the French and for purely commercial reasons suited us. It did not, however, suit the British groups who wanted the line to go through the British mandated territory of Palestine and finish at Haifa, despite the fact that at Haifa unsuitable winds and tides did not make for good anchorage and an expensive harbour would have to be built. Furthermore, while the line to Tripoli, being shorter, would need only four pump stations, the one to Haifa would need five. Technicians were sent out to survey the alternative possibilities and one wonderful report, which came bound in Moroccan leather complete with schedules, maps and detailed calculations, seemed to show that the cost of going to Haifa would not, after all, be as much as of going to Tripoli. This surprised us for a while until a closer examination of the figures showed a simple but highly significant mistake in the arithmetic. The authors had forgotten to divide an essential figure by two. Neither side seemed prepared to budge until at last the deadlock was resolved by compromise, which produced the worst of all worlds. On the suggestion of the Americans, it was agreed to have two lines. There was to be a

ILLUSTRATIONS

Hadji Avedik Agha Gulbenkian (my great-grandfather, who lived to be 106)

Calouste Gulbenkian—the last picture taken of my father

My mother

Aged 5, with Clemence

The Hon. Commercial Attaché to the Iranian Embassy, 1926

When I accompanied the Ambassador on presenting his credentials at Buckingham Palace in 1961 (wearing my white gloves!)

Three fashionable young men at Le Touquet, 1929. *Left to right:* Tommy ('my permanent best man') Frost, myself and Tommy Lavington-Jacks

'Gate-shutting' with the Whaddon Chase

Winners of the Cream Candy Cup at Richmond Horse Show, 1963

Talking to the present Archbishop of Canterbury at Lambeth Palace

Dining with the Catholicos at Etchniadzine

Thirteen at table—but I felt safe in such good company with *(seated, left to right):* the Bishop of Kensington, Bishop Manoukian, the Catholicos, the Archbishop of Canterbury (Lord Fisher) and Lord Radcliffe

Opposite: Relaxing at an oriental restaurant (in the City of London) and, *above,* relaxing at home

At the diamond wedding of my parents *(seated). Standing, left to right:* Kvork Essayan, Rita Essayan (my sister), Robert Gulbenkian (cousin), Mikhail Essayan (nephew), myself and my wife

The Old House at Hoggeston

joint line from Kirkuk in Iraq to a place called Haditha; from there one line would branch off to Tripoli and the other to Haifa, where the Anglo-Iranian and Shell wanted to build—and eventually did build—a huge refinery.

Ever since the post-war trouble between Israel and the Arabs the refinery has been shut, except for producing oil for local consumption, so it has been proved, belatedly, that even on political grounds the Gulbenkian point of view was the wiser one. The gift of hindsight, of course, allows one to dwell on other mistakes which were made, of which the most costly I can recall was over the Saudi Arabian concession, which was offered by Ibn Saud to the I.P.C. There was a snag, but not one which need have caused too much trouble. Ibn Saud had no confidence in any currency and sterling itself was feeling the strain at that time. The only coin recognized in the whole of the Arabian Peninsula was the silver Maria Thérèsa dollar, which is still being turned out by the Austrian Mint; it bears the head of Maria Thérèsa and the date 1780. Unfortunately to have paid Ibn Saud in silver would have meant tons and tons of it, so he asked to be paid in golden sovereigns, 20,000 of them. The oil groups were interested in getting the concession and would probably have agreed to Ibn Saud's terms, but the British Treasury stood firm on the principle that the pound sterling was just as good as the golden sovereign and refused to allow a British company to enter into a contract which provided for payment in gold sovereigns; the concession was turned down by the I.P.C. The French interests, the C.F.P., were fully entitled to take the concession, but the President, Colonel Mercier, a very able man but at times a weak one who was always seeking compromise, thought it a matter of principle that the C.F.P. should not go off on their own. In recent years, under pressure of events, they have developed a much more courageous policy, but the outcome of Mercier's weakness then was that the Standard Oil of California picked up the concession. Just how costly that mistake really was—initially the mistake of the British Treasury obsessed by ideas of prestige—can be measured by the fact that today that same concession produces more oil than any other concession in the Middle East except Kuwait; in 1963 it produced more than eighty million tons.

My trip along the southern stretch of the pipeline took me

through lava country; there was no road and it was the most back-breaking journey I have ever made. To keep out the dust, the windows of the car had to be kept shut and I almost suffocated. I had insisted on inspecting that part of the line because of earlier discussions at headquarters in London. The Iraq Government were very anxious to have a railway and they thought there was no need to pay for one because the I.P.C. would have to build a railway before they could build a pipeline. At the time, the I.P.C. engineers in London said the pipeline could be laid without a railway, by using high-powered Mack trucks, the last word then in heavy transport. The engineers were right; it could be done and it was done.

And what a job it was. I drove across the desert to watch the work, accompanied by the Chief Engineer, an American called Stuckey, a most agreeable and capable man. A telegraph line had been laid from Haifa along the proposed pipeline route to Kirkuk and driving was a matter of following the telegraph poles; there was no road. I started counting the poles.

'One, two, three, four, five . . . nineteen, *twenty*. That one's mine,' I said. I was thinking of the Gulbenkian 5 per cent interest in the I.P.C., notching it up as it were. That was how I first got the name by which my father was afterwards to be known: Mr. Five Per Cent. To see a 5 per cent investment in a company like the I.P.C. in terms of telegraph poles, miles of pipeline, coils of wire or Mack trucks is to give a solid reality to the entries on a balance sheet or those in a bank passbook. My father never saw the land from which so much of his wealth came; I am glad I was able to go there.

One of the most remarkable features of the laying of the pipeline was the energy and keenness of everyone on the job. This first twelve-inch line—the Spaghetti Line as it was called, in comparison with the thirty-six-inch pipelines of today—was built by the I.P.C. itself; subsequent increases were built by contract.

Driving across the desert it seemed at first as though there were just the telegraph poles and nothing else; no pipeline and no activity. Then, suddenly, a speck of dust on the horizon became a lorry, carrying lengths of pipe and a gang of up to twenty Bedouin under the control of an American foreman; he gave orders by blowing blasts on a whistle or by making signs with his hands, for he had no common language with his workmen. But they certainly jumped to it until the job was finished. As the lorry progressed the men on board heaved the piping on to the ground. As I waited and watched them I became aware of the lengths of pipe that had been dropped all across the desert and were now snaking across the sand. As we drove on, I saw the way the pipeline was being built. First, there were the gangs welding together the lengths of pipe, each welder working with a sunshade over his head. Then came the trenching machines, gnawing a continuous trench out of the desert, leaving heaps of earth along the sides of the trench. After that came a machine which wrapped the line in what looked like huge rolls of lavatory paper; these rolls were made of bituminous paper and their purpose was to prevent corrosion. Then came another machine to heave the pipeline into the trench, and, finally, one which buried the pipeline by shovelling the earth back into the trench on top of it.

I spent the night at one of the pumping stations which, with its high wall all around it, looked just like a Beau Geste fort; indeed, each of the pumping stations had been built in the same way, to withstand possible Bedouin raids. The actual building of them had been done, one might almost say, confidentially, to attract as little attention as possible. Security was not as good as it might have been and the possibilities of raids by the Bedouin were considered very real; it was amusing, however, to hear the French explaining how dangerous a southern line (which they had opposed) was, with the working gangs always exposed to attack by the Bedouin, and the English saying the same about the northern line, which they had opposed.

Each pump station had a landing strip with a wind-sock and rudimentary wireless communications which hardly ever worked. I was very interested, personally, in the I.P.C. air services which were something of a pioneering venture. That they existed at all was, I feel, due to Jules Meny, the representative on the I.P.C. Board of the C.F.P., the French company, and to myself. Meny, a small, very active and go-ahead man, had been an aviator in the First World War. I took up Dunkerley, the I.P.C. General Manager for the Middle East, on his first trip in an aeroplane. We took off from the Stag Lane aerodrome at Edgware, where De Havilland had their factory, for half-an-hour's flight and when he came down from this, his first flight, he was converted to the idea of flying. The I.P.C. entered into an agreement with Imperial Airways and a French company to run a few planes on charter for the I.P.C. Service. The planes, which flew up and down the pipeline during the construction period, saved a tremendous amount of time. I used one of them to fly to Kirkuk to visit the installations there. Kirkuk was distinguished by the splendid boulevard built by the previous general manager, Sir Adam Ritchie. He had justified it as being necessary for inland communications but it had provoked a great deal of criticism in London.

From Kirkuk I flew to Baghdad which, with its two bridges formed of boats, its royal palaces, minarets and palm trees, looks more romantic from the air than on the ground. Flying in across the Tigris it looked a wonderful city but, after landing and going by car into the centre, my illusions faded; there was a main street, but beyond that none of the Arabian Nights' glamour the aerial view had led me to expect.

I stayed in the I.P.C. guest house on the banks of the Tigris and it was there that I met my first sand-storm. One moment the air and sky were crystal clear and I could even see the airport some ten miles away across the completely flat landscape, Then, suddenly, it was misty; then the further bank of the Tigris began to disappear in a pale, yellow fog; the other side of the road was lost to sight and I seemed to be enveloped by an opaque vapour. All the doors and windows were shut but the sand worked its way through. I put a pencil down on the table as I strained to see out of the windows. Two minutes later when I picked it up again there was a patch on the table, bare of dust, where it had been lying. Eyes, mouth and nostrils, all were choked with the stuff.

In Baghdad I was under the care of the I.P.C. general manager there, Crawford Clark, who had been at the British Embassy in the city when it was still a High Commission. Clark took me out on the many calls I had to make, calls of both a business and a courtesy kind. I was received by the King, Faisal the First, whom I had met in London at the Hyde Park Hotel at the time of the Versailles Peace Conference. In his own country, he received me most graciously; I talked with him for about an hour and found him very well informed. I cannot write of my visits to Iraq in 1933 without also remembering those who, in one way or another, were to meet sudden death in later years. I felt deeply sorry when his son, King Ghasi, was killed in a motor accident in 1939. I felt appalled when his grandson, the young King Faisal II, was murdered in the Kassem revolution on Bastille Day, July 14, 1958. I used to see this young boy while he was at Harrow after the Second World War and he was always very charming and polite. There was the occasion at Lord's, for instance, when I did not see him in a group of schoolboy friends; he recognized me, however, came up, raised his hat most politely and greeted me as any well-brought-up young boy would greet an elder. I saw him once or twice later when he was on the throne and by then he had assumed a regal poise and graciousness.

His uncle, the Regent, and subsequently the Crown Prince Amir Abdul Illah, was a much tougher character, and his grand-uncle, Amir Zeid, was a much luckier one. Zeid was in London as the Ambassador at the time of the Iraqi Revolution and had received something like £120,000 from the young King Faisal to buy furnishings for the new palace which was being built for the King to live in after his forthcoming marriage to a Turkish princess. After the Revolution the Amir was able to use this money to live partly in Rome and partly in London, very quietly, of course, but quite comfortably. His wife, Princess Zeid, is Turkish and a prolific painter in modern style who has held several exhibitions in London and in Paris and successful ones at that. The Amir had a pleasing sense of humour and always sympathized with me for being terrified of my father. He said that as the youngest brother he had had to keep his arms folded in front of his elder brothers and was not allowed to speak until he was spoken to.

I had long talks with Jaafar Pasha and his brother-in-law, Nuri es Said Pasha. Jaafar Pasha was one of the few men who were decorated with both the D.S.O. and the Iron Cross during the First World War. He had been landed in Libya by German submarine from Turkey to stir up the Senussi against Egypt; he had been charged by a British cavalry regiment (with whom he was very willing to dine when, later, he was Minister in London) and had then gone over, at the time of the Arab rebellion, to the British side. He was always a very good friend of ours. I remember asking him to my flat at Hereford House for dinner at 8.30. When he turned up at eight o'clock he found neither my wife nor myself ready to receive him, not even for drinks. I dashed in to apologize but at the same time to remonstrate mildly that he was, after all, half an hour early; I may have pointed this out with little or insufficient tact, for his reaction was somewhat tart.

'What would you like me to do?' he said. 'Do you want me to go away and come back again at the right time?' I was blessed if I did! A most charming man and a great diplomatist; it was a tremendous loss to his country when he was murdered in the Rashid Ali rebellion.

As for Nuri es Said, he had been a friend of my family since he was a small boy in Constantinople, studying at the military school at Top Khane, and calling at my grandfather's office for his weekly pocket money. (My grandfather and his brother were the bankers of the Sultans; any financial business between Baghdad and Constantinople was transacted through their firm.) He had an unexpected liking for Havana cigars, for everyone in the Middle East smoked cigarettes, whether Arab or, as he was, Kurd. Whenever he was in London I gave him a box of my cigars which he much appreciated.

Nuri was a great friend of the British; they had saved his life more than once and he was genuinely grateful to them. He had fought for Arab independence during the first war with Lawrence of Arabia and the Amir Faisal. He was a small man with a rather pudgy face, a twinkle in his eye and a very great sense of humour. In London, he generally stayed at Claridges, where I used to call on him. Out of extreme courtesy, an Oriental tradition, he always waited for me by the door in the hall, and, much to the surprise of the hall porter, greeted me with the old Ottoman salutation, touching the ground, the heart, the lips and the forehead. I, of course, did likewise; then we used to shake hands and laugh. On one occasion when we were discussing the political situation in Iraq and the insecurity of the dynasty which rested on one small baby, the young King Faisal, he said, 'Our country is like a chicken with only one leg.' And so it proved in 1958. Nuri was the strong man of Iraq and, cunning old politician that he was, he thought that no matter what changes or upsets happened in his country he would survive them. Unfortunately, even he was lost in the 1958 Revolution: he was found, disguised as a woman, and shot. He was a great man and a fine friend.

The first rumblings of change could be heard in 1931 when I was in Baghdad. One small instance of that was the covert resentment encountered by the British Ambassador when he had an Arab village removed in order to extend the gardens of the British Embassy. The Ambassador undoubtedly improved what was already a beautiful residence in a beautiful situation, amply supplied with water pumped from the nearby Tigris, but he made himself less than universally popular with the Iraqis.

Sir Francis Humphrys had just taken up his post as Ambassador after having been High Commissioner and Commander-in-Chief in Iraq during the Mandate. In order to ensure that the British representative should also take precedence over all other foreign representatives it had been agreed that only Britain should have an embassy in Baghdad; other nations were restricted to a legation. Now Iraq had attained full independence and Sir Francis had a new role to play. But the evidence of his past remained with him and his wife. They both epitomized the British Raj. She was the daughter of Colonel Sir Harold Deane, the first Chief Commissioner for the North-West Frontier Province of India, and she had married Sir Francis while he, too, was serving on the North-West Frontier. He himself was a lieutenant-colonel, tall, with a grey moustache and military bearing, who had first received public attention when he was Envoy Extraordinary and Minister Plenipotentiary at Kabul, the capital of Afghanistan, and had successfully evacuated the pro-British Afghan Royal Family during a rebellion. To do so he had himself flown a plane through the high mountains of Afghanistan, which at that time was quite a feat.

At lunch at the Embassy, I met the then Prime Minister, Rashid Ali, who later rebelled against the British Mandate and the Hashemite monarchy and was exiled to Saudi Arabia. In the Second World War he was to try to hand over Iraq to the Germans but he failed and had to flee. I remember him chiefly at that Embassy luncheon because he was wearing a handkerchief round his neck and over his shoulders; he probably wore it when working to keep off the dust and had forgotten to remove it, but it did not go down well at the Embassy.

At that same lunch I met Sir Philip Cunliffe-Lister, whom I had met when he was Sir Philip Lloyd-Greame, and who was later to be known as Lord Swinton. He was then the Secretary of State for

the Colonies and he was accompanied by Tommy Dugdale, his
P.P.S. (who was Minister of Agriculture in Churchill's post-war
Government and became Lord Crathorne in 1959).

I flew from Baghdad to one of the stations on the northern pipeline where I picked up a company car to take me to Palmyra.
With me was Monsieur Despagne, the I.P.C. general manager in
French mandated territory, a courteous Frenchman who wore
plus fours; he made sure that we took a large stock of Evian Water
with us, for he had been in the desert before and was taking no
chances. We spent a night at one of the construction camps with
the French officer who was in charge of a detachment of troops
responsible for guarding the gangs of workmen. He offered next
morning to escort us with some of his men a few miles down the
road to the wadi crossing but Despagne said there was no need.
He was surer than I that there were no dangers involved and that
the officer's gesture was made merely out of courtesy; but, anyway,
nothing happened to us. We motored safely to Palmyra, in the
Syrian Desert, at the crossroads of important trade routes in
Roman times, and still showing the relics of that earlier prosperity.
Its wealthy merchants built temples and monuments to adorn their
city but so that posterity should never forget who built them they
ordered little ledges to be made halfway up the beautiful Greek
columns on which images of the donors were perched. These
ledges certainly spoilt the columns—at one time there were 750 of
them—but the monuments, the temples and the tombs, which the
merchants built for themselves outside the city, were well worth
seeing some 1700 years later, if only as the first example of
nouveaux riches. Sensitive to the feelings of historians and archae-
ologists, the oil interests took the pipeline on a detour of some miles
to avoid its passing through, or being seen from, Palmyra.

During my tour of the northern line, I was given, at one of the
stations, a telephone message that the *Sûreté*, the French C.I.D.,
wanted to talk to me. I wondered where and how I had fallen foul
of the police and concluded it must have been when I had not
stopped after colliding with that camel some days earlier. I went
to the telephone with some trepidation and called the number
passed to me. My anxieties were unnecessary. It turned out that
the French High Commissioner in Beirut, Monsieur Ponsot,
had heard I was in French Mandated Territory of Syria and

had called to ask me to lunch. I thanked him and heaved a great sigh of relief, making a mental note to keep an alert eye open for camels in future.

The High Commissioner's residency, the 'Résidence des Pins', as it was called, was some distance outside Beirut, overlooking the racecourse. It had been built as a casino and was an impressive place with large reception rooms; the approach to the house was by a winding road, uphill and about a mile long. I took a company car from Beirut. When we reached the bottom of the hill and entered the residency gardens, I saw a troop of horsemen, in what looked like Bedouin robes with red saddlery, galloping towards me. Their small grey Arab ponies were blinkered. From all sides they came at me and surrounded the car. I was really frightened.

'My God,' I thought to myself, 'one has heard enough about insecurity in these parts but fancy a raid by the Bedouin just outside the residency. They must think it's the High Commissioner in here; they want to kidnap him but they're going to kidnap me instead.'

After a minute or two, the Arab horsemen who had surrounded the car formed themselves into an escort and I noticed the kepi of the senior officer. I realized the horsemen must be a squadron of Spahis—French Moroccan troops. They escorted the car, at a canter, right into the courtyard by the front door of the residency. Very creditably, they lined up in two rows; the officer in front saluted with his sword, his troops presented arms with mousquetons, which, on horseback, is not easy. I could not for the life of me understand what it was all about. Thirty years ago I was certainly not pretentious enough to imagine that this escort had been laid on especially for my benefit. But, in the hall, awaiting the guests, was the High Commissioner's *officier d'ordonnance* (his A.D.C.), a very smart and dapper young man, and he explained what had happened.

'Tomorrow,' he said, 'Sir Arthur Wauchope, the British High Commissioner in Palestine, is coming here and we want to receive him with full honours; he will be escorted by a squadron of Spahis. But the captain in charge of the squadron wanted to have a rehearsal to see whether his troops would fall in properly on either side of the car and, as he knew there were people coming to lunch today, he took the opportunity of having a dress rehearsal.' Up to date in my life, that was the first and only time I have been escorted in my car by a whole squadron of cavalry.

A very good lunch was served, as in all official French residences. I had been warned, however, by my father's doctor in Paris before I left and by the I.P.C. officials in the Middle East, against the dangers of eating uncooked vegetables and so, at the French High Commissioner's table, I reluctantly refused a beautiful cos lettuce. But Madame Ponsot, always a perfect French hostess, saw me refuse the salad. 'You can eat that without fear, she said. 'It was grown in our own garden under my own supervision, especially for the High Commissioner who is very fond of salad. You need have no fear of cholera or typhoid.'

Whenever I recall my trip to Syria, I think of the four Ss: Syria, *Sûreté*, Spahis and salad.

Between the two wars it was suggested that I should take up politics. It was Sir Edward Keeling, a junior Minister in the Conservative Government of the day, who approached me, jokingly perhaps.

'Nubar,' he said 'you ought to go into politics.'

'But I'm not English,' I said.

'Never mind,' Keeling replied, 'we'll naturalize you. But you'll have to change your name twice.'

'How do you mean?'

'Well, I think you had better be called Gullybanks first of all and then Gumbley,' he said.

'Why on earth should I change my name twice? Why shouldn't I call myself Gumbley straight away?'

'Because you'll find that people will want to know what your name was before it was Gumbley. If you don't start off by calling yourself Gullybanks then you'll have to say your name used to be Gulbenkian. And then they'll know you're really a foreigner.'

I did not go into English politics.

My story nearly had a sudden ending on a summer's day in 1935. The stockbroking firm of Vickers da Costa chartered a plane to see the Silver Jubilee Naval Review at Spithead and invited some half a dozen of their clients, including myself, to join them. The idea was to board the plane, a de Havilland Dragon, at Heston, to fly over the Fleet and then to return in time for lunch. It sounded good fun to me. My valet at this time was called Hewitt and I told him to give me my old flannel suit, because it was a very hot day and whatever I wore was bound to get crumpled sitting in the aircraft. Hewitt was a rather pompous little Englishman who had been in the Royal service and could never forget it; nor would he allow me to forget it.

'Sir,' he said, 'their Majesties will be there: you must put on your *best* flannel suit.'

Although their Majesties were going to be two or three thousand feet below me, that was reason enough for Hewitt to insist that I should be suitably and respectfully dressed.

We took our seats in the Dragon and settled back for a morning's pleasure but we were quickly in trouble. Almost immediately after becoming airborne, the plane crashed, falling luckily on to a road near the airport. As I try now to set down what happened then I am bound to make the whole thing, including my own thoughts and actions, much more orderly than was actually the case at the time. But I remember seeing the pilot making signs to us from alongside the wrecked aircraft: he had scrambled clear immediately after the crash. Before any of us could get to the door, the plane burst into flames. Other passengers began to try to force open the door, but it was jammed; they were trying to break it down with the result that it was getting more and more jammed.

What did I think of when faced with what I thought was the certainty of death? If my mind was operating clearly there could be no doubt that I was to die. The plane had crashed; it was being eaten up by blazing petrol; the door, the one way to escape, was jammed. The flaming petrol reminded me of the last scene of Wagner's *Walkyrie*—or is this the kind of embellishment of one's thoughts that comes later? But I do remember thinking two things.

'They always say,' was my first thought, 'that when there is a crash and a fire people are killed by the crash and not burned alive; if that is right, then obviously this is entirely wrong. Here am I, *after* the crash, very much alive, but I shall be burned to death in three or four minutes and I shan't be able to tell the rest of the world what damned liars they are.' My second thought, and a somewhat irrelevant and grisly one, was that all my life I had been very fond of kebab (mutton roasted on a spit over live flames) and here was I going to end my life as a kebab.

Before the crash, I had hated the idea of death, though I had not feared it. Now, though I was not a particularly brave man—indeed rather the opposite—I neither feared dying and nor did the prospect of it greatly distress me. This is how I reacted despite my conscious recognition that I should be dead within minutes. My completely rational and calm reaction was: 'You must see about getting out of the plane.'

My first thought now was to reach the window and try to smash through it. But the window was small and I felt the sight of a rather stout, middle-aged Armenian gentleman half in and half out of the plane would be rather undignified as well as quite useless; so I proceeded towards the door. That is a euphemistic way of putting it, for, with the others already fighting to break down the door, my only way of getting near it was by crawling on all fours. I forced my way between the legs and managed to get hold of the latch, from which the paint had melted with the heat. Yet, again, contrary to the way one imagines these things happening, I was so absorbed and obsessed by the idea of getting out of the aircraft that although molten paint was now dropping on to my hands—and nearly thirty years later I have the scars to show for it—I felt not a thing. After a great deal of effort, I managed to force the latch up. The door flew open and we all fell out in a heap into a pool of blazing petrol. I scuttled away from the burning petrol and saw another man whose broken shin-bone was sticking out of his trousers and whose face looked just like a sponge. It was ghastly. I saw him again thirty years later at Ascot races. I would not have recognized him, as he was terribly disfigured, but he reintroduced himself to me and recalled the accident.

They say the devil looks after his own—which is a reassuring thought at all times—and I now had an example of it. I had taken precautions. It seemed to me that aeroplane accidents always took place on take-off or on landing so I had given my chauffeur standing instructions that, after taking me to the airport, he should always wait there for a short time until we were safely off the ground and away. Luckily for me, he had carried out my instructions meticulously. From the car park, he saw the plane crash, he saw smoke and flames come up from the wreckage and he set off straight away in the car.

The one lucky thing about the crash was that it had happened on a road so that my car had reached me within minutes of the accident. My chauffeur acted with superb presence of mind. He phoned my doctor and the London Clinic and he had me in London, and into the operating theatre, while, as I heard afterwards, my fellow-passengers were still waiting for ambulances. I was operated on for second-degree burns which can be very painful, and, at that time, the treatment was by Tanafax; the progress and achievements of Sir Archibald McIndoe were still to come. It was a week before I was allowed out of bed and then it was realized that I had dislocated my knee. It was several more weeks before I was ready to leave the London Clinic.

The first time I was permitted out of the hospital, on crutches, with bandages and slings, and accompanied by a nurse, I went by car to Heston Airport. I had been told that the only way to keep one's flying nerve after an accident was to keep flying, so I had decided to go straight up again. I chartered a small plane, similar to the Dragon in which we had crashed, and ordered my good friend, Captain Olley, to fly just over the spot where the Dragon had come down. Luckily, my nurse had never flown before. She was both air-sick and terrified and I had to look after her; that prevented me from thinking about my own fears. Ever since, although I was anxious for a year or two at the moment of take-off, I have been able to fly without undue strain. And I still enjoy kebab.

Among the things which have given me, at the time, the greatest satisfaction are things which are really, in themselves, very small. Some years before the war, for instance, I was about to ride in a point-to-point in the Whaddon Chase. I heard two yokels, outside the lavatory tent—I was inside—discussing the 'field' in the race in which I was about to take part.

'What about Gorblimey who's on number seven?' said one. 'With all 'is money 'e ought to 'ave good 'orses.' I was riding number seven.

' 'Im? 'E can't ride for little green apples.'

'Yus,' said the first yokel, 'but the bugger's got guts.'

The more sceptical of the two was right: I fell off the first time round.

I did not tell, in the previous chapter, the real reason why I took up hunting again. It all happened because Tommy Frost took Doré and me out to dinner at Sovrani's (now the Coq d'Or.) As Tommy always tells the story, I pressed on the fourth member of our party a peach or, rather, several peaches.

'Have a peach,' I kept on saying. 'Have a peach.'

So insistent was I that a great friend of Tommy's, called Herman Michelham, sitting at a neighbouring table, was quite ill at my exhibition of extravagance: he was always careful himself not to indulge in undue or unnecessary expenditure. The fourth member of our party on whom I pressed the peaches was a young woman in her late twenties. Her name was Diana. She was tall, chinless with protruding teeth, but with hazel eyes and a very good figure. She played quite an important part in my life for the next two or three years.

In the summer of 1930, Doré and I took a place in the country for a couple of months. It was quite a big place with a private golf course and three or four private tennis courts. Crawley Court, as it was called, was in Hampshire. It was a wonderful place for entertaining and entertainment was very much in the line of the people who owned it, Philipi, a well-known polo player, and his wife, Elita. (She was one of two daughters of Don Julio and Madame de Bittencourt, who were famous personalities in London just before the First World War, wealthy Chileans who arrived in England determined to marry off their beautiful daughters in the best possible way.)

We, too, entertained fairly continuously at Crawley Court, many of our guests being from the Corps Diplomatique. We had a private professional for golf, though the golf course was certainly not up to Sunningdale standards. We also had a tennis pro. He was stone deaf and this had a certain advantage, for, when he made up a doubles, or coached us playing a single, one could carry on quite an intimate and confidential conversation, secure in the knowledge that not a word of what was being said could be heard by him. This was helpful, especially if I was playing with Diana.

Diana, the girl on whom I had pressed the peaches, was another of our guests at Crawley Court.

Diana was very fond of riding and we used to go cub-hunting together. Diana, it was indeed, who caused me to take up hunting again. Diana it was, too, who was the cause of Doré divorcing me, although that did not actually happen until 1938.

I tried to be discreet but I was not always successful. There was the time, for instance, when Diana and I decided to spend a summer holiday, incognito, in Corsica. Our plan was to go by road, making a gastronomic tour on the way. In Corsica we were to stay at a quiet hotel where we should be unlikely to meet any friends and where we could enjoy the scenery, the bathing and a little boar-shooting without disturbance. In order to ensure the fullest discretion I did not even take my valet with me; that caused me discomfort but I had other assistance to compensate.

At that time, I owned one of the few SS Mercedes cars. They were the fastest cars on the market and I had taken mine, in full touring-trim with headlamps, wings and two people aboard, on to Brooklands racing track and was officially timed at over 100 miles an hour, a remarkable speed for those days.

One of our stops on our way through France was at Macon. We had decided to lunch at the Hôtel de l'Europe which Monsieur Burtin, whom I knew well, had just opened. I had first met Burtin in 1920 at Saulieu where he had the Hôtel de la Poste. He had come from the Kaiserhof Hotel in Berlin where he had been chef but he liked it to be known—at any rate, he did not contradict those who thought it—that he had been the chef to the Kaiser. When I first went to the Hôtel de la Poste at Saulieu he was delighted, although he was a Frenchman, to find in me someone to whom he could talk in German. That started me off on the right foot and I was always very well looked after by him both there and at the Hôtel de l'Europe at Macon. I was responsible for getting him his Michelin stars at Macon. He was a superb chef. He used to make a wonderful almond cake, a *feuilleté d'amandes*, and his *gratin d'écrevisses*, although imitated by many people throughout France, was really superlative. (The only place in the world I know which now comes near the same quality with that dish is the Auberge du Père Bise, run by Marius Bise, at Talloires.)

Diana and I had agreed it would be better to lunch late but even so I pulled up the car about 100 yards from the door of the Hôtel de l'Europe. Because it was a well-known restaurant there might be unwelcome acquaintances eating there and so I took the precaution of going in alone to spy out the land. The coast seemed clear and, as it was late, it was a fair bet that no one who was not there already would be likely to come in after us. I drove the car into the garage and settled down to enjoy good wine and excellent food.

When we drove out again we found the traffic held up by a procession along the banks of the Rhône, with peasants in local costumes and farm carts drawn by oxen. It was the *Fête de la Vendange*, very picturesque, very charming. We sat there comfortably enough for half an hour while the procession passed. It was not until two days later, in Corsica, that we caught up with the English papers. The first thing I saw, on the back page of *The Times*, was a half-page picture of the *Fête de la Vendange*, taken from the Rhône, showing the peasants, the farm wagons, the oxen —and my car and its occupants. The Mercedes was easily distinguishable because of the way the exhaust pipes were encased in large, shiny, chromium-plated pipes on the outside of the bonnet; it was said, vulgarly, to have 'its guts hanging out'. I had no beard in those days and, being in France, I wore no orchid, but thanks to the good photography of *The Times* neither Diana's nor my features passed unrecognized.

I certainly cannot blame Doré for our marriage breaking down. There is no doubt that she worked very hard to do her best for me and to make the marriage a success. It was entirely my fault that it failed. Being younger and more virile than I am now I succumbed to other charms.

The proceedings which ended my second marriage made good material for the newspapers and they were reported with big headlines. Perhaps I should have left the country—to shoot wild game in Africa, as all Englishmen are said to do when thwarted in love —and not come back until the hullabaloo was over. But, partly because I was working fairly hard and partly because it is not in my character not to face the music, I decided the only thing to do was to go on with my usual life. The day after the divorce proceedings were reported I went out hunting. I managed to raise four white horses from my stable, two for me and two for the charming lady for whom I had the privilege of providing a mount.

I explained that the white horses were a symbol of the purity of my past and of my future intentions towards the lady.

Hunting seems to have played quite a part in my romantic life. As I have said, I took up hunting again because I had met Diana. That, in turn, might be said to have led to my meeting Marie, for I first saw her while out hunting with the Old Berkeley. That was in 1934. She was a very attractive young woman on a chestnut horse. I discovered her name later; I found out, too, that she was the daughter of Louis de Ayala, the great champagne producer of Rheims. At that time, she was married to a man called Horace Samuelson.

Marie had been told of how I had been known to send a few orchids—some jealous person said 'coffin-loads'—to members of the opposite sex for whom I felt respect, admiration or desire. She took a bet that she would ride past me and that she, too, would receive a coffin-load of orchids.

She won her bet. She also ended up as my third wife but that was not until fourteen years later. We both had our respective matrimonial positions to tidy up and, with the coming of war and all its hazards, we saw no reason why we should go to all the trouble of washing dirty linen in public when it might turn out to have been unnecessary.

But hunting, which brought us together, nearly took her away from me. It was after the war, after we were married, when we were out with the Whaddon Chase. We were near Shenley when hounds 'found' and the field streamed off along the covert and galloped straight into a bog. There was a most appalling mix-up, with three or four horses coming down together. One of them (as I told in chapter eight) rolled over on its rider, Digby Whitehead, and killed him. Another was a small pony, ridden by a twelve-year-old boy who got up, shook himself and mounted again. The boy himself had been kicked by one of the horses but, apart from bruises, was uninjured. But his horse had galloped over my wife, Marie. She was lying unconscious, face down in the mud. Luckily, another member of the Hunt, a first-year medical student, Jane Scott Brown, the daughter of an eminent Harley Street surgeon, saw her in time and turned her head round to prevent her suffocating. She had bad concussion and injuries to the spine; even after a month in darkness she had to remain in hospital and it took her a year to recover from that accident. She is very lucky, and so am I, that she is still alive and apparently none the worse for it— except that she now bullies me more than she did before. It is a price I am very happy to pay. I have had good wives as wives go and as wives go they went, but this one, so far, even under great provocation, has stayed the course.

One day after the war and after Marie and I were married, she had an 'encounter' with Diana. Both of them were wearing leopard-skin coats. It was a situation to test their mettle. Diana struck the first blow.

'I shot mine,' she said sweetly. Marie gave her leopard-skin an affectionate stroke.

'I *poisoned* mine,' she said.

My relations with my father during these last years before the war were characterized by genuine affection on both sides marred by explosive conflicts. One demonstration of my father's affection for me may strike some as trivial, perhaps even sloppy and sentimental, but I was touched by it. He had asked me down to Cannes for a few days, partly for a vacation and a change of air but chiefly to discuss outstanding points of business with him. He had reserved a nice apartment in his hotel for me. He always wanted me to have a private sitting-room as well as a bedroom and bathroom and accommodation for my valet; but my apartment had to be somewhat smaller than his own for the sake of discipline. When I arrived in my rooms I found in a bowl on the table a rather bedraggled bunch of mimosa. It was only later I learned that, during his daily walk in the mountains behind Cannes, he had himself plucked that mimosa for his little son.

I have written earlier of Adjemoff's great influence over my father. It was Adjemoff who had advised him to be very generous with me and to let me have all the expensive luxuries I might want because the more extravagant the tastes I acquired the more I would remain bound to him. I hope he was wrong in that appreciation of my reactions and I think the story of my relations with my father, involving the break with him at the time of my first marriage and my later rows, prove this. Of course, I did profit financially from my father's generosity, although I like to think his attitude was inspired by his affection and devotion to me rather than by the calculated ulterior motive proposed by Adjemoff.

But what I wanted and what my father would not give me was independence and money of my own. Finally, I took a legal action against him for what he had promised me as my share of the profits of 'Pandi'—Participations and Investments of Toronto, one of the Gulbenkian subsidiary companies, which owned its I.P.C. interests and of which I was a director. That, at any rate, was the formal basis of the action; but the real cause of the big row between us was something infinitely less substantial.

One day I had had a particularly large amount of work to do in my father's office. I knew I should not have time to go out for lunch so I ordered a chicken in tarragon jelly with asparagus tips to be brought into the office. When the food was delivered, it was paid for out of petty cash without my thinking any more about it. Some weeks later, my father, as was his wont, was going through the petty cash book when he noticed the entry: '18*s*. 6*d*.—lunch for Mr. Nubar.' He was very angry.

'You have a very large allowance,' he said. 'Aren't you ashamed of yourself, charging your lunch to the office?'

As I had not really intended that the office should pay for it and as I had sent out for lunch only to make more time for my work I felt it was a most unfair remark. I, too, flared up. That was the start of the famous 'chicken row'.

The case came to court in June 1939. It went on for three days. I had obtained the court's order for 'discovery', a technical term which means that each side in a lawsuit must discover or disclose to the other side all the documents in their possession which may have some relevance to the point at issue. By virtue of the order I obtained, all the documents relating to my father's business from the time I had joined him on coming down from Cambridge until 1940 had to be produced. There were nearly a million of them and they weighed over a ton. This was a tremendous undertaking. My lawyers were of the opinion that the production of these documents and all the unwanted publicity that went with the case ought to be sufficient pressure to enable the friends of both parties to achieve a compromise. My father was also discussing this court order with his counsel and, while doing so, he turned round to one of them, John Foster, the famous Q.C., and said: 'Isn't my son clever to have thought of this idea?'

Foster replied: 'I thought you were here to fight your son and now you are praising him.'

'He's getting tough,' my father said. 'He's a chip off the old block.'

John Foster, who told me the story later, said he and the other counsel found that endearing; what a pity, he added, that the silly row had not been stopped before it reached the court. Actually, the action had been nearly settled and would have been if it had not been for the opposition of a young solicitor employed by my father. As it was, I finally withdrew the action but my father very kindly paid all my costs which amounted to something like £30,000. That was surely the most expensive chicken in history.

10

The Valet Went Too

IN THE summer of 1938 I became convinced of the imminence
of war. Most people approved the Munich agreement, but I was
one of the many who opposed it. I remember expressing these
views rather strongly at a meet of the Whaddon Chase at Beach-
ampton, for instance; I found little support.

'Nubar wants us to go to war for the "Czechos",' said another
member of the Hunt who was actually a Jew and very anti-Hitler.

A few days later at another meet in Addington Park, while
hounds were drawing the osier beds, I had a conversation with
Digby Whitehead, a good friend of mine.

'I don't see any likelihood of war,' he said. 'I'd lay a hundred
to three against it.'

'All right,' I said, 'you're on—I'll take you.'

I was right about a war coming soon, but happily I was wrong
in my apprehension about what would happen when war started.
I expected heavy bombing upon the outbreak of war and I had a
Wellsian vision of the terror-stricken populace fleeing the towns
and cities and pouring into the countryside in panic. I imagined
they might seize by force any big house and felt glad that I had no
such place of my own. It was with these fears in mind that I
took a very small workman's cottage at Weedon in Buckinghamshire, near the country town of Aylesbury, about forty-five miles
north of London. It had only two bedrooms and a bathroom and
four people could be seated with difficulty in the dining-room;
just the sort of place, I thought, which would escape the notice of
marauding, frightened refugees. In fact, of course, the heavy
bombing did not come until much later and, terrible though it was,
I had overestimated its effects and underestimated the fortitude
of the people of London.

Just before war broke out, the Government ordered an evacuation of London by people whose presence there was not essential—chiefly mothers and children. Arrangements had to be made to house them in the countryside and everyone was asked to do what he could to provide rooms. Apart from the cottage I had also taken, for the hunting season, The Firs, a big house at Whitchurch, which later was to become a secret meeting-place for Winston Churchill and Professor Lindemann (afterwards Lord Cherwell). I was able to put up a few evacuees in some of the cottages where the grooms lived; grooms were taken on for the hunting season and I had not recruited my full complement, so there were rooms to spare. The evacuees were there for some months. I gave the children rides on my horses around the yard, much to the disgust of my head groom. 'Bad for the horses, sir,' he said. 'And I'm afraid of the children falling off.'

There were certainly not enough rooms in private houses to take care of all the children who were being evacuated from London and, in all the villages around Buckinghamshire, schools and other public buildings were being taken over, temporarily at least. Much of this was being organized on the day before war was declared and, full of the general desire to take part in the 'patriotic' activities which were going on, I applied to the civil defence headquarters at Aylesbury to see what I could do. I was told to get in touch with Mrs. James de Rothschild, who had a load of blankets and mattresses which I was to collect and distribute in the surrounding villages. Being a hunting man, I knew the countryside well and I should have no difficulty in finding even the most remote villages.

Mrs. de Rothschild had a place at Waddesdon (with its priceless collection of French furniture, it now belongs to the National Trust) and, on the Sunday morning, I went there in my station wagon. In anticipation of the war, Waddesdon had been closed as a house and all the priceless works of art had been either covered with dust sheets or stored elsewhere; I think, eventually, they went to the coalmine in Wales which housed the National Gallery pictures and also my father's. When I got to Waddesdon, the load of blankets was not quite ready and I was shown in by the servants. They could not show me into the house because it was all upside-down, so I was asked to sit down in the servants' hall which, at Waddesdon, was a comparatively palatial place. I was given a whisky and soda and a wireless; it was on that wireless I heard the declaration of war by Mr. Chamberlain.

Although I was well over forty and I was not English I was anxious, as I had been in 1914, to do something positive to help this country where I had spent the greater part of my life and where I had been so happy. When commissions were opened to foreigners I applied for one, but I was turned down this time because of my age and my lack of military experience. Next, I decided to see if my knowledge of languages could be usefully employed. I used to be quite proud of the number of languages I could speak until, on one occasion, when asked how many I knew, my truthful answer met with this response: 'Ah, yes, as many as a good head waiter but not as many as a good *concierge.*' Since that day I have determined that wild horses will never drag from me the number. But, in the hope of doing some useful war service, I polished up my Turkish by taking lessons from a Turkish professor, called Ali Riza Bey, at the Oriental School of Languages. He was a small, tubby man, full of fun; I enjoyed the lessons and made quite a lot of progress; but it still did not help me. I managed, through the aid of friends (among them Padre Beauchamp, the head in the R.A.F. of the R.C. chaplains) to get an interview with the selection board for interpreters, but they turned me down as well. I was very disappointed at my lack of success and I still wanted very much to be able to do something. My chance finally came in a most unlikely way.

One day in the autumn of 1939 when I was out cub-hunting I saw at the covert-side a newcomer to the Hunt; I recognized his horse; he had hired it from a local Irish dealer friend of mine. He also had his spurs on upside-down; I remarked on this and started talking to him.

It came out that his name was Captain Eddie Hastings and he was stationed at Bletchley, a large country-house which had belonged to Lady Leon and had been taken over by the Government—for hush-hush work, it was said. No one knew exactly what went on there and everyone who did work there was very secretive about it. Captain Hastings was no exception; he was friendly, an agreeable conversationalist, but the model of discretion in his references to Bletchley. I told him of my difficulties in finding anyone who would let me do something for the war effort, of how eager and determined I was and how frustrated by official rejections.

'It seems there's always something not quite right,' I said. 'For one reason or another my Armenian origin goes against me.'

Captain Hastings nodded sympathetically. 'I know how you feel,' he said. 'I was talking to an Austrian the other day who has met the same kind of thing as you have. He felt pretty annoyed about it, too. He said he didn't see why he should be held responsible for being born in a particular bed in a particular place.'

After hunting I mentioned Captain Hastings to a friend, who said he knew him and quite a lot about the work he was doing at Bletchley. As soon as Hastings himself reached home I was on the phone to him. Without revealing my source of information, I told him what I had found out about him. He seemed impressed. We met a few times during the months that followed and he introduced me to others who worked with him at Bletchley, and a most interesting crowd they were. One was known as 'Christopher', another as 'Punch', a third as 'Uncle'. 'Punch' took me to lunch at the Thatched House Club at the bottom of St. James's Street and discussed my feelings about the war very fully with me, enquiring about my past experience and what efforts I had made to join the orthodox services. 'Uncle' gave me lunch at Brown's Hotel and, wartime or no wartime, an excellent lunch it was. He suggested I should go to Berlin to see what I could find out. My cover story would be that I was there to sell oil from Iraq which could be shipped by neutral tanker, ostensibly to Rotterdam or some other neutral port, while destined in fact for Germany.

But this projected trip came to nothing when it was recognized that the Germans were neither fools nor squeamish in dealing with those who tried to outwit them. The newspapers at the time reported the misfortune which befell an English agent who had gone to Germany. It had been arranged that English colleagues in Holland should drive to the Dutch-German frontier to pick him up there on his way back from Berlin. Unfortunately, the Germans had already heard of the plan. The Englishmen drove, as arranged, to the Dutch frontier and went freely up to the Customs post. The returning agent stepped forward to meet them and the Germans pounced on the whole bunch. A Dutch Customs official who tried to protest was shot dead and the Germans carried off, back into Germany, a very important agent.

I learned later for myself just how thorough the German Secret Service could be. In that first autumn of 1939, I took a weekend off from London, spending it in Luxembourg. I went down along the Moselle to the point where the lines of French and German troops facing each other ended and motored through Luxembourg and on to Brussels. I was absent from London only two or three nights in all and was very quiet about my trip when I returned home. My journey had nothing to do with anyone else; but I travelled in my own name and signed my own name at the hotels. Soon after the Germans took over Paris in the middle of June 1940, the *Kommandantur* sent for my brother-in-law, Kevik Essayan.

'What,' they wanted to know, 'was your brother-in-law, Nubar Gulbenkian, doing in Brussels last autumn?' Of course, he, poor fellow, had never heard of my being there and said so quite truthfully to the Germans, but it took him some little time to convince them of his ignorance.

Although I did not attempt the Berlin trip, the Bletchley crowd soon appreciated my potential value, which lay in my special advantages as an official of a neutral legation and as the son of my father. The first gave me a diplomatic passport and a valid official excuse for going to consult with the Iranian Legation in Vichy; this in turn gave me excellent cover for going to Vichy to discuss business affairs with my father. Both in combination provided a first-class two-tier 'cover' for anything else afoot. And so began a phase of my life which bore many resemblances to a Phillips Oppenheim novel.

It was July 1940. France had fallen and the French Government, after being chased round France, had finally settled down in Vichy. My father had intended staying in Paris throughout the war, but had now followed the fleeing French Government down to Vichy; this gave me a convenient and valid excuse for going there. Even so, no one could travel out of England at that time unless he had a very good reason indeed and the reason had to be that the journey was in the national interest. Captain Hastings fixed things for me so that I could take my valet, Bailey, with me. (After leaving my service following his row with my second wife,

Bailey had served the Crown Prince of Japan and had made enough money to set himself up in a pub at Ramsgate. When he was compulsorily evacuated from there after the Fall of France, he rejoined me, taking my cottage at Weedon in hand with his wife, and allowing me, in effect, to be a guest in my own home. Many an official eyebrow was raised at the idea of my taking a valet with me in wartime, but Hastings justified it on the grounds that if Bailey could not go with me I would not go at all—which made Bailey a 'key person' in the whole operation.)

We travelled down to Bournemouth by car, arriving there in the middle of an air-raid, and then spent a short night at the Royal Bath Hotel before taking off by flying-boat from Poole at the crack of dawn. The flight to Lisbon took some nine hours. We flew down the Channel, well within sight of German-occupied France, but escorted by R.A.F. Blenheims up to a point beyond the Scilly Isles where they peeled off and left us on our own.

We reached Portugal without incident. In the launch which took us from the flying-boat to the quayside, I came face to face with an old friend of my father's, a man I had not seen for years since he had given up his partnership in the firm of Bénard et Jarislowski. It was Jean Monnet, then on his way to America and now, of course, reputed throughout the world as the father of the famous Monnet Plan which has been the base of the whole revival of the French economy since the war.

Lisbon itself was a tragic sight, crowded with refugees from all over Western Europe, people desperate to get to America. Here, in one place at one moment, was an image of a whole continent in turmoil and fear, a world whose orderly ways had been disrupted as by an earthquake. Terror was written on the faces of these refugees, the imagined terror of what would happen to them should Hitler's hordes catch up with them. Many of the Jewish families had arrived in Rolls-Royces, cars which had cost so much and had represented so much and which were now two a penny: scores of them, it seemed, had been abandoned on the quayside by people whose turn had come for a visa and a passage across the Atlantic to safety. There was, then, nothing more precious that money could buy them and they gladly left behind them the symbols of their former comfort and status in exchange for what they thought was the assurance of life itself.

I booked in for the night in the only place available to me in that overcrowded neighbourhood, a third-rate but very acceptable hotel at Sintra. At dinner in the restaurant that evening I mentioned to the waiter that I was flying on to Spain the next day. His reply was something of a shock. He pointed out three Italians who were enjoying a very jovial dinner, consuming large amounts of wine, and said: 'There is your tribulation. They are going to fly you tomorrow.' Judging from their happy state, I well believed they would indeed be a 'tribulation'. But my Portuguese at that time was rudimentary and the waiter's English was not that good and I found out later that he was translating the word *tripulação*, which is Portuguese for 'crew'.

Next morning, Bailey and I boarded an Italian plane bound for Madrid and Barcelona on its way to Corsica and Rome. On landing at Barcelona we repaired to the Ritz Hotel which, years later, I found to be one of the most comfortable hotels in Europe. But in 1940 conditions in Spain were appalling. Not only were they still staggering from the Civil War, but they were also under pressure to export what they could to their friends, the Germans. Even at the Ritz food was scarce and, to give an example of the way standards had deteriorated, there was a large ink-stain on the carpet of the best suite in the hotel.

One evening, the waiter came to me, beaming with pleasure, and said, 'Oh, señor, good news, good news, we have meat tonight, what would señor like?'

'What have you got?'

'Anything the señor would like. What about a fillet steak?'

I ordered a fillet steak and in due course three waiters arrived bearing a huge silver dish with a heater. The cover of the silver dish was removed with a flourish and, lo and behold, as they say, revealed beneath was a succulent and sizzling steak. We had had nothing like it for weeks and I set about it with relish. It was perhaps a trifle sweet but very good. I called the head waiter and asked him whether the steak was the end product of the bullfight that had taken place the day before. He held up his hands in horror.

'Oh, no, señor,' he said, 'a bull would be much too tough—that is a *caballito*—a little horse.'

I do not know whether that was the first time I ever ate horse but it was certainly the first time I had done so knowingly; apart from the hunting-man's natural reaction against the idea, I must say I found it quite tasty.

The coachman, whose two-horse victoria I had hired to drive me around Barcelona, told me things were much better than they had been during the Civil War. Then, he said, he had had to feed his horses on wood shavings and I am afraid they rather looked like it.

I tried to find out whether any means of communication with France was open but no one seemed to know. I asked to be put through on the telephone to the French Consulate-General in Barcelona but, at first, either by accident or by German influence, I was connected with the German Consulate-General. When I did manage to speak to the French, however, I was advised to take the daily train to the frontier and then hope for the best.

The train was crowded and it was no easy job getting on it; to make matters worse, some considerable distance short of the frontier we had to get out. There had been vast floods and the railway bridge had been swept away. The train pulled up; it could go no further. The passengers, carrying their own luggage, had to cross the waters by a temporary foot bridge. Luckily, when we got to the other side, we were able to cadge a lift from a bus; it had been sent there to transport the crew of a Scandinavian ship which had been sunk and who were now being repatriated. This took us as far as Gerona, where we stopped for lunch. We had partridges. The rest of the journey, the last fifty miles to Port Bou and the French frontier, we did in style, in a delapidated taxi whose driver we persuaded, after much bribery, to take us. We had no difficulty at all at the frontier, either on the Spanish side or the French; my diplomatic passport saw to that. I was asked, however, to declare any foreign currency I was carrying. I had been provided with American money before I left England because I had refused to travel in wartime Europe without plenty of dollar cash. I now produced a 500-dollar bill which, apparently, was more than one was legally permitted to import into France at that time. This caused a slight complication but, as no one at the frontier post could offer to change that kind of money and the man in charge did not really care a damn what went on, we were allowed in.

France was in chaos. Demobilization was in full swing and the whole country seemed to be on the move, everyone trying to sort himself out and hoping to return to something called normal life.

Those who had taken to the road as refugees, in front of the advancing Germans, now wanted to go home again. Others who found themselves subject to the Germans in the Occupied Zone wanted to come south, even though the Germans, at this stage, were behaving with the utmost propriety and had given no hint of what was to come. Most of the French servicemen still wore uniforms for their journeys home from the war but with buttons and signs of rank ripped off.

No one knew how the trains were running but we managed to get one from the frontier to Perpignan, the nearest big town, and hoped to pick up another there. In the train one Frenchman said to another how brave and successful the Italians, who had just come into the war, had been.

'Why,' he said, 'do you realize they had conquered half of Menton before the Armistice!'

At Perpignan, I posted a few letters from 'Punch' at Bletchley (there was then no censorship of mail within the Unoccupied Zone). We had another long wait for a train; it was about midnight when we heard of a train leaving there for Montpellier, which would be a further step on our way to Vichy, so we boarded it. Or, rather, to be precise, Bailey put the luggage on board; while we were still on the platform, dashing up and down the length of the train, looking for a place, even if it was only standing room, the train started. I felt pretty silly left standing there on the platform at Perpignan with our luggage gone and not at all like the resourceful spies and Men of the Secret Service of whom I had read. I had only one consolation: I had always made it a rule to keep my money and my passport on my person and, so long as I had those, I supposed the rest did not really matter.

I was told there was another train coming through in about a quarter of an hour which was also going to Montpellier. This, at any rate, was more luck than we had any right to expect. I gave a tip to a porter and asked him to telephone through to Montpellier, explaining that my luggage was on the train and asking the station staff there to take it off and hand it over to me on arrival. I was merely going through the motions for I had no real hope of seeing the luggage again.

The next train was also packed but this time we did manage at least to get on board. I struck up a friendship with a formidable

American lady with a hooked nose, who had been travelling on behalf of the Rockefeller Foundation and was full of good works. When she heard I had come from England, she proceeded to harangue me about the 'dastardly action' of the British in sinking the French Fleet, the ships of their Allies, at Mers-el-Kebir. The news had just come through and the good American lady was even more righteously angry than the French. After her harangue, however, she became more friendly and we took it in turns, instead of standing in the corridor, to sit on the only available seat, which was that in the smallest compartment at the end of the carriage.

Already, France was suffering from the ignorance, or from the dissemination of deliberate misinformation, which was an inevitable consequence of her defeat. If the Vichy Government were going to secure the support of the French people they had to keep back certain news which could be inconvenient. In Vichy itself, for instance, I found no one—no member of the general public, that is—who knew that the British Fleet had given the French at Mers-el-Kebir the chance of sailing away under escort to the French West Indies. The inculcation of anti-British feeling was a necessary element of Vichy policy.

There were people, of course, especially in the Unoccupied Zone, who were anti-British and certainly there was strong feeling about the action at Mers-el-Kebir, as there was bound to be in view of the way the news had been presented, or misrepresented. On the other hand, I found much pro-British feeling. For instance, when I went to a post office to put through a trunk call—which meant showing my passport, for special permission was needed— the official, seeing I had come from London, said, 'If ever you go back there, tell them how much we admire them.'

When we arrived at Montpellier in the early morning, I hurried to the station-master in the forlorn hope of news of my luggage. To my surprise, he said they had had a telegram from Perpignan about it but that the train carrying it had not yet arrived.

'But I saw it leave Perpignan a quarter of an hour before this one,' I said, pointing to the train in which I had just arrived. I thought he was trying to deceive me in some way. 'I saw it leave with my own eyes.'

'Yes, sir,' said the station-master, 'but the train you caught passed the earlier one.' It was true enough and ten minutes later it came in on another platform and waving to me was a man with whom I had struck up an acquaintance at Perpignan; he had been guarding my luggage for me.

Reunited with my bags, I next had to find a train from Montpellier to Vichy; I was told there would not be one until late afternoon. As we had not slept for twenty-four hours and were quite exhausted, we did not mind a pause in our journey—provided we could find somewhere to lie down. That was easier said than done; indeed, we were told it would be almost impossible to find a hotel room and, of course, there were no cars or taxis in which to search for one. We trudged out of the station, drooping with tiredness, wondering where we were going to go and how we should get there. Waiting outside the station was a military van, with a soldier at the wheel; he was waiting for some colonel or other. He was about to be demobilized the next day and cared little therefore about colonels and military discipline; an illicit bargain was easily struck.

We now had transport but we still lacked a hotel room. Our soldier-chauffeur took us on a search around the town but, in the end, we found that the only place we could have a wash and a bed for a few hours was the local brothel. It was a good choice. The young ladies were very hospitable. There was no running water, but they brought us a basin, jugs of water and towels, breakfast of coffee, milk and rolls, and they made ready two beds with clean sheets. All very remarkable and highly commendable.

In the afternoon, we carried our luggage to a tram stop and took a tram to the railway station, where a diplomatic passport and a few well-chosen *douceurs* enabled us to get a compartment to ourselves in quite a decent train. But not for long. The train became very crowded and although the guard was prepared to shoo the people out of our compartment and back into the corridor, I felt it wiser and certainly more humane to allow a limited number in.

At about midnight we arrived at a station which I took to be Vichy but was in fact St. Germain-des-Fossés; Vichy was on a branch line some miles away. I managed to make a telephone call to my parents and my mother said she would send her car to pick us up; thanks to Diplomatic petrol, this was possible. We had an hour or more to wait at the station, whose platforms were strewn with sleeping bodies, mainly those of returning troops lying on their greatcoats. We were lucky enough to be given a compartment in a coach in a siding and we tried to doze off, having arranged to be called when my mother's car arrived.

In Vichy, my mother had reserved a room in a good hotel, the Ambassadeurs. Although, as I found out the next morning, it lacked running hot water, it was an achievement to have been able to have got us a room at all when Vichy was bursting at the seams. There was running water and electric light, even if the use of these, too, was restricted to certain hours. My mother, with her usual motherly love, had provided a loaf of bread, some butter, some ham, a wing of chicken, cheese, some fruit and a half-bottle of claret, in case her little boy was hungry. It is remarkable how strong an emotion mother love is and how, throughout my life, my mother has always looked upon me as a little boy: for my part, I have always felt for her the deepest love and a very real affection.

When we woke up next morning, Bailey (always a perfect gentleman's gentleman) could not wait to go and see my father's valet. 'I must borrow an iron, sir,' he said. There was no doubt that, at that moment, nothing could be more important to him. It had gone harshly across the professional grain for him to leave England without his seven-pound iron which, because of the limited weight of baggage we were allowed, I had forbidden him to take. Off he went to the Hôtel Majestic where my father had established himself and where Maréchal Pétain and the French Government had made their administrative headquarters, though not their residence.

Bailey found the valet, borrowed the iron and, proud as a peacock, had started on his way back to the Ambassadeurs when he ran into some German staff officers. He was so terrified at the sight of the German uniforms (and no wonder) that he dropped the iron on to the toes of one of them. Naturally, he thought he would be shot, not merely at dawn but forthwith. Fortunately, at that time, the Germans were anxious to promote good relations with the French population and even more so with the Americans who had not yet come into the war. As Bailey spoke only English and French, the Germans took him for an American and they assured him they understood the dropping of the iron had been an accident. Which was just as well, for, later that day, I found out the name of the staff officer on whose toes the iron had been dropped: it was von Brauchitsch, the German Commander-in-Chief. For a would-be secret agent, or, rather, for a would-be secret agent's valet, this could scarcely be rated the height of discretion.

As with everything else in Vichy at that time, it was extremely difficult to get transport of any kind. The only horse-drawn carriage had been commandeered by Mrs. Corrigan, an American who had been in Vichy for some time engaged in good works. Mrs. Corrigan had been well known in London between the wars as a Society hostess. Her parties were attended by the British Royal Princes and were extremely lavish. Each guest received a valuable present, for the men it might well be a gold cigarette case, for the ladies something equally extravagant. Mrs. Corrigan, however, had fallen foul of a good friend of mine, Valentine Castlerosse, the first of the Society columnists. Valentine looked and behaved like Henry VIII. He had a large but discerning appetite for wine, women and food. He had joined Lord Beaverbrook's staff just after the First World War and for some twenty years had written a weekly page in the *Sunday Express*, as well as contributing to the other Beaverbrook papers in a quite inimitable style. He was no respecter of persons and what he wrote was less than kind, though always as witty as pithy. On the other hand, if you were a friend of his, there was nothing that was too much trouble for him. Long after the war, Lord Beaverbrook and I were reminiscing about Castlerosse and I referred to the biting things he had written about Mrs. Corrigan.

'What Valentine wrote and we published about Mrs. Corrigan,' said Lord Beaverbrook, 'is nothing to what Valentine wrote and we did not publish.'

Although Mrs. Corrigan had collared the one-horse carriage and petrol was very short there were those who found their way round the problem. The Ministers of the Vichy Government looked after themselves all right, of course, and the Diplomatic Corps were allowed a minute monthly ration of petrol. The doyen of the Corps, the Papal Nuncio, was responsible for the distribution of the petrol coupons, although it was a young priest, one of the secretaries of the Nunciature, helped by a neutral diplomatist, the secretary to the Irish Embassy, who actually doled them out. This young Irishman was Cornelius Cremin, who later became the

Secretary of the Irish Department of External Affairs and was Irish Ambassador in London until early 1964—a good friend of mine. I went once on behalf of my father and I had some difficulty in convincing them that his request, or the amount for which he was asking, was a reasonable one. I had to point out, with some eloquence and passion, but really with utter irrelevance, that it was only thanks to him that oil had ever been found in Venezuela or the Middle East.

The Rumanian Military Attaché was highly popular when he succeeded in getting a twenty-ton tank-car, full of petrol, sent from Rumania for his own use and that of his friends. However, not surprisingly, that supply did not last as long as he had hoped it would; others, not in the privileged circle, decided to take a share without his permission and the petrol 'leaked' away.

In Vichy, I met for the first time young Victor de Metz, a highly intelligent man who later became the successful President of the Compagnie Française des Pétroles, our associates in the I.P.C., and with whom I had many negotiations and hard but friendly tussles up to 1955. He was none too pleased to hear from me that he and his Company, like all residents in France, had been declared technical 'enemies under the Act' by the British Government; it was not easy for him to understand that this had been done to protect his Company and people like him, including my father. Under this declaration any documents signed by the owners resident in France were considered invalid because their signatures might have been given under duress from the Germans; their interests in England, and subsequently in the United States, were taken over by the authorities (in England they were vested in the Public Trustee) and were looked after as they would have been for an infant or a lunatic. My father found the idea of being labelled an 'enemy' by Britain no more appealing than did Monsieur de Metz and, for all my attempts to explain it away, it rankled with him right up to his death.

Vichy was full of rumours and that was especially true of the Hôtel des Ambassadeurs into which the whole of the Diplomatic Corps accredited to the French Government had been crammed. They had followed the Government round when it was being chased by the Germans, from Paris to Tours, from Tours to Bordeaux and finally to Vichy, where they were to remain until the

Germans took over the Unoccupied Zone. All the French officials and the foreign diplomatists were very anxious to meet me and to find out what was going on in London. I had as much success in Vichy as the Man From London as I had a few days later in London as the Man From Vichy.

The general feeling in Vichy was that the war was over and it was only the stubbornness of the British which was dragging things on and making it uncomfortable for everyone else. Britain was dead but would not lie down. What is the good of it all, I was asked time and again.

'Whether England's dead or not,' I kept on replying, 'she certainly doesn't know it. The British are determined to *tenir le coup* —to see it through.'

The American Ambassador and the Canadian Chargé d'Affaires stuck up for Britain and, as time went on, they were to become the main sources of pro-British propaganda. (The American Ambassador, Admiral Leahy, played his wireless full volume with open windows so that passers-by could hear the B.B.C. news bulletins: in theory, at least, it was forbidden in Vichy to listen to the B.B.C., but everyone did and the B.B.C. was highly regarded.)

I prevailed upon Victor de Metz, in return for all the useful information I had brought to him, to let me have some petrol out of the private store the bigwigs of the Compagnie Française des Pétroles had saved for their personal purposes; he gave me two 50-litre cans, thus assuring me a much more comfortable trip back than I had had coming. So, after a few days in Vichy, Bailey and I set off for the Spanish frontier again. We spent the night at Port-Vendres, just a few miles north of the frontier, where our friends, the Adjemoffs, had taken a very nice villa, conveniently placed for their quick escape across the frontier if the Germans were ever to take over the whole country.

From Port-Vendres we drove to the frontier where the officials remembered me, my English valet and my 500-dollar bill, and they waved us through without any formalities. On the train to Barcelona, I shared a compartment with a French professor who was going to Lisbon to lecture on some aspects of French culture. As I was wearing the Legion of Honour and spoke decent French he became quite talkative and particularly so on the subject of the war and France's position in the world. He was not too happy about France's surrender and was trying to prepare excuses for it.

'I would say we are tired of getting our skins shot through for the sake of the English,' he told me. That was quite a common attitude of mind.

From Barcelona, Bailey and I travelled together in a Spanish aircraft to Lisbon. The most memorable thing about this flight for me was the sight of a man smoking on board the plane. This was the first time I had seen smoking allowed in the air and I asked the man to put his cigarette out. I told him of my crash in 1935 and of the dangers from fire.

'If the pilot or any other member of the crew asks me to stop I will stop,' he said politely. 'Otherwise, I intend to go on smoking.'

'Just look at my hands,' I said, showing him the scars which remained. He looked but went on smoking.

'All right,' I said, 'we'll all burn together.'

The plane put down at Madrid for lunch. Bailey and I left our hats on our seats but when we came back we found our places had been taken. I started on the men who had taken them, only to find they were members of the British Embassy in Madrid. They, too, backed down very quickly when they found we were from London and gave us back our seats.

When we got to Lisbon, trouble started. The Portuguese were very determined at that time to assert their neutrality and independence; they asserted it at Bailey's expense. The visa in his passport was good for one journey from London to France, through Portugal and the return through Portugal to London, or so we thought until a self-important official in Lisbon decided otherwise. The Embassy in London, he said, had no business issuing a visa for the return journey and Bailey should have obtained a separate visa to permit him to re-enter Portugal from Spain on the return journey. He threatened to put my poor valet on the plane which had brought us to Lisbon and send him back to Madrid. As Bailey had no Spanish visa to allow him to return to Spain, however, I had visions of him spending the rest of his life flying, to and fro, like Mahomet's coffin, between Madrid and Lisbon. At this point, I intervened, and I argued and protested with some success; enough, at any rate, to keep the Portuguese talking until the plane to Madrid had taken off. My success was a limited one, however; as there were no more planes to Madrid until the following day, they simply put Bailey into prison.

The best thing I could do, I thought, was to go into Lisbon and seek the help of the British Consulate. The official at the Consulate was most courteous but regretted that it was lunchtime; I would understand, he said, that nothing could be done until after lunch. I understood and went to the Restaurant Negresco. Who should be at the next table but René de Montaigu, the managing director of the Compagnie Française des Pétroles, who was on his way to America. He recommended the red mullet as a very good fish to eat in Portugal, for there one could have it very fresh. He was right.

After lunch, I went back to the Consulate where the assistant vice-consul was put at my disposal to try to find a solution to Bailey's plight. We succeeded but it was about nine o'clock at night before we got him out of prison. The poor man was very hungry for he had been allowed no food unless he paid for it and he had no money. Bailey has never quite forgiven the Portuguese for his day in gaol.

Back in London, I enjoyed a certain celebrity among my friends as the Man From Vichy and I had no difficulty in getting an audience for my stories. I was in the smoking-room at White's, recounting my experiences to a group, when a brass-hat with red tabs and rows of decorations came in. Jack Crawshay, with whom I had been lunching, greeted him and said, 'Sir, I think you would like to meet Gulbenkian who has just come back from Vichy.' The high-ranking military gentleman, whose name I did not catch, murmured a few courteous words and then started asking the usual questions.

'Are they sore with us?' he asked me.

'Yes,' I said, 'they rather think we let them down. For one thing they blame us for not sending the Metropolitan Air Force to help them.'

'What else did they say?'

'Well, they say the immediate cause of the débâcle was that Gort[1] marched north when he had been ordered to march south.' Jack Crawshay kicked me hard. The brass-hat flushed and after

1. General Lord Gort was Commander-in-Chief of the British Expeditionary Force in France in 1939–40.

a few more muttered words he walked away. As soon as he had gone, I said to Jack: 'What on earth did you kick me for?'
'That, you bloody fool,' he said, 'was Gort.'

I reported back to Eddie Hastings and his colleagues at Bletchley on what I had seen and heard in Vichy. They seemed pleased with the information and even more pleased with the ease with which I was able to come and go from Vichy. They decided that, using my two-tier 'cover' to justify other journeys to Vichy, I could help to organize the escape routes for British servicemen who had managed to get away from prisoner-of-war camps in Germany and were on the run or had been shot down over France. For further instructions, I was asked to go to a flat in St. James's Street near Lock's, the hatter's. I was admitted by a servant who, I had been told, had also been sworn under the Official Secrets Act. He showed me up to a well-furnished room on the first floor.

It seemed I was early, for no one else was there. Remembering the old advice that, when you have an interview, you should always have your back to the light so that the light is on the face of the man you are talking to, I selected a chair nearest the window and turned it round so that I had my back to the light and whoever came in to talk to me would have to face the light. It was 'Punch' who came in. Without hesitating, he went straight to the window and stood with his back to it, so that it was I who had to turn round to him and face the light.

'Now, let's go through the terms you can offer over there,' said 'Punch'. 'Twenty pounds for other ranks, forty pounds per officer.' This was the money which the British Government would pay to see their men taken safely, from Perpignan, over the Spanish frontier. Once there, the escapee would be put immediately in gaol by the Spanish authorities but not for long. All arrangements had been made to get the prisoners out of gaol and ultimately back to England, although, of course, it was the Spanish duty, according to international law, to intern them for the duration of the war.

We talked over the broad lines of what I was to do.

'Good,' said 'Punch'. 'But I must just check with the Treasury.' Apparently, even in wartime, the Treasury was still the watchdog of the British taxpayer's money and nothing could be done without Treasury consent. While I waited, 'Punch' telephoned the Treasury and received approval for the arrangements we had discussed.

And so my mission was agreed. First stop was Lisbon again. It was there I met my first 'contact'. I had a telephone call from a man I shall call 'Didi', who was a vice-consul at the British Embassy.

'I am a friend of Ann Tyrrell,' he said. 'I have heard you are in Lisbon and I was wondering if you would care to come along and have a drink.' We arranged for him to pick me up in a car in the corner of the Rossio, Lisbon's great square. I got into the car.

'Can I give you a light?' he asked me, proffering a box of Swan Vestas. I took my cue.

'I have just arrived by aeroplane,' I said, 'flying like a feather.' These were the code-words we had been told to use to identify each other. I was to refer to 'feathers flying' and he to 'Swan'. 'Didi' was a very cheerful, intelligent and dedicated man who lived for his job. When one met him alone, he was very witty and an excellent raconteur. In company he sat like a clam. When he came to see me at the hotel for the first time, he came up to my room but, before he said a word, he opened all the windows and then seated himself on the window-sill.

'Safer,' he said. 'No other way to guard against hidden microphones. Don't forget this trick if you have anyone else up here. If you sit like this, the noise of the traffic will drown your conversation. Now, come over here and talk.' 'Didi' would never be seen in public with me in Lisbon although he did not go so far in his discretion with me as did another of his colleagues who met his contacts only in the public urinal in the Rossio. He now gave me an address to call at in Perpignan where I should contact the man I had come to meet, the man who was to look after the final stages of the escape route.

Crossing into France again gave me no difficulty and I began to take for granted the fact that I had crossed into what was virtually enemy territory. When I got to Perpignan, however, and I walked round to the address I had been given, I found there was no garage there as I had been led to expect, and, for a while, I feared I should be unable to find my man. Then I remembered I had been told he owned a large garage, a Citroen garage. I discovered that the biggest garage in Perpignan was a Citroen garage. I telephoned there next morning and was told my contact was away and would not be back for a few days.

I left immediately for Vichy where I found that Father had thought it unwise for me to stay in Vichy itself and had reserved rooms for me and my mother at a little place about three or four kilometres away. It was run by a woman who was a very good cook, and, on Sundays, all the French Ministers, including Jean Borotra, the famous tennis player who was then Minister of Sport, used to come out to lunch there. Their official cars, three or four big limousines, were a familiar sight there and I was rather shocked when one of the Ministers, seeing a little car parked outside the restaurant, put the police on to the owner. He was the local doctor who was entitled to a certain amount of petrol for his professional duties but appeared to have used a drop of it to go out to lunch. That sort of incident did not make for the popularity of the Vichy Government.

After a short stay in Vichy, during which my father and I discussed various developments relating to the Iraq Petroleum Company and our business in London, including matters it was impossible to deal with in letters, I went back to Perpignan. Father lent me his car; he had been accumulating petrol, black market or otherwise, and had built up a reserve.

When I got to Perpignan, I telephoned the garage and spoke to my 'contact'. We arranged to meet at a café in the Route de Prades, on the outskirts of the town.

'How shall I recognize you?' I asked him.

'I shall be reading my newspaper upside-down,' he said.

When I arrived at the café, I saw a man sitting there, reading *Le Figaro*. As I watched him, he turned it upside-down and looked at it that way for about a minute. I knew this must be the man I wanted to see. I went up to him.

'Have you a Parker pen?' I said. 'A Parker Duo-fold?' This was the password. He acknowledged me. He was a dark man with glasses, very precise, very polite, and very tactful. He noticed that I wore the Legion of Honour but he said, 'I shall not, of course, ask your name.' He was known to the bright boys at Bletchley for he had worked with them before the Fall of France. He seemed to know them all personally and talked warmly about them. He gave me a message to pass on to one of the R.A.F. officers attached to Bletchley who, it seemed, had left his car in Perpignan.

'Tell him I've had it jacked up and put carefully out of the way. It will be all right and waiting for him after the war.'

We settled down to discuss the details of the deal he was prepared to do.

'You will get £40 for each officer and £20 for each man,' I said, 'but payment will be strictly by results. Agreed?' He agreed. The money he was to be paid would be accumulated in England so that at the end of the war he could expect to find quite a nice nest egg waiting for him.

'Where will the men contact you?' In his garage, he said.

'And when they contact you there, it's your job to arrange for them to get across the frontier safely. Once they're across your job is done. Is that agreed?'

All the other details were his own responsibility. It was none of my business, for instance, to know how much he had to pay to the men who did the work of smuggling the escapees across the frontier. They, too, were paid by results. Even though the Germans offered rewards for the traffic to stop there was no point in their offering a reward for people not to do it because the smugglers would take their money and do it just the same. Nor could the Germans hope to achieve anything by offering a reward for each escapee handed over by the smugglers because a smuggler would need to do that only once to find himself cut out of the escape route and his livelihood at an end.

I spent no more than twenty minutes at the café with my contact. He understood what was required of him and agreed to carry out his part of the bargain and added he hoped he would get a *décoration anglaise* at the end of the war. I took it upon myself to assure him there would be no doubt about it, depending on how successful he had been.

I am afraid that when the war was over I had other things to think about and I do not know whether his ambition was fulfilled, though at the time I did transmit his ambitions to Eddie Hastings. One of the things we arranged before we left London was that Bailey (although he did not know it and I have never told him) should be left in France to escape along the route I had organized.

In his place, travelling with me on Bailey's passport, should go some highly placed person, posing as my valet; I had found that passports were not examined with any real care by either the French or the Spanish frontier officials. As it turned out, the bigwig did not materialize and Bailey was able to return with me to Spain in comfort.

There were little snags on the way, of course. I found, for instance, that the train to Barcelona on the return trip started on the Spanish side of the frontier. To board it, I had to take a taxi from the French Customs over the pass down to Port Bou on the other side. That also involved passing through the Spanish Customs at the top of the pass. I arrived there in the taxi at about two o'clock; the train left at three. Unfortunately, all the Customs officials had gone to lunch. There was only a very subordinate *carabiñero* left in charge and he had orders not to allow anyone through until the chief of the Customs had finished his lunch. I protested and managed to persuade the *carabiñero* to let me talk on the telephone to the chief Customs man. Luckily, I remembered his name, Don Cesar, from the previous trip and this helped me to change his mind. I asked Don Cesar whether he regarded it as consistent with Spanish *hidalgia* to hold up a foreigner and diplomatist wishing to enter his country, to make him miss his lunch and also miss his train. That appeal to Spanish courtesy did the trick: Don Cesar gave instructions to the *carabiñero* to let me and my luggage through the barrier. We arranged that my luggage should be examined in the Customs House at the railway station but, by the time I reached the station, everyone had forgotten the arrangement; the Customs official there, seeing a foreigner arrive in a French taxi, took it for granted that I must have passed through the Customs at the top of the pass.

As soon as we arrived in Barcelona, I received a telegram asking me to go back to Vichy. I could not just catch the next train to France for I had to get new French and Spanish visas for the journey. The French visa was the more difficult one to get for the Consulate in Barcelona was not entitled to issue any visas without reference to the Embassy in Madrid. As the French Ambassador, André François-Poncet, happened to be a friend of my parents, however, there was no great delay. His reaction to the request, as I heard afterwards, was 'All right, he can have a visa, but he will have to do without his English valet this time. We really can't let an Englishman go into France again.'

While I was waiting in Barcelona for the visas, I went to a bull-fight. In the place of honour there were six German officers, tall six-footers, good-looking, very smart in their grey coats, towering over the Spaniards around them. During the messiest part of the third bull (a bull-fight, let us face it, is at times a messy spectacle) one of the stalwart Germans fainted and had to be carried out by his companions. A voice shouted out from the cheaper side of the ring: 'And those are the people who are going to invade England!'

I took the train back to the French frontier where this time I had managed to arrange for a car to meet me. I made one or two further contacts in Perpignan and then went on to Vichy once more.

On my way back, in the waiting-room at Port Bou, the frontier town on the Spanish side of the frontier, I listened to Marshal Pétain delivering one of his 'messages' over the radio to the French nation. His voice quavery, he tried to rally France behind the policy of collaboration with the Germans. He regarded it as inevitable and urged them not to oppose it.

'Until today,' he said, 'I have spoken to you in the language of a father. Today I speak to you in the language of a leader. Follow me. Put your faith in France eternal.' It was October 30, 1940. Pétain had just returned from his historic meeting with Hitler at Montoire.

I rejoined Bailey at Barcelona and we picked up a plane to take us to Madrid and Lisbon. We put down at Madrid, and, before taking off again for Portugal, we had to hand over all Spanish money, as the law demanded. Then bad weather caused the flight to be postponed until the next day and we all had to spend the night in Madrid. I went to the Ritz and it was not until seven o'clock the next morning when I was about to pay my bill before driving to the airport that I remembered I had no Spanish money. The clerk at the reception desk refused to take American dollars for he was liable to be shot, he said, for dealing in foreign currency. A fellow-passenger, an Italian, came to my rescue. He changed enough of my dollars into pesetas for me to settle my bill, changing them at the official rate which was about one quarter of the 'free' or black market rate. But I was grateful enough. He turned out to be the correspondent in Brazil of the Turin newspaper, *La Stampa*. I became quite friendly with him and saw a good deal of him in Lisbon. I had to put up with a lot of chaffing from the British there for 'hobnobbing with the enemy', but he was a most useful man who had his entrée at the Italian Embassy and gave me useful information about the Albanian campaign; he told me, for instance, how many divisions the Italian generals had asked for and how many they had not received, which explained the reverses the Italian Army suffered at that time. I knew quite a lot of people in Lisbon and I picked up a lot of information which I passed on to 'Didi'; he was good enough to say it was quite useful.

Getting a seat on a plane back to London was becoming more and more difficult; no matter what priority you boasted it seemed as though somebody else always had a better one. I was not bothered by the delay, though, for I had plenty of money and the idea of having, say, three weeks' holiday in Lisbon, with good food, lighting in the streets, comfort in general and, of course, no bombs, caused me no great pain. (The blitz on London was at its height then.) Only one thing, or rather one person, was missing.

I suggested to 'Didi' that, in return for all I was doing, it would be only fair that a certain lady in London, to whom I was very devoted, should be relieved of the daily horror of her Red Cross job and brought out to share a fortnight or so in Lisbon with me. 'Didi' agreed and sent a cable to 'Uncle' proposing she should be sent out because 'Orchid' (that was my code-name) needed her as 'a key person'. After waiting three or four days, we received a cable back from 'Uncle': 'TO WHAT USE WILL ORCHID PUT KEY PERSON?'

The lady in question (Marie, my present wife) had heard nothing of these exchanges, of course, and was most surprised to receive a visit in her London flat from, to use her own words, 'a little man who looked like an undertaker'. The 'little man' told her how sorry he was and that no matter how hard they tried they would be unable to fly her out to Lisbon. There was a seaplane only two or three times a week and he hoped she would understand it was impossible to find her a place on it. She, of course, did not understand what all this was about. The night before Marie received this unexpected visit she had slipped and badly sprained her ankle. She was hobbling when the man saw her. This fact was reported to 'Didi' who told me about it. Naturally, I wrote immediately to Marie, saying how sorry I was. It was years before she understood how I had come to hear of her mishap.

After I had spent a fortnight alone in Lisbon, I started agitating to get back to England. It is hard now to imagine why I wanted to return; my parents in Vichy were imploring me to stay out of England and I had plenty of money from my father's funds in America. Just the same, I wanted to go to London. Eventually I heard that 'Didi' had got me on a plane leaving at two or three o'clock the next morning, Christmas Eve. So he had, but to someone's else's discomfort. 'Tank' Chamberlain, who was the air attaché in Lisbon, had to explain very politely to a Japanese diplomatist, complete with thick glasses and typewriter, that unfortunately, owing to adverse weather conditions, extra fuel had to be taken on board and it would not therefore be possible to take him as well. While all Japanese and Chinese faces are deemed to be inscrutable, I somehow fancy I detected a gleam of jealousy in the eyes of this particular Japanese as, at three o'clock in the morning, he watched not only myself, not only my valet, but also the maximum amount of permissible luggage, being taken on board the seaplane without argument. For my part, I was glad to be spared the indignity of being off-loaded. It had often happened, I was told, that having got down to the seaplane base and being ready to board the aircraft, A was off-loaded almost at the last moment to allow B on board and, even nearer to take-off time, B was off-loaded to make room for C who had a still higher priority, the outcome for A and B being a taxi-ride together back to Lisbon.

I was not so sure I had been fortunate, however, when I saw the starboard outer engine propeller stop while we were going over the ocean. The pilot was determined to get home for Christmas and pressed on, even though we took fourteen hours instead of the usual eight or nine over the flight. By the time we were on the ground in England again it was dark and blackout time and a difficult drive from Poole to Buckinghamshire lay ahead.

With me was Ralph Eastwood, a King's Messenger, of whom I had seen a lot in Lisbon and whose wife, a lady doctor with a smart grey Bentley, known as 'Square-Faced Annie', I knew well from hunting with the Whaddon. Eastwood lived at Newport Pagnell so we shared a car from Poole to Weedon. We had hoped to get home by dinner-time but when we reached Oxford it was already half past eight. We had not much English money between us but we pooled all we had, some eighteen shillings, intending at first to eat within the limits of our money. I did not think much of this idea, for we were all ravenously hungry, it was Christmas Eve and we were back in England. 'Let's go to the best hotel,' I said. 'We'll have a slap-up dinner and a bottle of champagne to cheer us up and then we'll just hope they'll take a cheque. If the worst comes to the worst, we can only be arrested.' We went to the Mitre, enjoyed our food and champagne and got away with the cheque: there is nothing like a bold front when faced with adverse circumstances.

The next day, Christmas Day, 'Punch' came round to me from Bletchley for a first-hand report on all my activities. He seemed very pleased. I also returned to him in sterling the equivalent of the five hundred American dollars with which I had been provided before setting out. This surprised him.

'You needn't give it back to me,' he said. 'We don't want it back.'

'Well, I don't want it, either, thank you very much,' I said. 'I don't want to have it said I ever took a penny for what I have done.'

'Well, that's the first time I've gone back from seeing an agent with more money than when I arrived. I usually have to part with some.'

'Punch' asked me whether I had mentioned the work I had been doing either to my father or to 'the key person'. I told him I certainly had done nothing of the sort but that my father had warned me against doing this kind of work because he knew how I felt about being kept out of the Services and probably suspected that I was up to something. ' "If you are not doing anything for the British," he said to me, "then I do not see why they let you out of England so often." '

'Your father is no fool,' said 'Punch'.

I wanted to do other jobs for the Bletchley people but I was told I had already been to France too many times. 'If you go there too often, the Germans are bound to get you in the end.' The practice was to get new people—the most unlikely people among them—to do one or two jobs and then to discard them. (They roped in my sister to help at the other end, the Paris end, of the escape route I had organized. Her job was to see escaping British servicemen safely across the city, using public transport, before handing them over to another 'link' in the escape chain for the next phase in their journey to the south.)

I returned to my work of looking after the Gulbenkian interests, which were chiefly concerned with the I.P.C. interests whose headquarters were, of course, in London. I spent most of the rest of the war in England. I kept my cottage at Weedon; it was far enough away from the bombs and yet near enough for me to commute each day to London. I made it my home for the whole of the war and it was not until 1948 that I gave it up. Because petrol was short, I took up driving a pony to a rally cart or a pair of horses to a Bristol wagon. I drove from the cottage to Aylesbury station, took the train up to London and then drove back in the evening. That was how I first became interested in driving horses. I was able to go to friends who did not live more than ten miles away for lunch or dinner at the weekends but I have to admit I was more impervious then to the rigours of the weather; driving a rally cart can be a very cold drive, no matter how many rugs, wraps and capes one may have.

Marie shared my pleasure in driving horses—and still does. Throughout the war, she lived in London, in Chelsea Cloisters. She, too, had been convinced that war was coming and, for a year before the outbreak, she had trained to be a Red Cross nurse. She did a lot of useful work during the war and, during the thick of the air-raids on London, she manned a first-aid post. We saw as much of each other as we could.

Although my own work as a secret agent was finished, it did not mean an end to my acquaintance with other agents or with espionage in general. I went several times to Lisbon when my parents went to live there, staying there for three or four weeks at a time, and, without doubt, if you were looking for spies, then Lisbon was the place to find them. There were some people—one could scarcely call them spies—who made a good thing out of serving all countries impartially, people like Rapetti, for instance, the Italian head waiter at the Hotel Aviz. Rapetti made no secret of the fact that he did a profitable round after lunch each day, reporting on who was lunching with whom and recounting snatches of conversation he had overheard. He went to the P.I.D.E. (*Policia Internacional de Defensa d'Estado*), the Portuguese Secret Service, then to the German Legation, the American and British Embassies, and finally, from a latent sense of patriotism, to the Italian Legation. From each he received fifty escudos— then worth about ten shillings—a day. None of them minded that his information was not exclusive but it had to be accurate. He became very skilful at reporting objectively on what had happened and restrained himself from the natural inclination to embroider on what he had seen or heard.

Portugal's neutrality made Lisbon highly attractive to spies but had its frustration for others, among them a certain British Military Attaché there. I remember a luncheon party at which this man, a colonel, was complaining, ostensibly to me but really at a Portuguese general across the table from us.

'Really,' said the colonel, 'the Portuguese are supposed to be our oldest ally, but you would never know it here—they're far more concerned about staying neutral. Do you realize I've been here for months now and I still can't get in to see either the Minister of War or the Chief of Staff or the General Commanding, Lisbon? I can't get in to see any of the people I ought to have contacted.' The Portuguese general who was listening, as he was certainly meant to do, said nothing and I merely nodded.

'The other day,' the colonel went on, 'I thought I was going to be allowed to inspect the School of Cavalry—they'd promised me that—but what happened? At the last moment, they changed their minds and I was taken along instead to see Nuncio's horses— you know, the bull-fighter.'

'Very interesting,' I said.

'Well, yes, I admit it was,' he said, 'in fact, I enjoyed riding his horses very much, but that's not the point. I think the Portuguese are very silly not to see me—I believe I could help them.'

'You could help *them*?' I said. 'In what way?' Speaking even more obviously for the benefit of the Portuguese general, he explained.

'I have made a special study of the defence of Athens,' said the colonel. 'Don't you see that the defence of Athens poses essentially the same problems as the defence of Lisbon, in other words the defence against a land attack of a capital city built on hills, with access to the sea? I am sure from my study of the Athens defences, I could give them some extremely valuable advice.'

The Portuguese general spoke for the first time, in a quiet voice.

'Do tell me, my dear colonel,' he said, 'the war moves so quickly these days, you understand, and one isn't always able to keep up with it—do tell me, who is now in Athens?'

The Portuguese undoubtedly found neutrality profitable. They were very canny and coined money from both sides. It was Portugal's good fortune to be one of the few sources of uranium and this was a situation they happily exploited, allowing the British and the Germans to bid against each other, not so much for the sake of getting the uranium for their own uses, but to stop the other side getting it. The effect was to push up the price of uranium to astronomical heights and Portuguese peasants were selling their houses because they were built of stone which contained uranium.

Portuguese neutrality survived the war and, unlike Athens, Lisbon did not fall into German hands; there were those, however, who were fully prepared lest it should do so. All through the war, in the private yacht harbour at Alcantara, a sailing yacht of about twenty tons remained moored. It had an auxiliary motor and was always kept fully provisioned against the day that either the German army overland or German parachutists came to occupy Portugal. It was small enough not to attract special notice and fast enough to make a rendezvous with a larger ship after two or three days. It was a getaway boat for the American agents in Lisbon.

My parents left Vichy to live in Portugal when Iran was brought into the war on the Allied side in September 1942. It is amusing to recall that my father's strong inclination when he had to leave Vichy was to go to Switzerland and that it was I who urged him to go to Portugal; I am not sure I have had much gratitude from the Portuguese authorities for that. My father knew Switzerland as a civilized and comfortable place; I was the only member of the family who knew anything of Portugal, which was apt to be

considered, then, as the end of the earth. I pointed out that
Portugal had a better climate and that it offered at that time
more creature comforts, and that, unlike Switzerland, it was not
encircled: should the need ever arise, I said, it would be much
easier to get away to America. Unintentionally, the Swiss Minister
in Vichy added his weight to my persuasions. When he was
asked by his Government what he knew of my father, who had
made enquiries about the possibility of taking refuge in Switzerland, he made a very guarded report. Calouste Gulbenkian, he
said, was an Armenian financier whose business affairs had
international ramifications and while he was undoubtedly a very
wealthy man, no one knew exactly what he did or how. His
attitude was similar to that of a high authority in England, whose
disposition towards our family was not a friendly one, and who
said of the Gulbenkians that they were 'very sharp'. 'Papa is
sitting in Vichy in case the Germans win,' he said, 'and little
Nubar is sitting in England in case the Allies win—so whatever
happens, they will be on the right side.' It seems almost a pity to
disappoint people like that but I fear our movements were not
worked out in this case with any such cunning calculation.

When my parents left Vichy, they were treated with the greatest
courtesy by the French authorities. They were given petrol for
their cars and a special railway van was put at their disposal to
transport special effects which they wanted to take out of the
country with them. The French were very apologetic that they
were forced by circumstances to ask people, who had lived in
France for so long and were so well regarded there, to leave the
country.

In Portugal, my mother and father settled in hotels. Mother
had a suite with her maid at the Palacio in Estoril, which was
quieter than being in the centre of Lisbon, while Father had a
suite on the first floor of the legendary Aviz Hotel. It has since
been pulled down but it really was a fantastic place, reminding
one of Hollywood. It had been a private house and was now run
as a hotel by the brothers Ruggeroni, the two sons of the house.
They were Gibraltarians and staunch supporters of Britain and,
throughout the war, refused to take in either Italians or Germans.
This sometimes caused them a bit of trouble because, as Portugal
was neutral, they were not allowed to discriminate, but with the

small number of rooms it was not difficult for the reception manager to say the hotel was full; occasionally a German slipped in, however.

The hotel had only about thirty suites, each bedroom had its own bathroom and nearly every room had, too, a sitting-room. The maximum number of guests the Aviz could accommodate was about fifty and servants outnumbered guests by two to one. It was a place of unrepentant luxury. It had a large hall with a carpet into which one's feet sank and which felt about six inches deep. There was also a gate, ten feet high, with two large golden eagles on either side of it. The gate looked as though it was made of wrought iron but, on closer inspection, it proved to be of wood.

My mother used to come up to Lisbon two or three times a week and Father used to go out to Estoril about as often, so they probably met once a day. There were also quite a lot of important social engagements, which they attended together. Father hated these but, when it meant getting in touch with either high Portuguese officials or members of the American or British Embassies, he overcame his inherent reluctance to social life and played his part.

The routine of Father's life in Lisbon during the war was much as it had always been. He was called at about eight o'clock in the morning, read his mail and his papers and did his exercises and his toilet. He used to have massage and do twenty minutes' physical jerks. Although my father looked after his health and observed a well-regulated routine based on his own experience and on the advice of the best medical men in France, England and Portugal, he could not be called a hypochondriac. He never indulged the idea that he had an illness or that anything was wrong with him; on the contrary, he had a very strong will-power and he always said he felt young and well and would not tolerate the suggestion that he was ill in any way. (At various times, in my younger days, inspired by admiration of my father, I started doing physical jerks in the morning but I am afraid that at the end of a few weeks the amount had dwindled and its timing had become irregular until I finally relapsed into laziness. On the other hand, I have always taken more violent exercise in the form of riding and hunting and golf—for the pleasure of it and not solely for the sake of my health.) Then, after a rest, he dressed and came down. By now it was midday and time for his walk, usually in the outskirts of Lisbon but possibly at Estoril. He was taken there by car, a hired car. He did not have a chauffeur of his own because his French chauffeur had refused to leave France and he now found it much less bother to hire a car, paying a weekly or monthly sum, than having to cope with a chauffeur and his lodgings and the garaging of a car. He always had a good car but not an ostentatious one; not a Rolls or Cadillac but an American car of the calibre of a six-seater Buick. He was careful as ever to avoid waste. In the car there was a little book in which, in the morning and at night, when he had finished with the car, the speedometer reading was recorded and, thus, he was able to tell how many kilometres he had done. He was very careful not to pay for any additional use of the car during his absence. He did not check the book every day but the chauffeur always knew that he might.

For his staff in Lisbon, my father started with his Oriental chef, his two valets and the faithful secretary, Madame Theis, who used to accompany him in the car. He also took with him a folding chair and, after walking for perhaps an hour, he settled down in the folding chair, working, with his secretary, in the open air. He found it more and more difficult, though, to find a private spot, for people learned of his routine and he was generally surrounded by a crowd of small children. In principle, he would never refuse any of them a small coin but eventually, for his own comfort, he had to strike a bargain with them. They could stand around while he worked if they wished, he said. When he had finished, if they had made no noise, he would give each of them a coin; but, if any one of them disturbed him, then none of them would get anything. The children organized their own police system to protect their interests.

Gradually, the time at which Father was taking his lunch became later and later until, at one period, he was lunching at about three o'clock. That made life impossible for anyone who was with him and, ultimately, he realized it; he allowed my mother and me to lunch at the more normal hour of one or thereabouts, although we had coffee at his table with him. My father was a public curiosity in the Aviz restaurant because, being a small man, he had had a platform built in the corner of the room to give him elevation. Later, when (much against his will) his rows with the oil groups had become public property, 'Mr. Gulbenkian at the Aviz Hotel' was considered one of the tourist 'musts' of Lisbon, along with the monastery of the Jeronimos and a Portuguese bull-fight. He objected very strongly to that but there was nothing he could do about it. He usually lunched alone, or with his devoted secretary. Even when he entertained he did not like to have more than one person, either someone with artistic knowledge, such as John Walker, the Chief Curator of the National Galley of Art in Washington, or Kenneth Clark, who was director of the National Gallery in London during the latter part of the war, or one of the Portuguese experts, or an important business associate passing through Lisbon on his way to the U.S., the Middle East or Occupied Europe, whom he always contacted to find out what was happening elsewhere.

Portugal, for all its virtues in wartime, had at least one small disadvantage—the Portuguese language. My mother never managed to master it. I was staying with her on one occasion at Busaco, a country town about a hundred miles from Lisbon, known to history as the place where one of the grimmest battles of the Peninsula War took place but which has a marvellous hotel where during the last war people went to spend the summer.

She invited three cronies to take tea with her in her sitting-room. The tea arrived, including some rolls, but no butter. She summoned the waiter.

'Butter,' she said in English. '*Du beurre*,' she said in French. He showed no sign of understanding.

'*Burro*,' she said in what she thought was Portuguese. The waiter left the room. After she had waited some time and no butter had arrived, she became angry and called the waiter again. She repeated her order and once more the waiter went away. After another long wait, her telephone rang. It was the *concierge*.

'The *burro* is downstairs,' he said.

'I don't want to go downstairs for my tea,' said my mother, by this time very angry. 'I want the *burro* brought up here.'

'Madam,' said the *concierge*, 'we can't bring the *burro* up in the lift—it might be dirty.' It was some further time before Mother realized that *burro* is Portuguese, not for butter, but for donkey.

My poor mother who had always been hard of hearing was by

now very deaf, as Herman Baruch discovered to his embarrassment. Baruch was American Ambassador in Lisbon from 1945 to 1947, a most striking man, six feet six tall, with a white goatee beard and a somewhat cultivated resemblance to Uncle Sam. He was then a widower, very wealthy, fancied himself a great man with the ladies, surrounding himself with pretty secretaries and engaging a very attractive young woman to teach him Portuguese. Baruch entertained lavishly at the Embassy, but made a point of getting all his food and drink in from the United States, so that he should not be accused of aggravating such shortages as arose in Lisbon at that time. My mother was sitting next to him at the Embassy dinner table when Baruch told her in a quiet voice the story of the two lions outside the Capitol in Washington which are said to emit a very loud roar every time a virgin passes by. Mother could either not hear or not understand and asked him to repeat the story. He did so in a louder voice. Again, she asked him to repeat it. By now, he had almost to shout what had been intended as a rather *risqué* aside.

Baruch enjoyed himself as Ambassador but served his country conscientiously. One morning, I happened to telephone a friend of mine at Lisbon airport but was unable to speak to him because a special charter plane of the Crown Prince of Saudi Arabia had been diverted there with engine trouble. I gathered that the Crown Prince was going on his first official visit to America. I mentioned the incident to my father who told Baruch, of whom he was a good friend, a man with whom he loved to discuss business and other things. Neither Baruch nor anyone else among the Embassy staff had heard of the Crown Prince's journey to Washington or of his diversion to Lisbon. Although it was a weekend and the military and air attachés were playing golf, they were hauled back from the golf course, ordered into their uniforms and, with Baruch and my father, they paid an official call on the Crown Prince at the Palacio.

Baruch gave a dinner party that night at the Embassy for him and his entourage. The Crown Prince gave Dr. Baruch a gold-encrusted dagger as a present; in return, after some anxiety about finding something suitable, Baruch offered the Crown Prince the imposing, high-backed, canopied chair in which he had been sitting at dinner as guest of honour. The Crown Prince accepted it gratefully, on the condition that Baruch would arrange to have it shipped to Riyadh, the Saudi Arabian capital. This was difficult, for there were no scheduled shipping lines from Lisbon to the Red Sea; but it was eventually arranged. It was my father, however, who suggested to Baruch the necessary last touch.

'Before the chair is sent,' he said, 'you must have it heavily coated with gold leaf.'

I enjoyed my visits to Lisbon both during and after the war. Before the city began to spread, the countryside was near at hand for hacking; the air is beautiful, the view, from the hills overlooking the Tagus estuary and the sea, magnificent. I enjoyed, too, the highly cosmopolitan company, including that of so many of the exiled royal families of Europe.

There was Umberto of Italy who had been King for a few weeks; there was Admiral Horthy, the Regent of Hungary for the period between the wars; there was the Pretender to the Spanish throne, Don Juan, with his very charming family: his son Don Juan Carlos, who was a small boy then, very fond of riding and swimming and playing practical pranks on everybody, and who is now being groomed to take over from Franco; his young brother, Don Alphonsito, who died tragically, being shot accidentally by his brother; and his two sisters, of whom the elder, Doña Pilar, was a special favourite.

There was also Madame Magda Lupescu, not royal by birth, but royal by her eventual marriage to the former King Carol of Rumania, who had created her Princess Helen. Marriage would anyway have entitled her to be called Princess Magda of Hohenzollern but she wanted to be called Princess Helen of Rumania. (Was it to spite King Carol's first wife, who was born Princess Helen of Greece and who divorced Carol?) She achieved this by marrying King Carol on what was supposed to be her deathbed. The marriage took place in Brazil where, after a 'miraculous' recovery, she managed to get the Brazilian authorities to issue a resident's permit to her in the name of Princess Helen of Rumania and not in that of Princess Magda of Hohenzollern. Armed with this, she went to the Swedish Legation there, who were in charge of Rumanian affairs, and asked them to issue a passport to her. Faced with the *fait accompli* of the resident's permit, they had no option but to issue her a passport in the title of Princess

Helen of Rumania, a dignity to which she has clung tenaciously ever since. I found her a very intelligent as well as a good-looking woman. Conversation with her was always a great pleasure for she had had a large experience of life—both before and after her marriage—and she displayed a deal of wit in the way she recounted it.

I must jump ahead, briefly, to 1955 to recount the high peak in the life of the exiles in Lisbon, when Princess Maria Pia, the daughter of Umberto, the last King of Italy, married Prince Alexander of Yugoslavia. Royalties and ex-royalties flocked from all parts of Europe and there was wonderful rejoicing. The guests were asked to appear in morning coats, top hats *and* decorations; this caused one unkind person who had not been invited to the ceremony to compare it to an ex-Servicemen's parade in Whitehall. The wedding took place in a little church at Cascais; I was among the comparatively few who could be invited there. The ceremony was marred, however, by the fact that all the priests had cameras and the altar was almost overrun by photographers shooting the processions coming up the aisle and the ceremony itself.

Several hundred other guests were asked to the reception afterwards at the Palacio. Soon after the bride had cut the monumental wedding-cake with a sword, her veil was torn to shreds by guests who wanted small pieces of it as souvenirs.

Only sixteen people were invited to the family lunch in a private room. The Belgian Ambassador, Baron Suzette, representing King Leopold, the uncle of the bride, was one of these; his wife was not invited and she had to eat with the hundreds of other guests. I had to try to console her and, after a plateful of lobster, cold turkey and foie gras, she felt much better.

Like my father, I had cause for a particular private hate against Hitler. Between the two wars I had had great pleasure in building up a collection of wines. My wine merchants employed a Mr. Bamberger to go around the country making sales on their behalf and also buying wines from the cellars of people who had died and whose executors were selling them. When a big cellar came up for sale, there were often odd lots in it—say seven bottles of one wine, a dozen and a half of another, two of a third wine, many of them unlabelled—which were to be had at a very cheap price because no wine merchant would take them into his stock, not knowing quite what he was buying. I commissioned Mr. Bamberger to pick up any such odd lots for me. As a result, I had a wonderful heterogeneous collection and I had a lot of fun, from time to time, with kindred spirits, opening a bottle of my latest purchase. Sometimes it was as undrinkable as ink or vinegar, especially if it was a very old wine. On the other hand, I sometimes found myself in possession of a wonderful wine which was quite impossible to get elsewhere and which, having been undisturbed for decades, was in a remarkable condition.

My collection, which amounted to about a thousand bottles, was stored by my wine merchants, Mayor, Sworder and Co., in Budge Row, Cannon Street. During an air-raid on London in in May 1941, a bomb hit that cellar. What wine was not destroyed by the bomb was consumed by the fire; what escaped the fire was ruined by the firemen's hoses; what escaped them served as well-earned refreshment to the Salvage Corps. None of which could be helped but the consequence was that Hitler had deprived me of priceless wines at a time when wines were unprocurable in England and my 1000 bottles or so would have seen me comfortably through the rest of the war. I lodged a claim for compensation under the War Insurance Acts and, fairly quickly, was paid over £1000. I mention the figure to show the average quality of the wine for, in those days, £1 a bottle was a great deal of money to pay wholesale for wine. The £1000 I received should have been a consolation to me but it was really pretty cold comfort because I could not drink—or offer my friends to drink—the increase in my bank balance.

11
La Folie Gulbenkian

As SOON as things began to return to something like normal in France, my mother went back to Paris, to live again in the house in the Avenue d'Iéna. She had not liked Portugal much; apart from her difficulties with the language, she found Lisbon society was too confined for her taste. Paris was still suffering from power-cuts which put the lifts in the house out of order; my mother, who was now in her seventies, had to work out her routine so that she was on the ground floor during the cuts.

Father kept his base in Lisbon, partly, I think, because for tax purposes it was more convenient to have his domicile in Portugal, but also because he was in a comfortable rut and did not wish to get out of it again. He came back to France once or twice a year, at one time for a few weeks, at another for months. His movements did not conform to any set pattern; he was likely to spend the winter in Portugal and the summer in France, either in Paris, or, at the height of the summer, at Deauville, where he had acquired quite a large property called 'Les Enclos' or, to give it its local name, 'La Folie Gulbenkian'. This was actually an amalgam of a number of adjoining properties which he had bought in the 1930s to give himself a self-contained estate of a little under 100 acres.

Gulbenkian's Folly became a show-place. My father engaged Monsieur Duchene, the highly reputed garden architect who had replanned the gardens at Blenheim between the wars. Without question, Duchene was a most able man and possessed of a rich creative imagination; what he lacked, at any rate when dealing with my father, was any sense of the value of money. Beside the beauty of his artistic ideas, the cost was, to him, an irrelevance. He thought nothing, for instance, of spending hundreds, even thousands, of pounds to move one huge tree six feet in order to achieve a perfect alignment.

There were occasions when my father, however much he admired perfectionists, had to restrain him. There was, for instance, the bomb-proof gun emplacement, made of reinforced concrete, which the Germans had built during the Occupation. It stood on high ground and spoilt what was otherwise a wonderful view of the sea and the surrounding countryside; what was worse, the Germans had built it so well it was impossible to blow it up. When my father told Duchene to find a way of concealing it, the architect proposed transplanting a forest but even my father jibbed at that one and Duchene had to devise some less ambitious form of camouflage.

Father was very fond of that garden; he felt it was something he had actually created. He had been especially proud before the war of a forest of small but very valuable pine trees he had imported at great expense from, I believe, northern Europe. They had been laid out in geometrical patterns and if they had been allowed to grow up they would have been very beautiful. The Germans, however, cut them down and used them as Christmas trees and this provoked in my father the deepest, if not the most enduring, feelings of hate towards Hitler and the Germans.

There was one rather ludicrous aspect of Les Enclos: there was no house in that huge garden for my father to live in. There were several nice houses in which an average person would be very happy to live and where people like his agent and head gardener did live, but not a big house such as he wanted. He did talk about building one for himself but he never made his mind up where to put it. At one moment, he thought of having one on the high part of the property but he gave up that idea when he was told it would probably be too windy there. As a result of his indecision Duchene, the architect, had the difficult task of laying out the gardens so that they would be related to several possible focal points where a house might be built. Father spent at most a few weeks at Deauville each year and when he did so he made the Hôtel Normandie his headquarters. From the hotel he drove to Les Enclos, taking with him two folding camp stools, one for himself and one for his papers, so that he could sit in his garden and admire the view while he also attended to his business affairs. He liked to go down to the lower part of the property, where there was a small pond, to watch his animals, peafowl, ducks and all sorts of farmyard animals, which had to be very well looked after. I do not say their claws were manicured but it almost came to that. My father had to acknowledge some small embarrassment at the amount of money he spent in accommodating his peafowl in specially built and very ornate houses. The cost ran into several million francs but he did manage to justify it to himself by saying all the money came from war damage claims. This was quite true, for the property had been very badly damaged during the Occupation and he was entitled to reimbursement for money spent on restoring it.

Naturally, my mother wanted to see Les Enclos but, for one reason or another, she never got there; she died without ever having seen it. Today, it is one of the assets of the Gulbenkian Foundation and some of the Foundation Trustees have found a nice use for it as a luxurious retreat for themselves, their families and friends to enjoy Deauville in the season; it is one of the 'perks' my brother-in-law, Kvork Essayan, for example, as one of the Trustees, enjoys for his family. Mark you, my father's executors have been very economical. They have cut down the number of gardeners at Les Enclos from the sixty he employed during his lifetime to a mere forty!

In Lisbon, the routine of my father's life was much as it had always been, although the amount of time he spent over his physical jerks and the distance he walked was becoming shorter and shorter. But he still lived in the Aviz, he still had his special table in the dining-room, he still attracted swarms of small children when he worked in the open air and he still preferred to hire a car rather than run one himself.

I was now able to stay in Lisbon for much longer periods than during the war and my father seemed more anxious to have me with him. As before, I stayed either at the Aviz in Lisbon or at my mother's hotel—while she was still in Portugal—at Estoril. I preferred staying at Estoril because, as my father was never ready for discussions with me until twelve o'clock or sometimes even until after lunch, I had my mornings free and it was easier to go bathing and riding from Estoril. I generally lunched alone at about 1.30 and by the time I had finished lunch my father was ready to start his; in the evening I had dinner with one or other of my parents.

Even after I had married again and my wife was with me in Lisbon, we still stayed in an hotel, at Estoril. I suppose it could be said it is a Gulbenkian tradition to live in hotels. It may be more expensive (it probably is) and one may not have the comfort of living among one's possessions, apart from a picture or two or a favourite carpet, but it is more in tune with our restless Oriental background. Buying a house went against the grain for my father and although he had his large house in Paris he preferred, on the whole, to stay in hotels. He did think more than once of buying or renting a house in Lisbon but he never got beyond thinking about it. Similarly, whenever I go for a holiday, even an extended one, it hardly ever occurs to me to hire a place or to buy one but rather to live in an hotel, remunerating the staff generously in return for making a damned nuisance of myself, but having no bother or responsibility. After Marie and I were married in 1948, we lived at the Ritz in London.

I had none of the same difficulties with my parents over my third marriage as I had had with the first two. True, there was one moment after the war when my mother, an inveterate match-maker, told me she had found a girl of pure Armenian descent and background whom she considered a suitable wife for me.

'As I've managed to find my own wives up to now,' I said to her, 'I think I can manage to do so again.'

'I am not sure I agree,' said my mother. 'Considering you did not do so well with the first two perhaps you ought to let someone else do it for you this time.'

I felt, as a man of fifty, it was a bit late in the day for an arranged marriage. Although I did not actually refuse to meet the girl in question I skilfully avoided doing so and my refusal to marry her was accepted by both my father and mother without any emotional scenes. My mother had known my third wife-to-be, before the war, when Marie was still married to the father of her two boys. My mother liked her. Both she and my father came to appreciate that Marie was very devoted to me, was not of a 'scheming' nature and had an easy temperament; her manner was straight-forward and open. We were not able to tidy up the matrimonial position until after the war but when I told my parents of my intention to marry her they agreed without any fuss and bother. We were married in the Armenian Church in London. It was a very simple ceremony, attended by my sister; my wife's 'champagne' brother, Richard de Ayala; her sister-in-law; the Iranian Ambassador and his wife; Mr. Hacobian and, of course, my 'permanent' best man, Tommy

Frost; certainly there were no more than a dozen in the church. Afterwards we went to lunch at the Ritz. The head waiter wanted to put my wife in the chair next to mine, as is the custom with all newly-weds, but I thought it was a bit late in the day for that and not a little ridiculous; I sat opposite my wife, placing the Ambassador on her right and the priest who had married us on her left. My sister, very sweetly, kissed Marie on both cheeks and said, 'Welcome, my dear, into a very difficult family.' They have remained on very good and intimate terms ever since.

It was a pleasant change to have a wife of whom my parents approved and whose relations with them not only started off by being good but improved as time went on. Marie showed a lot of consideration and affection for my mother when we were in Paris. She spent a good deal of time with her, playing bezique and talking about clothes, jewellery and similar feminine interests in which my mother's pleasure never flagged.

One day in June 1952 my mother telephoned Marie, who was staying with me at the Hôtel Georges Cinq.

'Come quickly, quickly,' she said, 'it's very urgent. I want to show you something.' My wife dropped everything she was doing, took a taxi to the Avenue d'Iéna, wondering what on earth had happened.

'What is it?' she asked my mother, who was smiling when they met and looking anything but perturbed. 'What's the matter?'

'I said I had something to show you, my dear,' she said, 'and so I have. Look at this.' With great pride, she showed my wife a rather beautiful three-emerald brooch from Cartier's which my father had given her for their diamond wedding anniversary.

With my father, too, Marie always succeeded in saying the right and soothing things and, later, when he was ill, her Red Cross training came in useful for, now and then, she managed to arrange the pillows or bandages and make him a little more comfortable; he reckoned she made a better job of it than his professional nurses. Sometimes she used to sit half an hour or more with him, when he was in a semi-coma and when he felt that her presence was soothing to him.

There was a real, practical need for my frequent and prolonged visits to Lisbon, for almost to the end of his life my father was involved in the development of the oil resources of the Middle East and in his personal struggle with the giant oil companies. The war itself had had little effect on the Gulbenkian interests for, once the German threat to the Middle East oil-fields had been dispelled, production had really got going again. By going to live in Portugal, a neutral country, my father was no longer an 'enemy' under the Act. This meant that he was able to claim full compensation for the oil which the other companies in the I.P.C. group had taken during the war and to get virtually all he claimed, but not without prolonged negotiations. The French were less fortunate, for they had been labelled 'enemies under the Act' right up to the end of the war and they received only a derisory settlement of their claims.

But the war did bring about one development which threatened the Gulbenkian interests—and that was the strengthening of the ambitions of the American oil companies to expand their stake in the Middle East. From before the First World War and right up to the start of the second war Britain had undermined the dominant position of France in the Middle East and the Levant and had done it fairly successfully. Now the Americans started to do exactly the same thing to the British position. They were impeded, however, by the farsighted arrangements my father had made just before the first war and which had been confirmed by the so-called Red Line Agreement of 1928, the Agreement which said that none of the partners in the Iraq Petroleum Company could act independently inside what had been the Ottoman Empire. Strictly and faithfully applied, that Agreement could have precluded the Americans from taking an interest in Saudi Arabia, and so, quite bluntly and ruthlessly, but with the best of big business good manners, they set about trying to pull down the edifice conceived by my father.

They took up the attitude that as it was they who had won the war—which, by and large, is what the Americans say about all wars in which they have been connected, remotely or otherwise—the American oil companies should have greater freedom in the Middle East.

Mr. Sheets, of the Socony Company, and Orville Harden, a vice-president of the Standard Oil of New Jersey, came to London. Their two companies were the only survivors of the six American ones which had been shareholders of the Iraq Petroleum Company in 1928 and, though I could not be sure precisely what they were up to, I had a fairly good general idea. However, I had other matters to attend to in Paris. I flew there in a special plane for discussions with Victor de Metz of the C.F.P. I went first to our office in the Avenue d'Iéna where I was told that an agonized Mr. Hacobian had been trying to get me from London.

Ten minutes after my plane had left London, he had received a call from the two American oilmen, asking us to meet them; they had an 'important communication' to make, they said. Mr. Hacobian had gone to see them. The U.S. State Department of Justice, he was told, considered the Red Line Agreement of 1928 a restrictive agreement, contrary to American anti-trust legislation; therefore, they could no longer feel themselves bound by it. The Americans are a generous people but they are also people with a strong business sense and, as a nation, they are generally able to defend their commercial interests on ostensibly moral grounds. They had already offered compensation to Shell and B.P., the two British partners in the I.P.C., in the shape of long-term contracts and other arrangements for the protection of their interests; now the pressure was on the French and ourselves.

I went to see de Metz. I warned him I had news of some startling developments but proposed that we should deal first with the business for which I had originally flown to see him. This took about an hour or so, at the end of which he sat back, relieved, and said: 'Well, now, that's settled—what's this startling news you want to tell me?'

'Simply,' I said, 'that the whole basis of your participation and our participation in the Middle East has gone. The Americans have abandoned the 1928 Agreement. What do you think of that?'

De Metz took the news very calmly. The only comment he made was, '*On va voir.*'

However, he had no intention of waiting upon events. It was then eight o'clock in the evening. He sent for a secretary.

'I must go to London by the first plane in the morning,' he said. That was not possible and, for a time, it seemed as though we should be fog-bound in Paris; but the fog cleared and we were both able to attend a meeting in London the following day. The Americans were pushing for quick agreement. I protested that the big groups should not gang up against any one of the members of the I.P.C. Where there is a conflict of interests on an important matter like this, I said, we should surely work for a compromise settlement we can all accept. This had always been my father's approach.

Negotiations went on for years. At first, the French sided with us but they were under heavy threats from the others. The French wanted a lot of oil quickly for the benefit of their own economy; the only company in which they had an interest at that time was the I.P.C. and their partners threatened to hold up development in Iraq unless they fell into line with the American proposals. The French Government were watching jealously all Victor de Metz's activities on behalf of the C.F.P., the French company. General de Gaulle, who was in power in that immediate post-war period, before his voluntary exile to Colombey-les-deux-Églises, became angry when he heard that the I.P.C. was producing only a relatively small amount of oil and the French were making little progress in their claims for their share of the wartime production. He issued a series of peremptory instructions that the matter must be dealt with forthwith. Eventually, the French were persuaded to agree to the American demands; that left the Gulbenkians on their own.

We were determined to defend our rights under the 1928 Agreement, if necessary in the law-courts. Indeed, what would have been a world-famous lawsuit was prepared with Cyril (now Lord) Radcliffe, for so many years my father's friend and adviser, acting as our counsel. The preparation of this action went ahead concurrently with negotiations to end the dispute. The attempt to break the deadlock was initiated by Robert Cayrol, another good friend of our family. He approached me and suggested that, without binding, on the one hand, either his Company, the C.F.P. and the other Groups, or on the other, my father and our interests, we two should get together and see whether we could hammer out some sort of compromise.

We were both busy men so that most of these discussions took place at the end of the business day. Cayrol used to come round at about seven o'clock—to the Ritz when I was in London or to the Georges Cinq when I was in Paris—and we would have a good dinner together. There was no question of ice-cold negotiations but very friendly ones in which we sought a solution acceptable to all parties; true, we were careful to drink the same amount of wine to ensure parity. Session by session, we worked gradually towards a basis for agreement until at last we reached the stage at which we felt it worth while to bring in the others. We agreed to meet in the Aviz at Lisbon and to the Portuguese capital came Cayrol, accompanied now by his 'caravan'—as the representatives of the other Groups were called. I had informed my father fully of the proposed settlement, of course, and most of the details had been agreed before the meeting in Lisbon. Nevertheless, the lawsuit was still going forward and it was touch and go whether the case would open in the Law Courts in London before agreement was reached formally in Lisbon.

The clearing up of outstanding points in dispute was finally achieved. Now it was just a matter of getting the Agreements typed —they were quite lengthy ones—in readiness for a formal signing ceremony. We timed this for seven o'clock—seven o'clock on the Sunday evening. The lawsuit was due to begin the next morning in London. Once the Agreements were signed, telegrams could be sent to London to stop the action going forward; I had ordered dinner in a private room at the Aviz to celebrate the signing.

It was at five minutes to seven that father found one more point which had not been covered by the Agreements. Until that point was covered, he said, he would refuse to sign. To say there was consternation on the faces of all the men gathered there would be a piece of English understatement. But father was determined. Telegrams must be sent to London where the unfortunate Boards of the Groups involved had been kept waiting on tenterhooks for news that the Agreement had been signed. Now they must consider a new point and, in turn, send telegrams to Lisbon giving their acceptance or otherwise of the latest Gulbenkian demand.

The necessary wires were sent from Lisbon and we knew it must take some hours before we could expect replies. There was no sense in going hungry; dinner had been ordered for the celebration, so we sat down to eat it. There were some twelve of us at that table, all men, with the sole exception of Cayrol's wife: Cayrol had come to Lisbon in advance of the others and she had come with him. No doubt she had looked forward, as indeed I had, to a gay, convivial evening, but if ever there was a gloomy occasion, that was it. The meal was accompanied by long periods of silence, for no one felt inclined to make the conventional efforts at conversation when all our minds were turned to what might then be going on in London.

I realized hardly anyone was drinking, either, and my impression was confirmed the next day when I settled the bill for the dinner: just one bottle of champagne had been enough for twelve people.

It was after midnight when we received the replies from London: they agreed to father's last point. The unfortunate secretaries had to start typing hard once more so that we could still get the Agreement signed in time to call off the lawsuit. It was something like two o'clock in the morning when, finally, everything was in order. Father signed.

'Now then,' I said, 'let's have the champagne we didn't have at dinner and really celebrate. This, after all, is an occasion.' Everyone agreed but, unfortunately, the Aviz staff had gone to bed, the cellar was locked and there was no champagne. So, instead, we sent out to an all-night café and celebrated on sandwiches and cheap wine.

This was the Group Agreement of 1948. It was Morry Bridgeman, the present chairman of B.P., who said at the time, 'We have now succeeded in making the Agreement completely unintelligible to anybody.' Similarly, Sir Geoffrey Cross, q.c. (now a judge of the Chancery Division of the High Court), who had been a Gulbenkian counsel in these negotiations, said, 'No one will ever be able to litigate about these documents because no one will be able to understand them.' Geoffrey Cross, a man with a bald head and a twinkle in his eye, was one of the few counsel (Cyril Radcliffe was another) who was prepared to see his client's point of view even though the solicitor might not agree with it. He did not take the short-cut favoured by so many of his colleagues who say, in effect, to their clients: 'I am the great I am, Queen's Counsel, etc., etc. What you say is wrong, what I say is right and, if you don't agree with me, you must be stupid.' He would try to put the client's point more clearly and forcibly than the client could himself and then, if it was wrong, to demolish it to the client's own satisfaction.

Under the Agreement the Americans were free to go into and develop Saudi Arabia but the much more rapid development of Iraq oil was also assured. One of my father's chief fears had been that the Americans, for all their righteous talk about 'freedom' and 'competition', would expand Saudi Arabian production and deliberately restrict that of Iraq. As far as the Gulbenkian interests were concerned, apart from profiting from the increased production from Iraq (which meant of course a proportionate increase in the value of our 5 per cent holding), we were given as well a 'special allocation' of oil. This meant that over and above our 5 per cent we should receive a few hundred thousand tons of oil worth a few hundred thousand pounds a year more to us.

That was by no means the only time when the Americans' pursuit of what they considered their legitimate interests endangered the Gulbenkian interests and those of the British and French companies. There was the extraordinary proposal put forward by Mr. Sheets, of Socony, also very soon after the war, when I went to see him and Orville Harden about more general matters of world oil policies. Mr. Sheets, whom I can only describe as an American of the Americans, had what he described as 'a wonderful idea' to keep the Russians sweet politically. He said they should be given a share of Middle East oil and that should be done by building a pipe-line from the Kirkuk oil-fields across the mountains of the Caucasus into Russia. Such was the naivety of the Americans—and it was certainly not confined to Mr. Sheets or the oilmen—just after the war. This particular scheme was firmly squashed by the British Foreign Office but it gave the other oil interests some anxious moments.

Another example of the way the Americans were ready to promote their own interests at the expense of what they privately called the 'effete' British was to be seen later on when Mossadeq (who was no stranger to the American Ambassador in Teheran, Dr. Henry Francis Grady) nationalized the Iranian oil industry. The result of his activities was not merely to oust the Anglo-Iranian Oil Company, the British Government and the writer of these lines, to say nothing of inconveniencing His Imperial Majesty the Shah; nor was it only to give his country a much larger share in its own wealth than it had before: the ultimate outcome was also to place the running of the oil industry in Iran into the hands of a consortium in which, curiously, the American companies have a 40 per cent interest, the Anglo-Iranian another 40 per cent, the Shell have 14 per cent and the French (C.F.P.) managed to get 6 per cent.

My father and I regretted the upheavals in Iran which resulted in our losing our status as Iranian officials but they had no real effect upon us and there was little we could do about it, anyway. What I had not expected was to be asked to help the Mossadeq regime.

That is what happened after they had tried, without success, to sell the nationalized oil throughout the world. Early one morning at the Ritz, I received a telephone call from Teheran asking me to take charge of the sale of the whole of the Iranian production. The caller offered me almost any financial inducement or social advancement I might care to name. I thanked him courteously and told him that, naturally, I was highly flattered. I promised to consider the offer most carefully and to let him know the result of my considerations as soon as I had reached any. I went on 'considering' it for some three years until Mossadeq was finished, the Shah was back, the consortium had been formed and oil was flowing again.

Although both my father and I were rather hurt at the summary way in which we had been dismissed by the Iranian authorities, if only by a temporary regime, there would have been no difficulty in our resuming our positions after the Shah had returned to power. But my father could not forgive the slight, as he considered it; he refused to take up his position again and he forbade me to do so, either. I obeyed him while he was alive but when, after his death, I was asked once more to rejoin the Iranian Embassy in London, I accepted with pleasure.

Political upheavals in the Middle East are rather terrifying at first sight to those who have large investments there but my own analysis of the situation as a whole leads me to two conclusions. First, the governments and people of the Middle East must eventually have an increasingly larger share of their own wealth and the days of the capitalist entrepreneurs are coming, no less inevitably, to their end. My second conclusion is that, generally speaking, the Middle East authorities are not yet technically qualified or equipped to take over the running of the oil industry, particularly not the disposal of the oil throughout the world, and therefore, whatever upheavals and revolutions there may be, capitalists can temporarily allay their fears by realizing that it will be some time before the final eviction. What happened to Mossadeq in Iran, and what happened in Mexico a few years before, is good proof of this.

I well remember talking to Nuri Pasha about this and his saying, 'Gradually you will become well-paid contractors for the Government, but the bulk of the profits will come to us.'

It is only fair that capital should be remunerated because, if it is not, it will not take the risks. It is also true that, in a civilized society, one must abide, by and large, by the sanctity of contract. On the other hand, there is a case for a limit to the remuneration of capital. Before shedding tears over the fate of the capitalist entrepreneurs, including my own family, we ought to look at certain figures. From 1914 to 1953, for instance, the Gulbenkian interests never had more at stake in the Middle East, at any one time, than between half a million and one million pounds. Since 1955 alone, the Gulbenkian interests have been drawing something between five and six million pounds a year on that investment and it follows that the oil groups are making the same relative profit on their investment as the Gulbenkian 5 per cent. Those with interests in the Middle East who look ahead must know that, though their investment is one which must gradually disappear, even now any money put into that area of the world is generally amortised within a year or two and remains a good investment while it lasts.

It was not until after the war and after Deterding had died that there was a rapprochement between my father and the Royal Dutch Shell. It was chiefly due to John Loudon, the aristocratic Dutchman in charge of the Dutch end of the Group (and, since 1957, the senior managing director), who realized how silly and damaging the row was. Loudon is a 'Jonkheer', one of the few hereditary Dutch titles, but one which he never uses. He is a great gentleman with charming manners and a moral sense of what a position like his entails. He looks upon it as one of great responsibility, not only to his shareholders but to the world at large; this, of course, does not stop him from being a very sound and tough business man when the occasion demands.

The rapprochement took place as the result of a meeting in Lisbon. Joe Boyle, one of the directors of the Royal Dutch Shell, turned up in the Portuguese capital and went to see my father, as though merely to pass the time of day.

My father asked him, out of courtesy, 'How long are you staying in Lisbon, Mr. Boyle?'

Boyle was not a man who could dissemble for long and he answered, 'That all depends on you, Mr. Gulbenkian.'

He explained that the Royal Dutch Shell Group were reorganizing their various interests in Venezuela and they could do so only if they obtained the whole of the capital of the V.O.C., which meant chiefly the holdings of my father and General Aranguren, who each had three or four hundred thousand shares. (The extent of the General's holding was not realized at the time and everyone was under the impression he held no more than 100,000 or 150,000 shares at most. The balance did not appear until the takeover was complete.)

The Group offered to exchange the V.O.C. shares, which were standing at about £4 on the Stock Exchange, for Shell shares. My father refused to exchange paper for paper and said he would be willing to sell his shares for cash—the price being £6, the current price of Shell shares. He made a condition that the same offer must be made to General Aranguren, who had been his ally in his fight against the Group's handling of the V.O.C. for over twenty years. The General telegraphed back saying the shares were worth about £10 and it was quite wrong to accept the offer at such a low price. When my father decided to sell out, however, he followed suit.

These negotiations took some three or four weeks and, for all the efforts made to keep them confidential, rumours started to fly and the V.O.C. shares went up from £4 to £4 10s. When I was in London, I was bombarded with enquiries from people who wanted to know what to do. We had recommended V.O.C. shares for over twenty years and had been responsible for their buying them. The public had been our loyal supporters and had given us their votes at various shareholders' meetings over the years. We had always told them the shares were worth much more than the price at which they were standing because of the fact that they were not receiving the proper price for their oil. Once that was put right, we said, their value was bound to go up.

I was faced with a moral problem. On the one hand, I could not allow people, who had trusted the Gulbenkians, to sell out their shares at £4 10s., when I knew quite well that in a few days they would be offered £6. On the other hand, I did not want to let fall the slightest hint of what was going on. I managed, for some time, to dodge the questions with which I was bombarded until, finally, I was asked, 'Look here, are you selling any of your shares at the present price, after the big rise?' When I replied 'No', some people jumped to the conclusion that V.O.C. shares were worth buying and bought shares for themselves. I was blamed for this. But, to this day, I still do not know what was the proper attitude the

Gulbenkians ought to have adopted towards the people who looked to them for protection. At lunch recently, I entertained three men of vast experience and eminence—John Loudon, Head of the Royal Dutch Shell Group, Hugh Kindersley, a director of the Bank of England, who had faced a similar dilemma, and Lord Chief Justice Parker, a member of the Bank Rate Tribunal. I asked them what they would have done in my position; each of them recognized the dilemma and each of them said he would have done as I had done. The practical answer is that, when there is a takeover bid in the offing, it must be made public at the earliest possible moment to prevent the leaks and rumours caused by delay. In the end, the Gulbenkians got out of V.O.C., after a row stretching over more than twenty years, with a ten-million-dollar profit.

Although the Gulbenkian interests suffered no permanent damage from the war, my father could not forget that the British had declared him 'an enemy'. It rankled with him right up to his death and was responsible, I am sure, for his taking his pictures away from the National Gallery in Trafalgar Square and sending them to Washington. At one time, he had considered building an annexe to the National Gallery, a project to which he had been prompted by the Gallery's very go-ahead and diplomatic Director, Sir Kenneth Clark. My father's relations with Sir Philip Hendy, who followed Clark as Director after the war, were not as friendly as they had been with Sir Kenneth. Sir Philip always felt, quite rightly, that his duty, with the limited space at his disposal, was to show all the pictures, no matter where they came from, along with those of the same school already in the Gallery. My father, on the other hand, was most anxious that all his pictures should be kept together as a sort of Gulbenkian Bequest. But the relationship between Sir Philip and my father was a wholly correct one and their difference of opinion over the disposition of his pictures was certainly not the chief reason for them being sent to Washington. That happened as the result of a series of circumstances and despite the attempts of people like the Earl of Crawford and Balcarres and Cyril Radcliffe to dissuade my father.

He finally took that decision as the result of a visit to Lisbon by John Walker, then Chief Curator of the National Gallery of Art in Washington. Johnny Walker, who had been left very lame by polio, was a charming man who got on very well with my father. (He had married Lady Margaret Drummond, the Earl of Perth's sister, who retained her British nationality so that in the U.S. she could still keep her title as Lady Margaret Walker.) The American Ambassador, Dr. Baruch, gave a little dinner party for my father and myself and Johnny Walker. After dinner, we saw a colour film of the National Gallery in Washington; Johnny Walker had brought it with him to Lisbon especially for the purpose of showing it to my father. Walker recalled the story of how the late Andrew Mellon had been persuaded to build the Gallery by Duveen. Mellon had wanted to build it of limestone; Duveen said only marble, which would cost at least $5 million more, would be good enough. They took a ride around Washington in a car to discuss it. Duveen won. 'Thanks for the ride,' said Mellon. 'It has been the most expensive ride of my life.' Even then, Walker recalled, Mellon, who shunned ostentation, decided to use Tennessee marble because it did not look like marble.

Johnny Walker's film, a most attractive piece of work, did the trick. He was able to impress my father with 'the artistic and handsome manner' in which the 'children' would be housed. The pictures went from London to Washington.

On the evening of the 30th of June 1952, only three weeks after her diamond wedding anniversary, my mother had a dozen or so people to dinner at the Avenue d'Iéna. I was told afterwards how happy and gay she looked and how well. At the same time, I was in London and my wife and I had given a largish dinner party at the Ritz, for perhaps eighteen or twenty people. Our party, too, seemed to be a success, the food, wine and service leaving nothing to be desired and everyone enjoying themselves.

At eight o'clock the following morning, I was awakened by a telephone call from Paris. It was my brother-in-law, warning me of bad news; he suggested I should call my wife so that she could be next to me while he told me. As she had gone to bed tired and was still asleep, I said I would listen to the bad news on my own. He then told me that my mother had died about half an hour before. It appeared that she had called in one of the nurses who was in constant attendance upon her, but the nurse had only just had time to waken my sister before, in a matter of minutes, my mother died from heart failure. She had suffered that summer from the intense heat but, though she was seventy-seven and perhaps too stout (being, like her husband and her son, fond of her food), it never entered my head or anyone else's that anything like this might happen.

I woke up my wife with the news and asked her to phone for reservations on an aircraft to Paris. Then we found our passports were in the country so we had to arrange for a servant to bring them from Hoggeston to the airport. Even so, we still managed to get to Paris well before lunchtime. There, at Le Bourget, my sister, Rita, was waiting for us; she, like my wife, was dressed in black, while I had on a dark suit but only a black armband over my light overcoat. As I saw her waiting there I remembered how my poor mother, with her unceasing maternal affection, had insisted on taking us in her car to that same airport only the previous week, when we were returning to London after spending some time with her.

With Rita, we drove straight to the Avenue d'Iéna. My mother was laid out on her bed; it was strange not only how peaceful she looked but also how youthful. My wife noticed there were no candles either at the head or the foot of the bed and she went out to buy the three tall ones appropriate to the occasion.

As always, at such times, there were many things to be organized, the most important of which was the breaking of the news to my father who had gone to Deauville. The doctor who attended both him and my mother feared that the shock of her death might prove fatal to him; he was unsure of the best way in which to tell him. Finally it was decided that my wife and I, accompanied by the doctor, should take the car immediately to Deauville, some 130 miles away, to break the news to my father as gently as we could. The doctor went up first to his suite in the Hôtel Normandie to see how he was and to prepare him as carefully as he could for the bad news. Then my wife and I went in. My poor father was shattered; he broke down and sobbed bitterly. Although, during the sixty years of their marriage, they had very often led separate lives, it was remarkable to see how much my mother's death meant to him. Happily, my wife, with her Red Cross experience and her affectionate nature, was there to soothe him. There were still many urgent matters for me to deal with; where and how my mother was to be buried, for instance, and when the funeral service should take place.

It was over this that my last serious disagreement with my father began, the one above all others I could wish to have avoided but in which I felt myself bound to behave in the way I did. It is sad and ironical that the feelings of affection we both had for my mother caused this last row. I always used to say that a man may have many women in his life—I suppose I have had, one way or another—but he will have only one mother and, after her death, I felt it behove me to see that her wishes were carried out.

My father wanted my mother's remains to be embalmed so that a suitable joint grave, which they would eventually share, could be prepared. He had no clear idea where that should be but he knew he wanted them to be together, in what must be the finest of mausoleums. I knew that was not what my mother wanted. She had left very clear instructions that she should be buried at Nice in the south of France, in the same tomb as her favourite brother, Yervant Essayan, and my old tutor, Monsieur Devgantz, who had been present at her birth and who had been attached to the Essayan family for something like seventy years when he died in 1940. My mother had made me promise that her last wishes should be respected but it was a heartbreaking situation for me.

My father had known of my mother's wishes before I recalled them to him but I think he had been hurt and disappointed by them; he was prepared to forget or to ignore what she had wanted. He was also hurt by my insistence at doing as she wished although, before I took my leave of him, he had reluctantly withdrawn his objections. I left the doctor looking after him and then my wife and I took the car back to Paris to make arrangements for the funeral at the Armenian Church in the Rue Jean-Goujon in Paris, the church built by the Armenian millionaire, Alexander Mantacheff, some half a century before.

Announcements of her death and of the funeral service were published in *Le Monde* and *Le Figaro* and, within an hour of the first publication, the callers started to arrive. In accordance with French custom, all the blinds, curtains and shutters of the Avenue d'Iéna were closed and Rita and I had to receive the callers in one of the darkened drawing-rooms. The first was an official of the Compagnie Française des Pétroles who said that the President,

Victor de Metz, would come himself in two hours' time. Then, in the stream of people who followed, came our good friend, Robert Cayrol. I appreciated the goodness of people like him in coming, but, my word, I felt tired. I had taken turns with Clarisse Genie, my mother's former lady's maid, who, as I have said, was over fifty years in our service, to watch over my mother's remains during the first night, but I was now both physically and emotionally exhausted.

The funeral service was an even more wearying affair. The church was really a bower of flowers; every inch of it, the walls, the altar, everywhere, seemed to be smothered with them. In accordance with French custom, the wreaths, huge ones, five feet across, with broad ribbons inscribed in gold with the names of the people who had sent them, had to be laid outside the church on the pavement, once no more room remained inside for the flowers. The church holds 200 people and it was packed full. Everyone my parents had known, my mother's own large circle of friends as well as my father's business acquaintances, had come themselves or had sent their representatives. The Iranian Prime Minister, who was on holiday in Paris, attended. So did a number of ambassadors. Two men, Victor de Metz and Sir Oliver Harvey, the British Ambassador, came in top hats, a rare enough sight at that time in France. My sister and I, accompanied by our respective spouses and by all the uncles and aunts who had come to the funeral, had to line up with our backs to the altar and, for about an hour, stand there and shake hands as every member of the huge congregation filed by, murmuring their words of condolence.

After the service, mother's coffin was taken to the crypt of the church and as many of the flowers as the crypt would hold were heaped around the coffin. The following day, a specially chartered Viking of B.E.A., the inside of which had been draped in black and converted into a flying mortuary chapel, arrived from London. My wife and I now accompanied my mother's remains in the aircraft to Nice; Rita was too tired and stayed in Paris.

At Nice, a macabre delay took place. We had ordered the best coffin money could buy but it was so much larger than the standard size that the hearse which came to meet the plane at the airport could not take it. While we were waiting for another vehicle to be found, the coffin, which could not be left in the broiling sun, was wheeled into the shade, but the only shade available was in a hangar. Mechanics in their greasy overalls were working there and the hangar itself was no different from any other airport hangar, full of oil drums and the like. I wonder what those mechanics thought of it all. There was I, trying to shade my wife and myself from the unbearably hot sun with the umbrella with which my valet, faithful as ever to the British tradition, had armed me. Near to us huddled an army of priests and ecclesiastics who had come to carry out the Armenian burial service.

At last, a lorry arrived big enough to carry the coffin to the cemetery and it was possible to hold the service. Afterwards, again in accordance with custom, my wife and I took the priest and a few other friends who lived in Nice to a private lunch in a private room at the Negresco. With us, too, was Agathon, an old Armenian crony of mother's, who had volunteered to come down in the plane with us from Paris to help with all the practicalities; shattered as I felt by now, I was only too glad of his assistance. I can only describe the lunch as lugubrious, although at another time the food would have given me much pleasure: salade Niçoise; mostelle, a fish very delicate in texture and somewhat akin to whiting; lamb cutlets and ratatouille. But I was in no mood to discourse on the merits or the demerits of the particular dishes.

My mother had not left a will. She had intended to some years before, when she had been seriously ill in Portugal, but my father had begged her not to do so. He was afraid that he would be pestered interminably by members of her family pressing their claims upon him; but he swore to her by all he held most sacred that he would see her wishes were carried out. As so often, she gave way to him and instead explained what she wanted to be done after her death. Just to make sure that nothing was overlooked, however, she wrote a letter to her favourite brother, Yervant, whose tomb she eventually shared, setting out what she wanted. She recovered from that illness—she had been very well nursed by my father in his usual efficient way, engaging the best doctors and nurses from England, France and Portugal—but her brother had died before she did. The famous letter, which came to be known as her Last Wishes, found its way back into her own possessions. When she died my sister, who is a most practical person, opened her cupboards and desks. Rita distributed her clothes and personal trinkets to my mother's sister and nieces, paid her maid the legacy she had been promised, and bought a safe to house all her jewellery. Then she produced the letter which was to cause so much trouble and bad feeling between my father and myself.

The letter, apart from containing her testamentary dispositions, also made scathing references to other people who had been very close to my father and who had thereby caused my mother great unhappiness. There were other remarks, too, which were, in my opinion, very very private, which I am sure she would never have wanted my father to see and which, if he had seen, would have caused him great pain.

My father heard of the existence of the letter and demanded to see it. He took the attitude that, as head of the household, he should see everything which even remotely concerned him or the household. My brother-in-law, Essayan, who had always done his best, in his quiet and humble way, to further his own interests, tried to get hold of the letter to show it to my father. I had a big row with him and another with my father, who was not to know or to understand that I was trying to protect him; my father saw only a disobedient son frustrating his rightful wishes. In the end, however, he agreed that my mother's jewels should be at the disposal of her children so that they could sell them and carry out her wishes.

Mother had little money of her own. She received a small dowry when she married and she had received a part of her parents' fortune when they died. Most of the latter went in maintaining my grandmother when she escaped from Turkey after the 1914-18 war; she was practically penniless because the Essayan property was in Turkey, Rumania and Bulgaria and was not realizable.

My mother had pocket money and a dress allowance from my father, of course, but all her expenses, like the expenses of all his family, were defrayed by him. As a matter of principle, her expenses, like everyone else's, were questioned and checked by him. The only way of raising the cash for the legacies she wanted to give to her surviving brothers and sister was to sell her jewellery. After we had done so and paid the legacies, a balance of some £18,000 remained.

This money was set aside to go towards meeting another of her last wishes. She had set her heart on building a school or orphanage

—she was not very precise about it—for small Armenian children of both sexes, where they could be taught the Armenian language, Armenian traditions and Armenian history and folklore. She was anxious to prevent them from becoming entirely assimilated by the countries of their adoption, as is tending to happen to the second and third generations of Armenians who have settled in America, France, England and other countries of the West, although their faithfulness to their Church and their respect for their old traditions has been a rallying point. (I have learned to speak Armenian fluently, though I read and write it with the utmost difficulty, and I know in London many young Armenians whose parents were born in England yet have kept their Armenianhood very strictly and very proudly. The Kurkjian family are a praiseworthy example; my cousins, Virginie and Krikor Gulbenkian, are another.)

My father wanted to take charge of building the orphanage but I insisted it was the responsibility of my sister and myself; while the argument was going on he was gradually getting older and weaker and, in the end, nothing much had been done about it. The orphanage will be built, however, with the £18,000 left over from the sale of my mother's jewels, together with $100,000 I managed to squeeze out of the Gulbenkian Foundation for this purpose, and another $15,000 a year for its upkeep. I am afraid I have had trouble with my sister and her husband about founding this institution but I hope the last difficulties will soon be smoothed over. I seem fated to have rows with the living to defend the wishes of the dead, which is probably a very Quixotic and unpractical attitude on my part. How different, indeed, from that of my sister and brother-in-law who have a very much more practical outlook and have done, relatively, financially much better as a result. Of that, however, as all the best authors say, more later.

12
'Leave it to Radcliffe'

FOR one year after my mother's death, my wife and I wore black and we took not a single meal in a public place. I had the dark bronze bodywork of my car painted black and the light fawn upholstery also suitably changed. (This car was one I called 'Pantechnicon', designed to my own ideas of striking out on a new line. The work had been done for me by Hoopers, Royal coach builders for a century and a half, as soon as new cars were available after the end of the war. Hitherto, motor-cars had been merely an adaptation of the old horse carriage; I felt that a modern car should be streamlined, curved and should look as though it had been designed by someone who had never seen horse-drawn carriages and had been presented for the very first time with the task of building a body around an internal combustion engine. Rolls Royce were less than enthusiastic about the way I had discarded their beautiful bonnet, modelled on the Parthenon, and I am sorry to say the effect I achieved, while certainly striking and distinctive, was not an unmitigated success.)

To change the colours of one's car into those of mourning or, as my father instructed, to use black-edged office stationery for one year, may sound faintly ludicrous nowadays, but these gestures were inspired by genuine feelings and were in accordance with old Armenian traditions, similar to those which then prevailed and still do prevail widely on the Continent. In England, I know, as soon as someone dies he is buried, generally privately, and the memorial service is reported in *The Times*; a few weeks later and you see the deceased's nearest and dearest carrying on his usual life, perhaps wearing a black tie for a while but with no other outward sign of mourning.

Frankly, I am shocked at this but probably I am thought to be slightly ridiculous, in England, for my views. My own sister laughs at me because, ever since my mother's death in 1952, each year I have attended services held at her tomb in the cemetery at Nice on the 1st of July, the anniversary of the death, and at the beginning of January. So far, I have not missed one. My sister says it is a waste of time, a morbid display of grief and a form of self-advertisement; she has steadfastly refused to attend these services, even the one marking the tenth anniversary of our mother's death. We must agree to differ.

From the day my mother died, father started going steadily down; he was a broken man. Whatever ironical people may say or think, he was deeply attached to her in his patriarchal fashion, an attachment which was not qualified by the fact that he lived his life in his own way. It was very sad to see a man, who had been intellectually so brilliant, gradually weakening and sinking. At first, my sister was with him in Lisbon and I spent much of the time in London looking after the office and conducting the negotiations to dot the i's and cross the t's of the 1948 Group Agreement, which had laid down the basis of future developments in the Middle East. I maintained the closest touch with my father, however, and more and more he wanted the apple of his eye near to him—especially when his daughter, of whom he was also fond in his way, refused to spend the first Christmas after her mother's death with him. She did not get on very well in Portugal and she had become bored with living there. Father still had his staff, of course, including his very devoted private secretary, Madame Theis, who had been in his service for twenty years or more, but he wanted his family about him and most of all he wanted his son, despite the many disagreements we had had, including the most recent one over mother's Last Wishes. My wife and I were called—'summoned' is probably a more appropriate word—to his bedside and there we remained, virtually until his death.

We did manage one good break, a visit to Morocco in 1953. We sent out the car and a station wagon with the luggage by boat and we took the plane from Paris to Casablanca. Morocco, in those days, while the French were still in control, was a country of wonderful contrasts. The French had been very wise; they had built new modern towns about a mile away from the old Arab ones, new towns with wide boulevards and fine modern buildings, rather reminiscent of the Middle West of the United States. The Arab towns had been given drainage and were kept clean but the picturesque buildings, the very narrow streets and the clamorous bazaars, were left as before.

In Casablanca, I called on the various people who had been asked to help me and received their guidance on what and what not to do, on where visitors were welcome and where their cameras, at any rate, were not.

In Marrakesh, I had my first camel meat. The hump of a young camel is quite a delicacy but it needs to be stewed and made into a *tagine* with sweet and sour sauce and raisins, vegetables, pimentos and spices. Moroccan cooking is very good, though somewhat specialized; it does not resemble the other cooking of the Orient, neither Egyptian nor Greek, Turkish nor Persian. But the mixture of flavours is even more intriguing. Relatively simple dishes like the *pastilla*, a mixture of puff pastry, raisins, vegetables and meat, made in a circular receptacle with a conical lid of basketwork, gave me much pleasure. The customary drinks are, of course, black coffee or mint tea with a lot of sugar.

Marrakesh is a really beautiful city on the edge of the desert, its main tower, the Koutoubiya, the Mosque of the Scribes, standing out at a great height against the skyline, resembling the Tour Hassan at Rabat and the Giralda in Seville, having been built by the Al Mohads in the twelfth century.

We motored down to Agadir (later to be destroyed in the 1960 earthquake) and from there down to the far south of Morocco, nearly on the border of Spanish Rio de Oro. We went there to see the so-called Blue Men, whose name comes from the indigo they use, partly as a dye for their clothes, partly as an ornament to their bodies. We watched their women dancing a variant of the general Oriental belly dance: they did it kneeling. Its origin, we were told, was that it was performed in a tent where the men-folk watched, while reclining on cushions and carpets on the ground.

In the walled city of Ouarzazate, with its very imposing Casbah, full of dark rooms and earth floors, we were accosted by a personage in Arab dress who insisted on being our guide. He took us to his home, which was really a hole in the wall. We felt somewhat apprehensive. He gave us mint tea and showed us a large bowl containing visiting cards.

'All the famous people I have received,' he said. 'See.' Sceptical, I picked out a card at random: it was that of Patrick Balfour, now Lord Kinross, whom I knew very well as a member of my club.

The letters of introduction I had brought with me from Paris assured me of every sort of kindness and generosity. When we arrived in Marrakesh, for instance, the Pasha, the famous El Glaoui, who was Berber ruler of the Atlas Mountains and for years the supporter of French influence against the Arabs in the northern part of Morocco, was away. He knew of my arrival, however, and with true and lavish hospitality immediately sent me a present. My wife and I were upstairs in our apartment in the world-famous Mamounia Hotel when the concierge called us.

'Monsieur,' he said, 'there is a present here for you from the Pasha.'

'All right,' I said, 'please send it up.'

Five minutes later, there was a discreet knock at the door. An Arab in a flowing burnous came in, leading two little figures swathed from head to foot in black.

'Yes?' I said. 'What is it you want?'

'With the Pasha's compliments, monsieur,' said the Arab. 'He sends you two of his young dancing girls—he knows you will enjoy them.'

I knew I had to accept this present from a fellow Oriental, for it would have been a great insult to have refused, but what on earth could we do with them? I gave suitable baksheesh to the messenger and, after much salaaming, he retired—leaving us with a pair of dancing girls. I couldn't help remembering Mr. Jorrocks saying, 'Confound all presents wot eat' and wondered what he might have said about this present. My wife looked a little old-fashioned at me.

'We've got to keep them,' I said. 'We must.' She went on looking at me in the same way.

We kept them for a week. Luckily, they did not have very large appetites but, when the time came for us to move on, my wife put her foot down; she refused to continue our journey with this addition to our retinue.

'But we've got the station wagon as well as the car. There's room in the station wagon for them as well as the valet, the maid and the luggage. We could easily stow them in the back.' My wife shook her head firmly. Nothing doing!

'You must get rid of them,' she said. 'I don't care how but somehow they must go.'

Easier said than done. I could not send them back to the Pasha; it would have been heartless to turn them out on the streets; I knew of no one who could look after them properly and nor could I send them to an orphanage, for the only orphanages were run by Catholic Sisters. (I feared that the Sisters might have tried to convert them and this could have led to trouble in that part of the world.) Finally, I consulted the concierge, always a great help when in doubt.

'But, monsieur,' he said at once, 'if you will give me but twenty-four hours, I can sell them at a good price. After all, it is true they are second-hand, but they have been in the Pasha's harem.' The concierge was as good as his word. I was assured that the purchaser was a wealthy notable in the district, who had a good reputation for the way he treated his dependants, so I let them go without any twinges of conscience. The proceeds I gave to charity.

To be near my father, my wife and I stayed in Portugal for months on end. We made our home in the Palacio hotel at Estoril so that we could manage to have our own life as well as fitting in with father's wishes. Of course, when he became very ill, it could involve waiting around from lunch until six or seven in the evening before he was well enough to see me. The periods during which we could talk together became shorter and shorter, from half an hour down to five minutes or so. By then, he was wholly bedridden, kept alive by the constant attention of the best doctors and nurses and by the administration of the most modern drugs.

As he became more and more ill so he relied more and more upon my advice. He was always very generous in his praise of my business ability, and, in the last years of his life, he never took a business decision without first consulting me about it, nor one with which I was not in accord. While he was still well enough this meant walking with him, in the Bois when we were in Paris and, in Lisbon, in the Parque de Monsanto outside the city or up and down the terrace of the Aviz. Father never was an office man, he hated sitting at a desk, and he did as much of his business as possible walking with people in the open air: he discussed all his problems in that way.

He sought my advice on other matters, too. It was in 1953 that the British Government, on the prompting, I believe, of Cyril Radcliffe, offered him the K.B.E. This was the same time at which Jack Hobbs and Gordon Richards received their knighthoods. As soon as he heard the news from Nigel Ronald, the British Ambassador in Lisbon, he rang me up; I was in London at the time. He wanted my views. I told him that, in his position and at his time of life, it would look slightly ridiculous to be called Sir Calouste Gulbenkian. 'Sir Five Per Cent' did not sound right, either. He was happy to find that my opinion coincided with his own and, just as before the first war he had refused to entertain the idea of a peerage, so he turned down the K.B.E. Cyril Radcliffe had probably thought of the K.B.E. for him because the Portuguese Government, only a short time before, had given him the highest rank of the Order of Christ of Portugal. My father had wanted to decline this honour, also, but his Portuguese friends had advised him that, as he was living in the country, a refusal would look bad; he agreed and he was invested with the insignia of the Order at a private ceremony. No such considerations attached to the offer of the English honour and he spent a long time with the British Ambassador drafting a very courteous and respectful letter asking to be excused from accepting it.

Lord Radcliffe of Werneth, as he became in 1949 when he was made a life peer (in 1962 he received a viscounty and took the title of Viscount Radcliffe of Hampton Lucy), was perhaps the one other man, besides myself, whom my father implicitly trusted, at any rate during the last ten years of his life. He had discussed with him, as he had with me, the idea that had been forming in his mind from before the Second World War of leaving the bulk of his fortune to be the basis of a world-wide charitable Foundation, something which would be similar in scope to the Rockefeller or Ford Foundations in America or, on a much smaller scale, the Nuffield Foundation in England. Father had a great desire to ensure 'continuity' after his death—the continuity of the Gulbenkian family and of the Gulbenkian business and fortune. He contemplated Lord Radcliffe sitting 'in his chair' after he had gone, in supreme direction of the Foundation, acting in his name as he would have acted himself. I think he imagined himself looking down on us all with a benign eye.

Lord Radcliffe has the finest legal brain England has seen for over a hundred years. He is the first person since 1887 to go straight from the Bar, not to the High Court, not to the Court of Appeal, but to the House of Lords. He has been appointed chairman of one Royal Commission or official inquiry after another;[1] his powers of examination, exposition and expression are alike remarkable for their quality of lucidity. He came into the Gulbenkian orbit when he was a young junior counsel and was called in to help to advise on one of the various facets of the Gulbenkian activities. Father took a great liking to the young man, a liking which developed into friendship. In my action against the B.B.C. in 1962, Lord Radcliffe himself, giving evidence on my behalf, described his relationship with my father in these words: 'I was for many years his legal adviser when I was at the Bar. It ripened into personal friendship. Of course, when I ceased to be at the Bar, I ceased to have any formal legal relationship with him, but he regarded me as a friend and a consultant and adviser on many general things affecting his position, and I admired him very much. He was a very remarkable man, with many personal ways of great brilliance, and I was very fond of him.'

For my own part, I was not only very well aware of my father's intentions regarding the disposal of his fortune after his death but I was also entirely in agreement with them. I was quite happy to think that the bulk of his vast fortune should be used for charitable purposes and happy, too, that the responsibility for deciding how and where that charity should be dispensed should rest not upon me, not upon any one man, but upon a Foundation.

Father drew up his first will in 1950, when he was eighty-one. In it he gave expression to these intentions in the broadest terms but

1. Lord Radcliffe was appointed: Chairman of the Punjab and Bengal Boundary Commission, 1947; chairman of the Royal Commission on Taxation of Profits and Income, 1952; Constitutional Commissioner, Cyprus, 1956; chairman of the Committee of Inquiry into the Monetary and Credit System, 1957–9; chairman of the Committee of Inquiry into Security Procedures and Practices, 1961; chairman of the Tribunal of Inquiry into the Vassall Case, 1962.

it lacked any detailed indication of how the Foundation should be set up and administered. He said he 'relied on the family to realize the spirit of his wishes.' He also dodged all attempts to make him become more definite by putting the responsibility on to Lord Radcliffe. 'Leave it to Radcliffe,' he used to say, or 'Cyril Radcliffe will look after that.'

After the death of my mother and with his awareness of his own failing health, my father recognized the need to give more precision to his wishes. In June, 1953, he made a second will. I had known all about the contents of the first will; I knew less about the second.

I did know, however, that it gave firmer, but, as it transpired, insufficient definition to the kind of Foundation he wanted and that it named the initial trustees: Lord Radcliffe as the Chairman with the supreme direction, Kvork Loris Essayan, my brother-in-law who was also my father's confidential clerk and maid of all work, and Dr. José de Azeredo Perdigão, the local Portuguese lawyer, who had drawn up the will for my father. I was not named as one of the immediate trustees. The provisions of this will, the terms in which it was drawn up and the way in which my father's wishes for the Foundation were set forth in that document, have been the cause of much argument and controversy ever since his death. So far as I am concerned the argument remains unresolved and it has been the main purpose of these later years of my life to demonstrate that, since his death, my father's fortune has not been used as he would have wished and his Foundation has not taken the form he envisaged for it. But, if I am to explain why I believe that to be so and if I am to hope that I can persuade readers to my view, I must first return to my narrative and, in doing so, introduce and briefly characterize three men who have played a large role in this latter part of my story.

During those years when my father was in decline he looked more and more to 'his team' to run his affairs. This 'team' consisted of Mr. Hacobian and Mr. Denton of the London office, Charles Percival Law Whishaw, a London solicitor, Kvork Essayan and myself.

Charles Whishaw was born in Russia, as his father, grandfather and great-grandfather had been; his mother, a charming lady devoted to her son, was a German. After leaving Russia the family had gone first to South America, where his father had been in business since 1911, and later, in 1915, settled in England. Whishaw himself had been called to the English Bar. He never practised, however, as he gave up the idea of so doing before finishing his year as a pupil. Then he became a journalist, joining, in an editorial capacity, that rather dry publication, the *Law Journal*, but rarely contributing thereto. That sort of journalism offers very limited progress, either social or financial. Whishaw asked to be disbarred[1] and passed the necessary exams to become a solicitor which, I imagine, with his intelligence, he found no difficulty at all in doing. It was as a solicitor that he came into the Gulbenkian sphere. After the V.O.C. row, the firm of Freshfield, Leese and Munns—now called just Freshfields—became chief solicitors to the Gulbenkians. The senior partner at the time was Sir William Leese, who was solicitor to the Bank of England. He died in 1937. Leslie Peppiatt (a relation of Sir Kenneth Peppiatt, Chief Cashier of the Bank for fifteen years and whose signature used to appear on Bank of England notes) joined the firm in 1935. It was now the firm (and not the individual, as it had always been until Sir William Leese's death) which became solicitors to the Bank.

A member of this firm looked after our affairs. At first it was Duncan Smith, to whom I have referred earlier; when he died his place was taken by Cyril Nisbet who, though perhaps not possessing the brilliance or great experience of Duncan Smith, was very sound and conscientious and helped us very well. Nisbet was an officer in the Naval Reserve and he joined up immediately on the outbreak of war, giving gallant service throughout its duration. It was arranged that, while he was away, Leslie Peppiatt, by now the senior partner of Freshfields, should look after the Gulbenkian affairs. Peppiatt found, however, that these affairs took up a great deal of time and so he engaged Charles Whishaw, then a young man of under thirty, to help him. Whishaw was also called up soon after the outbreak of war, as a cavalryman. He knew a great deal about *haute école*, though whether this was of much help in the days of mechanized cavalry is doubtful. His call-up lasted a matter of minutes, as he had been reserved on Leslie Peppiatt's urgent request. He was released at once and returned to Freshfields, his 'reserved' status being granted no doubt because

1. In England it is not possible to be a member of the bar and a practising solicitor.

of the national importance of his firm's work for the Bank of England.

It was now that I met him, a man of average height, very thin, with a very long, cadaverous face and piercing eyes behind large glasses. I had to explain to him the intricacies of the Gulbenkian affairs. This was a tedious business although Whishaw, with his keen intelligence, grasped first the essentials and then the details with remarkable agility. After the fall of France it was arranged for him to represent the Custodian of Enemy Property in whom the Gulbenkian assets were vested. Inevitably, I saw a lot of him during those days and that, plus the way in which his mother, who was devoted to him, used to come and see him off and commend him to my care when we went together to Lisbon, induced in me a sort of fatherly interest in his progress and in his general well-being.

It might be said that my father gave an even more convincing demonstration of concern for his welfare—by going to gaol for him. That happened in Lisbon during the war. Father had reserved a room at the Hotel Aviz for Whishaw but, when the solicitor arrived, he was told he would have to be lodged in a neighbouring annexe because the greater part of the Aviz had been requisitioned by the Portuguese Government to provide accommodation for a visiting Spanish mission. My father felt that he himself had been slighted and became more and more angry, kicking up a fuss with the management, with Portuguese officials, with anyone who might conceivably have had any hand in the arrangements. In the end, the management reported the disturbance and the dispute to the police who quickly solved the difficulty by taking my father off to gaol to cool his heels and his temper. It is said—though this may be a piece of embroidery—that he was pushed into a cell with a negro and a murderer. He remained there only a few hours for his faithful secretary, Madame Theis, contacted the head of the Egyptian Legation in Lisbon, Fakhry Pasha, a good friend of my father. Fakhry Pasha, who was *persona gratissima* with the Portuguese authorities, appealed for my father's release and they readily agreed; he went himself in his car to the gaol and rescued my poor father.

This may or may not have increased my father's affection for Charles Whishaw (in fact he was quite philosophical about his experiences afterwards) but he did certainly respect his ability, an ability which I did my best to bring to my father's notice. What my father found less attractive about Whishaw was his anxiety, as an employee of the Bank of England's solicitors, to conform and to see that all his clients conformed, not only with the letter but with the spirit of the host of regulations which the Bank, as an agent of the Treasury, promulgated during the war. Whishaw's preoccupation during and after the war—in the circumstances a very natural one—was to avoid the risk of incurring the displeasure of the authorities in any way. A striking example of this—which could also have been a very expensive example—was his interpretation of what the Exchange Control regulations did or did not allow concerning the use of what were called at the time Heinz's 57 varieties of Sterling. There was one particular, very involved transaction my father contemplated which, put very simply, involved the use of some currencies to pay off sterling liabilities. My father's obligation to contribute to the development of the I.P.C. was a continuing one and involved large sums; hence the importance of the kind of currency transaction I have mentioned. I had read the regulations carefully and I had no doubt of the legality of what the Gulbenkians proposed to do and I was glad to be confirmed in my opinion by Cyril Radcliffe who gave it as his opinion, in quite categorical terms, that we were within the law. He added that if the authorities disapproved they could pass overnight a new regulation under the Defence of the Realm Act to prevent the transaction going through. Whishaw was not convinced and still opposed the operation, urging that this transaction although legal was not the type of transaction in which the Gulbenkians should become involved. My father always used to say that he employed and paid generously the best professional advisers, lawyers, accountants, etc., in order that they should find legal means of carrying out his wishes and not be merely obstructive or find reasons why he should not do what he wanted. If Whishaw's advice had been taken my father would have been the poorer by a million pounds. But Whishaw's advice was not taken and the course approved by Radcliffe was; it was also approved by the Exchange Control authorities who recognized that the regulations should not apply to such transactions outside the U.K.

That was one of many arguments between the Gulbenkians,

either father or son, and Whishaw. More than once father considered dispensing with his services but he remained aware of his intelligence and his brilliance. He discussed Whishaw with Cyril Radcliffe, who told my father, 'Don't worry about him—Nubar keeps a good watch on him.'

Sooner or later, whether they were on their way, or returning from America, Occupied Europe or the Middle East, the important men of the oil world passed through Lisbon and my father made a point of contacting them, inviting them to take lunch with him at his special table in the Aviz. In this way, he remained remarkably well-informed, which in itself was the cause of a further row with Whishaw. From an American returning home from a meeting of the I.P.C. Board in London, he heard news of importance to us. It was news to me, too, when my father passed it on to me and that meant only one thing: that Whishaw, who had been present at that meeting (I happened to be absent) was not reporting fully even to me, no doubt because of what he considered to be his responsibility to the British authorities.

There was the occasion after the war, when Whishaw acted as our instrument of communication in negotiations between the Gulbenkians and their partners in the I.P.C. It was my father's practice never to press any claim to a breakdown but, very able negotiator that he was, to make his demands step by step, so that having obtained satisfaction on one point he would raise another and yet another, thus achieving all he wanted or, at least, much more of what he wanted than he would have obtained if he had started by putting forward all his demands at once. At one stage of these particular negotiations the Gulbenkians had manœuvred themselves, more by luck than judgement as it happened, into the position where their partners could not carry out a certain reorganization without our co-operation. As that reorganization could bring about a saving of some millions of pounds a year they were most anxious to get our agreement. Father insisted that, if this reorganization was going to result in such immense benefits to them, he was entitled to a share of that reward. He could have asked—and probably got—more than his legendary 5 per cent but he was content to stick to that as usual.

Whishaw went back from Lisbon and transmitted what he had been instructed to say to the other groups in the I.P.C. After much protestation they agreed to the Gulbenkian terms. In one of these discussions, John Loudon, of the Royal Dutch Shell Group, told Whishaw he hoped this was the last demand to come from the Gulbenkians. Whishaw said, 'Yes.'

My father was very annoyed and, in accordance with the practice I have described, the next set of demands was produced. Whishaw felt that his personal word was at stake. He said he would not be a party to making these further demands.

There was another row between Whishaw and my father. One morning my father and his trusted old adviser, Mr. Hacobian, called Whishaw into the Salon Rond at the Avenue d'Iéna. My father asked me not to be present, for he wanted, as he said, to give Whishaw a 'good dressing-down', but he also wanted to 'spare his dignity'. Twenty minutes later, Whishaw came out to me, literally in tears and in a state of great agitation. I tried to comfort him as best I could, reminding him that my father was a hard task master and sometimes spoke unduly harshly, and even unfairly, to his subordinates.

Whishaw was quick on the uptake and resourceful; he was persuasive and had a winning way about him, except when dealing with subordinates. I was probably guilty of unwise conduct in not pandering enough to his self-esteem and in not hesitating to impose my views on him when I felt that the Gulbenkian interests demanded certain actions by him. During his later years, as I have already indicated, my father would never take a decision against my advice, even if other members of the 'team' disagreed with me. This made membership of the 'team' somewhat frustrating, no doubt. There was many a clash when Whishaw tried to appeal to my father, over my head, but always unsuccessfully, especially as the other members of the team were usually loath to express an opinion at variance with mine.

During the last year or so of his life, when he was a dying man, my father gave me many counsels; one of them was: 'Be kinder and more tactful to Essayan and Whishaw. After all, when I am not here, they will be useful *Korzik* to you.' *Korzik* is an Armenian word which means a tool or instrument. It would perhaps have better served my father's interests and his wishes concerning the Foundation had I been more tactful with my subordinates.

Kvork Essayan, my brother-in-law, was another member of the

'team'. Kvork, or Kevik as he was called (Kevik is the diminutive of Kvork, the Armenian equivalent of George), is not just my only sister's husband but also my second cousin, which was the reason for his having married her. His paternal grandfather was a rich Constantinople banker, a brother and partner of my maternal grandfather, but whereas my grandfather died in 1900, his lived until after the first war. Kevik's grandfather had been a great gambler on the Stock Exchange; he lost the bulk of his money and fell upon evil times. What he had not lost on the Stock Exchange he had to abandon when escaping from Turkey just after the 1914–18 war; my father helped him on his arrival in London. Essayan's other grandfather was Abraham Pasha who played quite a role in Egypt in the period just after the opening of the Suez Canal in 1869, for he knew how to obtain and remain in the good graces of the Khedive, as the ruler of Egypt was then called. He and his brother-in-law, Nubar Pasha, who became the prime minister to the Khedive Tewfik, prospered hugely and Abraham Pasha's daughter, Anna Karakechia, became one of the most sought-after of Armenian heiresses. She married Vahan Essayan, Harrow-educated son of the then rich Constantinople banker. Kvork Essayan was their child.

Unfortunately, Vahan Essayan, like his father, was bitten by the gambling bug. Kvork used to tell me of how, as a small child in Constantinople before the first war, he used to listen outside the door of the family card room where huge amounts were won and lost. The Essayans escaped from Constantinople and arrived in London virtually penniless; Vahan could look to his wife's jewels as his sole worldly possessions. My mother, who could be very kind-hearted, took them under her wing. She managed to sell the jewels at Mappin and Webb's for some ten thousand pounds; this was a godsend to the Essayans, grandfather, father and, therefore, son, too. Vahan Essayan then conceived a good plan to retrieve the family fortunes: he suggested that his eldest son, Kvork, should marry my sister, Rita.

I do not think Kvork was very anxious to contract the marriage but his family impressed upon him that only thus could his ageing parents be rescued from their misfortune; being an Armenian, imbued with fear and respect for his parents, he agreed. As for my poor sister, who was just eighteen at the time this plan was put forward, she hated the idea. She protested to mother and father and there were many distressing scenes, with heart-rending tears on her side. There had been two young men with whom she had fallen in love. The first, Serge André, a member of a very wealthy French petrol family, however, did not reciprocate her feelings and married someone else. (He suffered from frostbite incurred in the trenches during the First World War and died at an early age.) The other man was Nicholas Misu, the son of the then Rumanian Minister in London, himself destined for a diplomatic career. (What I chiefly remember about him is that he played tennis of a high Wimbledon standard, exploiting a particularly devastating drop shot.) My parents did not approve of him as a prospective son-in-law. They foresaw, or feared, that if their daughter married a diplomatist whose family were not wealthy there would be constant demands for financial assistance. Then, too, as parents, they did not like the idea of their only daughter living with her diplomatist husband in various parts of the world far from her family. Besides, neither André nor Misu was Armenian, so my parents decided in their wisdom that the fellow you knew was better than the fellow you did not know and that, anyway, given the dependence of the Essayan family upon the Gulbenkian money, Kevik was likely to make a compliant son-in-law.

My sister refused even to kiss her future husband until they were married. She insisted, as the price of her obedience to her parents' wishes, that she should no longer have to practise the piano for three or four hours a day. She also said she would not marry Kevik unless she had a new dressing-gown. With typical Armenian frugality, from the time we were children, when I grew out of a dressing-gown it was handed down to my sister; she had never had a new dressing-gown of her own. My sister was always complaining about Essayan, but, as I saw it, there was no point in resisting what was bound to be; I tried to convince her that what could not be altered must be endured.

By and large, like the majority of arranged marriages, their marriage has been, in its way, successful. They have produced only one child, Mikael, who has turned out a very nice boy and to whom I have acted, during the Second World War, *in loco parentis*. (He is now happily married, with two children, to one of the Guinnesses, not the beer family but the K.L.G. Sparking Plug one.

There is no peerage in that branch of the family but at least my nephew's brother-in-law is a Bart!) It is remarkable perhaps that my sister and her husband have stayed together for so long, for Rita is very gregarious, enjoying people and parties, whereas he has no taste for social life. My sister tells a story of how, when they were first married, there was a rare occasion when Kevik had an evening free from work and they had been asked to a party to which she had looked forward very much. She went to her room and put on her best bib and tucker; then she went to Kevik's room to see if he was ready, only to find him in bed. That was too much for her, and she seized him by the throat and tried to throttle him but he still refused to get up and go out. Eventually, they found the best arrangement was for each of them to live his own life.

My father was always cautious and, before allowing an official engagement between Essayan and my sister, he placed Kevik on probation, as it were. He decided that his potential son-in-law should work in the Gulbenkian office so that he could train him on proper lines and at the same time discover any hidden defects which might not have come to light. Thus it was that young Essayan appeared at the office for his first day's work, complete with a little black moustache and a straw boater. The moustache survived until after his wedding but the boater was hastily suppressed and an immediate visit ordered to a proper tailor. Kevik was sent to T. and F. French (now Kilgour, French and Stanbury Ltd.) of Dover Street, who, for many years, had been making my father's clothes, as they had those of Lloyd George and George Grossmith, the famous musical comedy actor.

I must say that, from the beginning, Essayan did his best to curry favour in his father-in-law's eyes. He had to work very hard in a hard school where he was allowed no latitude. Nor could he rebel, as I have done from time to time. In the same way as I was expected to be beside the telephone at my father's disposal, morning, noon and night, holiday or no holiday, so was Essayan, but he had the larger burden of being at two people's beck and call, not only being attendant upon his terrifying father-in-law but also his 50 per cent as exacting brother-in-law. What Essayan complained of, but in a very small voice, was that my father and I could spend the day away from headquarters in whatever way we wished, whereas not only had he to stay at the office all day but was expected to be ready for calls in the evening to tell us what had been happening. He was, indeed, the guardian of the fort *par excellence* and this, apart from any disinclination, prevented him from making any social plans. My father's theory was that, if Kevik was kept with his nose to the grindstone, he would have no time to do foolish things, or things of which my father disapproved—which, in my father's eyes, came to the same thing. If there were jobs to be done which no one else wanted to do, they were given to Essayan, some of them delicate, some of them unpleasant. He was an ideal assistant and a conscientious one. He was not particularly brilliant and sometimes, as we all can, he made some silly mistakes. One morning he came into me, as proud as a peacock, having worked out a complicated business problem and anxious to show me his findings. The details of the matter are unimportant; enough to say that he had based his calculations on the prices for refined oil instead of for crude oil. I pointed out his mistake to him. He turned as red as a turkey cock, a physical characteristic to this day for he suffers from high blood pressure and excess of cholesterol. For years, I had only to look at him and say 'crude oil' for him to hang his head and turn scarlet. On the other hand, he was left, during the German occupation, to keep an eye on the family home in the Avenue d'Iéna and upon its priceless contents, and this he did very successfully.

Kvork Essayan inherited the family passion for gambling. He escaped from the harsh discipline of the Gulbenkian office to his studies of the genealogy of horses and dogs on which he staked what were, for a person in his position, fantastic sums of money. Sometimes he won and, even now, he has in his rooms a photograph of a Derby winner which came home at a long price with £100 of his money on it. Like all gamblers, however, he landed himself in trouble. He was afraid of confiding in me, though I should certainly have helped him; instead he went around borrowing left, right and centre from my father's business friends. Inevitably, this eventually reached my father's ears and there was the devil to pay—on two counts. One, that he should gamble at all, for my father so abhorred gambling that the only cards in our household were the two packs of patience cards my mother had. Two, that he should have so demeaned himself as to borrow money from father's business friends. (I saved him from being posted as a defaulter on the turf, for my father's first reaction was that, if Essayan were posted as a defaulter, he would never be allowed to bet on the horses again. When I pointed out that there were always greyhounds to back (apart from many other ways of gambling) and that, after all, in itself gambling was not considered dishonourable in England, father paid up.)

It may well have been in reaction to the conditions under which he worked that Essayan got into one scrape after another. Often, when in trouble with my father (but not when his anxieties concerned the outside world) he came to me, asking pathetically, 'Save me, Nubar, please save me.' Whenever I could, I did.

The third person I must mention and one who has played an unexpectedly important role in the story of the Gulbenkian Foundation was the local Lisbon lawyer, Dr. José de Azeredo Perdigão. Dr. Perdigão, a very tall man in a country of small people, had the reputation of being a most astute lawyer and it was as such that he was recommended to my father when he came to Portugal. Dr. Perdigão was a man who had the interests of his country at heart; he also had a highly-developed sense of self-interest. It is sometimes said that I am an extrovert and that I court publicity; compared with Perdigão I am the shyest and most retiring of violets. He towers above his compatriots in physical stature and he loves, in season and out of season, to stand up among them, to make a speech and to be reported in the Press— particularly in the Portuguese Press, which can be relied upon to quote him extensively and never to criticize him. He had some endearing qualities, of which I was well aware in the days when we saw much of each other. For instance, he was devoted to his first wife and when she died he went into deep mourning for the regulation one year. He even had a shrine erected in his office with her photograph before which he used to pray. After a more than decent interval, however, his temperament and Latin blood caused him to enter once more into the state of holy matrimony. I do not know his present wife personally but, from all I hear of her, she is a kind person, deeply attached to her husband, yet still able to mimic him at times, very kindly and very gaily, for his own good. He probably takes it well for, while Perdigão has always taken himself and Portugal very seriously, he has shown a greater sense of humour than the average Portuguese in whom this quality is sadly lacking.

Of course, in any of the criticisms I may make in later pages of the Trustees of the Gulbenkian Foundation, I should make this distinction between Dr. Perdigão on the one hand and Whishaw and Essayan on the other; he had no moral obligations to my father such as they had.

All the present trouble really derives from my father's unwillingness and, towards the end, his incapacity to go into fine detail over the establishment of the Foundation. As Lord Radcliffe said in the B.B.C. case, '. . . it was not very easy in his last years, to get down to detail. I am not being vain if I say he really thought of it in terms of my taking over . . . he used to talk of my sitting in his chair; and he really saw the thing as being, both on the business side (which I was quite incompetent to control) and on the development of the Foundation, very largely put in my hands and worked up by me.' A little later in his evidence, Lord Radcliffe said this: 'It would be a mistake to think that Mr. Gulbenkian attached essential importance to making his Foundation a Portuguese Foundation. He was genuinely grateful to the country which had given him shelter when he left Vichy . . . and he was grateful to the Portuguese for the treatment he had received there in the last years of his life; but he had many other, and I think deeper, associations with other countries. I will just say this, that I do not think he envisaged it being tied down to Portugal quite in the way that it seems it has been. As for the rest, he did not evade but he really did leave all the questions very much to me. He kept on saying: "Well, you will be in my chair. You decide that and it shall be as you wish." He really had set his heart, almost as an obsession, on me really being there.'

I shall be dealing later with the circumstances in which Lord Radcliffe found it impossible to take over the supreme direction of the Foundation as my father had wished. At this point, I want merely to emphasize that when my father sought Dr. Perdigão's help in drawing up his will he certainly did not intend to bring about the situation which now exists. He decided on Portugal as the seat for his Foundation because of the advice he received from Dr. Perdigão. That advice was to the effect that if he set up the Foundation under Portuguese law as a charitable body then there would be no taxes or death duties payable on it. My father also had the firm impression that as there were no rules in Portugal about the way in which Foundations should be administered (as they were unknown in Portugal hitherto) he could be assured that the Foundation would be run as the Board of Trustees, under the supreme direction of Lord Radcliffe, determined and therefore, of course, in accordance with his wishes. It had never been suggested that, in return for its exemption from taxes and death duties, there would be any requirements for a Portuguese majority on the Board of the Foundation, or that the bulk of the money should be spent in Portugal. Yet this is what has happened.

There were so many things my father never got round to in those last days as his strength drained away from him. He was very frightened of death and kept on saying, 'There is plenty of time.' He put off, again and again, the drawing-up of the statutes by which the Foundation should be governed. He had intended to buy for his devoted secretary, Madame Theis, the house to which she could retire as she had always dreamed of doing, but that was something else which did not get done.

He also intended to alter the clause in his second will which did not include me as one of the original trustees of the Foundation because my attitude towards him had been, 'in several respects, lamentable'. This was his way of rebuking me for, as he saw it, my rebellion over my mother's testamentary wishes. In that same clause, he added that he regretted his reservations about me because my 'intelligence and business capacity' would otherwise have made me a 'very useful element in the execution of the will'. Cyril Radcliffe in London, who had seen the will, wrote an open letter to my father, urging him to amend that clause and warning him, if he did not do so, there would be trouble later. He gave it to me to take to Lisbon. When my father read the letter, he expressed at once the wish to amend the clause and to make me one of the original trustees of the proposed Foundation and told Essayan to summon Dr. Perdigão to make the necessary modifications. Unfortunately, he died before this important amendment to his will was made.

13
The Founder's Intentions

WHEN my father died my wife and I were in Baden-Baden, that *fin-de-siècle* resort in the Black Forest of Germany. His doctor, Professor Fonseca, had told us that, in his condition, he might die the next day or still be alive the next year; that being so, said the Professor, we should lead our normal lives. So we had gone to Baden-Baden for what had become, on doctors' advice, my annual cure, dieting and, for a few weeks, living a more Spartan existence. My sister came to Lisbon to be with father while I was away; we took turn and turn about so that one of us would always be there.

On the day my father died, Rita had gone into the country, leaving her husband behind as usual. Death came suddenly. Kevik had popped out of the hotel to buy a packet of cigarettes. When he returned, he found that Professor Fonseca had been summoned by Madame Theis and that, though everything possible had been done, the end had come, peacefully.

I caught the next plane to Lisbon, a S.A.S. flight from Frank-furt, and was in Portugal twenty-four hours after hearing the news from Kevik. It was late in the evening when we arrived in Lisbon; Dr. Perdigão came to the airport to meet us but Essayan had gone to bed. Perdigão courteously accompanied us to the Chapelle Ardente where my father, in his morning coat, the white handkerchief sticking out of his breast pocket, was laid out. What followed was rather ghoulish for, in accordance with Portuguese custom, the laying-out was a public affair offering, not just friends and acquaintances, but anyone at all, the opportunity of paying their last respects. As I took my last parting from my father, I did so not only in the presence of many other people but also while photographers were taking pictures of the scene.

We went from the chapel to the Aviz. Even before I had been

to see my father, Dr. Perdigão had tried to persuade me that I should read the will that night. I refused to do so until my father had either been buried, or cremated in accordance with his wishes; I thought such haste on Perdigão's part indecent. Now, on reaching the hotel, he awakened Essayan to get him to use his influence on me to read the will straightaway; I still refused. Essayan's first remark on seeing us was a complaint about my wife's show of mourning: in obedience to custom in Oriental and Roman Catholic countries she was wearing a black veil, hiding her face. Essayan said he did not want his wife to be bothered with wearing a veil but she would probably have to do so if my wife did.

The next morning Dr. Perdigão and Essayan returned to the attack with even more force, insisting that the will should be read without waiting for my father to be buried. It was also amusing to watch Kevik strutting about, saying, 'Now that your father's dead, you will find me a changed man.' I learned that Dr. Perdigão had summoned a press conference for the night before but, in view of my attitude, he had to put it off until the morning; he was not prepared to postpone it again. After more argument, I finally fell in with their wishes. The will was read and then Perdigão summarized its contents to representatives of the world's Press assembled in the Aviz Hotel.

The following morning, my father's mortal remains were put, at last, into a coffin and placed on board a special plane for Zürich, where he was to be cremated. (Portugal, being a Roman Catholic country, had no facilities for cremation and we had heard of the rather unfortunate fiasco which resulted when an attempt had been made there some years before to cremate an Indian maharajah in accordance with Hindu rites; the funeral pyre would not burn and there were no electric ovens to do the job properly.)

The Armenian Bishop in London who had come to Lisbon to perform the funeral ceremony was to fly with my wife and me with my father's remains to Zürich. There was a great concourse of people at the Lisbon airport paying their last respects to my father. Both Perdigão and Essayan turned up but my sister, Rita, overslept and did not get to the airport. Her husband, however, took advantage of my wife's black veil to introduce her to many people as his wife; she was too well brought up to voice her protest on such an occasion.

The urn containing my father's ashes was left at the crematorium in Zürich, awaiting a final decision about its destination. Dr. Perdigão had his own ideas about that and in September, two months after my father's death, he made another announcement to the world's Press, saying that my father's ashes would be brought to Lisbon and interred in a grave which had been bought by the Gulbenkian family in the British cemetery there. The ashes, however, stayed in Zürich for another ten months.

On the 20th of July, 1956, on the first anniversary of my father's death, the urn was flown from Zürich to London. It was taken immediately to the Church of St. Sarkis, the Armenian Church in London built by my father, where a plaque on the wall now marks its final resting place. There the memorial service, which I had arranged in advance, was held, and on the same day in Lisbon there was another ceremony. Dr. Perdigão made another speech, full of gracious, if somewhat florid, tributes to my father.

The arguments over what should happen to my father's remains had been resolved. I only wish I could have ended the struggle over the interpretation of his wishes for his Foundation as simply and as successfully.

My father's will provided very generously for myself, my sister and her husband and all the people and institutions to which he had been making allowances during his lifetime. The bulk of the fortune remaining after those provisions had been met was to be used to set up and finance the Gulbenkian Foundation. The will named three trustees for the Foundation, Lord Radcliffe, Dr. Perdigão and Kvork Essayan. It suggested that my nephew, Mikael, and myself should be appointed as co-trustees and advised the trustees to retain the assistance of people who were either, like Hacobian and Denton, in the Gulbenkian business, or like Thomson McLintock and Co., the chartered accountants, and the Chase National Bank (now the Chase Manhattan Bank) of New York, eminent in their respective spheres and possessed of the kind of experience and qualities which would be an invaluable help. Among these names was that of Charles Whishaw (who had been designated as an executor of the earlier, 1950, will but who was not named as an executor of the second will).

As the newspapers reported, I was invited, within a matter of days after my father's death, to become one of the prospective trustees. I did not accept immediately for, like Lord Radcliffe, I already had my anxieties about the way things were being done.

'I think that the actual first news about Mr. Gulbenkian's will in Portugal was not very happily handled,' said Lord Radcliffe, when examined, seven years later, in my case against the B.B.C. 'It was treated as if he had made a great donation to the Portuguese nation. I did not think that really represented the expressions of the will or his purpose.'

Knowing how deeply my father wished Cyril Radcliffe to 'sit in his chair' after he was gone, I decided my proper course of action was to refuse to commit myself until Radcliffe himself felt able to accept the trusteeship offered to him. Naturally enough, Lord Radcliffe was not prepared to give up all his other commitments and devote himself wholly to the direction of the Foundation until he was satisfied its constitution and its activities would conform to the ideas he had discussed with my father. He was never able to receive that assurance. From September, 1955, onwards, Perdigão, Essayan, Radcliffe and myself, as prospective trustees, held regular meetings to talk about the embryonic Foundation but we made no real headway. Dr. Perdigão was anxious to get on with the work of drawing up the statutes which would govern the administration of the Foundation. Lord Radcliffe was no less concerned to have the statutes drawn up but, as these had to be approved by the Portuguese authorities before the Foundation could be established, he felt we must first achieve a more precise understanding of how the Foundation would stand in relation to Portuguese law and of the attitude of the Portuguese Government.

My father had been persuaded to the idea of a Foundation with its headquarters in Portugal and subject to Portuguese law because he believed that in this way his fortune would escape taxation and would thereby remain intact for the use of the Foundation. Certainly, he had feelings of affection and gratitude towards the Portuguese for the way they had treated him during the war and during the last years of his life but, primarily, the establishing of the Foundation under Portuguese law was a matter of financial convenience, like sailing a merchant ship under the flags of Panama or Liberia.

Lord Radcliffe wanted to get two main questions settled and

both depended upon the interpretation of Portuguese law and upon the attitude of the Portuguese Government. How many of the trustees should be Portuguese citizens? What proportion of the Foundation's expenditure ought to be in Portugal?

Lord Radcliffe's failure to secure satisfactory answers to these questions caused him to abandon the idea of becoming chairman of the Foundation's Board of Trustees and of assuming its supreme direction as his old friend, my father, had wished him to do. That same failure and the consequent activities of the Foundation form the core of my criticisms of the trustees.

Cyril Radcliffe withdrew only after he had explored every means at his disposal to achieve a satisfactory conclusion. He obtained expert legal advice from two distinguished Portuguese professors. He had two long conversations with the Portuguese Prime Minister, Dr. Salazar. He talked with other Ministers of the Portuguese Government. He conducted a protracted and detailed correspondence with Dr. Perdigão, who, Lord Radcliffe initially believed, was acting as intermediary between him and the Portuguese Government. He had more discussions with the then Portuguese Ambassador in London. Right from the start until his decision in June, 1956, nearly a year after my father's death, not to accept the chairmanship of the Board, Lord Radcliffe and I were in very close touch; I knew in advance of each step he took.

I do not intend to present here an account of those exchanges and their conclusions in any great detail but I do want to trace the broad lines of the argument, if only to make my own conduct since my father's death easier to understand. Where I ascribe views to Lord Radcliffe, it is on the basis of my close association with him at that time, of the letters he wrote to Dr. Perdigão and of what he said in the B.B.C. case.[1]

Radcliffe was satisfied, after reading the 'learned and voluminous opinion' obtained from the two Portuguese professors, that there was nothing in Portuguese law which could impose restrictions upon the constitution of the Foundation as conditions for the exemption of the Gulbenkian fortune from death duties. Their opinion tallied with what my father had believed the position to be. On the other hand, Radcliffe, while insistent upon the inter-

1. The complete text of the Radcliffe-Perdigão correspondence is in the Appendix.

national character of the Foundation, was ready to mark the special relationship between the Foundation and Portugal by proposing that a minimum proportion of the Foundation's money should be spent each year in Portugal. He put forward proposals to Perdigão, Essayan and myself as the basis for the establishment of the Foundation in Portugal and he put these on record in a letter he wrote to Dr. Perdigão from London in January, 1956.

He proposed that there should be a Board of no fewer than seven members. Two of these places were to be reserved for members of the Gulbenkian family, so long as there were any willing and competent to serve. Two places were to be reserved for Portuguese citizens, with the suggestion that, if the size of the Board were to be increased, the number of Portuguese should be maintained in a ratio of one for every three places filled. Lord Radcliffe also proposed an absolute prohibition against the Board of Governors containing, at any time, a majority of persons of one nationality.

His second main proposal was for a minimum of 15 per cent of the yearly outlay of the Foundation to be spent in Portugal and its territories but that it should never be more than 20 per cent in any one year. There is no doubt in my mind that Radcliffe would have been happier to have fixed the minimum guaranteed percentage lower than 15 per cent; he did not really go along with the interpretation placed upon the wording of my father's will by the two Portuguese professors who read into it an express desire to favour Portugal when considering the Foundation's activities. However, he felt he must go this far towards a compromise, for the sake of achieving an agreement with the Portuguese Government, without betraying my father's intentions.

Radcliffe wanted an informal go-ahead from the Portuguese authorities on the broad lines of his proposals so that the work of drawing up the constitutional statutes of the Foundation could begin. It was this assurance that he sought in his conversations with Dr. Salazar and his Ministers and through his correspondence with Dr. Perdigão. But, as the months went by (with Dr. Perdigão at one moment claiming to communicate the views of the Government and the next denying they were any but his own), it became more and more evident that the chance of a meeting of minds was remote.

The Portuguese authorities insisted that a Foundation set up in Portugal must have a majority of Portuguese nationals on the Board. (They were prepared to allow equal representation between Portuguese and foreigners with Lord Radcliffe possessing the casting vote, as it were, for just so long as he was chairman, a gesture which Lord Radcliffe did not appreciate as much as Dr. Perdigão thought he should have done.) At one time they demanded, or Dr. Perdigão did, that not less than a third of the total income of the Foundation should be distributed in Portugal. Later, they dropped the insistence on any set minimum but, as they maintained their claim to a Portuguese majority on the Board, it is hardly surprising that Lord Radcliffe did not feel reassured about their intentions.

He objected strongly to the imposition of restrictions upon the Foundation which, he held, had no justification in Portuguese law but would amount to an arbitrary exercise of power by the Portuguese authorities. As for the argument put forward by Dr. Perdigão that Portugal had every right to demand from the Foundation, in return for exemption from death duties, monies comparable to the death duties from which the Foundation was to be exempted, Radcliffe pointed out that my father chose Lisbon as the seat for the Foundation precisely in order to secure that tax exemption; there could be no question of the Foundation drawing upon the wealth of Portugal or upon wealth accumulated under the protection of Portuguese law.

'What are the facts?' Lord Radcliffe asked in his letter to Dr. Perdigão of 27th February, 1956. 'Mr. C. S. Gulbenkian, a British subject, who had for the great part of his life been resident in England and France successively, took up residence in Portugal in, I think, the year 1942. During the rest of his life he remained resident there, and I am sure—for I knew him well—that he was scrupulous in meeting all legal obligations in the way of tax that the Portuguese State imposed upon him in that capacity. I believe, too, that it is generally accepted that he contributed on no small scale to charitable and other benevolent objects in Portugal: and he enriched the city of Lisbon with a munificent donation to the Art Gallery. But the great wealth that has passed to the Foundation and of which it is now to dispose was never made in Portugal nor did it accrue from operations conducted under the protection of the Portuguese State. On the contrary, it arose principally from oil interests in various parts of the world, and the protection of those interests was at no time a Portuguese concern. As you know, the Iraq Petroleum Company, the interest in which forms a considerable part of the wealth of the Foundation, is an English Company operating in the Middle East. Finally, no appreciable part of his wealth was ever brought by him into Portugal; or, consequently, will ever leave Portugal when it is expended by the Foundation in other countries. How then can the Portuguese Treasury be a loser, if the exemption from duty which the Portuguese law appears to offer is in fact obtained?'

I must leave the reader who would like to follow these exchanges more closely and to arrive at his own assessment of the rights and wrongs of the affair to turn to the material in the Appendix. I will permit myself merely this one comment: that whatever else may be said of Dr. Perdigão's epistolary style, his considerable audacity or his patriotism, his arguments are scarcely distinguished by their logic or consistency.

Logic, however, and, as I believe, right, were not to prevail. Lord Radcliffe reached the point where, having restated his proposals in most lucid and reasonable form, he received what was tantamount to their wholesale rejection; he knew, then, it was senseless for him to persist any longer. On the 1st of June, 1956, he wrote to Dr. Perdigão, formally stating his unwillingness to take up the Chairmanship of the Foundation, 'having regard to its Portuguese nationality. . . .'

As Lord Radcliffe said in answer to a question from Sir Lionel Heald in the B.B.C. case, '. . . I thought it was starting the Foundation off on a basis which did not represent the purposes of my old friend, the founder. In a sense one might say that the question of the composition of trustees was a formality, but I did not think it so, and I personally never envisaged that an international foundation, starting from scratch, as it were, of this kind, could be properly run for its international purposes unless one could gather from the world at large—possibly England, America, France and elsewhere—some people with some experience of the kind of conditions in the world and how to work it. I did not feel that it was right we should be compulsorily tied down to a majority of Portuguese citizens.'

A little later in his examination, Lord Radcliffe said, 'I did not feel the thing ought to start on the basis of being anything like a gift to Portugal of the benefits of the Foundation. There were claims by all different countries which he had many associations with and had lived in for many years. There were claims from France, where he had built his last house and had great admiration and contacts with. There were the Armenian people whom he had always, of course, with his origin, supported. And there were what I may call the contestants, claimants from the rest of the world. I did not want to be tied down, although naturally one would have had to make concessions, to any fixed dedication of part of the income to any one country.'

Meanwhile, discussions which had been going on for months about my own position under my father's will and about the terms under which I might become a trustee of the Foundation had reached a crucial stage. In a letter dated 24th April, 1956, signed by Dr. Perdigão and Essayan, I received a formal offer of a trusteeship and also proposals for reorganizing my interest in my father's estate. These offers were to remain open for acceptance for a period of one month. By the middle of May it had become clear that Lord Radcliffe would take no part in the running of the Foundation because of the attitude of the Portuguese authorities.

Now that the first of my father's wishes for the Foundation—Radcliffe's supreme direction of it—could not be fulfilled, what was the proper thing for me to do? It was very difficult for me to decide and I had a long tussle with myself in trying to make up my mind. As I have made clear, I shared all Cyril Radcliffe's misgivings for the future of the Foundation and I had to decide how best I could influence its activities. Either I could accept a trusteeship and try, from the inside, though almost certainly in a minority of one, to do something to see that the Foundation was run more as my father would have liked, or I could refuse to go in and leave myself free to criticize from the outside. I knew the former of those alternative courses would have involved me in constant rows with my co-trustees. That was not a prospect that pleased. On the other hand, once he himself had felt bound to refuse the chairmanship, Lord Radcliffe counselled me to become a trustee on the grounds that, however circumscribed my influence might be, I would be more effective if I were in than if I were out. Dr. Perdigão and Essayan had flown to London to demand my decision on their offer. We met at the Ritz Hotel. I tried, as I had from the start of our negotiations, to divorce the offer of the trusteeship from the offer relating to my entitlement to a share in my father's estate. They maintained their insistence that the one was dependent upon the other. We had a stormy and unpleasant session. I came to the conclusion, however, that disagreeable though it might be for all concerned, I should take Cyril Radcliffe's advice and join them, despite the danger that my doing so could make it seem that Radcliffe himself had been unreasonably difficult in staying outside. The following morning, the 23rd of May, at the office, I wrote a letter accepting the trusteeship, but making no mention of my entitlement to a share in my father's estate. I sent it to Dr. Perdigão. Within the hour, I received a written reply stating that the offer had expired at midnight and that, anyway, the offer of a trusteeship was dependent upon my accepting the other provisions relating to my entitlement under my father's will. What was abundantly clear, beyond the legal rights and wrongs of this particular exchange, was that, for the moment at least, my chances of my becoming a trustee were ended.

The necessary period of negotiation with Lord Radcliffe having ended, too, leaving them on their own, the two executors of the will, Perdigão and Essayan, wasted no time. They pressed ahead with drawing up the statutes for the administration of the Foundation. These, according to Dr. Perdigão, were months over-due in Portuguese law and only the benevolence of the Portuguese authorities, he said, had prevented the exaction of duties on the Gulbenkian estate.

On the 5th of July, only a month after Radcliffe had withdrawn, the Statutes of the Calouste Gulbenkian Foundation were published in Lisbon, under the signatures of Kvork Essayan and Dr. Perdigão. On the 18th of July, a decree law was promulgated by the Portuguese Government, approving the statutes. On the 20th of July, the first anniversary of my father's death, in that same ornate speech in which he lauded my father, Dr. Perdigão also announced the appointment of three more trustees of the Foundation to join Essayan and himself. Two of them were Portuguese, which was entirely in tune with Article 11 of the

Foundation Statutes: 'Since the Institution is Portuguese and has to operate under Portuguese law, the majority of the members of its Board must be of Portuguese nationality.' The third of the new trustees was Charles Whishaw, described by Perdigão, in the words of the official translation published by the Foundation, as 'a reputed British solicitor, and one of the most devoted collaborators of the late Mr. Calouste Gulbenkian'. The same Charles Whishaw whom my father had dropped as an executor.[1]

So now my father's great Foundation had five trustees, three Portuguese gentlemen, his former confidential clerk, Kevik, and Whishaw. The Foundation, whose activities should have been world-wide and whose administrators were to have been drawn from the world's most able and experienced men, and upon whose establishment we had had the advice of people like Arthur Dean, the distinguished American lawyer and business adviser,[2] and Dean Rusk, then president of the Rockefeller Foundation[3] (both of whom came to Europe specially for long talks with us about the problems of running a world-wide Foundation), was started upon its narrow road.

The trio, Perdigão, Kevik and Whishaw, were not quite happy, however. They had neither the man the Founder had named specifically as the one he wanted to run the Foundation nor the Founder's only son. There was, too, a complicated lawsuit looming ahead, which might well upset all their schemes. The will might be held void, in whole or in part. So, in November, 1956, Dr. Perdigão came to London with a firm offer to settle both the question of the trusteeship and that of my rights under my father's will. I was now offered the equivalent of some £25,000 a year over and above what they had offered me in the previous spring. (Radcliffe, in accordance with the terms of my father's will, had been offered £20,000 a year to assume the chairmanship of the Board of Trustees.) On the other hand, they were asking for my

1. Whishaw now claims that the reason his name was removed as an executor may be because my father thought he sided too often with me!

2. Arthur Dean has served his country, in various capacities, in the international field; in 1953–4, for instance, he was Special U.S. Ambassador to Korea, and for several years from 1958 onwards he represented the U.S. in Geneva at the nuclear test ban negotiations.

3. Dean Rusk left the Rockefeller Foundation to become U.S. Secretary of State in the Kennedy Administration.

formal and public association with their activities; the offer included £2500 a year as President of Honour of the Foundation,
but it was a Presidency, it was made clear, without any special
powers over the other trustees. We had more heated meetings
with draft and counter-draft agreements passing between us. The
talks went on into December, but at the end of them we had still
failed to reach agreement.

The way the Calouste Gulbenkian Foundation has been run,
the way it conducts its affairs and the way in which my father's
money has been spent, has confirmed the initial anxieties shared
by Lord Radcliffe and myself. I have felt it my duty to criticize
the trustees whenever their actions have merited criticism and
whenever an opportunity has presented itself to me. My criticisms
are based on fact and in my belief that my father's wishes are not
being carried out. If they had been carried out or if, at some
future time, the trustees should mend their ways and begin to
carry them out, then my criticisms, too, would cease. Indeed,
Calouste Gulbenkian's only son would be happy to applaud
publicly the administration of the Foundation; after all, οὔτοι
συνέχθειν, ἀλλὰ συμφιλεῖν ἔφυν.[1]

I have three main criticisms of the trustees which, simply
stated, are these: first, that far, far too high a percentage of the
Foundation's money is spent in Portugal; second, that the Foundation is not spending enough money; third, that the trustees are
much too secretive about the accounts of the Foundation. I am
not saying that everything the trustees have done, every grant
they have made, has been wrong or bad. Far from it. Although
they have made many grants, especially in the early days, of
which my father would have disapproved, it is always easy but
rarely profitable to criticize individual decisions. But let me
elaborate my criticisms so that the substance of them may become
apparent.

According to a report in The Times, based on an official statement released in Britain by the Foundation, the trustees, in the
first seven and a half years of operations up to the end of 1963,
had distributed a total of some £15½ million.

1. 'My nature is not to fight with people but to love them all.' Sophocles'
'Antigone'.

Of this (I am using round figures) £6,300,000 or 40·5 per cent had been spent in Portugal; £3,750,000 or 24 per cent in 'Iraq and other Middle East countries'; £2 million or nearly 13 per cent among the Armenian communities which were so very dear to my father; £1,900,000 or 12 per cent in Britain and the Commonwealth, and £1,600,000 or 10·5 per cent in 'other countries'.

This is the consistent pattern of the Foundation's activities from the start to the present time, with Portugal receiving very much more than any other two countries. I must say again that my father did not envisage his Foundation as favouring any one country or group of countries but of serving 'humanity' in general.

The Foundation has been well served by the committee which advises the trustees on the applications for aid from individuals and organizations concerned with the Arts in Britain. (The trustees may take the advice or ignore it, for they alone have the power to authorize a grant.) This committee which, apart from Whishaw, the Resident Trustee in this country, now consists of Lord Bridges, Lady Albemarle, Sir Dennis Proctor and Dr. T. S. R. Boase, seems to me to have operated with care and a real sense of responsibility.

In one of the books on the American Foundations I have read, the aims of a Foundation are neatly characterized: 'A Foundation should be a priming pump and not a reservoir.' A Foundation, in other words, should not try to undertake and execute a series of individual projects; it can only provide the stimulus, the helping hand by which people or organizations are encouraged to persist in their own endeavours. It must maintain general and comprehensive sympathies which find expression in grants for particular activities. It must be insatiable and restless in its search for suitable causes to aid: there is no shortage of them in the world.

Foundations are generally responsible to no one except public opinion and, if public opinion is to be brought to bear, it must know exactly what a Foundation is doing and how its money is being spent. I remember Dean Rusk telling me, during our discussions in London, that the safeguard for people who were running a Foundation and for the proper running of a Foundation was that the full light of publicity should be shed on all its activities. The Gulbenkian Foundation does not provide public opinion with the knowledge it needs in order to play its part effectively.

The Statutes of the Gulbenkian Foundation require the Board of Administration, each year, to 'make an exact inventory of the endowment of the Foundation and prepare a statement of all its income and expenditure'. They also require an Accountancy Checking Commission to make a yearly examination of this inventory and to produce an annual report to be published compulsorily at the expense of the Foundation. I claim that the trustees have made it not just difficult, but impossible, for anyone outside the Foundation to be adequately informed of its financial condition and behaviour.

In my case against the B.B.C., Mr. Donald House, a past president of the Institute of Chartered Accountants, was asked his opinion of the first report of the 'Audit Committee' or 'Accountancy Checking Commission' for the period from 18th July 1956 until the 31st December, 1957. This report was the only published information relating to the financial affairs of the Foundation up to the 10th July 1959, almost a full three years after the Foundation started its work. Mr. House was also asked to compare this report with annual reports published by the Nuffield Foundation, the Rockefeller Foundation and the Ford Foundation. I must try to summarize Mr. House's evidence, which was highly technical in places, but the full transcript is available to any who seek it and I have no wish or need to ascribe to Mr. House more than what he actually said; what he did say is entirely adequate for the purposes of confirming my own accusations against the trustees.

Mr. House said that it was impossible to discover from that report of the Accountancy Checking Commission what was the real value of the capital assets of the Foundation. A figure of some £4 million was given as the profits from these assets during the eighteen-month period, but the capital assets were given a nominal value of 100 escudos—about £1. Mr. House said that the reports of other Foundations dealt fully with the value of their capital assets. He also said that of the £4 million income from these assets, something like just under half was distributed to the Foundation. Now let me quote briefly from the evidence immediately following upon that answer.

Q. Is any information given as to how the remainder of that enormous income is dealt with?

A. Nothing beyond the fact that I believe they do say that it has been retained in the subsidiary companies for investment or otherwise to be dealt with to improve the assets of the Foundation.

Q. Is any information given as to how these subsidiaries operate?

A. None.

Q. Or their financial affairs?

A. None at all.

Q. So far as you know are there any published accounts relating to such companies?

A. None at all.

Q. Without that information do you as an accountant consider it possible to obtain any very fair notion of the financial position of the Foundation?

A. Not of the value of the Foundation.

In further answers to Mr. Mark Littman, Q.C., who conducted this phase of the case on my behalf, Mr. House said that the report did not give the kind of detailed information about how the Foundation spent and distributed its money as he found in the reports of other Foundations. He could find no schedule of investments such as he found in the reports of other Foundations. He could find no detailed analysis of the way in which some £150,000 was spent on 'administration, installation and operation expenses'. He could find no details of how much the trustees were being paid or how much was being earned by people holding office in the subsidiary companies.

Mr. House agreed that some two years after my appearance in 'Face to Face' in July, 1959, the Gulbenkian Foundation published a 'rather more comprehensive' report which gave a certain amount of information which had been lacking in the earlier report of the Accountancy Commission, but that it certainly did not fill all the gaps. Although the Foundation is not obliged by Portuguese law to publish detailed accounts or lists of investments, I hold that the practice of the Gulbenkian Foundation ought to be in line with the practice of comparable Foundations, such as the Ford and Rockefeller, and that this is certainly what my father would have wished, and Lord Radcliffe would have so insisted.

In the television programme 'Face to Face' with John Freeman, I accused the trustees of not giving as much information in their accounts as other Foundations did and of drawing remuneration in excess of the amount specified in the will. Despite the report to which Mr. House referred, which may or may not have been provoked by the broadcast, I see little reason to withdraw or modify my accusations.

There is further ground for my criticism of them in the amount of money the Foundation distributes.

The *Financial Times* states: 'By far the biggest increase in assets between 1960 and 1962 represented undistributed revenue of 1·7 million contos, equivalent to £21·25 million, or 75 per cent of total net revenue.'

This reveals an attitude of mind and a practice quite contrary to that of comparable Foundations, like the Ford and Rockefeller Foundations. In *their* accounts, the trustees of those other Foundations repeatedly affirm that it is the duty of a general Foundation to distribute as much money as it can. A Foundation, they point out, is not a profit-making organization to save and accumulate money; its purpose is to spend money as and when worthy causes appear and, when necessary, not merely to distribute the income of the Foundation but also to make inroads into capital. The administrators of the Ford and Rockefeller Foundations find there is so much work for their money to do in the world that they do indeed have to cut into their capital.[1] Even so, they are both still worth more than the original funds with which they were started and this, I believe, is the way in which my father's Foundation ought to be run.

1. In July 1962, a statement by the Ford Foundation's Board of Trustees, called 'The Ford Foundation in the 1960s', was issued. The following is an extract:

'While the Foundation's assets and income have increased since 1950, the demands on these resources have grown at a substantially greater rate. The Foundation, consequently, has not only expended all its income, but has invaded its capital, as of the spring of 1962, for an additional $525 million. The Trustees are prepared to continue invading capital, as necessary, to respond to opportunities for making advances on the vital problems of the period ahead. During the eleven years ending September 30, 1961, income after administrative expenses amounted to $1,081,100,000 and grants and appropriations during the same period amounted to $1,553,000,000. The 1961–2 appraisal was not undertaken because of any inability to spend the Foundation's income and capital; on the contrary, the staff faced a growing pressure of competing claims upon available funds. The examination has verified that opportunities for significant Foundation action (to say nothing of the many other worthwhile and urgent purposes for which funds could be spent) greatly exceed present income and assets.'

I am also very doubtful of the wisdom of the investments held by the Foundation. The Gulbenkian Foundation has neither sold nor reduced its holding in the Iraq Petroleum Company. On the contrary, it has been increasing its stake in the oil production in the various shaky sheikdoms of the Persian Gulf. I am aware that, earlier in this book, I commended investment in the Middle East, on a short-term basis, because of its rapid amortisation. It is quite another question, however, whether a charitable body, like the Gulbenkian Foundation, is wise to hold such an investment. I very much doubt whether, if my father had been alive and at the prime of his power, he would have committed himself so extensively to the I.P.C. I am bound to wonder whether the Board of the Foundation, with its majority of Portuguese gentlemen—two are lawyers and three former diplomatists—have the experience or the knowhow to run an intricate business such as my father's participation in Middle East oil has become. The risks that he took with his eyes open—and with all his intelligence and adroitness to handle whatever situation might arise—should not be taken, in my opinion, by those who have the responsibility for running a great charitable institution. The Ford Foundation started by holding only Ford Motor Company shares but, from time to time, the Foundation sells a large block of Ford shares and reinvests in different stock in order to diversify its holdings. The same thing applies to the Rockefeller Foundation whose original investments consisted of shares in the Standard Oil and New Jersey Oil companies. The trustees of the Gulbenkian Foundation would be well advised to heed these examples. They were approached some years ago with a view to exchanging their holdings in Iraq Petroleum Company for shares of Royal Dutch Shell, Standard Oil of New Jersey, etc., which of course command a ready market. It would be interesting to know how much better off the Foundation would have been today had the trustees taken advantage of these approaches. It is hardly helpful for the public to judge when the value of the I.P.C. investment is always put in the balance sheet at a merely nominal figure.

The trustees may not have always appreciated my efforts to help them but that has not deterred me. In 1957, however, both they and I had resorted to legal action to try to make our points.

They asked the Portuguese courts for a declaration concerning the will. For my part, I had already started proceedings in the English courts against the executors of the will and the administrators of it in this country. I also issued writs against Whishaw and Essayan, seeking to establish that the remuneration they were receiving from the Foundation in one way or another—in the region of £10,000 each a year—was grossly excessive and contrary to the wishes my father expressed in his will, where Essayan was to get £4000 a year.[1] The English courts decided that this was a matter for the Portuguese courts; and that was that.

Dr. Perdigão has done a number of things as chairman of the Gulbenkian Foundation which I am bound to find regrettable. This is particularly true in respect of my father's art collections. Much to Lord Radcliffe's annoyance (as he makes clear in his correspondence), Perdigão and Essayan, even before the Foundation had been set up, had started trying to get the treasures into Portugal. It was always my father's desire that certain unique French works should remain in France and be handed eventually to the French museums. Father was very fond of France, he had lived there for many years and had been very happy there. It was

1. In his will my father appointed Lord Radcliffe, Dr. Perdigão and Kvork Essayan as trustees. The will stated specifically how much they should be paid: 'The testamentary executors and trustees shall, for the carrying out of their relative duties, be entitled to a fixed annual remuneration . . . amounting to £20,000 sterling in the case of Lord Radcliffe of Werneth and to £4000 sterling in the case of each of the others, the former being under the obligation to devote all his time to the exercise of the duties entailed by the offices of testamentary executor and trustee.' The will provided, of course, for the reimbursement of travelling expenses and the like incurred as executors or, later, as administrators of the Foundation. It also adds this significant instruction: '. . . from the merging of the offices of testamentary executors and trustees with that of the administrators of the Foundation *no duplication or merger of fixed remuneration shall in any case result in their favour*'. The remuneration to be paid to the trustees named in the will was fixed by the will and although it states that any other trustees appointed should receive 'remuneration . . . such as may be fixed by the testamentary executors and trustees' I cannot accept that this justifies remuneration in excess of that stipulated for the original trustees. As for Essayan's remuneration, the will is wholly unambiguous in its language: he is to get £4000 a year and no more. Lastly, the will provided an annual remuneration of £20,000 for Lord Radcliffe if and when he assumed full-time duties as supreme director of the Foundation. There is absolutely no suggestion in the will that, in the event of his not being able to accept the office, a substitute should receive the same amount.

thanks to his co-operation with the French Government—co-operation which was of mutual interest—that he managed to hold his own against the attacks of the other oil groups in the I.P.C. dealings. For these reasons he had told many people of his wish that the French works of art should remain in France. I also felt strongly about it. There were the table and chair, which had been made specially for Marie Antoinette; the Houdon 'Diana'; the French silver by Germain and the portrait of Germain by Largillière. This portrait showed a large and beautiful silver tureen which came into the possession of the Portuguese banker, Ricardo Espirito Santo. (The name of his bank, the Banco Espirito Santo e Commercial, literally translated means 'The Bank of the Holy Ghost and Commercial'). Espirito Santo had tried very hard to obtain Germain's portrait and father had tried very hard to obtain the soup tureen, but neither of them would give way. Now both are in Portugal.

Perdigão, Essayan, and the Portuguese Ambassador in Paris, Dr. Marcello Matias (who had a charming Greek wife), worked hard and very skilfully to get the collections out of France. Perdigão and Co. were afraid that, for one reason or another, the priceless works of art (which included the pictures John Walker had in the National Gallery of Art in Washington of which he was chief curator) would be denied exit permits from France and America. Indeed, when the possibility of the French works leaving France was raised, the curators of the French museums protested most strongly and justifiably. At one stage, thanks to the intervention of that good friend of my father and of myself, Monsieur Cayrol, the French Government had placed an embargo on the export of any of the works of art then in France. But, during one of the innumerable changes of Government which took place during the Fourth Republic, Perdigão and Co. managed to get the embargo lifted, at first partially and then wholly. The house in the Avenue d'Iéna was stripped and, today, all of my father's collections are in Portugal. As a temporary home for them, the Foundation has bought an eighteenth-century palace on the Tagus at Oeiras, between Lisbon and Estoril. Being near the sea, it is apt to be damp there, but I believe a great deal of trouble has been taken about air-conditioning and so on in order that the pictures should be properly preserved. As a permanent home, they are building the Foundation Palacio on the site of what was the Feria Popular —the Popular Fair, rather like an Earl's Court in Lisbon—but it will take years to complete.

Dr. Perdigão obviously believes that charity begins at home. One of the first provisions of my father's Foundation was to equip the band of the *Bombeiros Voluntarios* (the local fire brigade) at Dr. Perdigão's village of Obidos with new uniforms.

No one would ever accuse Dr. Perdigão of diffidence or of afflicting self-consciousness. There was the occasion, for instance, when, with Essayan in attendance, he came to England to perform some ceremony concerned with the distribution here of a very small part of my father's money. A dinner was given for the visiting dignitaries and a highly-placed Englishman was deputized to sit next to Dr. Perdigão and entertain him. However, as Dr. Perdigão's English was, and is, only slightly better than the distinguished Englishman's Portuguese, conversation between them had to take place in lamentably-halting French. Then the Englishman conceived a way of relieving the strain. He praised Camões, the great Portuguese poet, author of that great epic poem 'os Lusiadas' and asked Dr. Perdigão whether in Portugal people learn Camões by heart in the way the English learn Shakespeare. Dr. Perdigão rose to the bait and proceeded to recite, or rather to spout, Camões, at first merely to his neighbours and then, carried away by Camões' magnificent stanzas, to the assembled multitude.

I am often amused by Dr. Perdigão. For instance, I have not begrudged him the variegated collection of medals and decorations he has picked up all round the world, the last ones, I believe, being the Order of Cedar of the Lebanon and that of Bernard O'Higgins of Chile. But there have been times when he has really got above himself. It is one thing to watch him revelling in the office of chairman of the Foundation; it is quite another when the Foundation began to be known as the Perdigão Foundation. That was a bit too much, however, even for Essayan and, I understand, he made representations to Dr. Perdigão which, for once, were effective. Much as I regret it, I have had to make some rather severe criticisms of Essayan's behaviour; I am therefore all the more happy I can pay him tribute on this occasion.

Perhaps Dr. Perdigão would like to find a way to stop the Press from publishing my criticisms or to prevent anyone else, for that matter, from saying anything which he, Perdigão, may not relish. Now I am very fond of Portugal, having spent a few pleasant years there during the last part of my father's life; I have been received there with universal kindness and hospitality and I am grateful to the Portuguese for the welcome they gave my father and mother when they went there from Vichy; but I am well aware that their way of life is somewhat different from that of the English people. For instance, the Portuguese Press is subject to very strict censorship. The censorship decides what is 'truth' and nothing but the truth according to the censors is published. This may well make it difficult for Dr. Perdigão to understand why the authorities, or perhaps the British Government itself, do not muzzle the British Press and, come to that, the British Law Courts.

But I have not given up hope that eventually Dr. Perdigão will come round to my way of thinking about the Foundation. To help him to do so, I am going to recall to him three quotations, with two of which, at least, he must be very familiar.

The first is from a letter written to him by Lord Radcliffe on the 27th February, 1956, in response to Dr. Perdigão's delineation of the conditions upon which the Portuguese Government would approve the establishment of the Foundation:

'. . . you must permit me to say, without reserve, that I can see no warranty for the requirement of the Portuguese Authorities that one third of the total income of the Foundation should constitute the "minimum limit for distribution in Portugal". If the Foundation were set up on this basis it would not be realizing the founder's intentions: it would be flouting them. It would not be carrying out the terms of his Will: it would be defeating them. Moreover, as I have shown, it would not be giving effect to the law of Portugal, to which he trusted and to which he gave his confidence: it would in effect be making a new law after his death, directed solely at his own Foundation. . . .'

Next I want to quote from the judgement given by Mr. Justice Glyn-Jones in my case against the B.B.C. on 27th July, 1962:

'No one knew better than Lord Radcliffe the mind of the testator. He felt that Mr. Calouste Gulbenkian had thought of his Foundation as truly international, governed by trustees of eminence and wisdom, selected on merit from any part of the world without regard to nationality, and looking with an eye of equal benevolence on the needs of all men of whatever country, colour, class or creed; and in Lord Radcliffe's opinion the requirements of the Portuguese Government went so far to destroy or diminish the international character of the Foundation and thus to defeat the testator's intentions as to make it impossible for him to accept the office of executor and senior trustee reserved for him by the Will. . . .'

Finally, I draw Dr. Perdigão's attention to the words of the Portuguese Decree Law No. 40690 approving the statutes of the Foundation and its establishment:

'. . . We have before us an outstanding example of the proper appreciation of the social function of wealth, as opposed to the selfishness which seems to be taking possession of the World and which tends to sacrifice the high ideal that wealth has its own moral duties which it can neither neglect nor deny. Nobody has understood this more clearly than that great creator of wealth, Calouste Sarkis Gulbenkian. This wealth, produced over so many years by his intelligence, energy and work, reverts eventually to humanity in the form of material and spiritual benefits.

'. . . He knew well enough the value of Portuguese peace and the guarantee which that peace would mean to the work which was to carry on his ideas. He fully appreciated the calm enjoyed amongst us, and valued the stability of the institutions and social balance which reflect our character; *he also knew the extent to which a founder's wishes, in similar cases, are respected in Portugal. The decision he made was indeed an act of faith and of confidence.*

'*The legitimate expectations of this man who made our country the custodian of so magnificent a legacy must not be defeated, and the Foundation's Administration, with a Portuguese majority on its Board, will do full credit to such trust, in the manner in which it will exercise its powers and by the care it will take in carrying out the Testator's Will. . . .*'

The italics, Dr. Perdigão, are indeed mine.

POSTSCRIPT January, 1965

I am glad to say, perhaps as a result of my agitation over the last nine years, Dr. Perdigão has recently published a Report of the President which does give a great deal of information which Mr. House, in his evidence in my B.B.C. case, said was so blatantly lacking. In that report, however, there are still no details of the market investments held by the Foundation and its subsidiary companies, such as those published by the Ford, Rockefeller and Nuffield Foundations. Nor is there any means of ascertaining what the trustees receive, either as emoluments or as expenses. Still, progress has been made and I am vain enough to think that what I have been doing since my father's death has at last had some practical result and I am sanguine enough to hope that this book will result in even more, so that my father's Foundation may, at last, sail serenely on the course he would have wished.

14
An Orchid a Day

———————

THE great difference in my life after my father's death was th
the overwhelming, ever-present influence of his personality ha
gone. Although he has been dead now for nine years I still feel h.
absence. As I have told in this book, I disagreed with him fron
time to time, chiefly, I suppose, because we were too much alike
and because of his strong, autocratic personality. But even today I
have this conscious awareness of loss.

Materially, his death has not made that much difference to me
but it does mean that, when I want to buy a new car or some
jewellery or a sable coat for my wife, I have no need to make out a
case to my father to get the cash. Yet so deep is the influence of his
training that I still go through the process of justifying the purchase, only now it is to myself.

To a large extent, I have retired from active business life; I no
longer have any working association with the oil companies.
Having retired, I ought to have plenty of leisure but, as has
happened to many of my friends, despite not having to arrive at the
office at a fixed hour and not having to pursue any rigid routine, I
seem to have much less spare time than I had when I carried quite
important responsibilities. Of course, a fortune does not look after
itself and, to keep in touch with my fortune and to see that it does
not gradually melt away, I have to keep an eye on my investments.
That means spending a fair amount of time with bankers, brokers
and with people who know what is going on in the world and, more
especially, what is likely to happen in the future. I also read a great
deal of current literature. Each day I read a Swiss newspaper, the
Journal de Genève, whose two leading articles give a succinct,
balanced, unpartisan view of world problems, such as I can find
nowhere else. I try to read the weekly edition of the *New York*

Times, with its admirable two-page summary of world news and also the *U.S. News and World Report*, another 100 pages once a week, for an interesting reflection of the American outlook—which, compared with the attitude of the *Journal de Genève*, is surprisingly narrow. In the quarterly reviews of the Big Five banks I sometimes find an interesting and readable article—in other words, one which is not too highbrow and not too lowbrow—on some economic facet of the world.

In reading *The Times*, I start, snobbishly or commercially, with either the Court Circular or the financial pages. I glance through the rest of the paper in order to have some idea of what is being discussed. I do not read the special articles first time round unless there is an article about hunting or country life. I read three out of the four leaders; I include the fourth leader, the least serious one, partly because I think it is always well written and partly, perhaps, because (as I told in chapter one) I was once mentioned there. I am not beyond skipping a heavy leader, particularly if it is about a subject in which I am not interested. Nor do I read the correspondence columns with any serious attention unless they contain a letter from someone I know. I do not see much of the rest of the British Press, except for the *Daily Express* and *Evening Standard*, where I read William Hickey and the Londoner's Diary, generally to see whether any of my friends are mentioned. As for myself, I am vain enough to subscribe to a cuttings agency and therefore, although it may be a little late, I usually catch up with what has been published about me, either in England or anywhere else in the world.

Apart from keeping up with the world for the sake of my own interests, there is also my work as honorary commercial attaché to the Iranian Embassy. I report on the economic trends in this country, on the course of the pound sterling and the trading prospects. But, for many years now, my duties have consisted less in dealing with routine enquiries from firms in Britain or Iran wishing to trade in the other country than of keeping members of the Embassy, from the Ambassador downwards, informed about the British outlook and the British way of life. So many things which have no importance in, say, Paris or Washington can be of the highest importance in London, and this can certainly include matters of behaviour, dress and national attitude. Again, from our very large circle of friends and acquaintances and at the much-maligned diplomatic cocktail-parties, one can pick up many scraps of information which, in themselves, seem of little importance, but when pieced together may give a good indication of what is pending in England or in some foreign country. At the time I am writing this, for instance, it is generally known that relations between Britain and France are not over-cordial. What neither I nor my Embassy had realized was that Anglo-French relations had deteriorated to the stage where wives of British Ministers had been advised not to go to France. This was a small piece of information which came my way accidentally and whose potential significance was considerable.

Having lived in this country for more than sixty years, I have my entrées into many circles and I am able, in an unofficial way, to ascertain what is being thought and said about Iran. Conversely, I can drop hints in this country about things being done here which are upsetting the Iran Government, small irritations, perhaps, which would assume a false importance if they had to be taken up officially by the Ambassador.

I have said enough to show that my work for the Iranian Embassy cannot be reduced to any formal catalogue of duties or responsibilities and, inevitably, my own social life overlaps into my business and diplomatic lives. When I give fairly large dinner parties—to members of the British Government, the Iranian Ambassador and those other Ambassadors who are influential because of their own personality, their knowledge of Britain or the country they represent—I am doing it as part of my responsibility to the Iranian Embassy but also, of course, for the pleasure I find in it myself. That is in tune with everything I do.

I should quite like to know what is going to be said about me when I am dead but, so far, I have failed to persuade *The Times* to let me see a draft of my obituary. I have pointed out that I should be able to correct any factual mistakes that may have crept into it but it seems they are prepared to take the risk of error. To begin with, I asked the editor of *The Times*, Sir William Haley—indeed, I asked him twice—but he told me it was out of the question, very courteously but very definitely. Then, at the yearly lunch given by Bernard Mills of Mills' Circus, I had the advantage of sitting

opposite Gavin Astor, the chairman of *The Times*. I asked him if
he could arrange for me to see my obituary.

'It's against our principles,' he said, 'but give Haley a good lunch
and see if you can get any change out of him.'

'I have already given Haley,' I said, 'both a good lunch and a
good dinner, but it's got me nowhere.' Gavin Astor was very
charming but no less definite than Haley. I have never known
anyone say 'No' to me so unambiguously, so categorically but so
courteously. Yet he asked me to lunch at *The Times* new building,
where the view of St. Paul's is really remarkable. Although I was
on a diet, I greatly enjoyed my lunch; excellent fried sole, fillet
steaks almost transatlantic in size, sweet, cheese, a light white wine,
a fairly heavy claret, good port, an excellent brandy and a Havana-
rolled cigar but—*no draft obituary.*

For one night, every few years, when the Master and Fellows
are good enough to ask members of the College to dine and spend
the night, I occupy P3, the same rooms in Great Court at Trinity,
which I had when I was an undergraduate at Cambridge nearly
fifty years ago. These are charming occasions. One is aware, as
always, of tradition, of the pictures of past Masters in the Hall, but
also of change, both in the College and the University, which
shows that they are very much a living organism. Nowadays, for
example, I find I can have a bath without having to walk a hundred
yards across the courtyard as I did when I was up: that is one kind
of change I welcome without reservation.

The last time I went up for one of these reunion dinners, I was
rather struck by the fact that only a lot of old fogies had been asked
—until I looked at myself in the glass. In fact, the other guests were
all my contemporaries: one is now the Lord Chief Justice Parker,
others are already *ex*-Ambassadors. It was after one of these
dinners that I fulfilled a life ambition. When I was an undergraduate, only Fellows were allowed to walk across the grass in the
Courts; now, here was a Fellow, taking me back from the Master's
Lodge where we had been conversing after dinner in Hall, across
that privileged grass, to my old rooms. (The Master's Lodge at
Trinity is a Royal residence and the story, possibly apocryphal, is
told of how Queen Victoria, when visiting Trinity, was met on the
threshold of the Lodge by the then Master with the words,

'Welcome, Ma'am, to my humble House.' To which the Queen replied, '*My* House, Master.')

I have all the money I could possibly desire. I am, as I write this, sixty-seven years old; I have no children and no expensive hobbies. I have never owned or wished to own, like Onassis, a 1800-ton yacht, nor even a 500-ton one. I do not have a picture gallery and I do not wish to own one. I do not own and do not wish to own a stud of thoroughbreds or a racing stable. So many people I know own race horses solely as a matter of snobbishness: they cannot even recognize their own horses when they see them. I am very fond of horses and I have a few hunters but I have them where I can see them daily.

Money, of course, is very useful just so long as it remains a servant and does not become the master. One really important thing that money can buy is—room for living. A man with money can buy room for himself and his family. He can choose when to be with other people and when to be alone; he does not have intimacy thrust upon him, he does not have to endure the kind of enforced and constant proximity which can produce rows. The rich man, one might say, can work at living. I should prefer to put it less pretentiously and just say that I enjoy life.

If I had any more money I should have to devote it to charity; I think I am better employed seeing that the money my father left is properly applied than by having more money myself. I recognized that if I were to have any chance of influencing the activities of the Gulbenkian Foundation, my views must be publicized and that they were more likely to be publicized if I myself were considered a figure of some public interest. That is why, in recent years, unlike some rich men and certainly unlike my father, I have welcomed rather than shunned publicity about myself. It was to get publicity for my views about the Foundation that I appeared in the television programme 'Face to Face' and it was chiefly in order to get publicity for the views of Lord Radcliffe and Mr. House—views which supported my case against the Trustees—that I took my action against the B.B.C.

Before I was invited to appear in 'Face to Face', the B.B.C. had asked me several times to take part in radio or television programmes. I had appeared only twice before on television. In 1958, at the time of the Papal Election, there was talk of the possibility of an Armenian Pope. The B.B.C. put on a programme about Armenia and asked me to take part in it as a well-known Armenian in London.

The other time I appeared was in the programme 'Tonight', together with a London taxi which I had had converted for my own use: that was the taxi with the special, custom-built, basketwork body which has often got itself into the newspapers. My idea was to have a taxi dolled up to make it more comfortable inside and less clumsy in appearance while enjoying its inherent mobility. It is quite a useful vehicle and, by now, it is pretty well known so that I never have any difficulty in finding it. Whenever I leave some function or ceremony, whether it be, say, a memorial service in Westminster Abbey for Hugh Gaitskell, a M.G.M. film première or a reception at an Embassy in Millionaire's Row, while other people are still searching for their cars, some kind person always comes up to me to tell me where mine is. It was to give a 'plug' to Jack Barclay, who supplied me with the car, and the small coach-building firm, Panelcraft, who did the work and put a lot of trouble and professional pride into it, that I agreed to appear in 'Tonight'.

Very different considerations were in my mind, however, when the B.B.C. invited me to be John Freeman's fifth 'victim' in the programme 'Face to Face'. Here was a programme which not only went out 'live' and unrehearsed but also had as its purpose, as John Freeman himself explained to me later, to reveal public figures as they really were and to debunk them. A half-hour's uninhibited investigation of character could be an embarrassing, perhaps painful, experience for the subject of the programme but, of course, from the audience's point of view, rich in entertainment. Its previous victims had been Lord Birkett, Bertrand Russell, Bob Boothby and Edith Sitwell, and it had a regular audience in the region of four million people.

This was the tempting aspect of it to me, a wonderful opportunity for me to air my views about my father's Foundation publicly, but I thought hard and long before I decided to accept. I talked to everyone I could about the programme and found that John Freeman had a reputation, in some ways an unfair one, for tearing his subjects to pieces. I was frightened that I might make a mess of the whole thing and, under harsh examination by Freeman, appear a greater fool than I may be. On the other hand, I was flattered that I should rate such an interview and I have always said, rather smugly, that if you do nothing of which you are ashamed you will not be ashamed of anything you have done; it follows that if you are open and straightforward and tell the truth you will carry more weight and, what is more, it will be much simpler than if you try to put on an act or to tell lies.

One reason why I hesitated, apart from my anxieties about my ability to give a good account of myself, was that I was hoping that *The Times* might take up the question of the Foundation. I had asked Cyril Radcliffe to arrange for me to meet Sir William Haley, the editor of *The Times*, and the three of us were to lunch at the Ritz. Until I had talked to Sir William, I did not wish to commit myself to 'Face to Face' lest by doing so I should cross wires with anything *The Times* might be persuaded to do. Haley, however, took the view that, while he might be very sympathetic to my point of view, there was nothing effective to be done in England. The British public, he said, would not get excited at having lost a Foundation with a £5 million a year income when there was nothing they could do about it and he did not want *The Times* to start a campaign which he felt in advance would not succeed.

Lord Radcliffe's advice about 'Face to Face' was positive. 'If you're willing to take the risk of making a fool of yourself,' he said, 'you have a unique opportunity of putting your views across to the British public. There could not be a better way of enlisting public opinion on your side.' Now that there was no hope of *The Times* taking up my campaign, I decided in principle to go ahead with the B.B.C. and take the risk of looking an idiot.

I went to Feliks Topolski's studio for him to make the sketches of me which would precede the programme. (One of these sketches now hangs side by side in the hall of the Carlton Tower with those Topolski did of Adenauer, Eisenhower, Macmillan and de Gaulle when each was the chief statesman of his country.) John Freeman and Hugh Burnett, the producer of the programme, came to see me at my flat at Arlington House, five days before the date fixed for the programme.

It was only after that meeting that I finally decided to take part in the programme. There were a number of points I wanted settled. The meeting went most amicably; I found both John

Freeman and Hugh Burnett very charming and anxious to get my final agreement to the programme. We had a drink and a cigar and John Freeman told me the kind of questions he wanted to ask me, without going into any detail about them because he wanted to preserve the spontaneity of the interview. We agreed that he should not ask me any questions about my work as a diplomatist for it would have been improper of me to talk about that. It was also agreed that he should ask for my views on the Gulbenkian Foundation: I was most anxious about this, for there was no other reason why I should accept the B.B.C. invitation to appear. I said that, instead of a cash fee, I wanted a tele-recording of the programme. Hugh Burnett promised to get me one. Actually, at that time the B.B.C. expected to sell a tele-recording to America for rediffusion throughout the United States, as some previous 'Face to Face' programmes had been.

On the evening of the interview I went to Lime Grove an hour or so before the programme was due to begin, to make sure, as Mr. Burnett put it, that the studio lighting on me was 'perfect', to have a little make-up and to have a drink or two with John Freeman and B.B.C. people before we did our stuff. I was very nervous but they did all they could to make me less so. We did not talk about the programme except that John Freeman told me what his first and last questions would be. Then we were off to the studio for the interview itself. I must say that, although I went into it with some trepidation, I found myself at home fairly quickly. I knew that among the material John Freemen had read was a biography of my father by Ralph Hewins and I foresaw that he would ask me questions about my father's private life which, in the ordinary way, I should have preferred to keep private; but I felt there was no point in denying the facts, which had already been referred to in two books.

What I did not know was that, following approaches made to the B.B.C. by the then secretary to the Gulbenkian Foundation in London, Freeman had been given the Trustees' side of the story, and I was somewhat off guard when he put it to me. Being unprepared, I had no chance to beat about the bush. Not that I wanted to, anyway; far better to tell the unvarnished truth.

The interview seemed, from all points of view, to be a success. The B.B.C. people, over a drink after the programme, were full of nice words of praise; the newspapers next morning were no less complimentary. Some of my friends told me that John Freeman had made one or two cracks at me in the course of the programme but I was not aware of them. So far as I was concerned, his manner had been very fair and I told him so in a letter afterwards. (We have met once or twice since and we have become quite friendly. One outcome is that I now take the *New Statesman*, which Freeman edits, and, while I do not agree with many of its conclusions, it is interesting to get his slant on current affairs. It enables me to look at the generally accepted views from a different angle; in rare cases, it exposes their falsity, but generally it confirms me in their correctness.)

There is no doubt that Hugh Burnett promised me a copy of the tele-recording of the programme and that his promise was broken. That was the whole basis of my action against the B.B.C. and the case in the Law Courts confirmed that I was right. But, of course, I was not trying, principally, to get at Burnett or the B.B.C. As I said at the time, they were unlucky enough to get caught in the middle of the arguments between the Trustees and myself.

I am quite sure the B.B.C. had every intention of giving me my tele-recording—and of selling the programme to America—until Whishaw stepped in. He told the B.B.C. he and the Trustees objected to what I had said about them and that they claimed my remarks were defamatory. The letters that passed between him and the B.B.C. explained why, at one moment, the B.B.C. were about to hand over the tele-recording to me and, the next moment, were saying I could not have it. He also stopped them from selling the programme to the United States. They acted in self-defence. The B.B.C., through Hugh Burnett, agreed that they had made a gentleman's agreement with me but, as the B.B.C. claimed they were not gentlemen, they claimed they did not have to carry it out.

The details of the action against the B.B.C. are unimportant, however. The case was a success, so far as I was concerned, because it enabled me to present to the general public my criticisms of the Trustees, backed by the powerful evidence of Lord Radcliffe and the views of Mr. House. My lawyers had warned me before we went to court that the Judge would fight 'like hell' against having to try what was, in effect, a libel action in reverse—the means by which I could publicize my charges against the Trustees—and that we should have great difficulty in bringing the evidence of Lord Radcliffe and Mr. House before the court, evidence which, on the face of it, had nothing to do with whether the B.B.C. broke their agreement or not. That was why my solicitors advised me to engage a counsel of great weight, a former Attorney-General like Sir Lionel Heald, who would be able to stand up against the Judge and would fight to show that to substantiate my allegedly defamatory criticisms of the Trustees was relevant to the case. It is in that sense that my case, which was very well conducted, was successful.

True, it cost me £10,000 in lawyers' costs. It cost the B.B.C. half as much. But both Cyril Radcliffe and Lionel Heald told me that if I had spent £10,000 on a public relations officer I could never have obtained as much publicity for my views and for those of Radcliffe and the past President of the Institute of Chartered Accountants. I also had the satisfaction of receiving a cheque from the Royal Courts of Justice for £2 which I have framed and which I keep on my mantelpiece as a memento of my success.

I had only one regret. The evidence given by Lord Radcliffe and Mr. House was faithfully reported by *The Times*, the *Guardian* and the *Telegraph* but, by and large, it was not colourful enough, apparently, for the mass circulation Press. My gastronomic predilections seemed to appeal more than my high moral principles and the Press were much more excited about what I had to eat than about the case. The trouble was that I believe, with Dr. Johnson, 'he who hath not wit enough to care for his belly would scarce have wit enough to care for aught else'. I saw no reason to munch a sandwich during the luncheon adjournment when I could have a decent cold lunch sent into the Courts. I arranged each day for food (but not alcohol) to be brought from the Caprice, the restaurant which is attached to Arlington House and which I often patronize. The Caprice is run by Mario Gallati, a restaurateur of the old school who can serve an excellent meal, if necessary at a reasonable price. He is well over seventy but has all the activity of a man twenty years younger.

Many people merely eat to live, but food plays a much more important part in my life than that. To eat well is not primarily a question of having the money. There is no greater mistake than to eat things out of season just because they are smart or expensive. I have eaten strawberries at Christmas in England, forced hothouse strawberries, which had no taste and cost more than their weight in gold. (That was before the aeroplane brought them from Kenya and California: now it is fairly easy to have good strawberries all the year round.) It all comes back to the question of taking care and trouble; this is something my father instilled into me. Gastronomy is an art as difficult to master as music or painting and, for me, much more rewarding. I certainly get more pleasure from working out a menu, discussing the pros and cons of each dish with a chef who knows his business, seeking the most pleasurable combinations and contrasts in its creation, than I do from listening to the best of Beethoven's symphonies which I just do not understand.

Alas, nowadays, life is too hurried and it is difficult to obtain good food, but luckily there are still some culinary artists who take pride and pleasure in their work. They are people who find the modern way of life disheartening; rarely do they receive either a word of praise for a particularly well conceived creation and successful realization or any word of complaint for some dish which has been prepared in a slipshod way.

Monsieur Vaudable, who owns Maxim's Restaurant in Paris (where, if they know you and you order in advance, you can still get a very good meal, well worth its astronomical price), tells a story of his visit to New York some years ago. He went to a well-known French restaurant there and ordered, from the head waiter, what sounded like a good meal. He had to send back one dish after another as being, according to his standards, entirely uneatable. He was unknown there and was regarded as a nuisance and a fusspot; the staff were glad to see him preparing to go. As he was leaving, however, the chef—also a Frenchman—came out of the kitchen, tears in his eyes. He shook Monsieur Vaudable by the hand and thanked him profusely.

'But I am afraid,' said Vaudable, 'that I cannot possibly congratulate you on your cooking.'

'Ah, sir,' said the chef, 'but this is the first time that anyone has noticed my cooking at all. It is so disheartening preparing food for people who don't know or care enough about what they eat either to appreciate the good or criticize the bad. How can I take trouble for the average people who come here?' The 'average people', I should add, were the wealthiest of America and that means of the world.

Not surprisingly, I am very much concerned in the choice of food for our guests when my wife and I are entertaining. This is particularly true of the dinner parties we give now and then at the Ritz. These parties, which I mentioned earlier, are on the formal side and are given to entertain our official friends, in return, for instance, for the frequent hospitality we receive from the various Embassies. We give a big one for each new, incoming Iranian Ambassador and our guest list includes other Ambassadors, Cabinet Ministers, distinguished lawyers, such as the Lord Chancellor and Lord Chief Justice of the day, or men of letters and high-ranking civil servants. When we first started giving this kind of party, we confined the number to around eighteen or twenty, which is small enough to allow the host to talk to each of his guests, but the trouble is that to be sure of getting a dinner party of eighteen you have to send out invitations to twice that number—with the result that sometimes, unexpectedly, we receive acceptances from between thirty and forty.

Parties of this size are a little unwieldy, even though we try to keep down the number at each table to eight or ten, with my wife hostess at one, myself host at another and the most important of our guests, or those best known to us, acting as host and hostess at other tables. For these parties the food is highly elaborate. I order it a week or more in advance, after a long session with Monsieur Schwenter, the manager of the Ritz, and Monsieur Vinet, the Ritz chef, discussions which often lead to special importations from Paris. The organization on the day gives us no anxiety for everything, from the arrangement of the flowers to the provision of the cigars, from the printing of the menu to the preparation of the table plan, is under the discreet eye of Bishop, whose invaluable help has been at my disposal for over forty years. His formal title is that of telephone attendant in the restaurant; he is also the *physionomiste* of the Ritz; he knows everyone who is or was anyone in London.

Intimate friends we entertain to dinner in our flat. We hold parties there about once a week and keep the numbers down to ten. The menus are often quite ambitious and, when our own kitchen staff are not quite up to the standard required, or are overwhelmed by our demands, my wife calls in a chef whom we have known for a long time, a man who loves to come to help prepare a particular meal but who will not take up permanent employment. Sometimes, though my wife does not like to admit it, we get a dish sent up from the Caprice Restaurant below.

Less elaborate are the meals we give in the country at Hoggeston, though my wife takes a great deal of care over them and especially discusses the meat with our butcher, Mr. Parrot of Whitchurch, whose family have served me well for over thirty years. We get all our poultry, including turkeys, locally, and the vegetables we try to grow in our garden; a vegetable, picked from the garden two hours before being eaten, is incomparably more fresh to the taste than one bought in the shops. Our country entertaining is weekend entertaining and our guests are our hunting friends and our neighbours, generally six or eight and never more than ten at a time, for that is the maximum number who will fit comfortably into our small dining-room. Once or twice a year we give a cocktail party for about 200 people, indoors around Christmas time, in a marquee in the garden in the summer. We never have anyone staying with us. However much we like our friends, someone sleeping in the house and having breakfast there seems to disorganize the household. (We never stay with friends, either, preferring the independence of an hotel.)

Weekends in the country, weekdays in Town, hunting in the winter, a few days at Cannes at Christmas, a cruise in the spring, two or three weeks at Cap d'Antibes in the summer: this is the pattern of my life nowadays, each segment contributing its own kind of enjoyment. The services held, twice a year, in July and January, on my mother's tomb at Nice, are the pivots to our travels.

When we go to the July service we book into the Hôtel du Cap d'Antibes, an extremely comfortable and really charming place at Eden Roc. It is a smallish hotel but with beautiful high-ceilinged rooms, a very decent restaurant by the sea, vast grounds and a private bathing spot with *cabañas* fitted with every modern convenience. The *cabañas* are well spread out so that none overlooks another and we can be entirely on our own, undisturbed by the crowds who, at that time of the year, may be on the public beaches or in their cars on the roads. There is bathing off the rocks straight into deep water. When I first went there, I used to climb down into the water by means of steps. Then I started jumping from the rocks which, with my size, was a not very pretty procedure; so although I was over sixty-five, I decided to learn to dive.

By dint of much practice with the *maître-baigneur*, I now manage to proceed from land to water, head first, without indulging to an excessive extent in what is rather inelegantly but very aptly called a 'belly-flop'. Next, I had a diving-board built up, over the rocks, so that one can take a running dive straight into the water instead of having to be careful about missing the rocks. Building the diving-board meant building up a lot of rocks to make it fairly solid; some wag saw it and dubbed it the 'Gulbenkian Foundation'—because, he said, 'Nubar runs and jumps all over it'. At first the diving-board was only a couple of feet high; then I felt rather bold and had another one put up, six feet high. Finally, to my wife's despair, I had a third one erected exactly sixteen feet high, immediately outside my *cabaña*. Only the *maître-baigneur* uses that one, although I did use it once, quite successfully, if somewhat ungracefully. I met the water in good style but what I did not realize at the time was that, just after I had taken off from the diving-board, the *maître-baigneur* gave my legs a push upwards to straighten my dive. This took place in the sight of quite a large crowd gathered there to see the inauguration of the latest and highest branch of the 'Gulbenkian Foundation'.

At Eden Roc, my wife has no housekeeping cares and, much of the time, we just laze and lie, in and out of the water. We have a lot of friends on the Riviera but we refuse all invitations. Only the telephone prevents us from being entirely cut off but, while I can talk to any part of the world within five minutes, 'any part of the world' usually leaves us in peace. That is a real rest and holiday and then, in August, when everyone else travels we find it quieter and more agreeable at home; that is the time, too, when our garden is at its best.

The garden at Hoggeston is not a big one and the house is certainly no mansion although it is quite large enough for us and extremely comfortable. A landscape gardener has made the most of the little land we have, cunningly devising walks and vistas which give a flattering as well as pleasing sense of space and distance. We also run to a pond—it would be too pretentious to call it a lake—and a pair of swans which, at certain times of the year, have been known to treat visitors, particularly those from Town, with something less than respect.

We bought the place after the war. The house is a former rectory but, as my wife had been married once before and I had been married twice before, I did not think it appropriate to live in 'The Old Rectory'; so we changed its name to 'The Old House'. There is another 'Old House' in the neighbouring village of Swanbourne and this was the only one the postman knew—with the result that, at first, our letters went to Lord Cottesloe, the charming old gentleman who then owned the Swanbourne house. There followed a very polite correspondence between my wife and Lord Cottesloe until eventually we met him. We are now very friendly with his son, the present holder of the title, who is chairman of the Arts Council, a vice-chairman of the Port of London Authority, chairman of the National Rifle Association and a great authority on shooting at Bisley where he has won many prizes and championships. He also possesses a wonderful cellar. When I lunched with him recently he opened a bottle—one of his last two bottles—of 1863 Château Yquem, which was a rich and rare experience. He gave me the original branded cork which was as good as the day it was first put in the bottle; I sent it to the Marquis de Lur Saluces, the owner of the Yquem vineyard whom I meet every year at Messrs. Lebegue's famous wine-tasting in their cellars near London Bridge. He sent me a case of magnums in return. A sound investment.

The rooms in the Old House at Hoggeston, having been built in the eighteenth century, are well-proportioned and one can sit there with pleasure (which cannot be said of our flat in London where, as with all modern flats, the ceilings are so low one has the impression they will fall down on one's head).

I like being in the country. I like being there at all seasons of the year. Apart from the more obvious pleasures, there are others which, for me, are associated with being in the country. When I think of winter weekends, for instance, I also think of muffins. I have been fond of muffins since the time when the muffin-man, complete with his bell, could still be heard in the streets of London and one could obtain a muffin at one's club. After the war muffins seemed to have disappeared completely. It was only with great difficulty that, for some time, I managed to get the chef at the Ritz in London to make me a daily supply but even those were not particularly good. Fortunately, a couple of years ago, I found a Swiss baker who lives in Marlow and, in the winter, he sends me a weekly supply of muffins.

In the summer, I like pottering in my garden or going to see my horses. On Sunday afternoons, I retire to a little summer-house, tucked away about fifty yards from the house, where I settle down with the Sunday papers, at the same time enjoying a pleasant view over the enclosed rose garden with the yew hedge and the herbaceous border beyond. I have arranged a simple system of communication between the house and the garden; this has inspired a story about Nubar Gulbenkian and his whistle which, like many other stories, has been distorted by the exuberance of the Press. In order to save the time of a servant looking for me in our pocket domain if I am wanted on the telephone or someone has called to see me, I have arranged that I should be called back to the house by a blast on a whistle. That was the first stage out of which a two-way system has developed. Now I, too, carry a whistle and I have a code by which, when I am in the garden, I can summon a servant: one blast for my butler, two for my valet and six for tea or drinks, according to the time of day. A whistle is more portable and more effective than a hand-bell and a bell-push may well not be handy.

When we first moved into the Old House my wife searched for a bell-push to install in the dining-room for summoning the next course but it seemed as though at that time a bell-push was not to be had. At one shop where my wife enquired, she received the retort, 'And what do you want a bell-push for—in order to ring and then answer the bell yourself?' Eventually she did find one of alabaster, at Asprey's of Bond Street, and she had to pay a correspondingly Bond Street price for it.

I am told that, as the result of newspaper stories about me, orchids and Nubar Gulbenkian are inseparable in the public mind. I am, indeed, extremely fond of orchids and I do make a practice of wearing one in my buttonhole every day of the year.

The orchid, of course, must match the occasion. When I go to the Harrow and Eton match at Lord's, being a loyal Old Harrovian, I must sport dark blue colours; I do not want mere cornflowers but a dark blue orchid. Anyone who knows about orchids will appreciate what a difficult demand I make upon myself for, although orchids are grown in practically all colours, a dark blue orchid is very rare; it would probably be true to say that I, alone, have been known to wear one. One day at Lord's, a friend asked me how I managed to get a dark blue orchid.

'Actually,' I told him, 'there is only one place in the world where blue orchids will grow. It is just a small piece of land, no more than an acre in all, in the northern Himalayas about fifty miles from Lhasa, and facing north-west. You could try transplanting the dark blue orchids that grow there, you could get cuttings or seedlings, but, I assure you, you would never be able to grow them in England.

'What I have to do,' I said, 'is to get the blooms transported by yak caravan. The first stage of the journey has got to be by yak caravan and not by aeroplane because the effluvium of the yak apparently contains some form of ammonia which, acting in combination with the lack of oxygen at that high altitude and with the orientation of that particular piece of land, allows the orchids to remain dark blue until they reach the plains of India. There, they are put on an aeroplane and sent to me.'

A journalist eavesdropped upon that conversation and, next day, the story appeared, in all its detail, in one of the papers. The truth about my dark blue orchids is, I fear, a little less exotic. The process takes not less than twenty-four hours. I dip a white orchid into a mixture of Stephen's Ink and water—I have got the mixture virtually right by now—let it dry, then shake it out gently —and I achieve a very adequate dark blue orchid.

The origin of my wearing an orchid dates back to the early 1920s. My father was toying with the idea of buying a country house in England, an idea he toyed with until the late 1930s. My poor mother and myself must have seen well over a hundred places, desirable or otherwise, within fifty or sixty miles of London, but none of them was what my father wanted and, in the end, he bought and made Les Enclos near Deauville. But, in the same way as he built his garden there before building a house for himself, so he started collecting plants for his country place in England before he had any country place. He went regularly to the Royal Horticultural Society Shows in Vincent Square and the yearly Shows at Chelsea. He was very friendly with the orchid growers among whom the best, at any rate for *odonto-glossum*, was Charlesworth and Co. of Haywards Heath, and whenever a new specimen was produced, which was particularly rare or had a beautiful flower, he was persuaded to buy it. He acquired a large stock of plants at livery with Charlesworth and Co. (although, as far as I can remember, the firm did not send him any bills for livery charges), and, from time to time, they sent him the blooms from his orchids. Because orchids are apt to flower at the same time and because there may be seven, nine or eleven blooms on one spike, orchids arrived *en masse* from Haywards Heath. After my mother and the house and possibly my father's lady friends had been provided with orchids, there were always some orchids left over and, once, 'little Nubar' was given one to wear in his buttonhole. That is how I started the habit.

To this day, Charlesworth and Co., a most efficient and extremely helpful firm, take a great pride in seeing I have a good bloom in my buttonhole every day of the year. They send me three blooms twice a week which, in addition to those I grow myself in my orchid-house at Hoggeston, see me through. They take a professional pride in supplying them and I believe I am an advertisement for the firm because I have heard of many people who are orchid-growers and have been told by Charlesworth that they supply me. They have sent them to me when I have been in various parts of the Mediterranean, in Istanbul, in Moscow, even in the Caucasus and the Caribbean. They pack them carefully, with the stems wrapped in little plastic bags containing damp moss and, although an orchid which arrives in that way is not as fresh as one which has spent only a single night in the post between Haywards Heath and Hoggeston, I am able to sport my daily orchid continuously and to maintain my tradition. Not merely do Charlesworth's make sure I have an orchid every day of the year, wherever I may be, which might seem achievement enough, but they also send me a *different* bloom every day of the year. What is more, if they have not yet produced a dark blue orchid, they did breed for me, at my special request about thirty-five years ago, a yellow orchid.

When I started to hunt with the Old Berkeley, whose colour is mustard yellow, someone said, on seeing me wearing my usual orchid, 'If you're going to sport an orchid at all, you ought to sport a yellow one.' There were no yellow orchids available then but I talked the matter over with Mr. Smith, who was the great man at Charlesworth's in those days. Mr. Smith said that, if I did not mind waiting for perhaps two or three years, and if I was not worried about the expense, he thought he could produce a yellow orchid. And so he did. Not only was I able to wear a yellow orchid when hunting with the Old Berkeley but, nowadays, when my wife and I are out with the British Driving Society, whose emblem is a yellow carnation (every member is given one by our President, Sandy Watney, of Watney, Combe, Reid, from his hothouses), Charlesworth's produce two identical yellow orchids for us to wear when our own *odontoglossum élise* is not in flower.

The one time when I do not wear my orchid is when I am in France, on board a French ship or French aeroplane, or at a French Embassy. It is the French custom, in France, for those who have been granted the Legion of Honour to wear the insignia of the Order in their buttonhole. I feel it is only courteous, to show the respect I have for the country which granted me the honour, to wear mine instead of an orchid. I wear it whenever I go to the French Embassy in London, although when in the street, or going on from there to somewhere else, I wear my orchid bloom on top of it; I do not wish to appear to flaunt my foreign decoration, as I should seem to do if I were to wear it in public in England. Unfortunately, a few years ago, I slipped up. I went to a party at the French Embassy and, as I shook hands with the French Ambassador, our old friend, Monsieur Chauvel, he said, very sweetly but quite unmistakably, 'Oh, my dear Gulbenkian, what a beautiful orchid you have on today!' I had forgotten to take my orchid out of the buttonhole on entering the Embassy.

I give my orchid to the hostess—and reveal my Legion of Honour—as soon as I board a French aeroplane. When flying by British aircraft, I take it out as soon as we are over territorial waters. I hope all this does not seem pompous or over-fussy for I certainly do not think of it that way myself; I feel it is only right that I should make these completely genuine gestures of respect and courtesy.

I am sometimes asked: 'You grow your own orchids? How do you grow them?'

'Orchids are like horses,' I say. 'On Sunday mornings, I go around my stables, accompanied by my stud groom who carries a skip containing carrots. As I get to each box, the horse puts his head out and, knowing the ceremonial, nuzzles towards me, lowering his head. I stretch out my hand, the stud groom deferentially hands me the skip, I take a carrot, give it to the horse, pat him on the neck and proceed to the next box. When we have finished going around the stables, I go around my orchid house, accompanied by my orchid-grower who carries a trug containing very succulent manure. On my entering the orchid-house, the orchids recognize me; they turn towards me and bow. Thereupon, I turn to my orchid-grower, who hands me the trug; I take a little pinch of manure and put it near the stem of the orchid. I pass on from orchid to orchid until all have received their special nourishment. That is how I grow orchids.'

Until Castro arrived, Partagas and Company, a small Cuban firm who were not a member of the Tobacco Trust, had been making cigars for me for over thirty years. They used to make them with the greatest care and then keep them for a year before sending them by air to me. I, in turn, kept them for a further year, at the end of which time I could look forward to a pleasant smoke, the cigars being not too strong, not as dry as some English people like nor yet as green as some Americans like them. It is true that, since Castro came into power and has taken over all the cigar factories, it has been difficult for me to get my cigars, but my experience also shows the futility of trying to impose a boycott. Just before the revolution in Cuba, I sent out an order for cigars. I received a reply after the Revolution which said that my order would be executed in due course and I would be told when they were ready for shipment. A few weeks later, I was told that my cigars would be shipped by Russian airline from Cuba to Czechoslovakia and then by Czech airline from Czechoslovakia to London. I was asked, however, to pay for them not, as hitherto, in U.S. dollars, because Cuba's accounts in the States had been blocked, but by a cheque on Canada in favour of the Moscow Narodny Bank, as the Canadians had not seen eye to eye with the Americans over their attitude towards Cuba.

I like to think that our winter hunting, which I enjoy enormously, enlivens the winter countryside as well as providing pleasure and recreation both to those who take part on horseback and those who follow by car or on foot. On the other hand I am very ready to understand there are others who do not enjoy it, in the same way as I do not enjoy music; what I regret is the intolerance the subject of hunting has bred in recent years. If the people who belong to the League Against Cruel Sports, in a reversion to the Puritan outlook, however misguidedly and illogically, wish to proclaim their dislike of foxhunting they are surely entitled to do so. But I dislike their interference with the pleasure of others, including myself. I do not force them to come out on a horse to hunt; they should not try to prevent me from doing so. Still, whenever I meet representatives of the League I am studiously polite to them, although some of my fellow hunting men have chided me for 'siding with the enemy'.

There was the occasion, for instance, in 1961 when I was gate-shutting: it was my turn to forego a day's sport and follow the end of the field to ensure that all gates were shut and farmers' cattle were not straying. Members of the League Against Cruel Sports were on the trail, too, and were doing their usual best to make a nuisance of themselves. While I was remonstrating politely with them and conducting a calm argument, one of them, a lady who lives locally and is well known to us, offered me a cup of coffee. Gate-shutting is a cold job and I gladly accepted the offer. To show my appreciation of their courtesy I summoned my second horseman who carries a large flask of port and brandy— some call it 'jumping powder'—and offered the flask to the lady. 'Won't you have a drop of fox's blood?' I said.

We usually get away for a cruise in March but, sometimes, we have time to go to the local point-to-point before leaving England. Although I have not ridden in a point-to-point since before the war and I am never likely to do so again, it is fun seeing our neighbours and now our neighbours' sons taking part and to chat to the farmers and the people who make up the English countryside of which I have grown so fond. We have had a series of Bedford vans on the top of which we have installed a platform with a balustrade: this makes an excellent grandstand from which to watch the racing. Inside the van we have our picnic and a bar where we entertain our friends and acquaintances. My wife has reduced the provision of our point-to-point picnics to a fine art. So much so that we reached the stage a few years ago when I was hard put to it to find a cause for complaint.

'No flowers,' I said. 'We ought to have some flowers.' (This complaint might be described as an example of my pantaraxia, a word I coined with the assistance of my young nephew, a Balliol scholar, deriving from παν—Greek for 'all'—and ταράσσω—'I stir up'. It means that I like keeping people on their toes, or I used to; I suppose I inherited it from my father.)

At the next point-to-point my wife produced a little pot of *plastic* flowers.

'Your flowers,' she said.

'What a wonderful wife,' I thought.

I am not very keen on racing and I am no gambler but I used to go to the Grand National for the 'atmosphere'. I found it either rained or there was a fog which obscured the course; since television has covered the race I have watched it from my armchair. I still go regularly to Ascot, however, chiefly to show off my wife's new hat, I think. Mark you, one gets a good lunch at Ascot. Cold lobster, cold salmon trout, cutlets in aspic, cold chicken, ham and tongue, strawberries and cream, trifle and jelly: all these sound commonplace but, when properly prepared and served, they can be very appetizing. If one has a private box with a luncheon room, one can eat in great comfort. Of course, private boxes are a long, long way from the paddock and the Royal Enclosure where all the snobs (including myself for once) like to be seen in respectful proximity to the Royal Family: it always seems to me one of the tragedies of life that at Ascot, where the best horses in the world can be seen racing, the great majority of the people never even see them, so busy are they looking at each other.

I believe in comfort and I have said before now that the aim of a wife should be to make her husband supremely comfortable. In return, he should be kind and considerate in private and he should respect and stand up for her in public; whatever he does, he should not cause her public humiliation or embarrassment. But, after all, he is the head of the household and the household should revolve about him; he is the breadwinner and, if the breadwinner is not comfortable, he cannot win the bread from which everyone else should benefit. The whole of his entourage should share his good fortune. For instance, on the few occasions when I have a bet, a winning one, my wife gets a little nonsense and all my servants get a little *douceur*. There are moments, though, when the head of the household finds himself meekly submitting to his wife. In a recent Grand National, a horse named Ayala was running. As my wife had been born de Ayala, I backed it with my usual £10 each way. It won at 66–1 and I was better off by about £900. But my wife, pressing the interests of the Red Cross to the fore, said: 'Ah, wonderful! We're needing a new ambulance for our Branch—your winnings will go very nicely towards it.' My contribution to a new ambulance, plus the odd fivers to the servants and drinks all round on several occasions, soon took care of the £900.

In 1963, my wife was made President of the Buckinghamshire County Branch of the Red Cross, a very high position, it seems. It involves her in attending meetings, presiding at parades, giving demonstrations of first-aid, thus occupying quite a lot of her time which her husband feels might be more profitably employed looking after his comforts—but she finds it enthralling and I am forced to admit her work is very useful.

There are limits to my enthusiasm, however. When my wife tells me she will be holding a Red Cross garden party at Hoggeston and adds, 'You will be welcome'—I clear out. Similarly, we have an understanding that I will make other arrangements for eating when she is having one of her 'hag lunches' and that she will not join one of my business lunches. All we ask of each other is a courteous warning in advance.

I enjoy myself. I enjoy life. I enjoy everything I do. So far as I know, I have always worked to the best of my ability and I have acknowledged the limitations of human existence. It is very easy to say 'So what?' to human achievement, very easy to question one's activities and to analyse one's motives and purposes to the point where everything one does can seem futile. It would be possible (but how fatuous) to point at, say, Winston Churchill, as an old man in decline and say, 'What do his career as a statesman, all his speeches, his books and his pictures add up to now?' There was a time when I subjected myself to that kind of examination and I realized that it must produce profound discontent, to which suicide was the only logical solution. So I stopped analysing myself. I stopped asking myself questions that could never have a satisfactory answer.

I do not have conclusive, satisfactory answers to questions about religion, either, but I observe the outward forms, as a matter of habit, of example, of tradition. As an Oriental, I have been brought up to show external signs of grief and this upbringing dictates my views on mourning. On Good Friday and Ash Wednesday, I keep strictly to the Eastern Christian's code of fasting, eschewing all forms of flesh; I eat fish, vegetables and vegetable oils, but no meat, eggs, butter, milk or anything of animal origin. This abstinence entails a certain amount of difficulty over meals but falls short of privation; after all, caviare, salmon, asparagus and suchlike are permitted. All food, however, must be cooked in water or olive oil and not in butter or milk.

(The strictness of the Eastern Christian religion in the observance of Lent is well illustrated by the story of Viralogieux, the grill-room chef at the Savoy, who died during the war. Before coming to England, he had been chef, in Tzarist days, at the Nobles' Club in St. Petersburg. His instructions were to conform strictly to religious regulations in preparing meals but when, during Lent, he managed to produce a *coulibiac* which was particularly tasty, one of the Grand Dukes congratulated him and asked him how he had managed to make such beautiful pastry without using butter.

'*Monseigneur,*' he said, '*le bon Dieu n'y regarde pas de si près*' —'the good God doesn't look quite so closely into everything'.

During Lent I brush my beard, my moustache and my eyebrows downwards and it is not until Easter morning that they are brushed up again—*sursum corda*. From Ash Wednesday I cut out all smoking until after lunch on Easter Sunday when I have my first cigar. This is good for my health for I am an inveterate smoker and I do not have the strength of will to cut down so that by the time Ash Wednesday comes around I am smoking far too many cigars and pipes a day. (I hardly ever smoke a cigarette except when I am waiting impatiently for my wife to put the finishing touches to her toilette, which is not that often.) For the first few days after giving up smoking I chew gum; I am told my temper is even viler than usual. My wife says that I stop smoking but she does the penance.

To an Armenian, his Church represents more than merely religion: it is also a symbol of his corporate and independent traditions. When their political independence and political existence disappeared half a millenium ago, it was to their Church that the Armenians turned as their rallying-point. It is through the Church that their classical language has been preserved. For these reasons, the first thing a wealthy Armenian does is to build a church in the town where he happens to be living. My father built and endowed the church in London in the 1920s and enlarged it as a thanksgiving for my having escaped death in my aeroplane accident in 1935. ('A cheap form of insurance,' said Whishaw.) Mantacheff built the church in Paris. Even today, in 1964, a rich Armenian, who was born in Southport, is building a church in Geneva. In Lyon, a church built by public subscription, by money collected over ten years, was consecrated in 1963.

Nevertheless, Armenian churches are not so widespread that there is always one handy wherever I may be. Because I am at Hoggeston at the weekends, for instance, I find it difficult to travel 100 miles on a Sunday morning to attend the Armenian church in London but I do go there on special occasions, such as the annual Requiem Masses for the souls of my grandparents—in whose memory the church was built—and that for my father. I am not, anyway, a constant churchgoer, although I make a regular practice of going to church on Christmas Day, Easter Day and Harvest Festival (our gardeners have the honour of decorating the font in our village church), if possible in the Armenian church but otherwise in whichever other Christian church is handy.

Once, between the wars, when I was flying in a small aeroplane I was caught in a thunderstorm. The plane was being thrown all over the place and I was convinced it would crash at any moment. I prayed to God to help me. When I landed, I was rather ashamed of myself; it was hardly cricket, I thought, when in great trouble to apply to God with whom, otherwise, one does not have regular intercourse. I learned my prayers and my scriptures from my nurses and governesses and only to a limited extent from my parents—they were not regular churchgoers, either, although my

father was a very devout man—but religion itself is, for me, something which is kept in a rather separate and mysterious compartment. It is not to be confused with ethics. Both religion and ethics
may dictate particular codes of behaviour but the reasons why one
adheres to them are different.

I cannot say truthfully that I am a believer but nor can I say I
am an agnostic or a disbeliever because my attitude certainly
cannot be summed up as disbelief. Some thirty years ago, observing
that some of my friends derived great consolation from their
beliefs, I determined to study religion more closely. First, I invited
to dinner the vicar of the Armenian church in London who was
later to become a famous Armenian ecclesiastic and patriarch of
Jerusalem. Why should I believe? I asked him.

'It is a matter of self-respect and pride for someone who bears
the name of Gulbenkian to be a son of the Armenian Church,' he
said. 'Your parents and grandparents have been devoted supporters of the Church and you must remember how many
Armenians have died for their faith.' That was an *argumentum
ad hominem*, but it did not give a logical explanation of the
mysteries of the Resurrection. I could not help remembering the
thousands of people who were killed in the debate over whether
the Holy Ghost proceedeth from the Father or proceedeth from the
Father *and* the Son—which is the main theological distinction
between the Eastern and Western Churches.

Next, I asked the local Anglican vicar in Buckinghamshire to
dinner. We had a heart-to-heart talk over the port and, later, over
the brandy and cigars. He enjoyed the dinner very much but most
of my questions he dismissed with the word 'Dogma!' He was an
elderly man who had been the incumbent there for some thirty
years and he gave me the impression that his conception of religion
amounted to no more than a code of behaviour, the leading of a
decent life or, perhaps, even more narrowly, living the life of an
English country gentleman. At the risk of being unfair, I should
say he would have thought it a more heinous offence for a man
to shoot a fox than to beat his wife.

My third tête-à-tête dinner was with a Roman Catholic bishop,
who was head of the R.C. chaplains in the R.A.F. He was an
Irishman, a very good man to hounds, a pillar and prop of the local
hunt; he rode at the age of fifty in point-to-points and had a

wonderful influence on his flock, both inside and outside the Church. He was essentially a humane and understanding man, though perhaps not of the highest intellectual calibre. He approached the matter of religion from yet another angle and told me to read a book by Beverley Nichols called *The Fool Hath Said*, which concludes that, while it may be difficult for one's critical faculties to accept all the tenets of the Christian religion, this is no argument for denying the existence of God. I think it was that book which, more than anything else, crystallized my attitude towards religion.

The Armenian Church is very much identified with the Armenian people and, to some extent, it is democratically controlled: the laity has a great deal to say in the selection of the religious hierarchy. The advancement of a priest to bishop, for instance, depends upon written evidence sent by the community he is serving and by the trustees of his church to the head of the Armenian Church, the Supreme Catholicos at Etchmiadzine in Armenia. The democratic principle may be admirable but it does have its disadvantages in practice. This is especially true of Armenians. As Boghos Nubar Pasha, who spent a lot of time and a vast fortune on Armenian affairs, used to say, the trouble with Armenians is that they are much too individualistic to combine for their common good. 'One Armenian,' he would say, 'is worth ten Englishmen. But,' he would add, 'ten Armenians are not worth one Englishman.'

My father became so weary of bickerings about the church he was founding in London that he made an arrangement whereby not only would he pay for all the cost of the land, the building of the church and the furnishing of it, but also for its upkeep. During his lifetime, he refused any contributions from the Armenian community and also created a trust fund of a few hundred thousand pounds to ensure that there would always be a sufficient income to maintain the church and to pay the priest's stipend. What was more, in contravention of the usual, democratic form, he arranged that the Patriarch of Jerusalem (then in British mandated territory) should appoint the priest without consulting the Armenian community in London, but that he must choose a man my father found acceptable. Today, there is a Board of Trustees, over which I preside, and it is to them that the vicar of the Armenian Church is responsible. Of course, he comes under the ecclesiastical authority of his theological chief, the Supreme Catholicos at Etchmiadzine. When a bishop in the Armenian Church is elevated to archbishop it is by the sole and direct authority of the Supreme Catholicos. Yet when the present Catholicos, His Holiness Vazgen I, was himself elected it was by a general assembly comprising representatives of Armenian communities throughout the world, an assembly of which two-thirds were laymen and only one-third clergy.

Because Armenians are held together by their Church more than by any political ties, the Catholicos may be said to be not only head of the Church but head of all the Armenian people. The Catholicosate at Etchmiadzine dates back to the first century A.D. and there has been an unbroken line of Catholicoi ever since. These days, in fact if not in theory, the secular authorities in Russia have some influence upon the election of the Catholicos. It was some years after the death of the previous Catholicos before the Soviet authorities would allow the election of a new one to take place and, during that period, there was only a locum tenens. Then the Soviet authorities relaxed their restrictions and gave Armenians from all over the world the special permission and facilities they needed to travel as representatives to Etchmiadzine for the election. In Tsarist days, the electoral body had to elect two candidates and the Russian Tsar decided which of the two should be appointed. The Soviet authorities do not assert this right, nor the right of veto, but it would obviously be tactless to try to elect a man who was not acceptable to the Russians.

I met the Catholicos for the first time when he visited England in October 1956, not long after his election. I was there when Dr. Fisher, the then Archbishop of Canterbury, accompanied him to the Church of St. Sarkis, the one my father built, and again at a dinner party given by Dr. Fisher to which he asked Lord Radcliffe and myself. (There were thirteen of us at table, something to which I would never agree in other circumstances, but as the head of the Church of England and the head of my own Church were both present, I thought it might be all right!)

Two years later, in the autumn of 1958, I made my first and only visit to Armenia, in order to take part in the celebration of the third anniversary of the enthronement of the Catholicos. The Catholicos invited delegations from all over the world to attend the ceremonies and I was invited, not as a member of a delegation, but in my own right. At that time, it was very hard to get visas to Russia but His Holiness had arranged all that and the Soviet Embassy granted visas to my wife, myself and also to my English valet. But, as I learned afterwards, they suspected that my valet, at that time a man named Welch, who had been with me five years, might be an agent of British Intelligence, and they made a thorough check on his military record—they discovered that he had been in both the army and the R.A.F.

We flew from Paris to Moscow and there we were met by a representative of the Catholicos. The proposal was that we should pay our own fares to Moscow but, thereafter, we should be the guests of the Catholicos; the practice, however, was to make a suitable donation to the funds of the Catholicosate to reimburse their expenses and, with people like myself who could afford it, to donate considerably more—rather on the Peter's Pence principle. I refused to be the Catholicos' guest in Moscow and I made my own arrangements with Intourist to take me around the city during the week or so we stayed there before going on to Armenia.

While we were queueing up outside the Kremlin, I heard two people in the crowd speaking Armenian. Quite excited, I turned to the Intourist guide and said, 'Did you hear that—those people over there are speaking Armenian?' Our guide, a Muscovite, well imbued with a sense of her own importance and of the superiority of Moscow over any other city in the Soviet Union, looked them up and down and said: 'Hmmm. Yes. They *look* like Armenians.' Undoubtedly, they were a bit scruffy.

My valet was also put in his place while we were in Moscow. He left the hotel one day with his key in his pocket. On each floor there was a sort of *concierge*, who was probably an Intelligence agent as well, to whom he was supposed to hand over his key. When Welch came back, he was in trouble with the woman I had seen acting as supervisor to four other women who were on their knees scrubbing out the bathroom.

'Don't you know we're honest people,' she said to my valet. 'What do you think we are—thieves? Why didn't you leave your key behind the same as everyone else does?'

To get from Moscow to Armenia meant a night flight, starting at about ten in the evening and arriving at about seven the following morning. The Ilyushin aircraft in which we flew was very reliable, rather like a Dakota, but slow and old-fashioned compared with the Tupoleff which had brought us from Paris to Moscow in just over three hours. The Ilyushin was used as a mail plane and every two hours or so we came down, to refuel and to unload and take on mail.

Our first stop, at about midnight, was at Kharkoff, where it was bitterly cold. There was an hour's wait and so, although we had had a bumpy flight there and did not feel very hungry, we went into the airport restaurant for something to eat. Now I thought I had learned something useful from my experience in Moscow. In all the best hotels there, there was a printed menu, in Russian, French, English and Chinese, containing about 200 items; the price was put against those items which were available. These menus, which were standard throughout Russia, were a great help to foreigners. In Moscow, I had become very Anglo-Saxon and decided, as my Russian is more than sketchy, that I had better learn by heart the names of a few pet dishes which I might wish to order. I knew the words for water, bread, tea, butter, meat, vodka but I soon reached the limit of my vocabulary and had to point to an item on the menu. There was one item on the menu, number forty-three, I think it was, which I had tried in Moscow: bacon and eggs. I had been surprised—being under the impression that there was great hunger in Russia—when I had been given three eggs with my bacon. I remembered that at Kharkoff where, having ordered the tea, lemon, brandy, bread and butter, I asked, like a good Englishman, for my eggs and bacon, but, because I did not feel like three eggs, I very carefully explained I wanted only two. '*Dwa*', I said and held up two fingers. The old woman with the shawl on her head who was waiting at the restaurant nodded her head, smiling. A little later back she came, with the tea, lemon, brandy, bread and butter and, to my horror, six eggs!

We had another stop for refuelling and for the loading and discharging of mail at Sukhumi. It was as we flew on from there that we saw for the first time the Black Sea, which is such a very dark blue that it is not mis-named. After flying along the Black Sea coast for a while, we crossed the Caucasus mountains, wending our way through valleys, until we landed at the airport at Erevan, the capital of Armenia, at seven o'clock in the morning. There were some 200 people waiting at the airport. They included people who had heard that the representatives of Armenian communities abroad, the Gulbenkians among them, were arriving that day for the great celebration. There was also a large official deputation to receive us on behalf of the Catholicos, the priests wearing their clerical gowns. (This might sound like stating the obvious but in Turkey, for instance, ministers of religion, whether Christian or Moslem, must not wear their religious robes in public. When I called on the Armenian Patriarch in Istanbul, one of his priests showed me around the church in his clerical garb but, when he wanted to take me to the Patriarch's palace, which was merely across the road, he had to change out of his priest's habit into civilian clothes.)

From Erevan airport we were taken into the city by the local head of the Intourist organization who was an Armenian from Cyprus and talked excellent English. My valet followed us with the luggage in another car to the hotel in the main square of Erevan. As in the rest of Russia at that time the authorities, in carrying out the vast task of reconstruction, had given priority to public buildings. The result in Erevan was an inevitable lack of balance in the pattern of rebuilding but the explanation was that the community came before the individual. The main square of the capital was most impressive, composed of new buildings, an hotel, called the Armenia Hotel, a museum and a cluster of Government buildings, all made of local tufa stone in the Armenian style of architecture. Tufa stone can be either pinkish or blueish; like the Armenian architectural style it is most distinctive. When I went to the Agricultural Exhibition in Moscow there was no mistaking from the outside which, of all the pavilions representing the Soviet Republics, was the Armenian one.

Our rooms in the hotel, a large sitting-room, large double bed-room and bathroom, were comfortable enough and all the staff— as elsewhere in Russia, there was an enormous number of staff— were very amiable and very anxious to please. Having travelled all night, in two-hour hops which made rest difficult, we retired to bed and I slept all day until teatime.

The next day, we drove out to Etchmiadzine to pay our respects to the Catholicos. What Rome is to the Roman Catholics, Etchmi-adzine is to the Armenians, the site of a church and monastery dating back to the fourth century and the seat of the Catholicos.

The Cathedral itself was at one time badly in need of repair and my father allocated in his will up to 400,000 dollars for its restoration: that was one specific provision he did not forget to make. Dr. Perdigão and Co. sent out a mission to see what work could be done. When they got to Etchmiadzine, the Soviet authorities had already carried out the structural work. It seemed at one time, however, as though the foundations of the Cathedral were sinking and that, in order to save it, the foundations would have to be strengthened. That, in turn, involved the diversion of an underground stream. (I believe the same problem arose over St. Paul's in London.) To divert the stream meant also altering the main drainage system of the town. The municipality were willing to bear an adequate share of that cost but the rest would have to be borne by the Gulbenkian Foundation. Whishaw opposed the project, arguing that my father wanted his money to be spent on the restoration of the Cathedral, not on making drains for the town. In the end, that work was not necessary, but there was still much to be done in the way of redecoration of the Cathedral and the Foundation has spent the money well. The Soviet authorities have done much to help, too, regarding the Cathedral as a historical monument and contributing to its restoration. A great deal of marble has been used for the inside and it gives a general impression of warmth, avoiding that cold, austere feeling which pervades the Gothic cathedrals of Britain and Western Europe.

The 'residence' of the Catholicos, when we visited him, looked little more than a cottage. It stood next door to his Palace which Mantacheff had built before the First World War but which had been requisitioned by the Soviet Army as a barracks; like all buildings the world over which have housed soldiers, it was in pretty poor condition. (It has since been restored and is now, I am assured, one of the most beautiful buildings in the whole of Russia and, once again, the official residence of the Catholicos.) His Holiness Vazgen I received us most graciously. He would not allow me either to kiss his hand or to kneel before him, although in public, of course, I did so in common with everyone else. When he relaxed at an informal meal he also showed himself a very good conversationalist and, as the man responsible for the financial affairs of the Armenian religious community, he was a good business man, too, excellently informed on world affairs.

While we were his guests, we sat down to meals, with as many as twenty-seven people, in a simple room with myself in a chair but with my wife sitting at the end of a long bench. Pots were put down on the table and a food called *herisse*, a Biblical food, was served from great bowls. *Herisse* is compounded of mutton, mutton fat and wheat, pounded for some twenty-four hours, at the end of which it looks, to be polite, something like porridge, unattractive to the eye but most enjoyable to eat. All the Armenians wondered what my wife, a non-Armenian, would make of it but she, too, enjoyed it greatly. All the cooking was done by the mother of the Catholicos, an old lady in her late seventies, with a shawl over her head. She also kept house for him, with at most one other woman to help her, but she showed not the slightest sign of being fussed. My wife had many meetings with her and, although they had no language in common, they were able to communicate a great deal of sympathy between them while speaking their own tongues.

Before the religious ceremony associated with the celebration, caviare and vodka or brandy was served to a small exclusive group which included my wife and myself. As this ceremony, during which a priest was consecrated a bishop, lasted five or six hours, the preliminary nourishment was most welcome, though the person most in need of it, I fancy, was the unfortunate bishop himself, who was not a young man and who was physically exhausted by the end. The ceremony began with a procession from the Catholicos' residence for the two or three hundred yards to the Cathedral. I had the high honour of being one of the four bearers of the canopy. On either side of the procession, throngs of people were kneeling; the Catholicos blessed them as he went past; some of them rushed forward to kiss his hand. The way was kept clear by police who also bowed or saluted as the procession passed. In the Cathedral, His Holiness, in resplendent robes, sat in a high throne opposite the altar; I sat quite close to him. Each time a member of the congregation, whether layman or cleric, passed in front of the throne, he put his right hand on his heart and bowed.

The priest who was being consecrated, Bishop Zgon of Baghdad (now in Milan), had to progress around the Cathedral on his knees. When the moment came for him to renounce the world, he had to remain kneeling before the altar with his hands high above his head for an unconscionable long time; the poor man was almost passing out from exhaustion. The male voice singing, for the most part unaccompanied but, occasionally, to the accompaniment of an instrument resembling a harmonium, was most impressive. (In the Armenian liturgy, the Lord's Prayer is always sung and not recited.) Before his induction, the priest wore a plain white surplice. After the induction was complete, he had the more gorgeous robes as of a bishop put upon him, and Kurkjian and I, as godfathers, helped to vest him. The robes of the bishops, the archbishops and of the Catholicos himself, varied in their splendour according to the countries from which they had come. It seems that the richer the country from which they came the less rich their robes and vestments were likely to be because, in those countries, the labour involved in making them would be much more expensive and also because, in countries like the United States, there would be less understanding of the traditions and techniques of embroidery and less skill in their application. A bishop from Iraq was likely to have robes which were that much more gorgeous and whose embroidery was that much more elaborate.

We made several visits to the Catholicos and, on one occasion, he himself showed us around the Cathedral. In all, we spent some ten days in Armenia, making excursions arranged for us by the Minister of Cults, Mr. Gasparian, whose responsibility in the government of the Soviet Republic of Armenia was to maintain a good relationship between the religious and secular authorities. The Soviets have very wisely encouraged the Armenians to feel themselves Armenians, to take pride in their nationality and in their history and traditions. As a geographical term, Armenia has varied greatly in size. At one time it extended from the Mediterranean to the Caspian but what is now Soviet Armenia is only a very small part of the territory which was once inhabited chiefly by Armenians who were scattered throughout the Middle East, and especially in Turkey, in large communities. After the 1896 massacres, however, and again the deportations of the First World War, the Armenians in Turkey were much reduced in numbers. So many of the survivors of local persecution emigrated, sometimes in conditions of extreme distress. In Russia, under the Tsars, the policy towards the Armenians was one not of physical molestation, but of assimilation. For example, although all Armenian names end in —ian, under the Tsars Armenians were forced to end their names with —off or —eff. The policy of Russification was fairly thorough but it did not prevent a number of Armenians pursuing very successful careers, not only in business, but also in the army and at Court. One of the great generals in the service of Alexander II, Loris-Melikoff, was an Armenian.

In the last war, an Armenian, General Bagramian, fought on the Russian side, while another, General Guderian, who had been brought up by German missionaries and taken back to Germany, became the world's expert in tank warfare and fought on the German side. Mikoyan has become the President of the Soviet Union after having survived miraculously all the purges which took place in Stalin's days; Parseghian is the best football coach in America. These are more instances of what I call the Armenian talent for adapting themselves to their environment. (Those Armenians who were unable to adapt are no longer with us.) Armenians in Turkey still feel inhibited about proclaiming their origins. In a restaurant there, the bandleader, an Armenian, came to my table to ask me whether there was any particular tune I would like to hear. I mentioned an Armenian tune. 'Well,' he said, lowering his voice, 'I would like to but it's not very advisable for us to play Armenian tunes in public.'

There seemed to be much more freedom in Soviet Armenia which, for Armenians, is, in some ways, what Israel is for the Jews. I could not help feeling a real regard for the patriotism of the people who were living there and for the energy with which Armenians who, for so many centuries, have been scattered throughout the world, were trying to build a new country for themselves. One day we were going by car to visit some ancient ruins. To get there we drove across the mountains along a road which had been very well engineered but upon which the surface had not yet been properly laid. Then we came to a large village, mainly consisting of single-storey houses, looking much alike, none of them with windows or roofs and with no one working on them. It looked as though whoever had started work on them had tired of the project and had moved on elsewhere. I asked what had happened. I was told the peasants who belonged to that village were all, at that time of day, working in the fields. But these unfinished houses were to be their homes. The authorities had given them all the plans, materials and technical assistance they needed to build the houses but they had to produce their own labour in their spare time to carry out the actual building.

Armenia has been gradually industrialized and, among their manufactures, is electric machinery of which the Armenians are proud and which is exported to as many as fourteen countries, I believe. A chart in the Museum of Industry in the capital shows just where their exports go. It is a rather barren, mountainous country but in the valleys they cultivate fruit; the apples and grapes are particularly good. I brought back for my sister an apple which, in size, was as big as the 'woods' used on English bowling greens. There are dozens of different sorts of grapes, black and white and pink: they make good wine and excellent brandy. At the 1958 International Exhibition at Brussels, Armenian brandies took the first prize, beating the best French brandies, to say nothing of those from Spain, Italy or Cuba.

I am related, through my wife, to the Hennessys in France and so I pulled Kilian Hennessy's leg about this. It seemed, I said, that the Armenians could turn out better brandy than he could despite the fact that his family had been doing it for seven generations and he had a blender who was of the eighth generation in the firm of Hennessy. Kilian replied that, if he ignored commercial interest, he too could produce a brandy just as good as the Armenian. But, he said, the Armenian brandy was made purely from fruit; no colouring matter or sugar had been added to the spirit which had been distilled from the grapes and allowed to mature. To make brandy of equivalent quality and purity in Europe, he said, and to make it a commercial proposition, would mean selling it at three or four times the current price—which would mean pricing it out of the market.

We saw more than our fair share of hospitals, clinics, sanatoria and convalescent homes, because my wife's Red Cross interests were known, in advance, to the authorities. It was in one of these hospitals that my self-esteem, as an Armenian, which had been slightly ruffled by the Intourist guide in Moscow, was restored. I said what I thought were a few appropriate words to a young ward maid engaged on some menial task. She did not answer. I repeated what I had said in a slightly louder and more distinct voice. Still there was no reply. I turned to the doctor who was showing us around—in Armenia, as in Moscow, most of the doctors seemed to be women—and said: 'Doesn't she understand Armenian?' The doctor lo okedat the ward maid and said: 'She? She is a Muscovite —she understands neither Armenian nor anything else!'

To hear people in the streets talking Armenian as their everyday language and to be hailed by them in Armenian made me feel at home, although I suppose we really had little in common, either in our way of life or in our modes of thought: I had been brought up to be utterly different from them. Throughout our time in Armenia we were given the red-carpet treatment and received with great courtesy and friendliness, yet I sensed an underlying criticism that I ought to leave the fleshpots of the West and return to help rebuild our Motherland. I have a sneaking feeling that, by accumulating a few pennies abroad and spending some of them in Armenia, my father and I did more for the country than we should have done if we had lived there the whole time or even if we had gone back there. That may be a specious argument to protect myself. My admiration for the people there was entirely genuine but that does not mean I wished to emulate them. I felt I belonged to Armenia but that, again, is just another demonstration of my ability to adapt myself to my surroundings. I seldom feel like a fish out of water.

I was very touched with the reception we received from the people in the street. They lined up ten deep outside our hotel to see us come and go, held back by a policeman specially detailed to clear a way for us through the crowd. There were the inevitable enquiries about relatives. Did we know a brother, a sister, a cousin who went to Europe? No, they were not quite sure where they were, or what they were doing. We understood their hunger for news but we were rarely able to satisfy it.

Wherever we went we were greeted by friendly shouts. There was no question of servility in the attitude of the people, nor of envy. They showed admiration for my father's achievements in the outside world and a pride that he was one of their compatriots. But I think, in one way, we certainly let them down. They had not expected me to dress more or less as they did and they were even more disappointed by my wife's well-cut tailor-mades and her little black dress. They thought a capitalist's wife ought to go about dressed like a fairy queen, dripping with mink and diamonds; they were surprised, perhaps relieved, but also disillusioned, to discover that my wife and myself were really quite ordinary human beings. (Of course, in the so-called classless society of the Soviet Republics, class has much greater privileges than in the West and it is accepted that it should have. In Moscow, for instance, the V.I.P.s were the only people allowed to have white-walled tyres on their cars and to circulate up and down the centre tracks of the wide avenues, clear of all traffic obstructions.)

It was during this visit to Armenia that my wife was able, for the first time, to see and think of the Armenians as a people. She found them a very warm, sympathetic people, with an extraordinary capacity for enthusiasm. An evening we spent in Erevan, listening to an Armenian opera, made a deep impression on her. During the performance itself the theatre was absolutely hushed, as though the whole audience were entranced, yet during the intervals the behaviour of the people was as robust and ribald as that of an English music-hall. After the opera was over, the people crammed into open lorries for journeys of many hours and many, many miles back to their homes. As they went, they sang the arias from the opera they had just heard.

I profited at second-hand from the Soviet recognition of privilege, when we visited Khor Virab, a place of pilgrimage. This meant going into a military frontier zone to which, normally, only the military had access. But I was given special permission and we set off, accompanied by Mr. Gasparian, the Minister of Cults. In Erevan, Russian troops were not normally seen. In the frontier zone, however, there were plenty of them and a lot of military traffic. Whenever our Ministerial chauffeur saw a vehicle, military or not, coming towards us, he drove right across the road to force the oncoming car to stop so that the Minister might not be inconvenienced by flying dust. Our journey had been announced in advance and check-point barriers had been opened before we appeared.

At Khor Virab, we saw the shrine to St. Gregory the Illuminator who, in the third century, was tortured and thrown into a dungeon for refusing the orders of Tiridates, the King of Armenia, to worship and honour the pagan goddess, Anahid. St. Gregory was imprisoned in that dungeon, which was a sort of pit or cave, for fifteen years. The only light came to him from the hole through which he was thrown. It was through this hole, too, that each day food and drink was lowered to him by a pious widow. The hole was just big enough for a person of the right shape to squeeze through and my wife, who is younger, more agile and thinner than I am, was one of the few on that visit to make the perilous journey down a ladder, with widely-spaced rungs, into the cave seventeen feet below. There she saw the shelf which, over the years, St. Gregory had scraped out of the rock face and the adjoining cave, which had no vent of any kind (and is nowadays lit by a single electric bulb), where he had made for himself a rough sort of altar.

The visit to Khor Virab also gave me my first sight of the River Arax, with Mount Ararat in the background. The river is about half a mile from the shrine but the way to it was barred by a mass of entangled barbed wire which formed the frontier with Turkey, although there were gaps in the wire through which the local shepherd could drive his flock to water. I saw no signs of sentries or of any military movement on either side but we saw watch-towers, one within sight of the other, which, we were told, were manned by frontier guards.

Mount Ararat is across the border in Turkey. Sometimes, particularly at daybreak or sunset, it was clearly visible, in every detail, from the Armenian capital; it was remarkable the way it appeared for about an hour and then was lost to sight again. Often, as I was informed, there is a mist and then there is nothing of the mountain to be seen. (It is said that Tsar Alexander III, autocrat of autocrats, made a special journey to Erevan in order to see Mount Ararat. He stayed there for three days but during the whole of that time the mountain remained invisible. He could wait no longer. 'It is true,' he said on leaving, 'that I have not seen Mount Ararat, but Mount Ararat has not seen me.')

The River Arax is for Armenians what Father Thames is for the English and what the Tiber is for the Romans. It is only a muddy stream, not more than a few yards across, winding along a rather barren valley. But to an Armenian it means something and to this Armenian, as I looked upon it for the first time, it seemed to mean a great deal.

This is a book, it may be said, of a rich man. But there is one person who is doubtful of my wealth.

When my step-grandson, aged six, who has been taught to call me Great Unc, came to lunch with me, he asked, 'Mummy, is Great Unc very rich?' His mother made the appropriate reply.

'Well, then,' said my grandson, 'why doesn't he buy a razor to shave his beard off?'

Veritas ex ore parvulorum.

Appendix

Correspondence between Lord Radcliffe and Doctor
José de Azeredo Perdigão on the constitution of the
Gulbenkian Foundation.

I

From Lord Radcliffe to Doctor Perdigão

16th January, 1956

Before we parted last Friday I promised that, when I got back to England, I would send you a letter putting on record the two proposals which I have made to you, Mr. Essayan and Mr. Nubar Gulbenkian as to the conditions upon which the Gulbenkian Foundation should be set up in Portugal.

As you know, I do not think that so small a number as our four selves would be satisfactory for a Board of Governors, even during the Foundation's initial period. I take into account the very great resources that it will control, the immense range of its intended activities, both in subject and in area, and the additional circumstance that it has an active business interest to manage apart from its responsibilities for distributing its wealth. I therefore feel that a Board of not less than seven governors must be envisaged, and what I propose about the Board of Governors is based upon this number of seven.

Upon that basis I have been anxious to make some suggestion as to the constitution of the Board which would recognize in positive form the fact that the Foundation, being created under Portuguese law and having its head office in Lisbon, will stand in a relation to Portugal that is different from its relation to any other particular country. I also think it appropriate to suggest that the Statutes regulating the make up of the Board should contain some special provision for the representation of Mr. C. S. Gulbenkian's family, if only because it appears from the Will itself that he envisaged that they should participate in the administration of the Foundation.

My proposals on this head therefore are as follows.

1. One or two places (as the case may be) on the Board should be reserved for members of the family of the Founder, so long as there are such members available who are willing to serve and are competent to do so.

2. Two places on the Board should be reserved for Portuguese citizens. If it should prove wise to increase the total membership of the Board above the number of seven, I would favour the adoption of a formula which secured one place for citizens of Portugal for every three places filled: so that on a Board of nine there would be three Portuguese citizens.

3. There should be an absolute prohibition against the Board of Governors containing at any time a majority of persons of one nationality.

With regard to condition 3 above, I can only say that, after giving the matter much consideration, I think that it is an essential condition for the proper functioning of this great Foundation. It is not for me to enter upon any argument as to the legal rights of the Government of Portugal to require that there should be a majority of Portuguese citizens upon the Board of Governors. But it seems to me clear that the Founder himself showed by his nomination of the original Trustees whom he hoped to secure for his Foundation that he had not in mind a majority of Portuguese citizens or any other national majority. Moreover, when I consider the diverse countries and peoples who will be looking to the Foundation in due course for some share of its expenditure in meeting their needs, I feel that I must adhere to the view that the requirement of any national majority, carrying with it the effective control of the working of the Foundation, would prejudice its best interests and lead to very wide misunderstanding in other countries.

I must now mention the other matter upon which I have made a proposal to my colleagues—that is, the distribution of the Foundation's resources. It may be that, theoretically, the Foundation should deal with all such questions as they arise, without the burden of any prior commitment. I am confident that, in practice, such a theoretical position could not be preserved. I will mention two reasons.

1. There is a possibility—to say no more—of very wide differences of opinion as to the proper proportion of the Foundation's expenditure

in Portugal as compared with its expenditure in the rest of the world. Such differences may be most sincerely and genuinely entertained. But, unless some attempt is made from the beginning to define the position, the Foundation's opening years of activity would be clouded with uncertainty and, quite possibly, with irreconcilable disputes. Every reference to this subject to which my attention is drawn, either in Portuguese newspapers or in public utterances, confirms me in this view. Indeed, to speak for myself only, I could not undertake the duties of Chairman of the Board without some clarification as between myself and my colleagues on the one hand and as between the Foundation and the Portuguese nation on the other.

2. The very terms of the Will, as interpreted to us by the valuable joint opinion of Professor A. Ferrer Correia and Professor A. Rodrigues Queiro, impose upon us the necessity of some such step. For the effect of their opinion is to tell the Trustees that in one aspect the duties of the Foundation are different in relation to Portugal from what they are in regard to any other particular country. For, whereas they are not obliged to undertake expenditure, in any other particular country unless they so decide, it is their duty always to exercise some activity in Portugal. But the Will does not give any guide to the Trustees as to the extent of that activity when compared with the extent of their activity in all countries put together, and unless some provision is made which can be accepted as a guide in the matter, I foresee endless un-uncertainty among different Trustees as to how to interpret their duty in the matter. To meet this, my proposal is that the Statutes should require the Foundation so to operate that as much as 15% of its total annual expenditure on grants is spent either in Portugal itself or in Portuguese territory. That guarantee gives Portugal a special position which no other country will enjoy.

As to this proposal, I would only add one or two observations before I close my letter.

Admittedly, the figure of 15% is arbitrary. In my view it gives to Portugal a very favourable allocation when the needs and requirements of the country and its territories are placed in opposition to those of all the rest of the world. If I were told that it was unacceptable as being too high and so compromising the position both of the Foundation and of Portugal, I would reduce it to 10% without misgiving. It would still be favourable. But, however that may be, I do want to point out that it is not in any way intended as the commencing figure of a bargain—a process which would, of course, be quite out of keeping in a matter of this kind.

I accept that, whatever figure is taken for the guarantee—and I have suggested 15%—, the guarantee can only cover a minimum, and I do not desire to give support for the argument that a minimum should also be regarded as a maximum—as does sometimes happen in these cases. To avoid any danger of this I would be ready to concur in a resolution of the Board of Governors to the effect that the 15% guarantee in the Statutes was not to be interpreted as prescribing a maximum of expenditure not to be exceeded in any case, and that it would be no derogation from their duty if in any particular year—not, of course, in every year—they expended in Portugal and its territories anything between 15% and 20% of the year's outlay. But beyond that I could not go.

Finally, there is the question of Mr. C. S. Gulbenkian's several collections. I do not think that it is possible to treat this question as altogether distinct from the other questions which I have discussed above. So far as I am concerned, I concur in the view that the collections —if, as I hope, it is possible to assemble them—should be housed permanently in Lisbon and that the Foundation should charge itself with the erection there of a noble Gallery designed for their reception. By doing so, it would give signal recognition to the special relationship between Mr. C. S. Gulbenkian, the Foundation and the country of Portugal, and it would be dedicating by the same act several million pounds sterling of its capital resources to the adornment of Lisbon itself.

I have recorded my ideas on these points in this letter, as you asked me to do. You are at liberty to show it to other persons as you think proper—indeed I hope that you will. Let me say in conclusion how grateful I am for the untiring and sympathetic interest that you have shown in formulating these early problems of the Gulbenkian Foundation, and how sincerely I confide in your good will to assist in bringing the discussions of them to a satisfactory conclusion.

II

From Doctor Perdigão to Lord Radcliffe

20th January, 1956

I thank you for your letter dated 16th January, in which you define your position towards the conditions upon which, according to your opinion, the Gulbenkian Foundation should be set up in Portugal.

I will give it my careful consideration and avail myself of this opportunity to thank you for the liberty you provided me with to show it to whom I might deem proper.

As soon as I am able to do so, I will pronounce myself definitely on the problems you raised.

I would like to thank you for your very kind words and say how very much we enjoyed, both my Daughter and I, the pleasure of having had you and Lady Radcliffe with us.

Renewing my homages to Lady Radcliffe . . .

III

From Doctor Perdigão to Lord Radcliffe

11th. February, 1956

Further to my letter of 20th. January last and with reference to the letter which you were kind enough to send me on the 16th. ultimo, I have the pleasure of submitting the views of the Portuguese Authorities, to whom I have transmitted the contents of your abovementioned letter.

It is only now, after my return from Paris, where I had to go in order to deal with some problems connected with the liquidation of the Estate duty and the classification of the works of art at the Avenue d'Iéna, that I am entitled to say in all assurance what the views of the Portuguese Authorities are.

Their justified reasoning is based on a point of fact and of law which can not be questioned:—that the Gulbenkian Foundation is a Portuguese institution of public interest. It is only due to this fact that the Portuguese law grants it all the fiscal privileges stated in the Opinion of the Coimbra Professors, Doctors Ferrer Corrêa and Rodrigues Queiró. Those privileges and exemptions are granted to Portuguese Foundations precisely because, in exchange of the activities of said Foundations, a direct benefit derives to Portugal. It would be unconceivable if the Portuguese legislation would grant a total tax exemption to foundations only Portuguese in name, i.e., to foundations that, although having its head-office in Portugal, were entitled to work mainly abroad. If such foundations could be deemed Portuguese, the Portuguese Treasury could be, and would certainly be, largely defrauded. I will give concrete examples of the possibility of such a defrauding.

A Portuguese citizen left his fortune to a Portuguese foundation, but with the obligation of delivering, say, 90% of its income to his Children. The Portuguese State, having not received the Estate duty nor the income tax due by the patrimony of that foundation, would only dispose of 10% of the income to use in works of Portuguese public interest.

Another case: let us assume that a British subject instituted in Portugal a foundation with international purposes, providing in his Will that the income deriving from the patrimony of his foundation would be distributed, say, 50% in England, 20% in France, 10% in Italy, 5% in the Middle-East and 15% in Portugal. Owing to the fact that the foundation was legally Portuguese, it would profit of all the referred tax exemptions, although Portugal would only receive 15% of the estate assets passed on to the foundation and only 15% of its income. It is quite evident that it would be nonsense to admit such hypothesis and, therefore, the legislator, by Decree no. 37.578 dated 11th. October 1949, mentioned by the Coimbra Professors in page 28 of their Opinion, does not grant in every case an absolute tax exemption.

In fact, the granting of that exemption depends on a decision of the Finance Minister—§ 1st., article 1st. of said Decree. And why this? Because, quite necessarily, the Finance Minister does not grant that exemption prior to the verification of the fact that the foundation is not only Portuguese in name but 'de jure' and 'de facto', i.e. that its activities are mainly in Portugal.

If the Gulbenkian Foundation was not Portuguese, i.e., if it could not be considered 'de jure' and 'de facto' a Portuguese institution of public interest, the Foundation would have to pay the estate duty of 42% on the value of the Estate assets, viz., 38% of a fixed tax on the values over 5,000,000 Escudos and 4% of an additional tax; besides this, the Foundation would have to pay taxes over propriety, capital and income mentioned in the Opinion of the Coimbra Professors.

Once the Gulbenkian Foundation is acknowledged as Portuguese, it will be exempted, as I have always said, of the referred taxes. This exemption depends, in what concerns the Estate duty, of a special announcement from the Finance Minister and, in respect of the income tax, it depends on the Foundation being in fact Portuguese. Thus, we have—and this is a fundamental point—that great and valuable fiscal benefits granted by the Portuguese law to Portuguese foundations, are based on the assumed existence in Portugal of a counter-value or exchange of benefits; this counter-value or exchange must be, at least, equal to the value of the benefits received.

Starting from this principle, which appears to me just, moral and legally based, the Authorities consulted are unable, much to their regret, to give their agreement to the points of view stated in your esteemed letter of 16th. January last.

However, both the Portuguese Authorities and myself, are deeply interested in trying to give satisfaction to your wishes, as far as it can be done, for we praise very high the value of your collaboration in the superior management of the Gulbenkian Foundation.

It was only due to this reason and, therefore, as an homage to you, that the Portuguese Authorities were prepared to condescend until certain limits which represent, in fact, a material and positive loss in relation to the benefits the Country might receive if the tax exemption was not granted. Thus, and starting from the principle that the Gulbenkian Foundation will be granted all the tax exemptions mentioned in the Opinion of the Coimbra Professors, (amongst which stands out the Estate duty), the referred Authorities establish, as a minimum limit for distribution in Portugal one third of the total income of the Foundation, thus remaining for distribution abroad two thirds of that income. Once more, I invite particularly your attention to the circumstance that the Portuguese Authorities have granted to the Foundation a tax exemption of a much higher value.

I dare referring you—and I do not wish to mention the case of England—to the fact that France will collect 50% on the value of all the assets there and this in spite of the Estate being abroad, while Mr. Gulbenkian's Estate was opened in Portugal, where he had in fact his legal and effective domicile.

I feel assured that you, with your wise intelligence and your high sense of justice, will conclude that the reasoning of the Portuguese Authorities on the subject deserves to be considered and accepted.

Let us see now the problem of the constitution of the Board of Trustees.

For the reasons mentioned in the Opinion of the Coimbra Professors and for the necessity of guaranteeing that a Portuguese foundation will be able to perform its activity mainly in Portugal (mainly in relation to any other foreign countries), the Portuguese Authorities wished a majority of Portuguese Trustees, as it happens with the nationality of the trustees of foreign foundation, whether their activities are only performed in their home country or abroad. But, both myself and the Portuguese Authorities are anxious to correspond with the greatest sincerity, as far as it can be done, to your wishes and, therefore, several solutions have been studied here in order not to impose a Portuguese majority on the Board of Trustees of the Gulbenkian Foundation, at least for as long as you perform the duties of its Chairman.

Therefore, the Portuguese Authorities would be prepared to agree that in a Board of five or seven members, two or three Portuguese were represented, respectively. In either case, the majority would be a foreign one, under your superior chairmanship, whose impartiality we all trust. You would therefore be, as the Chairman, a kind of arbiter between the points of view of the Portuguese and foreign Trustees, when they would not agree. This system however, I repeat, would last only as long as you were the Chairman of the Foundation. If, due to any circumstance, and whenever it happened, you would leave the chairmanship, it will be obligatorily performed by a Portuguese subject. This point of view of the Portuguese Authorities, to which I join with all my heart, represents a significative homage to you, to which you will be undoubtedly sensitive.

The aforementioned are the points of view of the Portuguese Authorities which, according to my opinion, have an entirely sound basis.

I apologise for the extension of this letter but I wished not only to state but to justify the points of view of the Portuguese Authorities in such a delicate subject. However, I feel happy with the results arrived to, especially because the Authorities of my country have shown a great spirit of compliance and, on the other hand, have taken the opportunity to display their high appreciation for you, to which I, personally, adhere with the greatest sincerity.

Renewing my best homages to Lady Radcliffe, believe me, dear Lord Radcliffe . . .

IV

From Lord Radcliffe to Doctor Perdigão

27th February 1956

I am now able to write to you fully in reply to your letter of 11th February, of which I have already sent a short acknowledgement.

I am most grateful to you for your detailed statement of the views of the Portuguese Authorities on the problems which concern the basic constitution of the Gulbenkian Foundation. I understand from your letter that you are in full agreement with those views and that they appear to you to be just, moral and legally based. It would be a matter of genuine happiness to me if I could share your feelings, for I am deeply concerned to find myself so much at variance with the Portuguese Authorities, whose judgement I esteem, and with yourself, whose sincerity of purpose in all these matters needs no endorsement from me. But I am sorry to say that in my view the conditions proposed for the constitution of the Foundation are not proper conditions, since to give effect to them would defeat the essential purpose for which my old friend, Mr. C. S. Gulbenkian, created his Foundation at all. As I am confident that the Portuguese Authorities do not contemplate for one moment that such a result should be brought about, it is evident to me that there must be some misconception in Portugal as to the purposes which he had in mind and as to the wording of his Will which gave effect to them. I think it desirable, therefore, that I should recall briefly how these matters stand.

Mr. Gulbenkian desired that his Foundation should be a Portuguese institution. By that he desired that there should be created under the law of Portugal and in accordance with the law of Portugal a perpetual Trust to which would be ascribed Portuguese nationality, so far indeed as the conception of nationality is applicable to such an institution. About those facts there has never been any dispute. But there is no warrant for inferring from his expressed wish to found a Portuguese institution that he thereby intended that its resources or any particular part of them should be given to Portugal in the special sense that they should be expended in Portugal or for the direct benefit of members of the Portuguese State. For in the same clause of his Will by which he directed the creation of a 'Portuguese permanent Foundation', having its domicile in Lisbon, he proceeded to declare that its purposes should be charitable, artistic, educational and scientific, and that its activities should be exercised not only in Portugal but also in any other country where its managers might think fit. These words are of no casual importance. In all the years during which he confided in me his ideas as to the eventual creation of a great public Trust—and they go back to 1937—I never heard him express an intention to favour specially any particular country. He spoke always of 'humanity' as his beneficiary.

Is there anything in the law of Portugal that prevents a foundation from being validly created in these terms and for these purposes? On the contrary, the learned and voluminous opinion which we have obtained from Doctors Ferrer Correa and Rodrigues Queiro asserts positively that the foundation so created is valid according to its terms. They have replied to our specific question (see Part XI):

'Portuguese law does not envisage any limitations either on the nature, number and size of the grants made by foundations in pursuance of their statutes or as regards the identity of the individuals and organizations for whom these grants are intended. *Nor does Portuguese law, directly or indirectly, distinguish or proscribe any necessary relationship between grants made in and out of Portugal.*

'The Government can place restrictions of this kind on the liberty of the Gulbenkian Foundation by making its recognition, which is indispensable and entirely discretionary, conditional upon the inclusion of such limitations in the charter, or by the decree approving the latter.

'It would be impossible for the Government, however, without betraying the spirit of the law now in force, to go to the point of ignoring the intention and wishes of the founder. These were clearly to the effect of setting up an institution which, while Portuguese, could none the less, upon decision of its directors, be active not only in Portugal but also in any other civilized country.'

The same point is repeated in para. 39 under heading XXIII:—'No specified part of the Foundation's income will have to be spent in Portugal, but its income must be used for the benefit of Portugal or of Portuguese institutions and citizens to the extent necessary not to betray the testator's idea and intention.' You will be familiar with the interpretation of that idea and intention which the learned professors have extracted from the wording of the Will itself. It is set out at the end of Part XI of their Opinion:—'Besides Portugal, accordingly, no other country where the activity of the Foundation has to be exercised is specified; but it cannot fail to be exercised in Portugal . . . The Foundation is free not to be active in Spain, Greece or the Argentine—that will be up to the administrators to decide; but it can never be free to leave Portugal and the Portuguese out of the range of its activities'.

I think myself that this reading of Mr. Gulbenkian's intentions as demonstrated by the wording of his Will might be criticised by other lawyers as attaching undue importance to circumstances, such as the seat of the Foundation and the system of law under which it is founded, which have no real bearing upon the question of its distributions: while the words 'not only in Portugal', to which special significance is attached, are inserted in their context rather to disclaim than to assert any special preference for Portugal. But these are debatable points

upon which I do not wish to enlarge. For, as you know, I have throughout been ready to accept and to be guided by our advisers' opinion on
this and to act accordingly. It was for the purpose of expressing it in
practical terms that I made my proposal that the statutes of the Foundation should guarantee to Portugal and its territories 15% of the income
expended in each year together with the permanent endowment of the
art collections. In making that proposal I was conscious that I was
going beyond any condition which the Will imposed or which the law of
Portugal required. But I thought that I could defend it as a reasonable
interpretation of the spirit of the founder's wishes and a not improper
concession to the peculiar situation which had been brought about by
his wish to have his international trust domiciled in Portugal and his
failure to take the necessary steps during his lifetime to make his wishes
known and to see that they were carried out. Certainly, I never thought
that it could be regarded as containing less than a generous recognition
of any claims of Portugal.

It has been a profound disappointment to me that my proposal has
been received as it has been.

You must permit me to say, without reserve, that I can see no
warranty for the requirement of the Portuguese Authorities that one
third of the total income of the Foundation should constitute the
'minimum limit for distribution in Portugal'. If the Foundation were set
up on this basis it would not be realizing the founder's intentions: it
would be flouting them. It would not be carrying out the terms of his
Will: it would be defeating them. Moreover, as I have shown, it would
not be giving effect to the law of Portugal, to which he trusted and to
which he gave his confidence: it would in effect be making a new law
after his death, directed solely at his own Foundation.

I must therefore say something about the reason which you give as
justifying this requirement. This reason is that the privileges and
exemptions granted to Portuguese foundations are granted to them only
because in exchange for the activities which they conduct a direct benefit
is secured to Portugal. Therefore, it is argued, tax exemption cannot be
granted to a foundation which, though having its head office in Portugal,
is entitled to work mainly abroad: and it is further argued that, if
the Gulbenkian Foundation is to receive tax exemption, it must
submit to having the legal fetter imposed upon it that it must
employ at least one third of its total income in this way for the benefit
of Portugal.

This argument appears to me to be wholly misconceived. Even if it
were well founded it would not be an argument for diverting the true
purposes of the Foundation; it would merely be an argument for the

Portuguese State taking away a proportion of the foundation's resources by way of tax explicitly and under that head. But in any event there are weighty reasons why it would be wrong to apply such an argument to the Gulbenkian Foundation. The matter is of very great importance both to Portugal and to the Foundation, and therefore I will take pains to set out these reasons in due order.

First, you must give me leave to ask you, where is it laid down in the law of Portugal that a foundation which exists for such purposes as those served by the Gulbenkian Foundation can only obtain tax exemption if it spends the main part of its income within Portugal? Such a rule is evidently unknown to the distinguished Portuguese lawyers who advise us; for having defined the duties of the Foundation in the terms which I have set out above they proceed to say (Part VI, para. 15):—'We deem it advisable to make it clear at the outset that the transfer of the testator's estate to the Foundation is not subject to the tax on succession and donations (Decree No. 37578 of the 11th October, 1949, Art 1(a)).' May I then take it that the Decree does *not* make any reference to such a condition as is now suggested?

Moreover, it is my clear understanding that Mr. Gulbenkian made his Will in the same belief that so long as he made a Portuguese Foundation the guardian of his Trust his estate given to the Trust would be exempt from death duty in Portugal. I gathered from him that you yourself had expressed an opinion to him to that effect: and I cannot believe that when in his Will he declared his Trust and required that it should be set up under the protection of the laws of Portugal he had any reason to suppose that after his death its operations could be subjected to an arbitrary condition of this kind.

Secondly, it is surely a profound mistake to suppose that no benefit accrues to Portugal from expenditure for the Foundation's purposes which is made outside Portugal or received by other hands than those of Portuguese organizations or nationals? In the field which the founder's money was destined to enrich—culture, science, education, charity—a distinction based upon purely national considerations becomes unreal. I would feel uneasy indeed about the future of the Foundation if we could not accept as a fundamental promise that Portugal is one of a community of Civilized nations the life of which is made fruitful by their participation in a common culture, and that each in truth derives benefit from the advancement or preservation of that culture in any other, just as all must benefit from anything that is done to stimulate the growth of the same culture in other countries which at present are less certainly related to this community. Surely we are not asked to suppose that Portugal derives no benefit if Foundation monies are spent, for instance, in the encouragement of literature and painting in France, in medical or other scientific research in England or Scotland, in the preservation or investigation of the monuments of antiquity in Egypt, Greece or Italy? To take a rather different example, does Portugal derive no benefit from money spent in the cause of education or charity in the Middle East, when we know that so large a part of the resources that make expenditure possible at all is derived, directly or indirectly, from operations in that area?

It is my duty therefore to submit this consideration to the Portuguese Authorities and to yourself in the most sincere confidence that it will be accepted. Any argument is misconceived which attempts to measure the Foundation's right to tax exemption by the amount of expenditure that may take place in Portugal or for Portugal in the literal sense. Though I have never expressed my intention or wish but that that amount should be substantial, it is to me very plain that the true benefit that accrues to Portugal from the creation of the Gulbenkian Foundation is that Lisbon has been made the seat, as Portugal has been made the patron, of this great benevolent institution to whose very existence it is fundamental that it should serve without impediment those humane purposes that transcend the physical boundaries of States. This is the ground upon which I would wish to claim for it the tax exemption which Portuguese law so enlightenedly affords.

Thirdly, I beg that the Portuguese authorities should not entertain the mistaken idea that if tax exemption were given to the Foundation despite the fact that it was entitled to work mainly abroad, 'the Portuguese Treasury could be, and would certainly be, largely defrauded'. I quote from the actual words of your letter. I realize, of course, that it is only through your kindness and courtesy in corresponding with me in English that the word 'defrauded' has been employed: but I must most explicitly reject any such imputation so far as concerns the Gulbenkian Foundation. Whatever might be the right point of view in a case where wealth made in Portugal or drawn from Portugal were to be used by a foundation for expenditure for the public benefit outside Portugal—and for the reasons I have already given I should not even then accept your major premise—the point in our case is that the Gulbenkian Foundation will be drawing neither upon the wealth of Portugal nor upon wealth accumulated under the protection of Portuguese law.

What are the facts? Mr. C. S. Gulbenkian, a British subject who had for the great part of his life been resident in England and France successively, took up residence in Portugal in, I think, the year 1942. During the rest of his life he remained resident there, and I am sure—

for I knew him well—that he was scrupulous in meeting all legal obligations in the way of tax that the Portuguese State imposed upon him in that capacity. I believe, too, that it is generally accepted that he contributed on no small scale to charitable and other benevolent objects in Portugal: and he enriched the city of Lisbon with a munificent donation to the Art Gallery. But the great wealth that has passed to the Foundation and of which it is now to dispose was never made in Portugal nor did it accrue from operations conducted under the protection of the Portuguese State. On the contrary, it arose principally from oil interests in various parts of the world, and the protection of these interests was at no time a Portuguese concern. As you know, the Iraq Petroleum Company, the interest in which forms a considerable part of the wealth of the Foundation, is an English Company operating in the Middle East. Finally, no appreciable part of his wealth was ever brought by him into Portugal; or, consequently, will ever leave Portugal when it is expended by the Foundation in other countries.

How then can the Portuguese Treasury be a loser, if the exemption from duty which the Portuguese law appears to offer is in fact obtained? You call attention to the fact that France will require a death duty at the rate of 50% on that part of the estate which is situated in France. But I must call attention in reply to the fact that Mr. C. S. Gulbenkian did not wish to establish his foundation under the law of France. The French law, I believe, promised no general exemption from death duties upon an estate transmitted to such a foundation. The law of Portugal, on the contrary, did promise just such an exemption and in the face of that Mr. C. S. Gulbenkian established his foundation as a Portuguese one. I must say with all respect that I consider it quite inadmissible that after his death the Minister of Finance should seek to introduce by administrative decision a substantive alteration of the purposes of the Foundation, which would not only distort them from what the founder intended, but would appear to be a material qualification to the Decree Law No. 37578 itself.

There remains the question of the constitution of the Board of Trustees. Here again I must say with much regret that I find the counter proposals contained in your letter to be without justification. If we consult the founder's own intentions there is no reason whatsoever to suppose that he contemplated any particular Portuguese representation among his Trustees, apart from your own valued individual contribution. If we deal with the matter more generally, as I think that we are entitled to, I am forced to ask for what purpose the Portuguese Authorities would wish to require that a foundation which is intended to serve worldwide purposes and will need to draw upon the judgment of persons of the most varied experiences and contacts, should be compelled to draw almost half its Board and, after me, its chairman from members of the Portuguese nation alone? The purpose of the Authorities, as I understand it, is explained in your letter: it is 'for the necessity of guaranteeing that a Portuguese foundation will be able to perform its activity mainly in Portugal'. Since I have explained at length my reasons for finding it quite impossible to agree that the Gulbenkian Foundation should be called upon to offer any such guarantees and since what I have already said will indicate how very inappropriate it would be to apply the provisions of Law 1994 of 1943 (dealing with public utility undertakings and companies administering public property or engaged in activities of essential interest to the national economy) to a trust such as this which is to serve the purposes of all nations, I know that I shall be excused from commenting in any further detail on this aspect of the question. I must adhere to my original proposal as set out in my letter of the 16th January.

I hope that the Portuguese Authorities and yourself will excuse the great length of this letter. It is due to my sense of the importance of the issues involved and to my most sincere anxiety to avoid a situation in which it has to be said publicly that there is an irreconcileable difference of view between them and you on one side and me on the other as to the proper way of realizing Mr. C. S. Gulbenkian's Foundation. I have therefore been at pains to set out in detail the reasons which would make it impossible for me to join in putting forward any statutes for the Foundation which incorporated the conditions proposed in your letter. I do not see how any executor or trustee could feel that he was carrying out the directions of the Will if he were to adopt such proposals. I am indeed grateful for your assurance that in formulating them the Portuguese Authorities have been anxious to make concessions to anything that may be special in my own position: but, grateful as I am, my own position is not really distinguishable from the obligation that I feel to try to see that the Foundation is set up as the Founder intended it.

I am sure that you will give my letter your full and sympathetic consideration. I am sure too that you will see that it is placed before the Portuguese Authorities as the reasoned statement of my views. I can assure them that I regard their point of view as entitled to every respect, but at the same time my knowledge of their sense of propriety and justice gives me confidence that this point of view will in due course be modified in the light of what I have set out above.

V

From Doctor Perdigão to Lord Radcliffe

7th March, 1956

I have received with thanks your letters dated 27th and 28th February last.[1]

I shall study the former with the care it deserves and will let you know in due course what I think about it; however, as regards the latter, I have duly noted the position adopted by you, my dear Friend.

VI

From Doctor Perdigão to Lord Radcliffe

15th March 1956

I have not yet replied to your letter of 27th February ultimo for, as you are undoubtedly aware, it deserves a very careful consideration, not only mine but also from the Authorities to whom the law grants the right of approving the Statutes.

In spite of your having expressed the opinion that you did not wish to take any active part in the routine work and affairs of the Heranca and Foundation prior to the settlement of the conditions for your acceptance of the Chairmanship, I would like to inform you of the negotiations which are taking place with the French Government, with the intervention of the Portuguese Embassy in Paris, concerning the authorization for the removal of the Collections from the Avenue d'Iéna to Portugal and the liquidation of the relevant estate duty.

With reference to these negotiations I have just received the attached note from the Ministry for Foreign Affairs. To this I have replied

1. The letter dated 28th February is not available but would not appear to be material.—N.S.G.

saying that I could not take any resolution alone and therefore was consulting the other Trustee in charge, Mr. K. L. Essayan.

I wrote yesterday to Mr. K. L. Essayan about the abovementioned note from the Ministry, as per enclosed copy.

I apologise for disturbing you with such matters, all the more so that I understood from the Press that you are kept occupied and preoccupied with other matters of great responsibility. But I do not wish to get accustomed to the idea of not having your valuable collaboration and of not knowing your views even with relation to problems which unfortunately have to be solved under the exclusive responsibility of the Trustees in charge.

With my very best homages to Lady Radcliffe and kind personal regards to yourself . . .

Enclosure 1   TRANSLATION

MINISTRY FOR FOREIGN AFFAIRS
General Direction of Politics   Lisbon, 13th March 1956
Proc. 380
No. 53
URGENT

To Dr. José Neves Raposo Magalhaes (Secretary to the Calouste Gulbenkian Foundation.)

Further to a telephone conversation between the Assistant General Director of Politics and yourself, I have the honour of submitting the following information given by the Portuguese Embassy in Paris:—

1—Our Ambassador in Paris talked with Mr. Janjard, General Director of Arts, Member of the Institute of France, who will pronounce himself at the Ministry for National Education on the leave of the Gulbenkian collections prior to the final decision being taken by the French Government.

2—At one moment Mr. Janjard raised the hypothesis of an agreement based on the delivery to the French museums of certain pieces, specially silverware, of which we already own in Lisbon similar ones, and others which belonged initially to royal collections or are worldwide known and unique, as the statues by Houdon.

3—Our Ambassador insisted on the position adopted initially viz. that the collections must leave as a whole to Portugal for this is the only way for France to give evidence to its appreciation for Portugal creating at the same time a moral credit near the Gulbenkian Foundation which would entitle France to receive in future the full recognition of the former, pointing out that the Foundation is unable to assume any written engagement as to the form adopted to this effect. In the event however of the French Government giving permission to the removal of the collections, a Note of acknowledgment would be sent, in which the Ambassador would express his feeling that the administrators of the Foundation would not forget such a generous gesture from France.

4—On the other hand, it was also stated to Mr. Janjard that he could trust our Government and the Trustees of the Foundation and that we would give the maximum publicity to the attitude of France in order to define from the beginning the moral rights this Country has to our gratitude.

5—Mr. Janjard will submit the case to the National Education Minister, whom the Ambassador will see later on.

6—Our Ambassador has always hinted the eventual offer to the French Government of the palaces at Avenue d'Iéna and Deauville.

7—Our Ambassador has been received since by Ramadier, Finance Minister, to whom he explained the mere outline of the affair, keeping a full talk for a new meeting, awaiting the Minister to have a personal knowledge of the matter. As it is quite normal in similar circumstances, Minister Ramadier expressed his good will but said that the problem will require to be studied on a legal plan by the General Direction of Taxes and Duties, hinting also at the Foundation's great resources.

8—He was answered that our legal advisers, after having considered the matter, had found our application practicable and thus it was submitted to the French authorities.

As to the Foundation's resources, our Ambassador commented that such fact advised that the question should be considered with a view to the future and not only to the tax amount to be discharged at the present moment. A new meeting was agreed to, after the General Direction of Taxes and Duties having considered the case.

9—According to what can be inferred from the aforementioned, our Ambassador has concentrated in two points which need to be adjusted with the Foundation—a vague promise of France being contemplated by the Foundation later on, if it allows the removal of the collections staying at present in Paris, and the idea of the donation to that Country of the Palaces owned by the late Mr. C. S. Gulbenkian in France.

In order to enable us to inform the Portuguese Embassy in Paris whether it must proceed with the present approaches based on those two points we would be greatly indebted for the Foundation's opinion on the matter.

*(Enclosure 2. This letter, as enclosed, was in French, but is here translated. The first enclosure is printed in the translated form in which it was sent to Lord Radcliffe.—*N.S.G.*)*

From Doctor Perdigão to Mr. K. L. Essayan

14th March. 1956

As you see, the matters awaiting a decision are now becoming urgent and in order to settle them, the position in which we find ourselves becomes more and more difficult, since Lord Radcliffe has not yet accepted the trusteeship and since the Foundation is not yet functioning fully.

This rapid march of events and the necessity for settling them forces me to take into consideration the situation as it is from the legal point of view, and that means that you, my dear friend, and I are the only persons fully competent and fully authorized [*responsables*] to carry out the provisions of the late Mr. C. S. Gulbenkian's Will and to solve all the problems arising from it.

We cannot maintain an equivocal attitude and persist in vague remarks especially with regard to official bodies and to negotiations which are being carried on to a considerable extent by the Governments themselves of the respective countries.

I am referring especially to paragraphs 6 and 9 of this communication from the Ministry of Foreign Affairs. Towards the end of this document the Ministry asks us if they may tell the Portuguese ambassador at Paris to carry on his negotiations basing them on the previous assumptions.

We must answer definitely and this I do not wish to, and indeed cannot do without having beforehand your agreement.

In these circumstances, I would ask you to give me your opinion on the matter, but as I never seek to avoid responsibility, I will tell you what I myself think.

Despite all the advantages accruing to us by the permission offered by the French for the exportation of the whole of the art collections and by the reduction to a minimum of the succession duty and the customs duties, it seems to me that the gift of the mansion in the avenue d'Iéna as well as that of the house at Deauville together with a guarantee that a percentage of the Foundation's revenues should be applied to French objects, would be a price too high to pay.

On the other hand, we must manœuvre skilfully so as to obtain what we want and at the same time, not to leave the Portuguese ambassador in the lurch for he, as you know even better than I do, has carried on the negotiations with an ability and an assiduity which merit our gratitude.

In these circumstances it would seem to me to be fitting to offer the French government the building at Deauville (for use as a rest home for French intellectuals and artists) and to undertake to put up suitable outbuildings [*pavillons*] and to make the necessary alterations. I think we could establish a programme for expenditure in this connection of a sum between 10 and 15 million escudos a year.

Of course it is not my idea that the Foundation should bind itself either in writing or by any other strict and very precise means, to carry out such an undertaking. The idea is to brief the Ministry of Foreign Affairs so that the Ambassador may be able to play his trump cards as and when he may see fit.

I should add also that I do not look upon the French business as something to be concluded separately. My idea is that if the French Government agrees to our requests, we should then make a public declaration of the decisions of the Trustees for the first general plan of the Foundation's activities. This plan would include, in addition to what I have just said concerning France, the building at Lisbon of our headquarters and of the Gulbenkian Museum, the setting up of the institution for Armenian children—to commemorate the late Madame C. S. Gulbenkian and to which Nubar referred—and the allocation to the London National Gallery of the sum of £1,500,000 payable in ten yearly amounts of £150,000, in accordance with the speech made by Lord Radcliffe on the British wireless, according to a cutting from the *Sunday Times* of 29th January last.

The revelation of such a general plan would tell the whole world that the Calouste Gulbenkian Foundation had begun its work in a setting worthy of what may be expected of it in the future. Of course the time and means adopted for making this declaration would be again agreed upon by the trustees.

This, my dear friend, is what I had to say to you stated with all the frankness you expect from me. I would be very grateful if you would give me your opinion just as frankly, and as soon as possible, both on the approaches to be made to the French government and on the plan I have just set forth.

VII

From Lord Radcliffe to Doctor Perdigão

22nd March 1956

I write at once in reply to your letter of 15th March, which reached me on the 19th. I feel that it is only fair that I should let you know without delay what are my views on the subject which you raise, although I recognize that, owing to the fact that conditions have not as yet arisen which make it possible for me to accept the responsibilities of the Chairmanship of the Foundation, I am imperfectly acquainted with some of the relevant matters that affect the future of the Gulbenkian Collections in France.

I think that I can best express my views for your assistance in the following short statements which I would gladly elaborate when circumstances offer.

1. I am in favour of the Foundation adopting a plan of trying to assemble the Gulbenkian Collections in a Gallery or Museum constructed for that purpose in Lisbon.

2. I must point out that I could not regard such a plan, if adopted, as anything but a decision of the Foundation itself as to the use and care of its own property. To locate and house its property in that way is not a fulfilment of any specific duty imposed by Mr. Gulbenkian's Will, nor would it be the realization of any plan which could be attributed to his wishes. I am confident that, if he had ever planned the assembly of his art treasures in Portugal, he would have spoken of that to me and taken an interest in the problems of siting and construction. So far from doing so, his mind up to the end was occupied with the project of locating his pictures permanently in Washington in an extension of the National Gallery there. He never finally decided to commit himself to that project, any more than he finally committed himself to his earlier plan of locating them in London. On the other hand, he did in a general way speak from time to time of a wish to have all his various art collections housed together in a gallery built for the purpose, as, in a sense, the house at 51 Avenue d'Iéna had been in earlier years. In these circumstances I think that the Foundation would be justified in making its own independent plan to locate the collections as a whole in Lisbon.

3. But such a decision amounts to the permanent installation in Portugal of a very important part of the Foundation's resources, to the exclusion of the rest of the world, except those who have the good fortune to visit Portugal, as I hope that many will. It would be wrong to decide upon it in isolation from the general question, still unresolved, what policy the Foundation should adopt, I trust in agreement with the Portuguese State, with regard to the use of any part of his other resources for the immediate benefit of Portuguese individuals or institutions.

4. It is for that reason that, when the four 'Trustees' (I use the word loosely) were discussing the general question in Lisbon last January and I ventured to make certain concrete proposals in the hope of forwarding the matter, I included a decision about the art collections as one of the important elements of that proposal. See my later letter to you of the 16th January.

5. As you know, those proposals are still under discussion. I must say in all frankness that it never occurred to me that, while the discussions were continuing, any steps would be taken by the acting Executors and Trustees to alter the position on their own initiative and, in effect, to seek to take on behalf of the Foundation one of the very decisions about its future policy that was an important part of our negotiations—both as between ourselves and as between us and the Portuguese Government.

6. I was therefore surprised and, I admit, somewhat hurt when I first learnt from a London newspaper that it was reported in Paris that the Portuguese Ambassador had been endeavouring to persuade the French Government to agree to an immediate export of the Gulbenkian collections to Lisbon. It seemed to me, not to say any more about my personal feelings, that that must be a matter for the Foundation to decide when properly constituted.

7. My view is, therefore, that any attempted arrangement to get the collections out of France is altogether premature and should not be proceeded with until the basic problem of setting up the Foundation has been resolved. When it has been, if I were connected with the Foundation, I would wish to study the matter closely before deciding that the Foundation should part with other important and valuable assets in France merely to purchase the right to move some of its possessions from France to Portugal. Could that be in the interests of the Foundation as a whole? Would the Foundation have the power or right to make absolute disposal of its assets in this way? I had previously understood from you that it was very doubtful whether it had any such powers of disposition. I do not say that something on these lines might

not be possible and justifiable. I do not yet know nearly enough about the whole question: but I do feel that it is out of order that the Foundation, not yet set up, should be committed in this way at this stage.

8. With very great respect to yourself and him, I do not think it right that you and Mr. Essayan should seek to decide Foundation questions of this kind before the Foundation itself has Articles legally approved by the Government, a legal existence and legal rights and obligations given to it by that approval, and a Board of Governors who can duly take decisions on its behalf. These are not questions of administrative or of the personal trusts—they are basic questions of Foundation policy. In my view the efforts of all of us should be directed primarily toward solving the difficult questions involved in setting up the intended Foundation—See Clause 10 (e) of Mr. Gulbenkian's Will.

9. For the same reason I deprecate most sincerely your suggestions to Mr. Essayan for some public announcement 'contenant les decisions des Trustees pour le premier plan d'ensemble de l'activité de la Fondation'. It would necessarily raise questions which I should be consulted about by many newspapers and others and to which I could not well give my usual answer that everything is under discussion and nothing definite is to be said. Take, for instance, the suggested donation to the National Gallery. I think it very kindly in you to think of following up a policy which I advocated for that body which has indeed created a good deal of attention and I am most grateful. More than that, I do certainly envisage that, when the Foundation gets to work, substantial contributions will be forthcoming to purposes in or connected with the U.K. But, if you ask me whether a grant on that scale to the National Gallery ought to have first priority, I would be bound to advise you that it should not. On the whole, I think that, even in that field, the British Museum has more urgent claims. Indeed, please consider this. I have accumulated in my rooms during the last eight months a very large number of applications, mainly from the U.K., for Gulbenkian monies. To all I have replied to date to the effect that I can do nothing at present but make a note of them, because the Foundation, which has to be constituted in Portugal, has not yet been set up and questions of the use of its monies are therefore premature. I have merely promised that all applications will be brought to the notice of the Trustees in due course. All these letters are available to be seen by you at any time, if you wish to do so, but at the moment I do not see any practical purpose in sending them to Lisbon since I have not supposed that the time has come for any decisions to be taken about them. But, if it were suddenly to be announced that a very large grant had been allocated to the National Gallery, the whole position would be altered. It would mean

that the Foundation was at work, even though it were not organized; that it was disposing of large sums; and that it had given absolute priority to certain objects. None of that seems to me to be in order.

10. I do trust therefore that you will reconsider the whole question of trying to get the Gulbenkian Collections out of France at this stage. I cannot at all see that there is any urgency in such a matter. So far as I know there is no proper place to receive them in Lisbon. There is no expert staff to be charged with their reception and care, no curator to assume responsibility to the Trustees for the important charge. The selection of such an official is no light matter in itself. Nor is the question of choosing a proper site for the intended Gallery. Even then, we shall need time and care before appointing a suitable architect who must obviously be looked for among the leading men in the whole international field. The whole project can only be considered as a long term plan to be considered as a whole. I agree, of course, that we shall have to know where the Foundation stands with the French Government as to the question of export before the rest is taken in hand. But I am certainly of opinion that its chances with that Government will be better if it can show that it has been established and intends to work truly for international purposes than if its claims are presented merely as a contest between Portuguese interests and French ones.

11. I am so sorry that I appear to criticise the line that you have taken. I only venture to do so because I am convinced that, even when our views differ, we both have at heart the true interests of the Foundation which Mr. Gulbenkian envisaged. I know too how enthusiastically you desire the assembly of the art treasures in Portugal and how much energy you have put into trying to bring this about. The basis of my criticism, as you see, is that it is premature to take action to bring this about.

VIII

From Doctor Perdigão to Lord Radcliffe

22nd March 1956

1. According to the promise set out in my letter of 7th instant, I will reply in detail to your esteemed favour dated 27th February last.

The delay in replying is due, partly as you know and partly as you may imagine, to the fact that my new functions as trustee of the late Mr. Gulbenkian, which I try to perform with the greatest care and zeal, have accrued to me such an amount of work that it is not always possible to reply as quickly as desired to your always esteemed letters.

Particularly in relation to yours dated 27th. ultimo, I wished to give the matter my deepest consideration in order not to say or do anything without a previous and full thought.

2. After the reading of your letter I found myself deeply concerned and decided, before any official approach, coming to you in order to try an adjustment of points of view, in a friendly and open talk.

As I have said before, I would find it very painful if an irreducible position was created between yourself and the representatives of the Portuguese point of view and I, for my part, will do everything within my power to prevent so.

Besides, I have always acted with the greatest care in order to avoid reaching a deadlock. Accordingly, upon receipt of your letter dated 16th January 1956, I saw some members of the Portuguese Government, but with the sole purpose of finding out what the prevailing positions and intentions were. After having seen that the general outline of the Government attitude concurred with my own ideas, I drafted my letter dated 11th. February last, of which I gave no previous notice to any of the authorities concerned. Therefore the terms and arguments set out in that letter are of my own exclusive authorship and responsibility.

I have acted accordingly, I repeat, in order to keep a certain amount of freedom of action and the possibility of submitting eventually, if necessary, new suggestions and proposals to the Portuguese Government. About some points of detail I deemed it was even more desirable to consult some qualified officers of the Portuguese public administration, whose points of view, although qualified, do not represent the very opinion of the Government.

Before your letter of 27th February last, I feel the need of giving you these explanations, all the more so that the contents of your letter impress upon myself the view that you felt I was being the mere transmitter of governmental messages, which is not exact and would move our exchange of points of view to the ground of a State affair with the relevant implications.

3. I wish to point out clearly from now, the following:

(i) I have never deemed really appropriate the inclusion under the Foundation's Statutes of any clause bounding the trustees' powers as to the distribution and application of the income proceeding from the Foundation's patrimony;

(ii) It was you, my Dear Friend, who were kind enough to suggest that we should secure to Portugal the application in each year, of a certain proportion of that income, and this as a consequence of your disagreement with the view that the Portuguese nationality of the Foundation would imply the majority of its trustees being a Portuguese one;

(iii) It was only due to No. 2 above that we discussed what proportion should be eventually granted.

4. In order that no misunderstanding may exist about what I wrote you on 11th February last, that misunderstanding being possible due to the circumstances of my writing in Portuguese and having not a sufficient knowledge of the English language to control a rigorous translation, there is still another point I wish to fix and enlighten.

But since goodwill and loyalty prevail upon our mutual relationship, everything can be explained.

The point I wish to fix and enlighten is the following.

I assume from your letter that you have interpreted mine in the sense that the Portuguese Government would not grant tax exemption to the Foundation unless a proportion of the Foundation's income of, at least, one third was secured to Portugal.

This is not however the case.

The Portuguese Government has not yet taken any position on the matter.

I expressed a personal point of view based on the logical reasons stated and on the opinion of the high officers of the Public Administration whom, owing to their qualified functions and competence, will have to give their opinion as to whether the Foundation has the necessary legal conditions to be deemed a Portuguese one thus having the advantage of tax exemption.

These fundamental points enlightened, I feel more at ease to continue our talk.

5. Due to what I have stated in the previous numbers and the relevant need of these explanations, I deemed more advisable not to show your last letter to any members of the Government or even to other Portuguese authorities prior to this conversation between us.

As it is quite natural I know better than you do the susceptibilities of my fellow-citizens and it is a duty of mine to avoid as much as possible them being hurt.

In the question we are dealing with the point to which the Portuguese Government pays more attention is the nationality of the Foundation. It is felt here that the conferring of the Portuguese nationality to the Foundation does not mean only the intention of enjoying the benefits accruing from that quality but implies also the acceptance of certain duties, especially those relating to the ties binding the institution to the Portuguese community.

The head-office is deemed unsufficient to establish that binding, especially since the first World War of 1914–1918, at which it was proved necessary to consider the nationality of the partners or, at least, of the administrators in order to distinguish the societies that should be regarded as enemies. It dates from then the trend, stronger and stronger every day, to determine the nationality of collective persons before other elements, besides the head-office, elements that should guarantee that the institution belongs effectively to the legal and political community under the laws of which it lives.

In the case of a Foundation it can not be seen what element can be required other than the Portuguese nationality of the majority of the administrators. With reference to this point I found near the members of the Government whom I have seen a strong firmness and do not see any probability of compliance. If I should be allowed to offer advice, I would suggest not to discuss this point any more.

In effect, the members of the Portuguese Government manifest a deep surprise, even a little shock, at the opposition laid down to what they feel is a logical and reasonable consequence of the Foundation's Portuguese nationality. The Portuguese majority of administrators secures, both in peace and wartime, the local defense of the interests of the institution and certainly is the best warrant as to the fulfilment of the Portuguese laws and even of the Government's benevolence. In the fact of denying the right to a Portuguese majority of administrators (already attenuated by a special compliance for as long as you are the Chairman, by a gesture of courtesy which you appear not to have appreciated to the very extent) the Portuguese see a proof of diffidence as to their capacity to participate in the administration of an institution with international ambit; you will undoubtedly realise that such diffidence is deemed deeply unpleasant and completely inadmissible.

It adds to this that I was unable to show to the referred members of the Portuguese Government a sole case of an international foundation in the administration of which the majority of people are not citizens of the country of the foundation's nationality and this fact aggravates the discriminatory aspect of the solution intented to the Portuguese.

Here it is, my Dear Lord Radcliffe, the reason why I deemed this point as absolutely essential in our talks with the Portuguese Government.

6. As to the point of the minimum proportion of income to be used in every year in Portugal—if its discussion proves necessary to be

carried on—I do not wish to leave out the justification of my personal point of view, which is the relation between the tax exemption of the Foundation must enjoy with the guarantee that an equitable part of the income proceeding from the Foundation's patrimony will be spent in Portugal.

The fiscal departments consulted feel, as I do, that if the Portuguese law grants tax exemption to foundations with the aims of charity or study, this fact is due to the assumption that such institutions will render services to the Portuguese community which will release the intervention of the State in the same direction with the relevant expenses.

Your argument that an ideal benefit will derive to the Portuguese State from the welfare of the whole Humanity and that such benefit justifies tax exemption, proves too much, for if we give to that argument its entire meaning, we will infer that the full activity exercised by the Foundation in Portugal will also turn to the advantage of the whole Humanity.

In fact taxes will always prove to be a sacrifice to which private wealth is subject. I have no doubt that the Princedom of Monaco Government feels a genuine satisfaction for not having to collect taxes from their subjects. But if the Princedom had no other receipts then taxes would be unavoidable. Your being an experienced politician, besides an outstanding jurist, know that the expenses of a State are not paid by ideal interests.

Thus a country only gives up the right to collect its taxes whenever it may derive another benefit out of the fact. Otherwise, the Government would be accused of negligence or dilapidation, especially when the country is a poor one, as it is the case of Portugal.

7. The 1949 Law did not consider the hypothesis of international foundations. Assuming that tomorrow an international foundation is established in Portugal having the purpose of exercising its activities exclusively abroad, it is quite evident that no legal or moral reason would justify the Portuguese State to abdicate from its own right of collecting, out of the patrimonies placed under its protection, by means of taxes, the fair proportion to pay, according to the principle of generality and equality of taxation, for the public expenses which guarantee the conditions indispensable to the social living and businesses.

The fact that I am talking to you avoids my expressing more details on the matter, for I am speaking to someone who knows every particularity of it.

Having dealt for so many years with points of law and having derived from them a certain sense of justice, it seems to me that in the expressed thesis, which I openly share, nothing exists to shock anyone, and that although the suggested proportion may vary, you will do well to insist that a guarantee should be given to the Government and the Portuguese public opinion as to the legal and moral base ∩f tax exemption.

8. Before I finish I wish to speak about the following points referred in your letter:

A) *the intentions, ascribed to the late Mr. Gulbenkian, as to*

a)—the countries where the Foundation should operate; and

b)—the constitution of its Board of Trustees;

B) *the non-existence, on the Opinion of the Coimbra professors, of the view that the granting to the Foundation of tax exemption would be subject to the application of a substantial share of its income in Portugal;*

C) *Mr. Gulbenkian having not foreseen such a condition, probably due to the fact of my having not enlightened him on the subject;* and

D) *Mr. Gulbenkian's wealth having not been made in Portugal.*

Because the length of this letter does not allow extensive divagations, it is my duty to tell you in a few words, my Illustrious Friend, the following:—

(i) If it is true that Mr. Gulbenkian wished his Foundation to exercise its activities not only in Portugal but in other countries, it is also true that his preference for Portugal, besides being perfectly justified, is declared in his Will and was expressed to me on many occasions;

(ii) If it is true that the majority of the trustees appointed by the Will is not Portuguese, it is undoubtedly true that, to the best of my knowledge (and I believe myself to be the most qualified person to interpret the thought which dictated the working up of Mr. Gulbenkian's Will) Mr. Gulbenkian has never envisaged the hypothesis of appointing other foreign trustees and, on the contrary, his intention of appointing more Portuguese trustees is unquestionable, since some approaches have been made to the effect during Mr. Gulbenkian's lifetime;

(iii) The omission you indicate on the Opinion of the Coimbra professors does not really exist, for the obligation of the Foundation to spend in Portugal a substantial proportion of its income, besides being the necessary presupposition of their reasoning, is the logical consequence of the testator having made a special reference to Portugal, this reference being the evident purpose of giving to my country an outstanding place in relation to any other countries;

(iv) When talking with Mr. Gulbenkian—and I gave him my opinion to the effect—it was always foreseen that the Foundation would enjoy tax exemption but, according to what I pointed out in No. 1 above, it was always assumed, both during those talks and in my above mentioned opinion, that the Foundation being Portuguese, its activities would be exercised in Portugal in the first place, as it has always been Mr. Gulbenkian's intention since he began to study with me the problems concerning the working up of his Will and the institution of the Foundation, as it was his intention that his Collections of Art should be brought together under the same roof, that roof being a Portuguese one;

(v) The fact that Mr. Gulbenkian's wealth is not the product of an activity exercised directly in Portugal is an argument which, with due respect—as it happens with the fact of Portugal belonging to the international community and thus deriving advantage from all the benefit the Foundation may grant to other territories—proves too much, for if we accepted it, we would have to infer that the major part of our late and dear friend's wealth should be spent in Iraq, which is certainly not on your mind. I would like to recall on the subject that:—

a)—Mr. Gulbenkian's income increased in no small way during the period he lived in Portugal; and

b)—it can be said that the administration of his wealth during that period was done almost completely by himself, in Lisbon, where he really owned besides a true business office, his domicile which he enjoyed in complete freedom, security and tax exemption.

9. Your letter suggests many other considerations, but I believe having replied already to the main points with the frankness, loyalty and consideration always prevailing in our mutual relationship.

Before I finish, I would like to have permission to make a call to your spirit of understanding and compliance.

My relationship of so many years with Mr. Gulbenkian gave me the exact notion of the interest he had for his Foundation. I believe the best homage to his memory is to secure as soon as possible the full activity of the institution. As a Portuguese subject I feel completely convinced that Mr. Gulbenkian did well entrusting his Foundation to the protection of the Portuguese flag and placing it under the aegis of the Portuguese laws. I know that, amongst my fellow-citizens, many personalities exist whose intelligence, experience, zeal and dignity are not inferior to those of other countries and who have full capacity to help you on the administration of an institution such as this. In all sincerity, I do not see therefore the slightest reason to the raising of a point about the solution of the outstanding problems which may drive you away of the Portuguese point of view.

I await your further indications in order to see again the members of the Portuguese Government.

I would like to recall that you promised me a long visit next Easter; I have no news about it.

With my homages to Lady Radcliffe and best regards to you . . .

IX

From Lord Radcliffe to Doctor Perdigão

16th April 1956

I am sorry that I have not been quicker in sending you a reply to your last letter of 22nd March; but, apart from the fact that I had several commitments to attend to over Easter, I have been finding it very difficult to decide what sort of reply it would be best for me to send if we are really to advance what we both have in mind, discussions about the constitution of Mr. Gulbenkian's Foundation.

I must say, quite frankly, that I was very much surprised to learn from your letter of 22nd March that I was not to take your earlier letter of 11th February as expressing anything but your own personal point of view on the questions dealt with. I think that, if you will re-read that letter, you will understand the reason for my surprise, because it did seem to say quite explicitly that you were expressing to me the views and, indeed, the requirements of the Portuguese authorities. As you will recall, my letter of 16th January, to which it was a reply, was written by me at your request, so that you should have something formal in writing which you could show to the Portuguese Authorities; and you asked Mr. Essayan and Mr. Nubar Gulbenkian to supply you with *their* written views for the same purpose.

It was perhaps natural therefore that, when I wrote on 27th February, I should suppose that our correspondence was being conducted on this level. I quite understand, from what you now tell me, that it was not. I am glad to have this made quite clear, as you have been good enough to do so, because it would be the most unfortunate thing if I were, through inadvertence on our parts, to attribute to the Portuguese Government attitudes or views which they do not in fact hold. But at the same time I realize with regret that, in the light of what you say, we we have not advanced in three months any nearer to the point which remains fundamental to the setting up of the Foundation, namely, what requirements is the Portuguese Government going to make in the Decree or other instrument that validates its statutes?

So I am afraid that there is no alternative to our returning to that subject. You tell me that the aspect of the matter to which the Government at present pays most attention is the nationality of the Foundation, and that they interpret that as involving that a majority of the Trustees should be persons of Portuguese nationality. But it is precisely such a requirement, the effect of which is to force upon the Foundation a constitution which conflicts with the scheme of arrangement made by the Founder's Will, that his Executors and Trustees ought to reject as unjustified and ought to join in persuading the Government to regard as unjustified.

I am confident that this point of view can be presented without wounding any national feelings or susceptibilities. Why should they be wounded by the suggestion that in making the necessary enlargement of the Board of Trustees the Founder's own pattern should be followed, in which there was one Portuguese national to two outsiders? The question, rightly presented, is not whether not having a Portuguese majority shows a lack of confidence in the ability of Portuguese citizens to assume responsibility for an international foundation—of course no such question arises at all—but whether the Portuguese Government would act rightly if they insisted on imposing a majority of Portuguese nationals upon an international foundation against the wishes, as I understand it, of all those responsible except yourself. I am very sorry, but I must continue to make it plain that in my view such a requirement would be quite unacceptable. On the contrary, I regard the proposal that I made in my letter of 16th January as a very adequate recognition of the Portuguese nationality of the Foundation. On the other hand, I would gladly consider the possibility of a board of nine, with three Portuguese nationals, if by increasing the number any possible injury to national susceptibilities were to be avoided.

On this subject, I think that you must have a little misled yourself and, perhaps too, the members of the Portuguese Government to whom you spoke, by the enquiries that you refer to as to the constitution of international Foundations in other countries. No-one doubts that, for instance, Mr. Rockefeller and Mr. Ford in the U.S.A., who were American citizens, chose other Americans to govern their Trusts and that the majority, if not all, of the Trustees have continued to be Americans ever since. Similarly, in Sweden Mr. Nobel, a Swedish citizen, placed his foundation, I believe, under the control of the Swedish Academy in Stockholm. But the point to attend to, if you wish to establish an analogy with the situation of the Gulbenkian Foundation, is whether, whatever the founder's wishes, the law of the American state concerned in the one case or of Sweden in the other made it *obligatory* that such a public foundation should be governed by a majority of its nationals. Did it? I believe not. If not, why should Portugal? So far as I can make out, such a requirement is exceptional in the countries of Europe. I do not think that it is part of the law of Italy, Belgium or Spain. It is certainly not part of the law of my own country. In France, an 'association étrangère' seems to be capable of being formed and recognized freely as 'une personne morale de droit privé'. Italy in fact affords a rather striking example of a charitable and cultural foundation, the Keats Shelley Memorial Association, which is entirely managed by foreigners, though its nationality as a foundation is Italian.

I feel sure that, if you think over this aspect of the matter, you will appreciate its relevance. In this connection I am obliged to correct something that you have said in heading 2) of paragraph 8 of your letter. It is an error to say that Mr. Gulbenkian 'never envisaged the hypothesis of appointing other foreign trustees'. You must be unaware of the offer that I made on his behalf to the late Mr. Frederick Grant Q.C. to accept a trusteeship in the proposed Foundation, an offer which only fell through because Mr. Grant decided to accept the Chairmanship of the Iron and Steel Foundation. You must be unaware also of the talks that I had after that, with Mr. Gulbenkian's approval, with another person in this country who is still alive. As to the approaches made during Mr. Gulbenkian's lifetime with a view to appointing more Portuguese trustees, I think that you are referring to one approach that was made to a very distinguished Portuguese lawyer. This was in fact made on my suggestion in accordance with the policy that I consistently urged upon Mr. Gulbenkian to the effect that, if he wished to establish his foundation in Portugal, he should take the necessary steps to set it up during his lifetime and should secure the services of a number of persons of unquestioned standing, both in Portugal and in the outside world, to be its guardians. I am still confident that that is the right policy though, unfortunately, we have to evolve it for ourselves, as he died without putting his plans into final shape.

As to the question of dedicating a defined portion of our annual expenditure to the service of Portugal itself, you rightly say that this arises from a proposal made by me during the course of our January discussions. But the proposal was not connected with my disagreement with the view that the Foundation ought to be controlled by a majority of Trustees of Portuguese nationality. My reasons for making this proposal are set out under the third paragraph of my letter of 16th January, if you will refer to it. I still think them reasons of weight. It was your letter of 11th February that informed me 'for the reasons mentioned in the Opinion of the Coimbra Professors, and *for the necessity of guaranteeing that a Portuguese foundation will be able to perform its activities mainly in Portugal* (mainly in relation to any other foreign country) the Portuguese Authorities wished a majority of Portuguese Trustees . . .' For my part I shall always regret to see the question of the proper constitution of the Board of Trustees made dependent upon the question what proportion of expenditure ought to go directly to Portugal.

There is, I believe, as there has always been, general agreement that some such expenditure should be expected and that it should not be negligible or merely formal. I am afraid, as I have already indicated at length in my letter of 27th February, that I cannot attach weight to the argument that the proportion of expenditure ought to be fixed by a calculation based on the rate of death duty that might in other circumstances have been exigible and I do not think that I need return to that subject as the Government, if I understand you rightly, does not make the claim. Nor need I return to express my inability to accept your statement that it was Mr. Gulbenkian's intention 'that his Collections of Art should be brought together under one roof, that roof being a Portuguese one'. I have already written to you fully on that point in my letter of the 22nd March, and, if I may speak frankly as a friend, it would be a great mistake to make any public attribution of such an intention. It will be sufficient if the Trustees in due course can arrive at such a solution on their own responsibility.

I quite appreciate the feeling that you express that it is not really appropriate to include in the statutes a clause binding the Trustees' powers as to distribution and application of income. There is much force in what you say. What I am primarily concerned with is that we should start with some definite understanding on the point that will be a basis for what the Foundation sets out to do. Whether such an understanding is best incorporated in the statutes themselves or can more suitably be recorded in some other instrument is a matter which well deserves discussion. But I think that some understanding we must have.

I hope that you will think that I have now dealt fairly with the various points that you have raised in your letter. What I am hoping to do, as you know, is to clear the ground sufficiently in the initial plans for the Foundation to enable me to give up my various other commitments and to devote my time to taking up the responsibilities of its Chairman. I am afraid that we have not got very far yet in that direction. You mentioned to me the possibility of my coming out to Lisbon at Easter. I would of course have gladly made arrangements for so doing if our correspondence up to that date had led me to think that I could forward matters by personal discussion. But so long as I am offered the picture of a Foundation under the control of a Portuguese majority expected or required to devote one third or more of its annual income to expenditure inside Portugal, I feel reluctantly that there can be little advantage to be served by my presence in Lisbon. I await therefore a further letter from you in reply to this before I determine any future movements.

X

From Doctor Perdigão to Lord Radcliffe

17th April 1956

I have not yet replied to your letter of 22nd March last, which I do now, for I kept the hope of meeting you at Eastertime, what would have enabled us to discuss the problems raised in your letter under a less formal plan.

2. Although I have deeply appreciated your having confirmed once more your agreement to the effect that the late Mr. C. S. Gulbenkian's collections of art should be brought to Portugal, I wish to point out that I do not adhere to the point of view which you expressed that Mr. Gulbenkian had no precise and definite ideas on the matter and envisaged until his death different solutions.

I wish to say once more that I have a quite different opinion on the subject and that I have always interpreted Mr. Gulbenkian's statements and confidences on the sense that it was his wish that the collections should be brought together in Lisbon.

Besides, I do not see what other destiny could be given to them under the Will.

3. Also I can not leave unmentioned what seems to me the basis of the general argumentation of your letter, mainly your allegation that Mr. K. L. Essayan and myself are exceeding the limits of our functions

as Testamentary Executors, for we have taken attitudes and action, especially those concerning the removal to Portugal of the collections at the Avenue d'Iéna, which are a right of the Foundation, which, according to yourself, is not yet established.

4. May I say in all sincerity that I deem your censure unbased. I am answering for myself alone for I believe that Mr. Essayan has already told you, personally, what his views were.

5. In effect, having accepted the duties of Testamentary Executor and Trustee, I am obliged, I should even say binded, to fulfil the obligations necessarily inherent to them. This is a moral duty which I am quite unable to exempt myself from without betraying the trust Mr. Gulbenkian placed on me, but if anybody could feel that such a moral duty was not enough to determine my acting the way I have acted up to now, there would remain the very wording of the Will and the law to make me do so.

6. In fact the Will established, under clause 10, a Portuguese Foundation and provides its Portuguese nationality and Lisbon head office. And I maintain, based otherwise on the most competent Portuguese legal doctrine that, according to the Will and the testator's death, the Foundation is instituted and perfectly individualized since Mr. C. S. Gulbenkian's death.

7. On the other hand, clause 16 shows that the duties of the Testamentary Executors and Trustees are precisely the same, since they are '*at the same time*' one and the other, they perform '*a double function*' and have the 'largest powers granted by the English law' to the effect.

8. Following next, in clause 17, '*the Testator gives special permission to his Testamentary Executors and Trustees to take possession of the whole estate, wherever it may be*' and '*to dispose freely of the same assets in order to the full execution of the testamentary provisions*'.

9. Please note, my dear Lord Radcliffe, that while clause 14, which deals specifically with the administration of the whole estate assets, refers only to the *Trustees*, clause 17, when granting the powers to take possession and dispose of the estate assets, mentions the Trustees and the Testamentary Executors, as if the Testator were afraid that due to any reason the Foundation should be unable to start functioning immediately after his death and foresaw the hypothesis of the Executors having beforehand the necessity of disposing of the whole or part of its assets.

10. What has been done up to the present, to the effect of securing the removal to Portugal of the collections at the Avenue d'Iéna, is no more than the action necessary so that the Executors may take possession of the assets and dispose thereof, *in order to the execution of the*

Will's provisions, since the same Will establishes the Foundation's head office in Lisbon. Besides, as we all have admitted, the late Mr. C. S. Gulbenkian wanted his collections to be brought together under the same roof, which can be no other than the Foundation's. I do not need therefore to go further on the matter, renewing the arguments already expressed, either verbally or written, and which deserved the concurrence of everybody.

11. But I feel quite sure that Mr. K. L. Essayan and I have been fulfilling the Will thoroughly and, more than that, the Testator's intentions, which I knew well; I feel I must point out that this was the most convenient opportunity to deal with the removal of the collections from the Avenue d'Iéna, since we were compelled to deal with the liquidation of the estate duty in France and the negotiations we had to conduct to the effect were providing us with the opportunity of binding the two matters, in order to get the most advantageous results to the Foundation.

Besides, you are not considering the fact that we—Mr. Essayan, myself or the Portuguese Ambassador in Paris—were not the ones who took the initiative of those negotiations and that we were led to them by the French authorities when they showed officially the wish to examine the collections at the Avenue d'Iéna to the effect of classifying eventually some pieces which they knew as existent or supposed existed within the same collections.

On the other hand, you know quite well that the French authorities required that the Foundation should pay the rate of 50% of estate duty on the value of the pieces and that, due to the referred negotiations which you blame, we have sound hope of securing, *on the Foundation's benefit*, a considerable reduction of that rate.

This is how the problem emerged and we were obliged to resort to the good offices of the Portuguese Ambassador in France in order to try to avoid that the French Government should collect the tax of 50% on the value of the collection and at the same time should retain an important part of it in France, fracturing it.

Besides, neither Mr. Essayan nor myself did, directly or indirectly, any *definite proposal* to the French Government and what I expressed in my letter of the 15th. was a mere *suggestion*. If I had the intention of putting it into effect without your agreement, I would have not consulted you on the matter.

12. You, my dear Friend, base your criticism to my action, qualifying it as an excess of powers, on the circumstance of the statutes having not yet been drawn.

13. I ask you to note that this work is not yet done because of you,

since the great esteem Mr. Essayan and myself feel for you is the sole reason which has prevented us from dealing with this matter prior to your acceptance of the Foundation's Chairmanship, an occurrence we all wish so much. I feel sure that you will acknowledge that a purely legal interpretation of the Will would not oblige us so far.

We call your special attention to what is provided by clause 10, line e), of the Will.

But if we have taken such an attitude—exclusively due to the great esteem we feel for you and to the wish of doing everything within our power to secure to the Foundation the benefit of being directed by your great capacity and wise intelligence, I repeat—it seems to me that it is not fair for you to resort to our attitude to criticize the policy we have been following so far.

14. This position, as regards the liquidation of the estate duty in Portugal, becomes particularly serious and therefore I call your special attention to the matter.

According to the Opinion of the Coimbra professors and as I have said several times, *prior to that Opinion, the granting of the estate duty exemption made by the Portuguese Government to the Foundation depends upon the previous approval of the respective statutes by the Government.*

The Portuguese law—article 32 of Rule dated 23rd December 1899 —grants, to the effect of submitting to the competent fiscal authorities the balance of the estate, in order that they may collect the tax due, a 60 days term as from the date of the communication, which has to be made within 30 days following the death.

The 60 days term may be prorogated one or several times, but never beyond six months—para. 4 of said article 32.

Therefore, within the maximum limit of eight months as from the communication of death being made to the Fiscal Department and of nine months as from the date of death itself, we had to finish the estate's balance and to ask for the approval of the Foundation's statutes to the effect of the estate duty exemption being granted.

The first term is finished and has already been exceeded, without us having submitted to the Government for approval the draft of the statutes and, consequently, we run the risk of the Fiscal Departments— unless there is an exceptional intervention of the Finance Minister, which I have already asked for—collecting the tax due in relation to the assets already stated within the legal term.

As you see, our position is not easy, and to make it even more difficult we have the contribution of your having not yet accepted the

Foundation's Chairmanship and the fact of the actual Trustees, due to that circumstance—an outstanding one for months—, not having wanted to exercise the powers they are entitled to according to the Will and the law, although they could legally do so.

The fact of your postponing your decision successively, can not be allowed to make the actual Trustees run the risk of failing the fulfilment of their duties.

May I remind you that the Will, when foreseeing that you, due to your official position, would only discharge your office at a later date, at an undefined time, imposes at the same time to the other Trustees the quick fulfilment of the Will. This duty, as it could not be otherwise, if not derived from the Will, would be derived from the law.

Looking forward with great interest to the pleasure of hearing from you soon, and asking you to be kind enough to convey to Lady Radcliffe my very best homages . . .

XI

From Lord Radcliffe to Doctor Perdigão

25th April 1956

Thank you for your letter of the 17th April. I appreciate from what you say that you would like a reply to it as soon as possible, so I am writing without further delay.

I have carefully re-read my own letter of the 22nd March in case I had said anything in it which made it necessary for you and me to enter upon a discussion as to the legal powers which you and Mr. Essayan possess as the acting Executors and Trustees under Mr. Gulbenkian's Will. So far as I know, there is not and has never been any dispute as to the extent of those legal powers. The view that I pressed upon you is that, when the question of the location of the Gulbenkian collections is at once an important question of Foundation policy and at the same time an important element in negotiations, still unresolved, as to the basis of the Foundation, it could hardly be right for you and Mr. Essayan to go ahead and decide that aspect of the matter on your own responsibility.

I should have thought that that view could hardly be rejected as an unreasonable one or as an unfair attempt on my part to interfere with the proper discharge of your legal duties, either as Executor or Trustee. Such language seems to me quite inapplicable to the situation. And I am afraid that I cannot follow your argument that because it was the duty of the Executors to take possession of the Testator's assets, as no doubt it was, it was therefore their duty to remove the French collections from France to Portugal. Surely you would not suggest that it is impossible for the Executors or Trustees of the Foundation to have effective possession of property, unless and until it is physically situated in Portugal?

I am sure that it is desirable that I should make quite plain what is the situation as I see it, so that there can be no possibility of misunderstanding between us. Reading the Will as a whole, quite apart from what one may know of Mr. Gulbenkian's own intentions, I think that it is the primary duty of the Executors and Trustees (a) to carry out the necessary acts of administering the estate and (b) to get statutes prepared and approved by the Government which will give the Foundation a constitution, including its legal powers, a Board of Administrators, and regulations to govern its actions. Without those, it may exist juridically but it can hardly operate effectively as a juristic person.

Of course, I share your regret that no statutes have yet been drawn up or approved by the Government. Like you, I wish that they had been. But I do not think that it will forward our discussions if we try to argue as to who is responsible for this unfortunate situation. Since last January at least I have been making certain proposals as to the form of the Statutes which you, if I understand you, are still unwilling to agree with. Considering that I regard such proposals as essential to the proper setting up of the Foundation, it seemed to me an obvious act of courtesy, both to my future colleagues and to the Portuguese Government who would have the function of approving them, that I should make known my views in advance. It would hardly have been reasonable or polite to allow Statutes to be drawn up or approved which did not provide for what I regard as essential, and then to announce that I was unable to accept the responsibilities of Chairman of the Foundation because the statutes were not in a satisfactory form.

My views as to what is essential have not changed. What is it then that you desire to do? Do you and Mr. Essayan wish to put forward some proposed statutes and, if so, in what form? Do you intend to provide for the Foundation being governed by a Portuguese majority or to what alternative scheme do you wish the Foundation to be committed? For my part I find it impossible to understand how, in the light of Mr. Gulbenkian's Will, his Executors could actually propose that the Foundation should be governed by a Portuguese majority; and, as I have several times pointed out, a block of three Portuguese to four non-Portuguese is equally inadmissible as a fair reflection of the Founder's intentions.

To my mind no satisfactory constitution can be produced for the Foundation until it has been possible to enter upon close and, if necessary, lengthy discussions with the Portuguese Government as to the numerous points upon which a Foundation, so unique in character and so vast in its potentialities, may require special provision. When these have been worked out, a Decree-Law approving the Statutes would seem to be appropriate, if I understand our Advisers' Opinion. But all such discussions can only be without utility until some assurance has been obtained on the two points that are of basic importance, the set up of the Board and the allocation of revenues.

I would be so glad to hear from you soon in reply to this and to my recent letter of 16th April, for, like you, I am much concerned at our lack of progress and the ambiguous position in which, consequently, each of us is placed.

XII

From Doctor Perdigão to Lord Radcliffe

11th May 1956

I acknowledge receipt of your letters dated 16th and 25th ultimo.

The latter contains a set of interrogations which brings down the whole subject of our already lengthy correspondence to two essential points:—the constitution of the Board of Trustees of the Calouste Gulbenkian Foundation and the eventual guarantee as to the distribution in Portugal of a fixed proportion of the Foundation's income.

I will only reply in this letter to those two essential points, leaving out for further correspondence the clearing up of the other matters dealt with in your referred letters. I believe this is the right method since, naturally, only those *essential points* were dealt with by myself with the Portuguese Government.

2. Beginning my reply to you I feel the hope that we may be able to

reach quickly a definitive clearing up of those problems thus making rapid progress towards the approval of the Foundation's statutes.

Not that I am impatient or felt, at any time, the discussion you raised irrelevant or inappropriate. But I am seriously anxious as to the eventual consequences deriving from the fact of the Testamentary Executors, owing to the delay of these discussions, having been unable to fulfil some of their duties, within the legal periods. As I have had the opportunity of explaining in my letter of 17th April last, we reached in the meantime the termination of the period due for the statements for estate duty purposes to be made. The course of action of the liquidation has its legal procedures which obviously go on by themselves. The law foresees only the prorogation of the term up to six months and we have already attained that limit. I have asked the Finance Minister for an extraordinary prorogation but was informed privately that, owing to the fact of the non-existence of a legal basis to authorize it, all we can have is a *real* stop for some days on the liquidation course, time enough to finish the outstanding negotiations to the effect that the Executors, in accordance with yourself, may submit to the Government's approval the draft of the Foundation's statutes.

By allowing such stop, the Government displays a manifestation of courtesy towards ourselves, to which I feel we ought to correspond by not delaying things very much. If the tax department concerned proceeds in such cases to the immediate liquidation in relation to the values already known, proceeding later to the additional liquidations gradually as the new assets come to be stated or known.

If such was the procedure in our case, we would have to pay *full* estate duty in relation to the assets already stated, since, as you know, the granting of the exemption depends upon the previous approval of the statutes.

For these and other reasons, some accruing from the Will itself—paragraph e), Clause 10—and others deriving from the law—for instance, from article 1903 of the Civil Code which fixes a one year period, as from the testator's death, to the fulfilment of the Will—I begin to feel really anxious about the problem of the drafting and approval of the statutes.

3. You wish to know formally Mr. K. L. Essayan's opinion and mine, as well as the Government's, on the points you deem, quite rightly, essential.

By conveying to you the views of the Portuguese Government, I give you my own, since, quite apart from the fact of my Portuguese citizenship, and placing myself exclusively in the position of Testamentary Executor of the late Mr. Gulbenkian, I must say, for conscience sake, that I consider the points of view expressed by the Portuguese Government fully reasonable and well based and thus am in entire agreement with them.

If you should eventually have any doubt about Mr. Essayan's views he is the most appropriate person to enlighten you.

As I explained in my letter of 22nd March last, I had tried till then to know the Government's views through approaches made to some of their members and enquiries to high officers of the Administration. What I will tell you now is no more just my personal opinion about what the Government's views on our problems may be, but their own opinion.

4. You say in your letter of 16th April last that you are unable to accept *'the picture of a Foundation under the control of a Portuguese majority expected or required to devote one third or more of its annual income to expenditure inside Portugal'*. For a matter of principle, the Portuguese Government show themselves intransigent about the Portuguese majority, but confirm their full agreement to the effect that one of the places designed for Portuguese managers on the first Board should be held by you, dear Lord Radcliffe, what would have therefore as a result a foreign majority at the beginning, exactly in the period in which the basis and rules of the Foundation are to be laid down.

If I am allowed to do so, I would like to point out that this is therefore, for the hypothesis of increasing the number of Trustees, the picture correspondent to the one provided for by the Will:—You as the Chairman, a foreign member (Mr. K.L.E.) and a Portuguese member (this friend and admirer of yours). According to my proposal, which deserves the approval of the Portuguese Government, you keep, as it could not be otherwise, your position of Chairman and the number of foreign and Portuguese members is increased in the same proportion.

Consequently, apart from the Chairman, there will be an equal number of Portuguese and foreign members, exactly as it is provided for by the Will. Thus, if there is ever any fundamental difference between the Portuguese and foreign points of view, you would be the arbiter. This represents, on the Government's part, a proof of the highest trust, to which I join, fully confident that you, on the discharging of your office, will never let yourself be influenced by any considerations connected with nationality, as it will happen with myself.

I say it in all sincerity: I do not see, on the Government's part, any attitude which may be considered as not respecting fully the liberty of choice and future action of the Trustees.

5. As regards the second point raised, the Government do not even take notice of any proposal of guarantee and therefore do not impose anything connected with the expenditure in Portugal of the Foundation's income. The Government by so doing do not obey, on the contrary, to what you appear to think, to the secret hope of getting a higher proportion than that stated in your proposal, through a Portuguese majority (which will not exist at the beginning, owing to a gesture of trust of the Portuguese authorities towards yourself), but to the wish of removing any question of material interest from the negotiations.

The fear you show of a control practiced by '*a Portuguese majority expected or required to devote one third or more of its annual income to expenditure inside Portugal*' appears to me entirely unbased and unjust.

I say it in all frankness: although your contrary position to the principle of the existence of a Portuguese majority of trustees in a distant future and your preoccupation of fixing a limit to the proportion of the expenditure to be made inside Portugal, may be a consequence (and I do wish to believe it) of a mistaken interpretation of your view points, the truth is that they look like a distrust towards this country, based upon I do not know what and which can not leave the Government unshocked.

To whom, like myself, it was granted the privilege of dealing the matter with the Portuguese Prime Minister and has seen the broad and balanced way through which he has defined the position of his Government, it is rather difficult to deem unreasonable the only guarantee asked for, according to the spirit of the Portuguese law, about the Foundation's nationality. Besides the Government, in order to prove their full exemption, proposes that in the decree approving the Statutes it should be stated that as long as the Chairmanship of the Foundation is discharged by the person appointed by the testator, there will only be an equal number of Portuguese and foreigners.

Here it is, dear Lord Radcliffe, the last word of my opinion, expressed now in a definitive way after a previous assurance that the position of the Portuguese Government remains the one I foresaw in the approaches referred to in my letter of 22nd March last to you:—full liberty to the Foundation and its trustees, but assuming that the Foundation's nationality is defined by the arrangement of its administrative board, as I proposed in my letter of 11th February last.

With my kindest personal regards, and asking you to be good enough to convey to Lady Radcliffe my most respectful homages . . .

XIII

From Lord Radcliffe to Doctor Perdigão

1st June 1956

I have received and given very careful consideration to your letter to me dated 11th May. I appreciate that its purpose was to deal exclusively with the two points which I have stated to be, in my view, the essential ones in any consideration of the set up and constitution of the Gulbenkian Foundation.

The first one relates to the constitution of the Board of Trustees. On this I read your letter as stating that the Portuguese Government with whom lie the right and duty of approving the statutes that will govern the existence of the Foundation, are not prepared to modify their requirement that the Board must contain at all times a majority of Portuguese Nationals, except that, so long only as I am Chairman, 'one of the places designed for Portuguese Managers' (I quote from para. 4 of your letter) should be held by me.

I have explained at some length during our earlier correspondence why I do not regard this requirement as one which is appropriate to the special circumstances of the Foundation or is likely to conduce to its best interests. Nor does it appear to be in accordance with the practice of other countries in dealing with foundations or other organisations for charitable or public purposes that bear the stamp of their nationality. In this letter, therefore, I will confine myself to saying that, much as I regret it, I cannot find it possible to alter my views as to what is right on this point, though I have been glad to give full weight to the sympathetic and persuasive manner in which you have presented the case for the opposite view, with which I know that you are personally in agreement.

On the second point, I regret again that it is not found possible to meet in some way the proposals that I have made. It is distressing me to find that these proposals are ascribed to suspicion or distrust on my part as to the Government's intentions. Let me say without qualification that the cause of them does not lie in any such feelings. But it seems to me, if you will forgive my bluntness of speech, only common-sense that a Foundation controlling such very large resources and having before it a quite uncharted course of experience, both in dealing with its own and other Governments and with members of the public in many countries, should wish to come to some understandings with the domestic Government on such vital questions as taxation, foreign exchange, distribution of funds etc. I do not have it in mind that the statutes are necessarily the best place for this kind of provision, indeed I am ready to believe that they are not: but it does seem to me that it is only the reasonable course that those responsible for setting up the Foundation should try to secure a clarification of their position on these matters before they start.

Here again I do not think it desirable to repeat what has been said before on this topic. I know that it is not an easy one, but I can not say less than that I am so much disappointed that my proposals should meet with no response at all and that they should be ascribed, unfairly, as I think, to nothing but an unmerited suspicion of the Government's intentions.

I share to the full your feeling that we cannot delay indefinitely the decisions that are required as to the setting up of the Foundation. Apart from the importance of finalising the death duty charge, to which you draw attention, it is undesirable that the Foundation should not be in a position, within a reasonable space of time, to give practical evidence of its existence and its activities. I think therefore that we must regard your last letter, expressing as it does the considered view of the Government in reply to my proposals, as having brought the stage of negotiation to a close.

In order, therefore, that you and Mr. Essayan should feel free to take action forthwith as the present acting Executors and Trustees I think that it is right for me to say explicitly that I am not willing to take up the Chairmanship of the Foundation, having regard to the constitution that would be attached to it by virtue of its Portuguese nationality, and that I agree accordingly that it is for you and Mr. Essayan, in association with Mr. Nubar Gulbenkian, as is, I believe, your intention, to proceed with the drawing up of the Foundation's statutes and their submission to the Portuguese Authorities for approval.

If I say simply that I am very sorry that I cannot come to any other decision than that which I have taken, you will understand, I am sure, that I do not say more since there is no purpose in enlarging on this aspect of the whole matter. But we have come to a deadlock on a question of principle and I think that it would only lead to greater difficulties later if we did not recognise it.

I can assure you that I have nothing but the most earnest wishes for the success of the Foundation as a benevolent institution of world-wide importance and I shall always take a lively interest in the work that it accomplishes. So far as I am concerned, I have no wish to make the present situation the cause of a complete severance of my connection with the Foundation, and any help that I can give in any branch of its work would be gladly given, so far as I could render it consistently with the claims on my time that are made by my present duties and other special commissions that may be entrusted to me from time to time. We spoke generally of the possibility of working out an association on these lines during our recent meeting in London: and at the moment I cannot say anything more definite with regard to it than that I both hope and think that it may be possible.

Index